A New Testi

May We See
Christ?

WARREN HENDERSON

May We See Christ? – A New Testament Journey
By Warren Henderson
Copyright © 2020

Cover Design: Ben Bredeweg
Editing/Proofreading: Dan Macy, Brenda Henderson, and Kelsi Henderson

Published by Warren A. Henderson
3769 Indiana Road
Pomona, KS 66076

Perfect Bound ISBN: 978-1-939770-62-2
eBook ISBN: 987-1-939770-63-9

ORDERING INFORMATION:
Copies of *May We See Christ? – A New Testament Journey* are available through www.amazon.com/shops/hendersonpublishing or various online retailers worldwide.

Table of Contents

A Word of Testimony

Dear reader, I would like to share with you the incredible experience I had in preparing the book you hold for publication. The Covid-19 crisis that is gripping our planet had the effect of clearing my speaking schedule, except for electronic ministry. Zero travel! On April 4, 2020, I began a writing project, but after a frustrating day, I knew the Lord was not in it, so I stopped and deleted *my* work – a wasted day. I had known for some time what the Lord wanted me to do, pen a Christ-focused New Testament devotional, similar to *May We See Christ? – An Old Testament Journey*. But this was a huge task that would require perhaps a year of hard work to finish, so I had been balking at the idea. Nonetheless, on Monday, April 6th, I yielded to the Spirit's prompting and began working on my assigned task. Day after day, and every day, I labored long hours without ever once feeling fatigued. Though plagued by an ongoing fever and headache during this time my ability to concentrate was actually enhanced. I was happily shut in with the Lord and was enjoying every moment of it. The days passed by so quickly, that the entire incident now seems like a blur, but one I will never forget! Thank the Lord, this book was written, assembled, and laid out for publication in 21 days (2 Chron. 29:36). It was sent out for proofreading on the morning of April 27th. What is too hard for the Lord to do? Nothing! It was an absolute privilege to labor with Him, especially since He enabled the work to its completion. Wherever you are at in your spiritual journey, take it from the author, resisting the Spirit's prompting is utterly foolish and never ends well, but going on with our wise Lord will always honor Him!

Other Books by the Author

A Heart for God – A Devotional Study of 1 and 2 Samuel
Afterlife – What Will It Be Like?
Answer the Call – Finding Life's Purpose
Be Holy and Come Near– A Devotional Study of Leviticus
Behold the Saviour
Be Angry and Sin Not
Conquest and the Life of Rest – A Devotional Study of Joshua
Door of Hope – A Devotional Study of the Minor Prophets
Exploring the Pauline Epistles
Forsaken, Forgotten, and Forgiven – A Devotional Study of Jeremiah
Glories Seen & Unseen
Hallowed Be Thy Name – Revering Christ in a Casual World
Hiding God – The Ambition of World Religion
In Search of God – A Quest for Truth
Infidelity and Loyalty – A Devotional Study of Ezekiel and Daniel
Israel's Kings – A Devotional Study of Kings and Chronicles
Knowing the All-Knowing
Managing Anger God's Way
May We See Christ? – An Old Testament Journey
Mind Frames – Where Life's Battle Is Won or Lost
Out of Egypt – A Devotional Study of Exodus
Overcoming Your Bully
Passing the Torch – Mentoring the Next Generation for Christ
Relativity and Redemption – A Devotional Study of Judges and Ruth
Revive Us Again – A Devotional Study of Ezra, Nehemiah, and Esther
Seeds of Destiny – A Devotional Study of Genesis
Sorrow and Comfort – A Devotional Study of Isaiah
The Beginning of Wisdom – A Devotional Study of Job, Psalms, Proverbs,
    Ecclesiastes, and Song of Solomon
The Bible: Myth or Divine Truth?
The Evil Nexus – Are You Aiding the Enemy?
The Fruitful Bough – Affirming Biblical Manhood
The Fruitful Vine – Celebrating Biblical Womanhood
The Hope of Glory – A Preview of Things to Come
The Olive Plants – Raising Spiritual Children
Your Home the Birthing Place of Heaven

The One-Year Journey

One day near the end of Christ's earthly pilgrimage, certain Greeks arrived at Jerusalem to observe the Passover feast and to worship God. But their souls were yearning for something beyond religious formality; they asked Philip, *"Sir, we wish to see Jesus"* (John 12:21). Philip discussed the matter with Andrew and then both men conveyed the request to the Lord Jesus. The Lord responded to their sincere appeal by saying that He must die soon to be able to share eternal life with them. Those who would receive Him for salvation and then live in obedience to Him would experience the fruitful benefits of His resurrection life:

> *The hour has come that the Son of Man should be glorified. Most assuredly, I say to you, unless a grain of wheat falls into the ground and dies, it remains alone; but if it dies, it produces much grain. He who loves his life will lose it, and he who hates his life in this world will keep it for eternal life. If anyone serves Me, let him follow Me; and where I am, there My servant will be also. If anyone serves Me, him My Father will honor* (John 12:23-26).

At this particular moment, each of us is as close to the Lord Jesus Christ as we desire to be. The Lord is a perfect Gentleman; He does not force Himself on anyone. Our patient Savior is always ready to extend knowledge, grace, wisdom, mercy, and forgiveness to those genuinely seeking Him. Whether saved or lost, God is calling and pleading with each of us to trust Him more and to experience Him more profoundly, but He does not force anyone heavenward against his or her will. God does, however, through His Word and His Spirit, aid a true seeker every step of the way into a deeper knowledge of Himself and His purposes.

God the Father loves His Son and desires for us to know, appreciate, and love Him too. The New Testament discloses God's ultimate revelation to mankind in a person: God's incarnate Son, Jesus Christ, is God's message and Messenger to humanity. Christ's life, His sacrifice, His death, His resurrection, and His ascension all speak to us of God's mighty, selfless Conqueror, now exalted to His throne. Christ freely offers light, love, and life to all who will receive Him and then promises to lead them ever heavenward.

By the illuminating assistance of the Holy Spirit, we are able to understand that all of Scripture speaks of Christ to some degree. The New Testament superbly declares to us the meanings of numerous Old Testament types, symbols, and allegories of Christ. Hence, the best reason to embark on this one-year journey is to more clearly see, know, and love Christ. We will not value Him at all until we esteem Him above all! May the Lord richly bless your daily contemplations of the Savior as you eagerly peer into God's oracles and witness the glory of His Son.

— Warren Henderson

Seeing Christ in the Gospels

The word "gospel" is found 101 times in the New Testament. In the original language, the noun form *euaggelion* simply means "a good message," while the verb form *euaggelizo* refers to "announcing the good news," or "to evangelize." The gospel message is good news from heaven to all humanity. The good news is that, through Christ, God's peace would come to mankind, or as the angelic host declared to the bewildered shepherds near Bethlehem so long ago, *"Glory to God in the highest, and on earth peace, goodwill toward men!"* (Luke 2:14).

As one examines the four Gospels (Matthew, Mark, Luke, and John), it is quickly observed that deliberate variations, exclusions, and inclusions of content exist within each account. There are different styles of language and arrangement of subjects. The Spirit of God obviously never intended for there to be a multiplication of narratives, but rather a necessity for variation. Likewise, the Holy Spirit made no attempt to convey a complete biography of the Lord's life, for lengthy gaps of personal history are apparent.

A brief breakdown of the content matter within the four Gospels will clearly demonstrate this point. Of the eighty-nine chapters in the four accounts, eighty-five pertain to the Lord's last three years on earth, and twenty-eight of these focus solely on His final week of ministry, His crucifixion, and His resurrection. Therefore, roughly one third of the four Gospels is devoted to the specific details surrounding the events of Calvary. The Gospel focus is a Person, not a biography of a person. The Gospels contain both the wisdom of God in sacred expression and what the Father longs for us to appreciate – the profound excellencies of His Son. C. I. Scofield summarizes the main purpose of the four Gospels:

> The four Gospels record the eternal being, human ancestry, birth, life and ministry, death, resurrection, and ascension of Jesus the Christ, Son of God and Son of Man. Taken together, they set forth, not a biography but a Person. ... The four Gospels, though designedly incomplete as a story, are complete as a revelation. We may not know everything that Jesus did, but we may know Him. In four great

narratives, each of which in some respects supplements the other three, we have Jesus Christ Himself.[1]

God's written "good news" to mankind is presented from the four unique vantage points of Christ found in Matthew, Mark, Luke, and John. Many have tried in vain to fully harmonize these Gospel accounts, but they cannot be fully harmonized; each Gospel stands alone as an inspired testimony of a unique theme of Christ's life and ministry. On this subject, Samuel Ridout remarks as follows:

> Had God intended that we should have but one narrative, He would have given us the record of the life of our Lord in that form. Our attention, therefore, should be directed to each separate Gospel to ascertain, as far as we may, its general character; its main theme; its point of view; the manner in which it presents our Lord.[2]

Clearly, the intended purpose and distinct content of each of the four Gospels must be understood to more fully appreciate what God has *spoken unto us by* [His] *Son* (Heb. 1:2). J. G. Bellett notes:

> The four Gospels are coincident testimonies to the Lord Jesus Christ, and valuable as such. But we are not to read them as merely explanatory or supplemental. We get a complete view of our Lord Jesus Christ only by discerning their distinctness in character and purpose. Even in the histories of men we may perceive this. One biographer may give us the man in his domestic, another in his political life; but in order to be fully acquainted with him, we must see him in both of these, and perhaps in many other connections. And one of such biographers will not only select particular facts, but notice distinct circumstances in the same facts. The same thing we see in the four Gospels.[3]

Generally speaking, Matthew and Luke do not strive to record events in sequence, but in accordance with their associated themes of royalty and humanity, respectively. For this cause miracles, discourses, events, and related facts are grouped together to ensure the fullest development of the deliberate theme of the Holy Spirit. Mark provides the most concise and most chronologically accurate Gospel account; He is upholding the "doings" of the Lord. John would be the next most chronological account of the Lord's ministry but is characterized by vast gaps in the life of Christ. In summary, it is the differences within the Gospels that call our attention to particular topical truths.

Matthew and John were personally discipled by Christ, while Mark and Luke were not. God employed quite a variety of writers and styles to portray His Son to the World. Two were apostles; one was a Gentile believer, and one a later Jewish convert to Christ. One of the apostles and one of the non-apostles recorded the events, generally, as they happened, while the remaining two upheld the richness of distinct presentation.

The unique Gospel themes preclude a full harmony of facts but serve as an invitation to appreciate the distinct glories of Christ's holy character, divine essence, and selfless ministry. As one slowly rotates a prism immersed in white light, various colors are refracted through the prism, such that the color one actually sees will depend upon the viewpoint from which one gazes upon the prism. Same prism, same light, but distinctions in radiance are observed from various on-looking positions. As we view the Lord Jesus Christ by the light of divine revelation, we learn to appreciate the fullness of His matchless splendor from the diverse Gospel illuminations. The Son is thoroughly and altogether lovely, as the Father fittingly proclaims to us through the four Gospel records.

But why did God choose to reveal His Son to us through four gospels? Why not use seven, the number of perfection, to present His Son to humanity instead of four? In Scripture, the number "four" is the number of *earthly order*, as created by God. For example, on earth we observe four seasons, four directions, four divisions of day, four phases of the moon, four realms of life (on the earth, under the earth, in the heaven, or in the sea), and four divisions of humanity (kindred, people, tongue, and nation).

How does *four* then relate to God's presentation of His Son to humanity? When the Son exited the dimensionless and timeless realm of majesty on high and descended to the earth, He willingly placed Himself under earthly order. As a man, He became subject to the natural laws of creation, even though, as God, He still maintained the order of all things (Col. 1:17). Consequently, the Lord never allowed

5

His deity to satisfy His humanity beyond the normal scope in which all humanity experiences the daily blessings of God.

Many other means are employed in Scripture to convey relevance to the Lord's condescending journey to earth for the sole purpose of suffering death, that mankind might have an opportunity to be restored to a holy God. For example, the Lord Jesus referred to Himself more often by the title "Son of Man" than by the title "Son of God." In so doing, He was not calling attention to His divine essence but to His lowly position and ministry on earth. The Spirit of God, throughout the Bible, consistently represents the glories of the Son, while being *earthly-connected*, by employing the number *four*.

Accordingly, the four Gospels uphold the brilliancy of the Lord both from a different perspective and to a unique earthly audience. The following table provides a short summary of these distinctions to enhance our appreciation of Christ's presentation to mankind.

Perspective	King	Servant	Humanity	Deity
Audience	Jewish	Roman	Greek	The World

The Father provided perfect representation of His Son through four unique vantage points of His greatness. *Four* is the number pertaining to earthly order. It is the best number to declare the "good news" message – the goodness of God to mankind. The Son willingly laid aside His outshining glory and departed from His celestial home. He became subject to creation order and took the place upon an accursed tree for every man, woman, and child that would ever live. There, rejected and abandoned, the billows and waves of divine judgment broke upon the Savior as every human sin was judicially accounted for. As a result of Christ's finished work, man now has the wonderful opportunity to be forgiven, redeemed, justified, and eternally restored to God. The Gospel of Jesus Christ, from every viewpoint, is "good news" indeed!

> The more you know about Christ, the less you will be satisfied with superficial views of Him.
>
> — C. H. Spurgeon

New Testament Devotions

January 1 – The Four "Beholds"
(Gospel Introduction)

So that man would not miss God's coming Messiah, there are four unique "behold" statements in the Old Testament. These prepare the way for Christ's first earthly advent, and each one emphasizes a distinct Gospel theme. Each "behold" declaration is a unique invitation by God the Father for all humanity to gaze upon and admire His dear Son.

> *Behold your King* (Zech. 9:9) – Gospel of Matthew
> *Behold My Servant* (Isa. 42:1) – Gospel of Mark
> *Behold the Man* (Zech. 6:12) – Gospel of Luke
> *Behold your God* (Isa. 40:9) – Gospel of John

What is additionally fascinating is that the same Old Testament declarations which prepared the way for the Lord's incarnation are repeated in the New Testament as explicit confirmation that Jesus Christ was the direct fulfillment of these Old Testament proclamations:

> **Behold! My Servant** *whom I have chosen, My Beloved in whom My soul is well pleased! I will put My Spirit upon Him, and He will declare justice to the Gentiles* (Matt. 12:18).

> *Then Jesus came out, wearing the crown of thorns and the purple robe. And Pilate said to them,* **"Behold the Man!"** (John 19:5).

> *Now it was the Preparation Day of the Passover, and about the sixth hour. And he said to the Jews,* **"Behold your King!"** (John 19:14).

> **"Behold**, *the virgin shall be with child, and bear a Son, and they shall call His name Immanuel,"* which is translated, **"God with us."** (Matt. 1:23) – *literally* **"Behold your God!"**

When the Lord is presented in a position of authority (as King in Matthew and as God in John), the possessive pronoun "your" precedes the title, but when the position of a lowly servant is stated, as in Mark, the pronoun "My" appears. When the Lord is introduced in the intermediate stature, as a man in Luke, however, the neutral "the" is applied. This arrangement declares the various positional glories of the Lord's ministry and how He would willingly relate to mankind on an equal footing.

January 2 – The Four "Branches"

(Gospel Introduction)

In addition to the four Old Testament "behold" statements to prophetically speak of God's Son coming to be the Savior of the world, four Branch declarations align with the same unique vantage points of Christ as presented in the four Gospels:

"Behold, the days are coming," says the Lord, "that I will raise to **David a Branch** *of righteousness;* **a King** *shall reign and prosper, and execute judgment and righteousness in the earth. In His days Judah will be saved, and Israel will dwell safely; now this is His name by which He will be called: THE LORD OUR RIGHTEOUSNESS"* (Jer. 23:5-6, also see Isa. 11:1).

Hear, O Joshua, the high priest, you and your companions who sit before you, for they are a wondrous sign; for behold, I am bringing forth **My Servant the BRANCH** (Zech. 3:8).

Then speak to him, saying, "Thus says the Lord of hosts, saying: 'Behold, **the Man whose name is the BRANCH***! From His place He shall branch out, and He shall build the temple of the Lord'"* (Zech. 6:12).

In that day **the Branch of the Lord** *shall be beautiful and glorious; and the fruit of the earth shall be excellent and appealing for those of Israel who have escaped* (Isa. 4:2).

As with the four Old Testament "Behold" declarations, these four divine titles of the Lord Jesus perfectly align with the four Gospel presentations of Christ:

To David a Branch … a King – Gospel of Matthew
My Servant, the Branch – Gospel of Mark
The Man … the Branch – Gospel of Luke
The Branch of the Lord – Gospel of John

By the light of nature we see God as a God above us, by the light of the law we see Him as a God against us, but by the light of the gospel we see Him as Emmanuel, God with us.

— Matthew Henry

January 3 – The Four Faces
(Gospel Introduction)

All creation, visible or invisible, provides a wonderful testimony of God's greatness (Rom. 1:20; Ps. 103:22). Included are spiritual beings in heavenly realms, which continually declare the glory of God and praise His name (Ps. 103:20). Scripture informs us that classes of spiritual beings do indeed exist in heaven for this very purpose. Besides Michael the archangel, there are cherubim, seraphim, the four living creatures, and a host of innumerable angels with various functions. Furthermore, God describes to us what many of these spiritual beings do and how they appear before God's throne in heaven. All things recorded in Scripture have a divine purpose, so why did God go to the effort of affording these details? What is it that He wants us to learn?

Clearly, God the Father is calling our attention to His Son through the appearance of these created beings. When the cherubim and seraphim cover themselves, it is for the purpose of concealing competing glories in God's presence – only God's glory is to be appreciated; He alone is to be worshipped. However, when the feet, eyes, or faces of these creatures are described, it is because they are not covered and, in fact, should not be, for some emulated glory of Christ is being visually proclaimed. Interestingly, the cherubim (Ezek. 1 and 10), the seraphim (Isa. 6), and the four living creatures (Rev. 4) all disclose that these beings have the same faces – four kinds of faces, to be more exact. Apparently, the cherubim each have all four, that is, the face of a lion, the face of an ox, the face of a man, and the face of an eagle. The faces of these beings reflect the same glories of the Lord Jesus that are presented in the main themes of each Gospel. The *lion* is the king of the beasts, which reflects Matthew's perspective. The *ox*, as a beast of burden, is harnessed for the rigors of serving, and pictures Mark's presentation. The face of the *man* clearly agrees with Luke's prevalent theme of the Lord's humanity. Lastly, the *eagle* flies high above all the other creatures – declaring the divinity of the Savior.

Lion – King – Gospel of Matthew
Ox – Servant – Gospel of Mark
Man – Humanity – Gospel of Luke
Eagle – Deity – Gospel of John

January 4 – From One to Four
(Gospel Introduction)

There was only one furnishing to be within the *Most Holy Place* of the tabernacle, the Ark of the Covenant. God dwelt above the Mercy Seat that covered the Ark of the Covenant. There was but *one* Most Holy Place, *one* Ark and *one* Mercy Seat, but moving from the glorious presence of God to the realm occupied by men, a steady presentation of the number *four* is plainly observed.

Four different colored fabrics were woven together to make the tabernacle (the ceiling), which then had three more coverings placed upon it to make a total of four layers. The inner veil hung upon four pillars (Ex. 26:31-32) forming a barrier between the Most Holy Place where God dwelt and the holy place where the priests entered twice daily. The veil itself was woven with four different colored fabrics and displayed the figures of cherubim; cherubim each have four wings. Moving into the holy place we notice that the Golden Altar of Incense has four horns extended upward from the altar. Both the holy ointment, dabbed on parts of the tabernacle, and the incense, placed twice daily by a priest upon the Golden Altar, were composed of four spices each.

Venturing eastward through the holy place into the courtyard, four more horns are noted upon the Bronze Altar. Peering eastward beyond the Bronze Altar, the only entrance to the tabernacle courtyard is seen, which is formed by "hangings" upon four pillars. Like the tabernacle and the inner veil, the "hangings" were also woven from four different colored fabrics. Lastly, the priests were to only offer four creatures on the Bronze Altar: the bullock, the lamb, the goat, and the turtledove.

The number one expresses God's dwelling place in the tabernacle and represents His abode in heaven. The Son of God departed heaven and became subjected to earthly order, as expressed by the number four. Hence, the number four pervades the journey from God's presence to man's realm of life on the earth. This is the path that the Son of God traveled to become the Son of Man – God's sacrificial Lamb. John tells us that the spirit of antichrist is to reject this truth:

Every spirit that confesses that Jesus Christ has come in the flesh is of God, and every spirit that does not confess that Jesus Christ has come in the flesh is not of God. And this is the spirit of the Antichrist, which you have heard was coming, and is now already in the world (1 Jn. 4:2-3).

10

January 5 – The Veil of Four Colors
(Gospel Introduction)

The writer of Hebrews informs us that Christ's own flesh was a veil (Heb. 10:19-20). Coverings in Scripture both reveal and conceal things. The Lord's flesh concealed the outshining glory of God but allowed His divine moral excellencies to be viewed by all. *"And the Word became flesh and dwelt among us, and we beheld His glory, the glory as of the only begotten of the Father, full of grace and truth"* (John 1:14). The night before the Lord Jesus died, we read of Him speaking to His disciples:

> *Jesus said to him, "Have I been with you so long, and yet you have not known Me, Philip? He who has seen Me has seen the Father; so how can you say, 'Show us the Father'? Do you not believe that I am in the Father, and the Father in Me? The words that I speak to you I do not speak on My own authority; but the Father who dwells in Me does the works. Believe Me that I am in the Father and the Father in Me, or else believe Me for the sake of the works themselves"* (John 14:9-11).

The veil of the Lord's flesh is pictured in the inner veil of the tabernacle. This veil hung upon four pillars; each pillar consisted of wood (speaking of Christ's humanity) overlaid with gold (declaring Christ's deity). God dwelt on one side of this veil and man on the other. What a depiction of the Messiah – He would be both God and man. He was both the Son of David and David's Lord (Mark 12:35-37).

As previously mentioned, the veil was woven with four colored fabrics, the basic four colors of all the coverings throughout the tabernacle. William MacDonald comments:

> The four colors of materials in the tabernacle with their symbolic meanings also seem to fit the evangelists' fourfold presentation of the attributes of our Lord! *Purple* is an obvious choice for **Matthew**, the Gospel of the King. Judges 8:26 shows the regal nature of this color. *Scarlet* dye was derived in ancient times from crushing a cochineal worm. This suggests **Mark**, the Gospel of the bondservant, *"a worm and no man" (Ps. 22:6)*. *White* speaks of the righteous deeds of the saints (Rev. 19:8). **Luke** stresses the perfect humanity of Christ. *Blue* represents the sapphire dome we call the heavens (Ex. 24:10), an attractive representation of the Deity of Christ, a keynote in **John**.[4]

11

January 6 – Repent and Believe
(Gospel Introduction)

One of the most beautiful panoramic views of the differing vantage points of Christ is seen in the Gospel message itself. There is but one gospel message, yet each writer highlights varying aspects of the Gospel as it directly relates to his associated theme.

Matthew's authority theme stresses "repentance" eleven times, but only three times does he speak of the necessity to believe in the Lord Jesus (e.g., Matt. 4:17). In fact, in Matthew, the Lord spends more time criticizing the Jews for not believing John's message of repentance than for not believing upon Him.

Mark stresses the need to both repent and to believe in Christ to be saved, but there is clearly a heavier focus on believing (e.g., Mark 1:14-15). He speaks of believing in Christ nearly a dozen times and of the necessity to repent only four times. As Christ is not lauding His kingly authority in Mark, repentance is of a secondary emphasis. Accordingly, it would require real faith to believe on a lowly Servant for salvation.

Luke speaks of believing in the Lord five times but addresses the matter of repentance fourteen times. The beloved physician instead employs terms in his Gospel which appeal to human need and suffering, such as "perishing" (Luke 13:3, 5). "Perishing" speaks of dying, and Luke speaks of it more often than the other gospel writers. On behalf of Christ, Luke petitions the sick, the suffering, and the brokenhearted suffering under the effects of sin. The Lord feels our painful infirmities caused by sin. He desires to save the sinner from eternal judgment and also to relieve the agonizing aftermath of sin.

John's Gospel expresses the heavenly perspective of the gospel message. While Matthew and Luke stress repentance, for one must acknowledge their sins before salvation can be obtained, John simply declares the overall spiritual situation: In God is life, and apart from God is death (John 1:3-4). Speaking of Christ, John writes: *"All things were made by Him"*; John stresses the fact that man is spiritually dead and must be born again (John 3:3) and made alive (John 5:21). How is this accomplished? By believing (John 3:16, 3:36, 5:24). Consequently, the words "repent" and "forgive" are not found in John's account, but the matter of believing is emphasized ninety-nine times! Man is dead in the world. Eternal life is only in Christ. Do you believe this?

The Gospels Illustrated

Perhaps the following improvised story will help better explain how each Gospel writer relates to the gospel message preached by Christ. Imagine a man fishing on a large flat rock adjoining a fast-flowing river. He is a stranger to the area, but while driving along the river, he spotted what he thought would be a great fishing hole. He couldn't resist the temptation, so he quickly pulled over and grabbed his fly rod and tackle box. His first cast lands a sizable brown trout, and while leaning over to pull it from the water, he slips off the rock he has been standing on and falls into the frigid water. The situation is desperate because the man does not know how to swim and the cold, deep water is quickly numbing his muscles. Fortunately for him, a huge log is floating down the river near him, and with a few desperate lunges, he is able to grasp it. Although he is debilitated from his near drowning experience, he musters up his remaining strength to cling to the tree. Though chilled to the bone, he begins to calm down and breathe a bit easier; he feels safe and is confident that he will eventually float near the shore.

His brief moment of composure is interrupted by cries from behind him. He glances over his shoulder to see five individuals running along the shoreline; one has a long rope in his hand. As they draw nearer, he is able to discern their warning – "huge waterfall ahead" – "certain death!" The man, not being familiar with the river, has no idea whether this information is true. Since he cannot see the approaching doom, he remains determined to grip his only means of safety, the log. One individual on the shore, named Matthew, yells out, "This man with the rope is the park ranger. He can save you from going over the waterfall, but you must let go of the log." Another man, named Mark, cries out, "Yes, when this man throws you the rope, you must let go of the log to grasp the rope; he will then pull you to safety, for he is strong and able."

The third man, Luke, shouts, "You will perish if you don't let go of the log and grab hold of the rope. This man with the rope knows how cold and afraid you are, and he can help you." Finally, the fourth man, John, declares, "Your situation is desperate. You are going to die. You must grasp the rope and trust this man with your life – he has saved everyone who has ever trusted him."

13

Repentance is stressed in the letting go of the log, which might be named "Infant Baptism," or "Good Deeds," or "Church Attendance." Believing is demonstrated by the grasping of the rope that is anchored to a secure object. Repentance literally means "to turn," and demonstrates an understanding of our desperate situation; we are sinners and could plummet into hell at any moment. We are merely one heartbeat away from eternity. Repentance is agreeing with God about our spiritual condition, that He is right about this matter of sin and then standing with God against ourselves (2 Cor. 7:10).

Repentance loosens its grip on self-pride, self-works and human traditions and chooses to grip the *"the truth and the life,"* the Lord Jesus. Repentance and faith are different but very much connected on the same hinge of truth. If the man only lets go of the log, he would still perish, either by drowning or over the falls. To be saved, one must let go of the log, then grip the rope. One cannot grip the log and the rope simultaneously; that individual would still go over the falls. *"For by grace you have been saved through faith, and that not of yourselves; it is the gift of God, not of works, lest anyone should boast"* (Eph. 2:8-9). To be saved, the man had to reckon his condition as desperate, understand he had only one means to safety, then act upon that means which required letting go of the log and grasping the rope. Salvation is obtained only by grace through faith, but repentance must precede an exercise of faith. Because the reality of having no other escape from certain death is understood – true saving faith has a continuing quality. Though doubts may creep in from time to time, true faith abides, for it reckons the seriousness of the situation to be real. Genuine faith holds onto the rope which is eternally secure in Christ.

Each evangelist is proclaiming the good news of Jesus Christ but from different perspectives. It is all the truth, related, and all one message, but it is uniquely presented for the purpose of seeing the fullness of Christ as God the Father wants us to appreciate His Son.

> The gospel is not good advice to be obeyed; it is good news to be believed.
>
> — Harry Ironside

> The great question is not, "Will not the heathen be saved if we do not send them the gospel?" but "Are we saved ourselves if we do not send them the gospel?"
>
> — C. H. Spurgeon

January 7 – Why Is Matthew First?
(Matthew Introduction)

Why is Matthew the first book of the New Testament? The opening sentence both introduces the theme of Matthew and answers this question: *"The book of the generation of Jesus Christ, the Son of David, the Son of Abraham."* The principal topic is the direct fulfillment of the Davidic and Abrahamic covenants through Christ. These were unilateral covenants that God had made with David and Abraham but never had been completely fulfilled. For the Jews, the hope of permanent royalty from *a man after God's own heart* and the acquisition of blessing promised to *the friend of God* were paramount.

The genealogies of Matthew 1 served as proof to the Jews that Jesus, through Joseph, was a direct descendant of David and, thus, the legal and rightful heir to David's throne. As to not distract from his theme of covenant fulfillment, Matthew begins with Abraham, not Adam, in rendering Christ's genealogy. Luke's genealogy of Christ, however, is for a different purpose. Luke upholds Christ as the "Son of man," or more specifically, the "Son of Adam." In so doing, Luke shows Christ to be the "Last Adam," God's replacement representative of righteousness and the literal fulfillment of the prophesied Messiah being derived from the "seed of a woman" (Gen. 3:15-16). God thought it critical for mankind to understand that the Messiah would not be of the seed of fallen man, yet His royal lineage would be established through a man, Joseph, back to Solomon and finally David. The two genealogies accomplish this: Luke focuses our attention upon the Lord's humanity derived from Mary by the power of the Holy Spirit, while Matthew demonstrates Christ's official authority through Joseph.

The Hebrew Bible concludes with genealogies from Adam to the point in time in which God invoked 400 years of silence concerning His rebellious covenant people. This prophetic hush was broken with the announcement of the Savior's coming to earth. In Matthew 1, the genealogies pick up again after the centuries of silence and lead the Jews to their predicted Messiah, the Lord Jesus Christ. He would be the literal fulfillment of God's promise to David of an everlasting throne (2 Sam. 7:13). Matthew completes what Chronicles only partially disclosed, and bridges the remaining gap between the first Adam and the last Adam, who would restore righteousness and rule forever.

15

January 8 – "From That Time"
(Matthew Introduction)

When Christ walked upon the earth, the Jews had been without their own king for more than six centuries. Four different Gentile empires had ruled over them during that time, most of them cruelly. The Jews longed to be liberated from Roman oppression and to be a self-governing nation again. From this political ideology, the prophesied Messiah was coveted, but from a spiritual sense, the heart of the people had drifted far from God over the centuries of exile and silence. The *"feasts of Jehovah"* had become the *"feasts of the Jews."* The legalistic traditions of the Pharisees controlled the people harshly and perverted the clear teachings of the Mosaic Law. Their oral laws had declared it wrong to serve others or to do good deeds on the Sabbath day and upheld that it was more honorable to give money to God than to use it for the proper care of aged parents. So, when their long-awaited Messiah did arrive, His message of repentance and spiritual transformation was not only unwelcome but flatly rejected – it was not what the Jews wanted, but it was exactly what they needed.

Often Scripture provides its own outline of a particular passage or book. The phrase *"from that time,"* found only twice in Matthew's Gospel (4:17 and 16:21), properly divides the book into three main sections: *"From that time ... Repent for the Kingdom of heaven is at hand"* (Matt. 4:17). *"From that time forth began Jesus to show unto His disciples, how that He must...suffer"* (Matt. 16:21). Accordingly, Matthew 1:1 – 4:16 forms an introduction, while Matthew 4:17 – 16:20 presents the Jewish Messiah, and Matthew 16:21 – 28:20 records the rejection of the Jewish Messiah. The last section begins after Peter's confession of Jesus, as Christ and the Son of God and just prior to the Lord's transfiguration. Matthew first records the Lord informing His disciples of His future suffering, death, and resurrection at this time.

After being anointed by the Holy Spirit, the Lord labored in Galilee for about two years, then in Decapolis for six months, in Judea for three months, and then withdrew to Perea for the final four months, prior to returning to Jerusalem for the Passover and crucifixion. Hence, Matthew 4:17-16:20 covers nearly two and a half years of history, while the last section in Matthew (16:21-28:20) spans the final seven or eight months of the Lord's sojourn on earth.

16

January 9 – The Spirit of Prophecy
(Matthew Introduction)

Matthew labors in his Gospel account to validate Jesus Christ as the Jewish Messiah – He was born of the Jews and for the Jews. He frequently quotes Old Testament prophecies to show that Jesus Christ literally fulfilled them. Where John repeatedly connects Christ to the completion of Old Testament "types," Matthew meticulously demonstrates that Christ is the culmination of prophecy, or as John would later write, *"For the testimony of Jesus is the spirit of prophecy"* (Rev. 19:10). Bible prophecy finds its center in the Lord Jesus Christ.

Because Matthew directly relates Jesus Christ to Old Testament declarations, the word "fulfilled" appears sixteen times in his Gospel. Fourteen of these references are clearly messianic, compared to eight in Mark, Luke, and John combined. It is noted that well over one hundred first advent prophecies concerning the Messiah are found in the Old Testament and that Jesus Christ fulfilled them all. The statistical probability of such a feat is astronomically impossible, but not for God's chosen Son.

In the first two chapters alone, Matthew refers to Christ fulfilling five Old Testament prophecies relating to His birth and childhood.

Behold, the virgin shall conceive and bear a Son, and shall call His name Immanuel (Isa. 7:14). **Jesus was born of a virgin.**

Bethlehem Ephrathah ... out of you shall come forth to Me the one to be Ruler in Israel, whose goings forth are from of old, from everlasting (Mic. 5:2). **Jesus was born in Bethlehem.**

When Israel was a child, I loved him, and out of Egypt I called My son (Hos. 11:1). **Jesus lived in Egypt to escape Herod's wrath.**

A voice was heard in Ramah, lamentation and bitter weeping, Rachel weeping for her children, refusing to be comforted for her children, because they are no more (Jer. 31:15). **In pattern, Herod murdered the baby boys of Ramah in an attempt to kill Jesus.**

There shall come forth a Rod from the stem [netzer – Nazarene] *of Jesse, and a Branch shall grow out of his roots* (Isa. 11:1). **Jesus would live in Nazareth.**

17

January 10 – Two Witnesses
(Matthew Observation)

Under the Mosaic Law, at least two witnesses were required to substantiate a legal claim or allegation (Deut. 19:15). While offering instructions on how to reconcile an offense with a brother, the Lord acknowledged the importance of two witnesses to confirm the truth. *"But if he will not hear, take with you one or two more, that 'by the mouth of two or three witnesses every word may be established'"* (Matt. 18:16). Matthew is the only Gospel writer to record these statements of the Lord Jesus.

As Matthew is mainly addressing a Jewish audience, he is conscious of this legal regulation in his writing. Though the other Gospel writers neglect this detail, he often identifies the existence of *two* witnesses to legally substantiate important events of the Lord's life. Matthew records that there were:

two demon-possessed individuals cured by Christ in the country of the Gergesenes (Matt. 8:28);

two blind men healed by Christ near Nazareth (Matt. 9:27);

two of John's disciples who came to inquire of Jesus (Matt. 11:2);

two blind men healed by Christ leaving Jericho (Matt. 20:30); one was Bartimaeus (Mark 10:46);

two false witnesses at His trial (Matt. 26:60);

two Gentile witnesses of nobility attesting to His innocence. (Both Pilate and his wife declared Christ was a righteous man – Matt. 27:19, 24.)

Matthew's focus on *two* witnesses is unique, for none of the other Gospel writers were compelled by the Holy Spirit to record the above details. Through compliance of the Law, Matthew shows us that there was ample and adequate testimony of Christ's ministry.

January 11 – Matthew's Mountains
(Matthew Observation)

Symbolically speaking, mountains refer to "kingdoms" in Scripture (e.g., Isa. 2:1; Jer. 51:25; Mic. 4:1). Daniel invokes this imagery to speak of the Lord Jesus coming into His kingdom after all Gentile powers had been judged (Dan. 2:44-45). Daniel describes King Nebuchadnezzar's secret dream to him as being a tall image composed of various metals. Suddenly, a stone from heaven struck the image in the feet and caused it to fall and crumble into powder. The wind blew away the debris, then the stone grew to become a glorious mountain.

Daniel explains that the image is a blueprint of five world empires that would be permitted to rule over God's covenant people from that timeframe forward. Each of these kingdoms would exist before Christ's return to establish His own kingdom on earth: Babylon, under Nebuchadnezzar's leadership was the head of gold; the Medes and Persians were the chest and arms of silver; the bronze torso and thighs represented the Greeks; the two iron legs, the Roman empire; and the ten toes of clay and iron, the final Gentile empire rising out of the old Roman Empire and controlled by Antichrist.

The stone that was not cut with human hands (an expression of deity) and that came down from heaven to strike the image in the feet represents Christ's Second Advent to earth. At that time He will wipe out the Antichrist and his armies (as pictured in the image's feet) and establish a worldwide kingdom of peace and righteousness (Rev. 19).

John applies this same metaphorical meaning in Revelation 17 where seven mountains are described as seven world empires, five of which had past, one was, and one was yet to come under the Antichrist. The Egyptian and Assyrian empires preceded the Babylonian empire.

Matthew, upholding the nobility of Christ, references mountains to signify His forthcoming earthly kingdom. Though all the Gospels record the Lord venturing up and down mountains during His ministry, the other writers, for the most part, do not apply the symbolic representation during key events as Matthew does. Examples include: Sermon on the Mount (Matt. 5-7): No mention in the other three Gospels. Transfiguration (High Mount – Matt. 17:1): No mention in John. Olivet Discourse (Matt. 24:3): No mention in Luke or John. Galilee Commission (Matt. 28:16): No mention in the other Gospels.

January 12 – Ministering Angels
(Matthew Observation)

Angels are rarely mentioned in Mark and John, but Matthew and Luke refer to them 43 times, yet from different viewpoints. In general, Matthew refers to these spiritual beings as messengers of God (mainly communicating through dreams) and as subordinates doing the Lord's bidding. Luke emphasizes their various ministries, including praising God, being His messengers, and being witnesses to His earthly operations. Perhaps Mark does not refer much to the ministry of angels because the ministry of the humble Servant of Jehovah is primary. In John, the Lord Jesus, the Supreme Son of God, is entrusted with all the work; no one else, not even the disciples, share in the Lord's ministry.

The authority theme of Matthew is upheld in the Lord's relationship with the angels, as He often commands their activities: *"The Son of Man will send out His angels, and they will gather out of His kingdom all things that offend"* (Matt. 13:41) and *"For the Son of Man will come in the glory of His Father with His angels, and then He will reward each according to his works"* (Matt. 16:27, also 24:31, 25:31).

Luke is the only Gospel writer to record that an angel assisted the Lord in the Garden of Gethsemane (Luke 22:43). The purpose of this visit was to "strengthen" the Lord. Luke uses *enischuo*, which means "to invigorate or make strong" to describe the ministry of the angels to Christ. Luke draws our attention to the Lord's frail humanity to demonstrate that, like us, He also was prone to weariness, thirst, hunger, emotional distress, etc. Contemplating Calvary had agitated the Lord's soul, but an entire night of prayer had quieted His heart, though it left Him physically and emotionally exhausted.

Though the "strengthening" language is consistent with Luke's "Son of Man" theme, it would be out of place in Matthew. Once in Matthew, after the forty-day period in which Satan unsuccessfully solicited the Lord to sin, we read of angels "ministering" or "serving" the Lord (Matt. 4:11). Only Matthew records the Lord Jesus rebuking and commanding Satan to go at the end of the forty days of testing. The word translated "ministered" in Matthew is *diakoneo*, which means "to be an attendant or wait upon." It is the same Greek word from which the church office of deacon is derived. As King, Christ commands and is waited on by subordinates.

January 13 – Righteousness
(Matthew Observation)

Matthew emphasizes God's righteousness in a way that substantiates mankind's inherent unrighteous state, humanity's need to be righteous, and man's natural propensity to boast of self-righteousness. Of the twenty-nine times that the words "righteous" or "righteousness" are found in the Gospels, nineteen reside in Matthew.

Blessed are those who hunger and thirst for righteousness, for they shall be filled (Matt. 5:6).

Blessed are those who are persecuted for righteousness' sake,
For theirs is the kingdom of heaven (Matt. 5:10).

But seek first the kingdom of God and His righteousness, and all these things shall be added to you (Matt. 6:33).

For I did not come to call the righteous, but sinners, to repentance (Matt. 9:13).

The subject of righteousness unquestionably relates to Christ's legitimate claim to the throne of David, from which He will establish an endless rule of righteousness. The kingdom manifesto in Matthew 5 demands righteous subjects for this kingdom, for Christ's kingdom will be thoroughly evidenced by the righteousness of God. By such association with Him, God's holy character demands dedicated and yielded subjects. *"Be holy, for I am holy"* (1 Pet. 1:16). *"Serve God acceptably with reverence and godly fear. For our God is a consuming fire"* (Heb. 12:28-29). The Jews rejected both Christ's righteousness and His call to righteousness and are, to this day, a suffering people waiting for their Messiah. The refined Jewish nation will acknowledge Jesus Christ as Messiah at His Second Advent to the earth (Zech. 12:10). Isaiah describes Messiah's righteous ministry at that time:

But with righteousness He shall judge the poor, and decide with equity for the meek of the earth; He shall strike the earth with the rod of His mouth, and with the breath of His lips He shall slay the wicked. Righteousness shall be the belt of His loins, and faithfulness the belt of His waist (Isa. 11:4-5).

January 14– Thrones and Altars
(Matthew Observation)

Scripture often presents what seem to be unconnected and even contrasting subjects in tandem so that a fuller spiritual teaching might be better understood. One such topical pairing in Scripture is the connection between God's *throne* and God's *altar*. The word "throne" is found five times in the four Gospels; four of these occur in Matthew. Likewise, the word "altar" is rendered eight times altogether in the Gospels, with six of these references being in Matthew. What meaning is being conveyed through more frequent reference to *thrones* and *altars* in Matthew? Though the Old Testament contains several references to this association, the example within Isaiah 6 is adequate to demonstrate the spiritual meaning.

Isaiah beheld the majestic glory of God's throne (Isa. 6:1-7). His response to the revealed holiness of God was *"Woe is me, for I am undone."* At that moment, he was not mindful of what he had or had not done, nor of what he should have done, but of his spiritual position before Almighty God. When man stands before the throne of God, there is no excuse, nowhere to shift blame; we all stand condemned: "I am a sinner, and I am guilty." But as soon as Isaiah acknowledged his condition before God, God's response was immediate and effectual. A seraph hovering about the throne of God swooped down and snatched a hot coal from off the altar and pressed it to Isaiah's lips to show God's ability to purify sinners. Through the altar, Isaiah received grace, found a holy standing before God, and was prepared and readied for service.

Matthew's message to the Jewish nation is twofold – "the throne of Christ" and "the altar of Christ." Anyone acknowledging His divine righteousness will also be compelled to repent and embrace God's altar, the finished work of Christ at Calvary. This is why righteousness and repentance are so duly stressed in Matthew. The throne must be understood first, or the altar will have no meaning or benefit. Only when man understands his lost and unsaved state before God can he be found and saved by God. For those awakened to their depraved and destitute state, God points the way to restoration – the cross of Christ. For *"we have an Altar"* (Heb. 13:10), but it is completely outside Judaism and any system of human works and requires an individual to identify with Christ and, thus, bear His reproach (Heb. 13:10-13).

January 15 – "The Son of David"
(Matthew 1)

Clearly, God's covenant with Abraham had not been completely fulfilled, for the Jews were under brutal Gentile rule and were clearly not the esteemed people of the earth. Secondly, they have never possessed, at any time during their entire history, more than about ten percent of the land promised to Abraham by God in Genesis 15. Through Christ, the Abrahamic covenant would be fulfilled. Listen to the prophetic words of Zacharias, the father of John the Baptist:

*Blessed is the Lord God of Israel, for He has visited and redeemed His people, and has raised up a horn of salvation for us in the house of His servant David, as He spoke by the mouth of His holy prophets, who have been since the world began, that we should be saved from our enemies and from the hand of all who hate us, to perform the mercy promised to our fathers and **to remember His holy covenant, the oath which He swore to our father Abraham**: To grant us that we, being delivered from the hand of our enemies, might serve Him without fear, in holiness and righteousness before Him all the days of our life* (Luke 1:68-75).

The order of mention in the first verse of Matthew is important: the "Son of David," then "the Son of Abraham." Normally, when these two chief patriarchs of the Jewish history are mentioned, Abraham is referred to first, for he walked upon the earth more than a thousand years before David was born. The order arranged by Matthew, however, introduces us to the "authority" theme of his Gospel. And who better than Matthew, a Jewish official, a tax collector, to address the official glory of the Lord Jesus as rightful heir to David's throne.

The "Son of David" refers specifically to the office of king, but the Lord has not yet returned to the earth to establish His kingdom (Rev. 3:21). Matthew upholds the official glory of Christ as King; this is the prevalent theme of his testimony. Ten times he refers to Christ as the *"Son of David."* This is in contrast to Mark, Luke, and John, which contain only five references to this title (see Matt. 12:23 and Luke 11:14). Matthew is properly placed first among the Gospels: the Lord Jesus will fulfill God's covenants to David and Abraham by reigning on the throne of David in righteousness and over all nations forever.

January 16 – "The Son of Abraham"
(Matthew 1)

The reference to the "Son of Abraham" in Matthew 1:1 is of a much wider scope than the reference to the "Son of David." Through the son of Abraham *"shall all families of the earth be blessed"* (Gen. 12:3). Paul speaks of Abraham as the spiritual father of all spiritual seed and of the eternal blessings which God promised to Abraham that are likewise offered to all those, who like Abraham, would simply believe God's word (Rom. 4:13-16). This is God's means of saving souls throughout all human history, whether Old Testament or New Testament. There may be varying messages of repentance and obedience to heed, but justification only occurs by grace through faith in what God proclaims is our responsibility. As with Abraham, only by faith can the work of Christ be accredited to our personal account:

> For what does the Scripture say? "Abraham believed God, and it was accounted to him for righteousness." Now to him who works, the wages are not counted as grace but as debt. But to him who does not work but believes on Him who justifies the ungodly, his faith is accounted for righteousness (Rom. 4:3-5).

If we want to work for our salvation, God is faithful to pay a fair wage; however, *"the wages of sin is death, but the gift of God is eternal life through Jesus Christ our Lord"* (Rom. 6:23). It may not seem logical, but God just wants us to recognize that we cannot save ourselves and that we must accept His free gift of salvation as the only means to be reconciled with Him. Man's lingering guilt provokes him to do something to earn God's favor, but God is unimpressed with such attempts. The gospel message candidly proclaims, "You can't *do* anything to be accepted by God: it's all been accomplished in Christ – you must only believe." Faith is a living trust in God, which ascends beyond what our five senses or reasoning can verify. We become Abraham's children when we exercise his type of faith (Gal. 3:7)!

In Christ, we see the very best aspects of both Jewish patriarchs. As the Son of David, Christ was the righteous king and a man after God's own heart, and as the Son of Abraham, He was a friend of God and a great man of faith – He lived to do the Father's will (John 6:38).

January 17 – The Lethargic Jewish Attitude
(Matthew 2)

By their response to the eastern magi and to John's ministry the Jewish nation clearly indicated that they were not looking for their Messiah, as least in the spiritual sense. Unexpectedly, several foreign diplomats arrived in Jerusalem inquiring, *"Where is He that is born King of the Jews? For we have seen His star in the East, and have come to worship Him"* (Matt. 2:2). After some investigation by the scribes, the magi were informed that Bethlehem in the county of Ephrathah was to be the birthplace of the Messiah. If the Jews had been yearning for Messiah's coming, they would have known His birthplace and then accompanied their foreign visitors to search for and find their prophesied king. But Herod told the wise men to *"go and search carefully for the young Child, and when you have found Him, bring back word to me, that I may come and worship Him also"* (Matt. 2:8). Did Herod really want to worship Messiah? No, he later proved that his only reason for directing the magi as he did was so he could locate and murder any rival to his authority. The heart of the Jewish people was so far from Jehovah that they had no desire or love for His Messiah.

Being warned in a dream, Joseph removed his young family to Egypt. Later, after the death of Herod the Great, Joseph returned his family to the land of Israel, but being again warned in a dream, he turned aside to live in Nazareth, for he feared Herod's son Archelaus. In a poetic sense, the Savior, in those early years, retraced the very steps of Israel's infant history (Canaan to Egypt in distress, and back to Canaan after the enemy had been vanquished).

Notice that earthly kings were responsible for the early movements of the Lord Jesus. His original pilgrimage to Bethlehem in the womb of Mary resulted from the registration decreed by Caesar Augustus. The Lord's hurried departure to Egypt resulted from the evil Herod sought to do against Him, and the Lord traveled to Nazareth because Joseph feared Archelaus. To demonstrate the sovereign power of God, the highest human authorities on earth worked to accomplish the foreordained counsel of God. Through the presence and administrations of these three kings, the Old Testament prophecies pertaining to Christ's birth, foreign travels, and hometown were all fulfilled.

January 18 – The Kingdom Offer
(Matthew 3)

The authority theme of Matthew is quite obvious in Christ's preaching and parable telling. How did the Lord commence His public ministry? John the Baptist had been preaching to the Jews: *"Repent, for the kingdom of heaven is at hand!"* (Matt. 3:2). Although Herod silenced John by incarceration, he could not thwart the Messiah from taking up John's message. Matthew records the Lord's first words of public ministry: *"From that time Jesus began to preach, and to say, 'Repent, for the kingdom of heaven is at hand'"* (Matt. 4:17).

The Lord Jesus was the literal fulfillment of the kingdom message John had been proclaiming. John *"was a burning and a shining light"* (John 5:35), but his brilliance was destined to be quenched as soon as the "Light of the World" (John 8:12) showed forth His illumination. With John in prison, the King of the Jews began to directly call His subjects to repentance, which meant they needed to acknowledge Him as the sinless Messiah and their rightful King.

In Matthew, God is still dealing with Israel as before at Mt. Sinai, on the ground of responsibility. Messiah had come. Would they accept or reject Him? The Kingdom Message itself was the culmination of a Jewish dispensational economy that began on Mt. Sinai – the giving of the Law to Moses – and would conclude at Mt. Moriah – the crucifixion of Christ. Fifty days later, the dispensation of the Church began, and both the message and the recipient of the message changed.

Matthew, more prominently than the other Gospel writers, shows the offering of Messiah, the Jewish rejection, and the consequential setting aside of Israel that the Gentiles might receive grace. *"Jesus Christ was a minister of the circumcision for the truth of God, to confirm the promises made unto the fathers; and that the Gentiles might glorify God for His mercy"* (Rom. 15:8-9). The Lord's ministry is mainly focused upon the *"lost sheep of the house of Israel,"* a term only found in Matthew (Matt. 10:6, 15:22-28). As long as Christ was on the earth preaching *"the kingdom of God has come,"* the disciples were instructed to only preach to the Jews – the kingdom Gospel was a specific message (a presentation of Messiah by words and signs) to the Jewish nation.

January 19 – The Gospel of the Kingdom
(Matthew 4)

The "Gospel of the Kingdom" and the "Gospel of Grace" preached now in the Church Age are both founded in God's grace and both require personal faith to appropriate God's blessing, but each has a distinct message, beneficiary, and dispensational focus. Arthur Pink notes the dispensational distinction of the gospel message:

> *"And Jesus went about all Galilee teaching in their synagogues, and preaching the Gospel* [not, be it noted, the "Gospel of the Grace of God" – Acts 20:24; nor "the Gospel of Peace" – Eph. 6:15; but "the Gospel"] *of the Kingdom, and healing all manner of sickness and all manner of disease among the people"* (Matt. 4:23).[5]

Failure to draw a distinction between the gospel message of the Kingdom, preached by Christ to the "Lost House of Israel," and the Gospel of Grace, preached presently during the Church Age, will result in doctrinal error. The gospel commanded to be preached now was not publicly proclaimed during Christ's ministry on earth, for if Satan had known what God was accomplishing through Christ, the princes of the world *"would have not crucified the Lord of glory"* (1 Cor. 2:8). Of course the sufferings of Christ were predetermined by the counsel of God before the foundation of the world (1 Pet. 1:19-20) – thus God, not Satan, is responsible for Calvary.

Furthermore, the Lord Jesus visited Paul personally to convey to him exactly what the gospel message during the Church age would be: *"I declare to you the gospel which I preached to you ...that Christ died for our sins according to the Scriptures, and that He was buried, and that He rose again the third day according to the Scriptures"* (1 Cor. 15:1-4, also see Gal. 1:6-12). Spiritual application within the Sermon on the Mount for believers today will certainly be gleaned, but the literal intent of the message was for Israel. The hope of the Jew is to see their Messiah reigning on earth and to be nationally restored with God, as His covenant people. The hope of the Church will conclude prior to this fulfillment, when the Lord Jesus descends to the clouds and "catches up" the Church to be with Him in heaven (1 Thess. 4:13-18). The church has a heavenly hope; the Jews have an earthly promise.

January 20 – "The Kingdom of Heaven"
(Matthew 4)

The phrase "kingdom of heaven" is found thirty-two times in Matthew but nowhere else in all of Scripture. This peculiarity must be associated with the theme of his Gospel. The similar and associated term "kingdom of God" is applied fifty-four times in the Gospel accounts, but only appears five times in Matthew and merely twice in John. What is the significance of these phrases, and how do the two terms relate to each other?

Centuries of debate on this subject prove insufficient to answer this question fully. The terms are used interchangeably by the Lord during the Sermon on the Mount and the Lord's discussion with His disciples concerning the rich young ruler who valued his wealth above following the Lord (Matt. 19:23-24). These instances seem to indicate that there is minimal difference in the meaning of the terms, or perhaps, an interrelated meaning (one term being a subset of the other). Some Bible scholars note a distinction in that the kingdom of heaven is a subset of the kingdom of God. The "kingdom of heaven" in this case refers to the realm of human profession in which one acknowledges the sovereign rule of God or "the kingdom of God." C. I. Scofield writes:

> The kingdom of heaven is similar in many respects to the kingdom of God and is often used synonymously with it, though emphasizing certain features of divine government. When contrasted with the universal kingdom of God, the kingdom of heaven includes only men on earth, excluding angels and other creatures. The kingdom of heaven is the earthly sphere of profession as shown by the inclusion of these designated as wheat and tares, the latter of which are cast out of the kingdom (Matt. 13:41), and is compared to a net containing both the good and bad fish which are later separated (Matt. 13:47).[6]

Certainly, there is a realm of human profession within the kingdom of heaven, which is composed of true believers and mere professors, but there seems to be no tangible disagreement between the kingdom terms. Regardless, it is important to understand that the "kingdom of heaven" and the church are not synonymous terms, for the kingdom of heaven contains both the children of God and the children of the devil, while the universal church is only composed of true believers.

January 21 – The Temptation (Testing) of Christ
(Matthew 4)

If the accounts of Matthew 4 and Luke 4 are examined closely, one will notice that the order of Satan's specific attacks upon Christ is different. The order maintained by each writer is for the purpose of upholding the prevalent theme of each Gospel. In Matthew, Satan first asks the Lord Jesus to turn the stones into bread, then bids Him to cast Himself down from the pinnacle of the temple, and thirdly offers to Christ all the kingdoms of this world, if Christ will only worship him. Luke's order, however, is first the request to turn the stones into bread, then the offer of earthly kingdoms, and finally Satan adjures Christ to cast Himself down from the pinnacle of the temple to prove that the angels will protect Him. Why the different order? Arthur Pink explains:

> The reason for this variation is not hard to find. In Matthew, the order is arranged climactically, so as to make Rulership over all the kingdoms of the world the final bait which the Devil dangled before the Son of David. But in Luke we have, no doubt, the chronological order, the order in which they actually occurred, and these correspond with the order of temptation of the first man and his wife in Eden, where the appeal was made, as here in Luke, to the lust of the flesh, the lust of the eyes, and the pride of life (see 1 Jn. 2:16; Gen. 3:6).[7]

Sovereign design accounts for the variation of the temptation accounts, which serves to further declare the wisdom of God and the distinct glories of His Son. Luke's order of temptations is chronological, while Matthew arranged it climactically unto kingship. It is worthy to note that John does not record the temptation of Christ, as that would be contrary to his theme. John presents Christ as God made flesh (John 1:14), and as James insists, *"God cannot be tempted"* (Jas. 1:13). This fact refutes any degrading doctrines that pertain to the Lord's ability to sin or to His members having the capacity to be enticed to sin. He was not only sinless, but His nature was impeccable; there was nothing in Him that could respond to sin (Heb. 4:15).

> If Christ is impeccable in heaven because of who He is, then it is also true that Christ was impeccable on earth because of who He was.

— John F. Walvoord

29

January 22 – The Sermon on the Mount
(Matthew 5-7)

The Sermon on the Mount is the manifesto of the King, literally the kingdom's constitution. Matthew (chapters 5 through 7) documents the Lord's lengthy dissertation to His subjects, as Israel's yet-to-be-enthroned King. Luke records a portion of a similar message (approximately thirty verses) given on a different day, while Mark and John do not mention it at all. Thus, the Sermon on the Mount strongly fits with Matthew's perspective of the Lord Jesus Christ. Even the Jews that listened to the Lord Jesus understood the tone of His exhortation, in which He would say fourteen times, *"I say unto you."* At the conclusion of the sermon, we read *"that the people were astonished at His teaching, for He taught them **as one having authority**, and not as the scribes"* (Matt. 7:28-29). The King spoke as the One in authority!

Within this lengthy discourse recorded in Matthew, the Lord addressed the ideal character and conduct of the subjects of His kingdom and what their circle of influence and testimony ought to be. Luke's focus pertains more to the lifestyle of the disciples in personal witnessing. For example: in Matthew, the Lord pronounced a blessing upon *"the poor in spirit"* (Matt. 5:3), but in Luke the blessing is to *"the poor"* (Luke 6:20).

Much of the Lord's declaration conveyed a flat rejection of the traditions and practices of the Pharisees. In the closing, He told the people that they were now accountable for what they had heard: Would they follow Him and build their lives upon His teachings, or would they continue to follow empty religious traditions and human reasoning (i.e. building their house on a foundation of sand)? When the storms of life would come, the latter would prove to be a total "washout," while those who built upon His word (the rock) would stand fast and enjoy an abiding peace in life, despite difficulties.

The Sermon on the Mount will be the constitution of the millennial kingdom, once Christ returns to earth to establish it. Although it is true that those in the Church Age who have the Holy Spirit indwelling them should be exhibiting behavior consistent with the Kingdom Constitution, the kingdom exists now in only that spiritual sense; the literal sense is future. The Kingdom Gospel message was delivered to Israel as an appeal to repent and receive Jesus as Messiah and King.

January 23 – Futile Doings (Part 1)
(Matthew 6)

Sadly, throughout much of Israel's history, the nation did not yearn to know God or to obey Him, and because there was no inward reality of faith in what they were doing, God was largely unimpressed. This sorrowful affliction infests much of the Church today. Religious people, ignorant of who God is and what He says, are trying to impress Him through good deeds, instead of through devotion settled in truth. As Paul puts it, this is *"having a form of godliness but denying its power"*; he then exhorts sound believers, *"from such people turn away"* (2 Tim. 3:5). Believers should not be rubbing religious shoulders with those whom God detests, nor engaging in superficial practices they endorse.

For example, why did the Jews think that fasting would somehow prompt God's favor (Isa. 58:1-8), when He had required them to corporately fast only one day per year? The Law did not require the Jews to *"afflict their souls,"* except on the Day of Atonement (Lev. 16:31). Because of this unique distinction, the Jews in New Testament times commonly referred to the Day of Atonement as *"the fast"* (Acts 27:9). Yet, because of its significance to God, the Day of Atonement was supposed to be a day of rest (as a Sabbath day), a day of fasting and of solemn reflection and repentance before the Lord.

However, for most of Israel's history, "the afflicting of the soul" had just become religious fluff and was void of the inner reflection and repentance as God desired on the Day of Atonement. God's commanded fast was to cause His people to pause and consider whether or not they were obeying His Law. God sent His prophets to point out to Israel the futility of their vain fasting and then the Lord Jesus did the same during His ministry. Believers in the Church Age would do well to heed His rebuke also. The Lord told His disciples:

When you fast, do not be like the hypocrites, with a sad countenance. For they disfigure their faces that they may appear to men to be fasting. Assuredly, I say to you, they have their reward. But you, when you fast, anoint your head and wash your face, so that you do not appear to men to be fasting, but to your Father who is in the secret place; and your Father who sees in secret will reward you openly (Matt. 6:16-18).

January 24 – Futile Doings (Part 2)
(Matthew 6)

We may glean several important points concerning the type of fasting that pleases God from the Lord's directions about fasting (Matt. 6:16-18) and Isaiah's rebuke of Israel about vain fasting (Isa. 58:1-8).

First, notice that the Lord said, *"when you fast."* This affirms that fasting should be a normal part of the believer's life. Second, fasting is not simply debasing one's self or appearing sad to appear spiritual to others, but rather a time of intense inner reflection and focused listening. Fasting for public display is contrary to its purpose and therefore negates its benefit. Hunger pangs remind us of our dependence on the Lord and lengthy times of introspection result in mental clarity to see things as God does. Third, Isaiah reminds us that heartfelt affliction of the soul would result in just and good conduct: the oppressed would be freed, those who were hungry would be fed, and the poor would be clothed. So then, Isaiah asked his countrymen, *"Is your fasting what God has chosen?"* (Isa. 58:6). Isaiah's response in the next verse indicated that the answer to his question was "no," as he suggested that the type of fasting that would be acceptable to God would emphasize moral transformation rather than ceremonial fanfare.

The Lord Jesus declared a similar message to hypocritical and ceremonial Israel during His first advent when He quoted Hosea 6:6 (on two different occasions): *"I desire mercy and not sacrifice"* (Matt. 9:13, 12:7). Fasting should result in a greater awareness of God's will and in a moral transformation. If our fasting does not lead to changed attitudes and behavior, then it did not achieve God's intended outcome.

Let us remember that vain, especially non-commanded, religious activities do not prompt God's blessing, but humble acts of righteousness done in the name of Christ do, because these reflect His gracious and lovely character to others.

The Church would be wise to consider the Lord's rebuke of Israel's futile practices. God is not impressed by religious ritual, developed church tradition, sanctimonious form, and denominational smugness, but rather with personal living fostered in divine truth (Col. 2:20-23). May we not get sucked into meaningless modern-day legalism, but rather engage in *"pure and undefiled religion before God"* (Jas. 1:27). Only having a love relationship with Jesus Christ can produce that kind of religion!

January 25 – Christ Before Others
(Matthew 10)

The Lord Jesus tells His audience of the type of devotion He expects from those who follow Him: *"He who loves father or mother more than Me is not worthy of Me. And he who loves son or daughter more than Me is not worthy of Me"* (Matt. 10:37-38). That the Lord was to have the first place in a believer's heart was not a new concept to the Jewish mind, for Moses had declared the same truth long ago.

Moses anticipated the most tragic circumstance which might lead some Israelites to forsake Jehovah for false gods – the influence of loved ones (Deut. 13:6-8). Moses painstakingly included a variety of close relationships, so that everyone would understand that there were no loopholes in his decree: *"If your brother, the son of your mother, your son or your daughter, the wife of your bosom, or your friend who is as your own soul, secretly entices you, saying, 'Let us go and serve other gods'"* (Deut. 13:6). The difference is that the Law commanded that if any Jew enticed another friend or family member to forsake the Lord for false gods, they were to be rejected and put to death. In the Church Age, false teachers are to be rejected and avoided.

Although false teachers are not stoned presently, the Lord affirms the same high level of devotion expected from God's people in any dispensation. In the parallel text of Matthew 10:37, the Lord Jesus said, *"If anyone comes to Me and does not hate his father and mother, wife and children, brothers and sisters, yes, and his own life also, he cannot be My disciple"* (Luke 14:26). In comparing the passages, we understand that the word for "hate" expresses a comparison: our love for the Lord should be so great that any natural affection would, comparatively, seem like hate. The Lord was weary of shallow followers; He wanted true disciples. He desired quality in consecration, not a large quantity of half-hearted patriots.

When it comes to misplaced affections and devotions, there is no middle ground with the Lord. The Lord expects our love for Him to be so astounding that by comparison our affections for anyone else would seem like hate! To love anyone or anything more than the Lord is a form of idolatry and proves we are not worthy of Him. God desires His people of all ages to be totally committed to Him and to love Him above all else.

January 26 – A Blind and Deaf Servant
(Matthew 12)

The Pharisees were enraged after the Lord healed a man's withered hand on the Sabbath day. Matthew tells us that they began plotting against Him, desiring to destroy Him (Matt. 12:14). Rather than being amazed by the miracle or rejoicing with the healed man, they longed to kill Jesus for doing a good deed on the Sabbath. But the Lord knew all about their plans, so He withdrew from the area and continued preaching to the multitudes and healing those with infirmities (Matt. 12:15-17). It was at this time that the Lord Jesus quoted Isaiah 41:9 and 42:1-4 to His audience. He was God's Servant and their Messiah, and therefore, a Conqueror, but as they had witnessed by His ministry, He was gentle and tenderhearted towards them:

Behold! My Servant whom I have chosen, My Beloved in whom My soul is well pleased! I will put My Spirit upon Him, and He will declare justice to the Gentiles. He will not quarrel nor cry out, nor will anyone hear His voice in the streets. A bruised reed He will not break, and smoking flax He will not quench, till He sends forth justice to victory; and in His name Gentiles will trust (Matt. 12:18-21).

Now notice what Matthew records directly after this declaration by the Lord Jesus: *"Then one was brought to Him who was demon-possessed, blind and mute; and He healed him, so that the blind and mute man both spoke and saw"* (Matt. 12:22). The miracle itself became an extension to the same text that the Lord quoted. After concluding the Messianic portion of the prophecy, Isaiah then describes Israel's demeanor towards Him: They would act like a blind and deaf servant (Isa. 42:18-19). God's indictment against His people is candid: *"Seeing many things, but you do not observe; opening the ears, but he does not hear"* (Isa. 42:20). Matthew's placement of Isaiah's prophecy accomplished two things: First, Jesus Christ is identified as God's Beloved Servant who had been anointed by the Holy Spirit. Second, the healing of the blind and mute man provided hope to Israel. In a coming day, God's Servant will heal His unfaithful servant, the Jewish nation, of their spiritual blindness and then Isaiah predicts that all they will want to do is talk about the Son of David. All their questions will be answered and they will praise their Messiah – the Lord Jesus Christ.

January 27 – The Unpardonable Sin
(Matthew 12)

The Lord had a stern message for the Pharisees; they had committed the unpardonable sin: *"I say to you, **every sin and blasphemy will be forgiven men, but the blasphemy against the Spirit will not be forgiven men**. Anyone who speaks a word against the Son of Man, it will be forgiven him; but whoever speaks against the Holy Spirit, it will not be forgiven him, **either in this age or in the age to come"** (Matt. 12:31-32). First, notice that different forms of sin and blasphemy exist and that forgiveness for these is possible. Second, a specific sin entitled *"blasphemy against the Holy Spirit"* is unforgivable, and this specific sin relates to a particular age. "In this age" relates to the public ministry in which Christ was presently engaged. "The age to come" relates to His Second Advent to restore Israel and establish His kingdom on earth. In between these ages of Messiah's initial offer and rejection, and second offer and reception, is the Church Age. During the Church Age, Christ is not personally on the earth declaring the "Kingdom Gospel" message to the lost house of Israel and working miracles to authenticate His message. During the tribulation period, the kingdom message will be again preached (Matt. 24:14), and Israel shall be converted (Zech. 10:12, Matt. 24:30).

The specific sin that the Pharisees had committed was to ascribe a miracle which Christ had done through the power of the Holy Spirit to Beelzebub, the prince of the demons (Matt. 12:24). These hard-hearted, stiffed-necked religious leaders had not only rejected the gospel message of Christ and His miracles, but they rendered insults in return for His acts of love and kindness. Because of their intense disbelief which was expressed in disdain for the Person of Christ and the working of the Holy Spirit, they had ruthlessly insulted God. Their rejection of Christ was so intense that the Holy Spirit would no longer work with their consciences to lead them to salvation. Without His help it is impossible for anyone to believe the gospel message (1 Cor. 2:9-13). They were already dead in their sins and condemned. (Everyone is born "condemned already" in Adam; John 3:18.) Though the sin of disbelief still occurs today and keeps people from being saved, this specific unpardonable sin cannot be committed today, for the Lord is in Glory and not before us, pleading, preaching, and doing miracles.

January 28 – Seeing Is Not Believing
(Matthew 12)

The word "miracle" is not found in Matthew's Gospel; rather, the miracles that the Lord performed are referred to as "signs." Signs of what? The signs witnessed by Israel were irrefutable evidence proving that Christ was who He claimed to be – the Messiah. The Lord's preaching and signs composed the kingdom message to the Jews. Though the signs provided proof that Jesus was the Christ, they would prove insufficient to cause the people to trust the Messiah for salvation. *"Without faith it is impossible to please Him* [God]*"* (Heb. 11:6), and faith requires the soul to venture beyond what the senses can verify.

The Lord Jesus stated that it was the unrighteous who wanted to see a "sign or a wonder" in order to believe in Him. He called these "sign seekers" an evil generation (Matt. 12:38-39). Even those people who had witnessed the miracle of the feeding of the 5,000 were pestering the Lord the very next day: *"What sign will You perform then, that we **may see it and believe** You?"* (John 6:30). Did they not recall the miracle the day before? Did they not fill their bellies with a boy's multiplied sack lunch? The Israelites saw miracles every day in the wilderness for forty years, yet it did not increase their spirituality – for they constantly murmured against God and His leadership. This shallow spiritual mentality was clearly evident while the Lord Jesus was hanging on the cross: *"Let the Christ, the King of Israel, descend now from the cross, that we **may see and believe**"* (Mark 15:32).

Peter shows us that true spiritual faith opens our eyes to understand the spiritual things of God. When the Lord asked His twelve disciples if they, too, would turn away from Him, as many had done, Peter responded, *"Lord, to whom shall we go? You have the words of eternal life. Also we have come **to believe and know** that You are the Christ, the Son of the living God"* (John 6:68-69). The unrighteous want a sign to believe, but the righteous believe to understand. Until we exercise faith, we will not understand from where we came and to where we journey. *"By faith we understand that the worlds were framed by the word of God, so that the things which are seen were not made of things which are visible"* (Heb. 11:3). Oswald Chambers puts the matter this way: "I must know Jesus Christ as Savior before His teaching has any meaning for me other than that of an ideal which leads to despair."[8]

January 29 – "Yes Be Yes, and Your No, No"
(Matthew 12)

In the Old Testament, swearing to validate a promise was quite common among the Jews. The normal Hebrew word for swearing, *shaba*, which means "to swear'" or "to take an oath," is found 180 times in the Old Testament. It was done to strongly affirm a promise or statement by using the Lord's name. In the New Testament, however, the Lord Jesus traversed the high moral ground on the subject of swearing. He instructed His disciples, *"But let your 'Yes' be 'Yes,' and your 'No,' 'No.' For whatever is more than these is from the evil one"* (Matt. 5:37).

The disciple of Christ does not need to swear to validate his or her words; the merit of everything said should be wholesome, accurate, needful, and gracious without adding God's name to it. Hence, the Lord issued a stern warning:

> *But I say unto you, that every idle word that men shall speak, they shall give account thereof in the day of judgment. For by thy words thou shalt be justified, and by thy words thou shalt be condemned* (Matt. 12:36-37).

Not only will our ungodly speech be judged in a coming day, but we will have to give account of all our idle chit-chat also (i.e., words having no value for eternity). Swearing involves tying God's name to our statements in an attempt to better validate what we say – to heighten the credibility of our words. The believer should not engage in such practices, for to do so would certainly bring low the name of God. Listen to James' warning for this sin: *"But above all, my brethren, do not swear, either by heaven or by earth or with any other oath. But let your 'Yes' be 'Yes,' and your 'No,' 'No,' lest you fall into judgment"* (Jas. 5:12). Demeaning the name of the Lord by swearing falsely is a terrible thing.

As we are forgetful creatures and are rarely perfect in our speech, it behooves us to refrain from swearing oaths which we will most assuredly fall short of keeping. Certainly, the rash vows of Jephthah (Judg. 11:29-40) and Herod (Acts 12:20-23) serve as historical examples of the heavy price to be paid when one foolishly swears to God to do something.

January 30 – "The Sign of Jonah"
(Matthew 12)

Jonah is a type of Christ in many respects. First, like Christ, Jonah was from Galilee (Gath-Hepher was only three to four miles from Nazareth). Second, the Jewish leaders were in error when they said to Nicodemus: *"Search and look, for no prophet has arisen out of Galilee"* (John 7:52). In their proud religiosity, the Pharisees probably ignored Jonah because he preached to Gentiles; they simply could not bear the thought that God's grace should benefit publicans and sinners. Likewise, the Sanhedrin despised Jesus from Galilee and His mission. Third, the Lord referred to the "three days" Jonah was in the belly of the great fish to foretell His death, burial, and resurrection. However, our Lord tasted death in all its appalling reality as the righteous judgment of God against sin, your sin and mine (Heb. 2:9), whereas Jonah suffered for his own disobedience.

Hence, the Lord Jesus offered a prophetic sign to the Pharisees: *"For as Jonah was three days and three nights in the belly of the great fish, so will the Son of Man be three days and three nights in the heart of the earth"* (Matt. 12:40). Later, the Lord clarified the exact meaning of His earlier statement about His own resurrection: He would be *"killed, and be raised up **on the third day**"* (17:23; NASB), but also be *"killed, and **after three days** rise again"* (Mark 8:31). The Lord Jesus implies that these are interchangeable expressions though appearing contradictory to us. In fact, most references speaking of the resurrection declare that it would occur **on** the third day (Matt. 17:23, 20:19; Luke 9:22, 18:33) or **in** the third day (John 2:19-22). The Lord Jesus used Jonah as a type to signify to the Pharisees what was going to happen to Him: three days and three nights Jonah was in the belly of a great fish, likewise for three days the Son of Man shall be in the earth (the grave).

Matthew 27:63 shows that the Pharisees understood the Lord's vernacular concerning His resurrection. He said, *"After three days I will rise again,"* but they asked for a guard to the secure the tomb **until** the third day. If the term "after three days" was not interchangeable with "the third day," the Pharisees would have asked for a tomb to be guarded for four days, but they did not do so. The term "one day and one night" was a Jewish idiom for indicating a day, even when only a part of a day was indicated.

January 31 – Christ Feeds the Multitudes
(Matthew 15)

On two different occasions, the Lord Jesus performed miracles to feed the multitudes that were listening to His message. First, He fed about 20,000 people by multiplying a boy's sack lunch of two fish and five loaves (Matt. 14:17-21). After receiving what was available, the Lord gave thanks for the fish and the bread, broke the bread, and gave the fragments to the disciples to be passed out to the people. After everyone had their fill, there were twelve baskets full of fragments that remained. There was a basket for each serving disciple, and each received an abundant portion after their service was completed. This is a wonderful illustration that our serving must precede our reward for serving and it will be far more than we deserve! Second, the Lord Jesus fed perhaps 15,000 people with a few small fish and seven loaves. Again after giving thanks, the Lord broke the bread, and distributed to the disciples who passed it along to the crowd. After the meal was over, there were seven large baskets full of food left over (Matt. 15:32-38).

The prophet of Elisha is a type of the Lord Jesus in the Old Testament. While Elijah publically confronted Israel's idolatry (as John the baptizer did), Elisha was a champion of the people; his ministry was personal and mainly to meet the needs of individuals. 2 Kings 4 records a similar miracle performed by Elisha that the Lord Jesus performed in feeding the masses. It is the only one of its kind in the Old Testament, which further heightens our understanding that the ministries of Elijah and Elisha were foreshadowing the future ministries of John (Christ's forerunner) and then Christ Himself. Elisha took the firstfruits offering of the man from Baal Shalisha (twenty loaves of barley bread and a sack of ripened grain) and multiplied it so one hundred hungry prophets could have their fill. Similarly, there was bread remaining afterwards. Both, the Lord and Elisha demonstrated through their miracles that it is God alone who controls earth's resources to bless His people.

While it is not likely that we will be feeding crowds by multiplying sack lunches, believers do have the opportunity to share with others and leave the implications with God. He is able to bless our generosity and cause us to flourish in order to enable us to give even more (Eccl. 11:1). There may not be twelve baskets remaining after such ministry, but we still get to observe God's working through us nonetheless.

February 1 – Christ's Transfiguration
(Matthew 16)

When applied metaphorically, mountains symbolize governmental authorities or kingdoms. Both Isaiah and Micah foretold of God's glorious mountain on earth, speaking of Messiah's future earthly kingdom (Isa. 2:2; Micah 4:1-3). There was an instance in the latter days of the Lord's ministry in Decapolis when the brilliant outshining of His glory was witnessed by three of His disciples. This event is referred to as the Lord's "transfiguration" and foreshadows the prophetic fulfillment of Isaiah 2:2-5. Matthew describes the scene: *"Jesus took Peter, James, and John his brother, led them up on a high mountain by themselves; and He was transfigured before them. His face shone like the sun, and His clothes became as white as the light"* (Matt. 17:1-2). One can only imagine the dazzling glory of the Lord on this high, remote mountain and apparently at night (Luke 9:32-37).

In the preceding verse, the Lord Jesus had said, *"Assuredly, I say to you, there are some standing here who shall not taste death till they see the Son of Man coming in His kingdom"* (Matt. 16:28). Years later, Peter confirmed what was represented by this incident: *"the power and coming of our Lord Jesus Christ"* – the revealing of *"His majesty"* (2 Pet. 1:16). For a brief moment the disciples were given a foretaste of the coming kingdom.

Matthew explains what happened next: *"And behold, Moses and Elijah appeared to them, talking with Him. Then Peter answered and said to Jesus, 'Lord, it is good for us to be here; if You wish, let us make here three tabernacles: one for You, one for Moses, and one for Elijah'"* (Matt. 17:3-4). But it was not time for the kingdom to be established. Peter's suggestion of erecting three tents showed a lack of discernment for the Lord's proper place in the kingdom. Yet, his unintentional blunder was immediately checked when a sudden bright cloud overshadowed them and God the Father declared, *"This is My beloved Son, in whom I am well pleased. Hear Him."* The disciples fell to the ground in fear, but the Lord touched them and when they looked up, they only saw the Lord and in His normal appearance. There is a glorious earthly kingdom coming in which Jesus Christ will be wonderfully recognized as Son by the Father. He will rule the earth with the full glory, honor, and authority as God's faithful Son.

February 2 – God's Design for Marriage
(Matthew 19)

Children were crucial to Jewish family life. Inheritance and clan leadership were passed down to male children. This is why Elkanah likely married Peninah; Hannah, his first wife, could not bear him children (1 Sam. 1). At this time, men did what was right in their own eyes (Judg. 17:6). Later, kings often had multiple wives to ensure there were plenty of males who could survive, if a rival tried to seize the throne by massacring the kingly line. Though a practical solution from a human perspective, polygamy was not God's intention for marriage.

God instituted His Law with the Israelites to show them that they were inherently sinful, condemned before God, and needed a Savior (Rom. 3:20; Gal. 3:24). The Law put constraints on their sin and warned them against behaviors that displeased God. For example, God's design for marriage did not allow for divorce, but because of the hardness of man's heart, God permitted divorce in the Law with constraints (Matt. 19:8). Likewise, polygamy was not God's plan for marriage, but at that time He only warned against it and put constraints on it (Deut. 17:17, 21:15). Through the Mosaic Law, God proved to the Jews that they were Law-breakers and thus deserved judgment. However, with the Holy Spirit's coming to indwell believers in the Church Age, the Lord Jesus again confirmed God's standard for marriage: *"He who made them at the beginning 'made them male and female,' and said, 'For this reason a man shall leave his father and mother and be joined to his wife, and the two shall become one flesh'? So then, they are no longer two but one flesh. Therefore what God has joined together, let not man separate"* (Matt. 19:4-6). Unless a marriage covenant is dissolved for the case of adultery, any man marrying another woman commits adultery with her (Matt. 19:9). The Lord reposted God's original marriage design which banned polygamy.

The fact that a man would be disqualified from church leadership if he was a polygamist tells us what marital pattern is important to God. The apostles only had one wife or no wives (1 Cor. 9:5) and those in church leadership or in the office of deacons could not be polygamists (Tit. 1:6; 1 Tim. 3:2, 12). Scripture records no example of any Christian engaging in the practice of polygamy; monogamy, however, is repeatedly shown to be the proper pattern for marriage (Eph. 5:31-33).

February 3 – Only God Is Good
(Matthew 19)

Matthew records the dialogue of a rich young man who wanted to be justified before God and thereby be assured of heaven:

Now behold, one came and said to Him, "Good Teacher, what good thing shall I do that I may have eternal life?" So He said to him, "Why do you call Me good? No one is good but one, that is, God. But if you want to enter into life, keep the commandments." He said to Him, "Which ones?" Jesus said, "'You shall not murder,' 'You shall not commit adultery,' 'You shall not steal,' 'You shall not bear false witness,' 'Honor your father and your mother,' and, 'You shall love your neighbor as yourself.'" The young man said to Him, "All these things I have kept from my youth. What do I still lack?" Jesus said to him, "If you want to be perfect, go, sell what you have and give to the poor, and you will have treasure in heaven; and come, follow Me." But when the young man heard that saying, he went away sorrowful, for he had great possessions (Matt. 19:16-22).

Many think that they are good by their own standards of evaluation, but since only God is *good*, the Lord Jesus challenged the young man to think of goodness according to *divine standards*. The Lord then used God's Commandments to bypass the intellect to speak to the inquirer's conscience. The purpose of the Law is to show us our sin and that we might understand that only God is good (Rom. 3:9-12).

Sadly, the Law did not achieve its intended purpose in the rich young ruler's heart. Instead of feeling guilt and impending judgment, he pompously declared that he had kept all of the Law, which he ironically broke by that false assertion. Our gracious Lord did not rebuke the young man for his audacious statement, but instead set about to show him who his god really was. After being told that he needed to sell his possessions, give the proceeds to the poor, and follow Christ, the young man departed in sorrow, for he was wealthy. Money was his god; he valued it more than treasure in heaven and following the Lord.

For those of us who have reckoned ourselves as needy sinners and have received the Savior, we can exclaim with David: *"O taste and see that the Lord is good: blessed is the man that trusts in Him"* (Ps. 34:8). Truly, God is good and does good (Ps. 119:68).

February 4 – The Lord's Anger
(Matthew 21)

Then Jesus went into the temple of God and drove out all those who bought and sold in the temple, and overturned the tables of the money changers and the seats of those who sold doves. And He said to them, "It is written, 'My house shall be called a house of prayer,' but you have made it a 'den of thieves'" (Matt. 21:12-13).

Although the Lord Jesus is rarely spoken of in Scripture as being angry, it is evident that His righteous anger flared on some occasions. The Lord glorified the Father when He made a scourge to drive the animals and their masters from the temple and threw over the tables of the moneychangers. These racketeers had turned the temple into a place of commerce and thievery, but the Lord restored it to a house of prayer. The Lord Jesus cleansed the temple twice, at the beginning and near the end of His early ministry (Matt. 21:12-13; John 2:14-17).

While angry with the Pharisees, the Lord healed a man on the Sabbath day to challenge their shallow spiritual existence (Mark 3:5). With utter contempt, He later warned them of impending judgment (Matt. 23:13-36). At other times, the Lord's anger did not result in direct action; instead He relinquished the offense into His Father's care. The Lord shows us that there are times to defer from righteous anger to accomplish a greater good: *"The discretion of a man makes him slow to anger, and his glory is to overlook a transgression"* (Prov. 19:11).

Perhaps the greatest example of this kind of temperament was when Christ offered intercession for the very wretches that had nailed Him to the cross. *"Father forgive them* [i.e., suffer their offense]*; for they know not what they do"* (Luke 23:34). The Greek verb rendered "forgive" means to "release and let it be" (see Matt. 27:49). This verb is in the imperfect tense, which means Christ repeatedly pleaded with His Father for a certain timeframe not to take action against the sneering rulers, the mocking soldiers, the blasphemous criminal, and the rebuking crowd (Luke 23:35-40). Although these were profane crimes, the Lord was abdicating His lawful claim for justice in order to achieve a greater good: "Father, do not judge this now – let it be." Similarly, we honor God when our anger becomes selfless and is released to uphold His honor and to benefit others. God is not mocked, and His judgments on our behalf will benefit us much more than our anger ever could.

February 5 – Only One Marriage in Heaven
(Matthew 22)

Contrary to the Mormon and Islamic views of heaven, people in heaven will neither be male nor female, at least in the way we understand the genders to exist today. There will be no marriages (save the Lamb with His saints) or sexual activities in heaven as some world religions tout. The Lord confirmed this truth while responding to a fictitious scenario posed by the Sadducees, a religious sect which formed part of the Jewish judicial court called the Sanhedrin. The Sadducees did not believe in the supernatural, and thus mocked the doctrine of resurrection. They asked the Lord Jesus about a woman who had been married to seven different men (she was widowed seven times and never married to more than one man at once): *"In the resurrection, whose wife of the seven will she be? For they all had her"* (Matt. 22:28). Rather than reiterating what they had already rejected, the Lord used the opportunity to affirm the truth of resurrection:

> *You are mistaken, not knowing the Scriptures nor the power of God. For in the resurrection they neither marry nor are given in marriage, but are like angels of God in heaven. But concerning the resurrection of the dead, have you not read what was spoken to you by God, saying, 'I am the God of Abraham, the God of Isaac, and the God of Jacob'? God is not the God of the dead, but of the living* (Matt. 22:29-32).

Those who experience resurrection will not be gender-significant. They will be like the angels, who are neither men nor women, although when they present themselves in human form to deliver God's messages, they have always appeared as men (e.g., Gen. 18). Male and female genders were God's design to provide complementing companionship in marriage and for the purpose of procreation (Gen. 1:28, 2:18). In heaven, the need for reproduction will be eliminated as everyone will be eternal. Moreover, our communion with God in heaven will far exceed anything we could have ever experienced in an earthly relationship. Accordingly, we will be completely satisfied with being in fellowship with God and desire nothing else, including marital relationships. One of the clear warning signs of a false teaching is the notion that fleshly desires will be satisfied in heaven, or even worse, that such things are a part of some supreme deity's reward system.

February 6 – The Lord of Titles
(Matthew 23)

Interestingly, there is no example of a disciple of Christ anywhere in Scripture having a title of position before his or her name, for all such titles are reserved for Christ. "Lord" and "Christ" are predominantly associated with the name Jesus after His resurrection.

Men covet titles so that they might be honored by others – it is a natural pull of our fallen nature. But those who worship Christ must not dishonor Him by stealing His glory. Listen to the solemn words of the Lord Jesus on this matter:

> *But you, do not be called "Rabbi"; for one is your Teacher, the Christ, and you are all brethren. Do not call anyone on earth your father; for one is your Father, He who is in heaven. And do not be called teachers; for one is your Teacher, the Christ. But he who is greatest among you shall be your servant. And whoever exalts himself will be humbled, and he who humbles himself will be exalted* (Matt. 23:8-12).

Disciples of Christ do not seek the praise of men or titles of position before their names, but as previously noted, all titles of status and all praise are reserved for the Lord Jesus Christ. John the baptizer, speaking of Christ, declared the proper obligation of all true believers: *"He must increase, but I must decrease"* (John 3:30).

Many of the common expressions we use to refer to each other or to individuals in Scripture do not conform to the same scriptural etiquette upheld by the Holy Spirit in conveying honor to the Lord. For example, we do not read of "Doctor Luke," but "Luke, the beloved physician." Nor do we read of "the Apostle Paul" but "Paul an apostle of Jesus Christ." No "Saint Matthew," no "Elder Peter," no Pastor …, no Minister …, no Deacon…. Men love titles, yet Scripture provides none, except for the Lord Jesus Christ.

Terms of association or endearment for believers, such as "brother" or "sister," are warmly permitted: Paul is referred to as "brother Paul" (Acts 9:17, 22:13; 2 Pet. 3:15), Apollos as "brother Apollos" (1 Cor. 16:12), and Timothy is spoken of as "brother Timothy" in Hebrews 13:23. The Holy Spirit shows us that how we address the Lord and others does matter. May each of us esteem the Lord more and human titles and praise less; only Christ is to be revered by us.

February 7 – They Sung a Hymn (Part 1)
(Matthew 26)

Having instituted the Lord's Supper on the eve of His crucifixion, Matthew records that the Lord sang a hymn with His disciples before departing to the Mount of Olives (Matt. 26:30). If following the Jewish tradition, this hymn would have been the final song in the Jewish *Hallel* – Psalm 118. This song celebrates God's patient faithfulness to Israel, and previews a future day when Israel will be restored to God and honored by all nations. Fittingly, it is also the final Messianic poem in the book of Psalms. The psalmist concludes by requesting continued salvation and prosperity for the people at the hand of the one who *"comes in the name of the Lord"* (Ps. 118:25-29). Because this psalm was sung at Passover, its lyrics would have been on the minds of the people when Christ entered Jerusalem on what is commonly referred to as Palm Sunday. Thus, it was no accident that the psalm was openly shouted by the people when the Lord descended the Mount of Olives into Jerusalem a few days before His crucifixion: *"Blessed is He who comes in the name of the Lord"* (Ps. 118:26). Jesus Christ is the one who comes in the name of the Lord, offering life and blessing.

Psalm 118:22 is quoted several times in the New Testament, where it is evident the reference to the rejected Cornerstone relates to Israel's refusal of Jesus Christ as their Messiah. The psalmist says, *"this is the day which the Lord has made"* (Ps. 118:24). The Lord Jesus Himself acknowledged that this verse spoke of Him (Matt. 21:42; Luke 20:17), as did the apostles (Eph. 2:20; 1 Pet. 2:6-7). After being rejected by the Jewish nation, the Lord suffered and died at Calvary and was resurrected to the highest station in heaven, and in a future day He will return to the earth to establish His throne as Israel's King.

The Hebrew word *yowm*, normally translated as "day," appears frequently in the Old Testament; however, only about twenty times is it used in the Hebrew expression that correlates to the English phrase, "on that day" or "this is the day." In Psalm 118:24, the specific day referred to had been marked on God's calendar since before the foundations of the world were laid – it would be the day in which propitiation for humanity's sins would be offered by His own Son (Heb. 2:9; 1 Jn. 2:2). If following the Jewish tradition, it seems likely that the Lord with His disciples sang of this special day, just hours before Calvary.

February 8 – They Sung a Hymn (Part 2)
(Matthew 26)

It is hard to imagine what thoughts went through our Savior's mind when He with His disciples sang Psalm 118 at the conclusion of the first Lord's Supper. The day that the Lord had made was the day that redeeming blood was to flow from Immanuel's veins to ensure the redemption of all those trusting in His message of salvation. Animal sacrifices were bound by a cord on the north side of the Bronze Altar before their throats were slit and the blood was collected and applied to its horns or poured out at its base. Incredibly, the psalmist wrote of this spectacular day:

The stone which the builders rejected *has become the chief cornerstone.* **This was the Lord's doing***; it is marvelous in our eyes.* **This is the day the Lord has made***; we will rejoice and be glad in it* (Ps. 118:22-24).

Blessed is he who comes in the name of the Lord! *We have blessed you from the house of the Lord. God is the Lord, and He has given us light;* **bind the sacrifice with cords to the horns of the altar.** (Ps. 118:26-27).

After rehearsing in song with His disciples what was about to happen to Him at the cross, the Lord then expressed His resolve to honor God: *"You are my God, and I will praise You; You are my God, I will exalt You"* (Ps. 118:28). And the Lord Jesus did just that!

Ironically, the Church often sings the latter portion of this Psalm as a praise chorus, without regarding its proper context. In other words, we are applying a different meaning to it than what the Holy Spirit intended. While it is true that the Lord is sovereign over each of our days, the focus of our joy is not *our day*, but *the day* Christ was rejected of men and judged by God for our sins. The content of this psalm is a capstone on the revelation of all the fullness of Christ and His work mentioned in the other Messianic Psalms. May we treasure the full value God breathed into the text of Psalm 118 three thousand years ago and, like the psalmist, let us rejoice and be glad in what God has accomplished through Christ!

February 9 – The Greatest Commandment
(Matthew 22)

Though the dispensation of the Law has been replaced with the stewardship of grace, the Law still declares God's moral standard for right and wrong today; the Ten Commandments show us our sin (Rom. 3:20) and affirm that we need a Savior: *"Therefore the law was our tutor to bring us to Christ, that we might be justified by faith. But after faith has come, we are no longer under a tutor"* (Gal. 3:24-25). The Lord Jesus affirmed nine of the Ten Commandments (keeping the Sabbath day holy would no longer be required in the Church Age). Yet, the Church continued to follow God's pattern of committing one day in seven to rest (Gen. 2:1-3) and also to revere God. To preclude mixing of grace and the Law, believers met weekly on Sunday (Acts 20:7).

The first two of the Ten Commandments relate to the subject of recognizing God as Creator and not worshipping creation. The first commandment is: *"You shall have no other gods before Me"* (Ex. 20:3). Moses explained how one obeys this commandment – it is by believing in the one true God and giving Him first place in your life (Deut. 6:4-5). The Lord reiterated this teaching: *"'You shall love the Lord your God with all your heart, with all your soul, and with all your mind.' This is the first and great commandment"* (Matt. 22:37-38).

On another occasion, the Lord Jesus explained the commandment's meaning: *"He who loves father or mother more than Me is not worthy of Me. And he who loves son or daughter more than Me is not worthy of Me. And he who does not take his cross and follow after Me is not worthy of Me"* (Matt. 10:37-38). When it comes to having no other gods besides the Creator, it means that He has first place in everything.

The second commandment is: *"You shall not make for yourself a carved image"* (Ex. 20:4-5). Today, many reject the gospel message because they embrace a self-concocted god, an imaginary image of god which fits their liking and will condone their ethics. This idol may not be a golden calf, but neither is it the Lord revealed in the Bible.

The first two commands alone prove that we all have offended God. Others include: Do not blaspheme God or use His name disrespectfully. Honor your parents. Do not murder. Do not commit adultery. Do not steal. Do not lie. Do not covet (lust for what is not yours). No one could keep this Law and that was the point – we need God's grace in Christ!

February 10 – The Olivet Discourse
(Matthew 24)

The Tuesday before Calvary (three days prior to the Lord's death) was an incredibly busy day for the Lord Jesus. Besides mastering the verbal challenges of the Herodians, the Sadducees, the Pharisees, the scribes, and a lawyer, He also spoke the "Woe" message to the Pharisees and conveyed several parables. After these events, the Lord departed with His disciples to the Mount of Olives for a time of private ministry. At this time, He proclaimed to them important details concerning the future of Israel and the time of His Second Advent to the earth. Because this teaching was privately given on the Mount of Olives, it is often referred to as "The Olivet Discourse."

As with the "Sermon on the Mount," Matthew records the specific details more prominently than the other evangelists (Matt. 24-25). Both Mark and Luke devote one chapter each to the narration (Mark 13 and Luke 21), while John does not mention the discourse at all. Much of the detail contained in Matthew 25 is completely unique to Matthew.

The Olivet Discourse again is *strictly* Jewish, for the Church will already be in heaven before the events of the Tribulation Period begin to unfold. The Olivet Discourse provides escalating signs of the coming Tribulation Period and describes events in the first half, mid, and last half of this horrendous time on earth. Then the Lord spoke of His Second Coming to the earth to judge the wicked.

Only in Matthew do we read the words: *"Then the King will say to those on His right hand, 'Come, you blessed of My Father, inherit the kingdom…'"* (Matt. 25:34). *"And the King will answer and say… to them on the left hand, 'Depart from Me, you cursed, into the everlasting fire prepared for the devil and his angels'"* (Matt. 25:40-41). The message resounds with a theme of watchfulness throughout: The Jews should not be deceived by the forthcoming Antichrist but should instead wait for the Lord Jesus to return to judge the wicked and to establish His kingdom. *"Watch therefore, for you do not know what hour your Lord is coming"* (Matt. 24:42).

Around the dial of a clock in a church in Strasburg, Germany, are these words: "One of these hours the Lord is coming." We do not know when; it may be today; it may be now! Therefore, let us be watchful servants while we wait for our Beloved to come.

February 11 – The Danger of Sign-Seeking
(Matthew 24)

While the Lord Jesus was speaking to His disciples on the Mount of Olives, they asked Him to reveal to them *"What will be the sign of Your coming, and of the end of the age?"* (Matt 24:3). The Lord then identified many signs associated with the coming of the Tribulation Period, the first half of the Tribulation Period, the Abomination of Desolation in the middle of the Tribulation Period, then the Great Tribulation (speaking of the last half), and of His second Advent.

While speaking of signs associated with the Great Tribulation, the time when the Antichrist will be gaining followers on the earth and slaughtering those who will not take His mark (Rev. 13:15-18), the Lord gave this warning concerning signs:

> *For then there will be great tribulation, such as has not been since the beginning of the world until this time, no, nor ever shall be. And unless those days were shortened, no flesh would be saved. ... "If anyone says to you, 'Look, here is the Christ!' or 'There!' do not believe it. For false christs and false prophets will rise and show great signs and wonders to deceive, if possible, even the elect* (Matt. 24:21-25).

In the Tribulation, the beast and the false prophet will be working great signs and wonders to deceive the inhabitants of the world (Rev. 13). The devil is a powerful being that can do what from our lowly vantage point seems impossible. This is why believers are not to trust in their senses, but are to use Scripture to judge all things. The truth is in the whole and if we have rightly divided the Word of Truth and hold it, we will not be deceived. Accordingly, the Lord told the sign-seeking Pharisees that *"An evil and adulterous generation seeks after a sign"* (Matt. 12:39). Signs (what our senses affirm) can be fabricated by the devil, but God's word is from Him alone and thus is always truth.

One cannot escape trusting in something to interpret life. The atheist trusts science (what can be observed or demonstrated) to explain the meaning of life. It will be shown in the Tribulation Period that those who reject God's revelation of truth will fall for anything; they will not be established (Isa. 7:9). Life without God as the center of existence is meaningless. Without God, man has no ontological compass to reckon anything true, and therefore, he cannot be guided into what is certain.

February 12 – Tomorrow Will Be as Today?
(Matthew 24)

Both Isaiah and Ezekiel rebuked Israel's leaders during their prophetic ministries for being blind and oblivious to God's ways. Isaiah even likened them to watchdogs who only wanted to sleep and eat, rather than to bark and warn of danger (Isa. 56:10-11). Israel's priests and Levites were to guide the people Godward as good shepherds, but instead their own lust for gain and pleasure had blinded them to God's coming judgment. They thought, *"Tomorrow will be as today, and much more abundant"* (Isa. 56:12). The Lord Jesus said that the same kind of foolish mentality would be evident at His second coming. No matter the age, self-seeking, self-sufficient, and self-exalting people do not discern that God's judgment is coming.

The disciples asked the Lord about the end of the age and His coming. The Lord responded by describing escalating signs of the coming Tribulation Period and detailing the events that will occur during that time. The Lord concluded by giving the following warning:

> *But of that day and hour no one knows ... but as the days of Noah were, so also will the coming of the Son of Man be. For as in the days before the flood, they were eating and drinking, marrying and giving in marriage, until the day that Noah entered the ark, and did not know until the flood came and took them all away, so also will the coming of the Son of Man be* (Matt. 24:36-39).

At the Lord's second advent the behavior of man will be similar to that in Noah's day. Sexual perversion and unceasing wickedness will characterize man prior to judgment. Man will be living for all the pleasure life can offer and have no remorse for the Creator's grieving heart. Noah's contemporaries lived as if they had flood insurance, but the only insurance was the ark. Likewise today, in our post-Christian society, man lives for the day, not realizing that judgment is coming and that the good news of Jesus Christ is the only means of escape.

This is why the Lord did not tell His disciples to be looking for the Antichrist, but rather to be intently watching and waiting for His unannounced return to the air to take the Church home (1 Cor. 1:7-8; Phil. 1:6, 10; 1 Thess. 5:9; 2 Thess. 1:10). Israel's religious leaders were living for the moment, not for eternity; let us not be like them!

February 13 – The Sheep and the Goats
(Matthew 25)

The revelation of future things revealed by the Lord Jesus on the eve of His death to His disciples on the Mount of Olives is generally chronological. He reveals signs that will commence before, during, and after the Tribulation Period, which will conclude with His second advent. At that time, He will judge the nations, and those following the Antichrist (the goats) will be executed, while survivors who were kind to the oppressed Jews and did not take the beast's mark (the sheep) will enter Christ's Kingdom (Matt. 25:31-46). This ended Christ's teaching to His disciples on future events (things that would pertain to Israel).

This was not the first time that the Lord had taught His disciples about *The Judgment of Nations* occurring at the end of the Tribulation Period. In the seventh of the Kingdom Parables found in Matthew 13:47-50, the Lord casts a net into the sea (depicting the nations – Rev. 17:1, 15) and then sorts through His catch. Those who did not follow the Antichrist are separated from those who did. The "good" are permitted into His kingdom; the "bad" are committed to eternal judgment. The net represents the influence of the kingdom gospel message that will be preached worldwide during the Tribulation Period (Matt. 24:14). This message consists of a warning to not worship the Antichrist and a declaration that judgment of the wicked and Christ's kingdom are coming soon (Rev. 14:6-12). The fish represent the living Gentiles who are saved during the Tribulation Period.

The Judgment of Nations is done suddenly and the general populace will not be expecting it (Matt. 24:36-41). Those unfit for the kingdom will be abruptly removed from the earth. The Judgment of Nations is also pictured in Daniel 2:35, 44-45 and described in Revelation 19:20. Daniel informs us that there will be a 75-day interval between the destruction of the Antichrist at the battle of Armageddon and the beginning of the blessings of the Kingdom Age (Dan. 12:7-13; Rev. 17-21). This time period is necessary to cleanse the earth of the defilement and the devastation which occurred in the previous seven years. After all evil has been purged from the planet and it has been rejuvenated by Christ to nullify the effects of sin, Jerusalem will be the seat of God's glory on the earth. Christ's name will have been vindicated and the Church will rejoice, rule, and reign with Christ.

52

February 14 – The Suffering Servant (Part 1)
(Matthew 27)

The Lord suffered three religious and three civil trials in less than twelve hours. Pilate, being unable to persuade the Jews to turn from their bloodthirsty intentions, even had Christ scourged in an attempt to appeal to human sympathy, but the Jewish crowds had none for Christ. In order to prevent a riot in a city likely having four times its normal population because of the Passover, Pilate sentenced Christ to death by crucifixion. Matthew records what happened next:

> *Then the soldiers of the governor took Jesus into the Praetorium and gathered the whole garrison around Him. And they stripped Him and put a scarlet robe on Him. When they had twisted a crown of thorns, they put it on His head, and a reed in His right hand. And they bowed the knee before Him and mocked Him, saying, "Hail, King of the Jews!" Then they spat on Him, and took the reed and struck Him on the head. And when they had mocked Him, they took the robe off Him, put His own clothes on Him, and led Him away to be crucified* (Matt. 27:27-31).

Isaiah foretold that God's Servant would be faithful to live out what He was asked to do no matter the personal cost to Himself. In the prophecy, the Servant conveys His determination to expend Himself on Israel's behalf (and on ours too) despite the human brutality and divine judgment He knew He would suffer:

> *I gave My back to those who struck Me, and My cheeks to those who plucked out the beard; I did not hide My face from shame and spitting. For the Lord God will help Me; therefore I will not be disgraced; therefore I have set My face like a flint, and I know that I will not be ashamed* (Isa. 50:6-7).

This prophecy tells us that Christ knew beforehand that He would be scourged, beaten in the face, and spat on. Matthew records the direct fulfillment of these prophesies in his gospel account (Matt. 26:67, 27:26, 30). Thankfully, two thousand years ago, the Lord Jesus did not enter into His rest until He had secured ours, through the shedding of His own blood. We worship a brave, tenacious, and sacrificial Savior!

February 15 – The Suffering Servant (Part 2)
(Matthew 27)

Besides Isaiah's prediction that Christ would be determined to go to Jerusalem to suffer, the prophet also reveals the intense focus beyond Calvary that Christ would have: *"Therefore I will not be disgraced; ... and I know that I will not be ashamed"; "He is near who justifies Me";* and *"Surely the Lord God will help Me; who is he who will condemn Me?"* (Isa. 50:7-9). The Lord Jesus shows us that trusting in God's promises results in present joy. He had God's promise that He would not be left in the grave, but would be exalted to Majesty on high:

> *Therefore my heart is glad, and my glory rejoices; My flesh also will rest in hope. For You will not leave my soul in Sheol, nor will You allow Your Holy One to see corruption. You will show me the path of life; in Your presence is fullness of joy; at Your right hand are pleasures forevermore* (Ps. 16:9-11).

> *Looking unto Jesus the author and finisher of our faith;* **who for the joy that was set before Him endured the cross**, *despising the shame, and is set down at the right hand of the throne of God* (Heb. 12:2; KJV).

The assurance of God's Word brought Christ hope for the future and an infusion of joy while bearing tremendous pain and suffering. Assuming personal ownership of God's promises will infuse joy into any situation. *"For we were saved in this hope, but hope that is seen is not hope; for why does one still hope for what he sees? But if we hope for what we do not see, we eagerly wait for it with perseverance"* (Rom. 8:24-25). During the deepest trials of life, it is possible to have present joy in God's future promises. So while the Servant-Messiah understood that He would suffer much to convey God's message of love and life to Israel, He also knew that His Father would also vindicate Him. The suffering Savior knew God's word, obeyed God's expressed will, and trusted in God's promised help. He had every confidence that those who would reject and oppress Him during His first advent would stand before Him to be judged in a coming day. They would become nothing, like an old garment that moths have feasted on (Isa. 50:9). What an example for us to follow!

February 16 – The Great Commission
(Matthew 28)

And Jesus came and spoke to them, saying, "All authority has been given to Me in heaven and on earth. Go therefore and make disciples of all the nations, baptizing them in the name of the Father and of the Son and of the Holy Spirit, teaching them to observe all things that I have commanded you; and lo, I am with you always, even to the end of the age." Amen (Matt. 28:18-20).

The Great Commission demonstrates God's great love for the lost and the fact that He wants to see as many as possible redeemed by the blood of His dear Son (2 Pet. 3:9). Believers are to be witnesses for Christ in the world (Acts 1:8). The Greek text of Matthew 28:19 conveys the idea, "as you are going make disciples"; there was never any doubt in the Lord's mind that His disciples were going. In the book of Acts we see that local churches, not mission boards or parachurch organizations, sent out missionaries to evangelize those who had not yet heard the gospel message. Each local church supported and watched over their workers. The missionaries of the book of Acts did not raise funds in order to be sent; rather, they *were* sent and the Lord provided for them as they went (Acts 13:1-5, 14:26, 15:40). They were to live by faith and, when necessary, to work with their own hands so that their motives for service would not be questioned by the people they were trying to reach (Acts 18:3; 2 Cor. 11:7-9).

There are many ways in which God's desire to reach the world with the gospel has been distorted. One of these is the popular idea that only those with the gift of evangelism are responsible for the Great Commission. Others teach that a person is not saved until he or she becomes a member of their local church. The call, then, is "Come to a church meeting to hear the gospel and get saved"; the attitude is "you come" instead of "we go." Consequently, a significant portion of the world's population is not being reached for Christ. The Great Commission does not center in inviting people to a meeting, but rather imploring them to repent of their sins and receive Jesus Christ as their Lord and Savior. Inviting the lost to come to a future meeting does not convey to them the urgency of their situation – today is the day of salvation, not next Sunday! Also, let us remember that meetings of the church were intended for the edification of believers (1 Cor. 14:22).

February 17 – Concluding Without an Ascension
(Matthew 28)

Matthew's overall framework has been to present Christ as the King of the Jews. In upholding Christ's nobility, Matthew has invoked several distinguishing key words and phrases that are either peculiar to Matthew or more prominent than in the other Gospels: "king," "throne," "altar," "righteousness," "kingdom of heaven," "hell," "dream," "prophet," "fulfilled," "two," "I say unto you," "son of David," and "from that time." Matthew now closes his account also in a peculiar way as compared to the other Gospels.

Matthew began his gospel record by focusing the Jews upon the Lord Jesus as the Son of David, the rightful heir to the throne of David. He will close his Gospel in a figurative manner that beautifully climaxes this realization. Does he conclude, as Mark did, by recording the ascension of Christ back to heaven? No. You will find no ascension of Christ in Matthew.

What we do observe is Christ positioned on a mountain in Galilee imparting directions to His disciples. As mentioned earlier, mountains, in the figurative sense, symbolize kingdoms in the Bible. From a Jewish perspective, this scene is the climax of Matthew and completes the theme that he began in the very first verse. It is only made possible through the finished work at Calvary. Just before the curtain draws closed, we get a futuristic representation of Christ's kingdom established on earth.

> *Then the eleven disciples went away into Galilee, to the mountain which Jesus had appointed for them. When they saw Him, they worshiped Him; but some doubted. And Jesus came and spoke to them, saying, "All authority has been given to Me in heaven and on earth. Go therefore and make disciples of all the nations, baptizing them in the name of the Father and of the Son and of the Holy Spirit, teaching them to observe all things that I have commanded you; and lo, I am with you always, even to the end of the age"* (Matt. 28:16-20).

The subjects of the kingdom are before Him and resolutely worshipping their King (Matt. 28:17). God will keep His promise to Abraham, to David, to the Jewish people, and to all those who heed the gospel message and enter by faith into the kingdom of heaven.

February 18 – Mark's Theme
(Mark Introduction)

Approximately ninety percent of Mark has parallel content in Matthew and Luke, yet the flavoring of these commonalities is different and more chronologically presented. Mark is the most brief and condensed of the Gospel accounts; very few key words or phrases are used repetitiously to accentuate certain points or to provide an outline of his work. In Matthew and Luke, angelic messengers and prophetic pronouncements through human agents introduced the Savior, but not in Mark. His introduction is quite concise: a few verses to describe the ministry of John the baptizer and the Lord's baptism and temptation, but by verse 14 of the first chapter, the Lord is preaching the kingdom gospel message and pouring Himself out to humanity. The fact that Mark so abruptly brings us to the beginning of Christ's ministry fits well with his theme – Christ the humble and industrious servant of God.

Mark contains few parables, four to be exact, whereas Matthew contains many more. Mark focuses more on the busy life of Christ in doing miracles and ministering to the brokenhearted and the down and outers. Mark depicts Christ ministering to God's chosen people, while Matthew reveals Christ as testing Israel. Mark is addressed to a wider audience, the Romans, while Matthew is distinctly Jewish. At the time that Christ walked upon the earth, the Roman Empire was about 120 million people strong, and half of these were slaves. Unfortunately, slavery was the reality of that day; therefore, his Roman audience would readily understand and relate to the tenor of Mark's record.

Because Mark presents Christ as a lowly servant, almost no authoritative decrees by the Lord are presented; that would be out of place in Mark. No sentence is passed on Israel. No "woe" message to Pharisees or stinging "woe unto you" decrees are issued by Christ in Mark; these well mark Matthew. There is no Christ weeping over Jerusalem, as in Matthew. The Lord Jesus cleansed the temple twice during His three plus years of public service, once at the beginning and once at the end of His ministry. Concerning the first event, Mark merely records that the Lord entered into the temple, but nothing is said of His driving out the moneychangers or turning over their tables. In Mark, Jesus is serving man, not pronouncing judgment upon him.

February 19 – Mark's Omissions

(Mark Introduction)

Examination of the four Gospels reveals that Mark chose not to include certain material in his account in order to better maintain his theme of "The Lowly Servant of Jehovah." Perhaps the first obvious omission is that Mark includes no genealogies. In fact, no mention is made of Christ's birth or childhood. This omission is in keeping with the perspective of Christ's serving ministry. In Mark, it would not be genealogies or childhood history, but what the Lord did for others that established His credentials as the Servant of Jehovah.

Because the Lord Jesus is presented as ministering to instead of commanding others, no mention is made in Mark of the Sermon on the Mount; no Kingdom Manifesto is declared. Hence, authoritative expressions are seldom found in Mark, as compared to the other Gospels. Divine or exalted titles pertaining to the Lord Jesus are also rare in Mark. He is not called Emmanuel – "God with us." Of the twenty-eight times Jesus is referred to as "the Son of God" in the four Gospels, only three are found in Mark.

In Mark, the Lord is referred to by the reverent title "Christ" only twice. Matthew refers to Jesus as Christ four times in the first chapter alone. The Lord Jesus is referred to as the "son of David" only once in Mark; Matthew applies the title ten times.

Also, no enlisting of Jesus as king is found in Mark. Mark is the only writer to refer to the Lord as *"the son of Mary"* (Mark 6:3). The Lord was born into His mother's low social status, ensuring He was acquainted with a simplistic and austere way of life. The Lord Jesus, as God's Servant, knew firsthand about hard work and redeeming time.

Though brief in introduction, Mark safeguards against having a degraded view of God's lowly Servant in his opening verse: *"The beginning of the gospel of Jesus Christ, **the Son of God**."* Humanly speaking, it is natural to adopt a smug attitude about someone serving you, but Mark ensures that his readers understand that this was willful condescension by the Son of God. For this reason, the Lord never speaks of "My Father" or "Our Father" in Mark's record; His humble service to man, not His relationship with the Father, is paramount. But to ensure no confusion on the matter, Mark immediately guards against undermining the deity of Christ.

February 20– A Busy Servant
(Mark Introduction)

Twelve of Mark's sixteen chapters begin with the word "and," and the overwhelming majority of the verses in Mark begin with conjunctions and adverbs such as "and," "now," and "then." For example, Mark 1 contains 45 verses, and 35 of them begin with "And…." More specifically, many verses in Mark begin "And Jesus…" or "And He…." Mark is careful to present a serving Savior to his audience: "And Jesus was doing this, and Jesus was doing that."

But he doesn't stop there. In order for the reader to gain a higher sense of the Lord's exhausting ministry, he adds further description to the verbs describing the Lord's service, employing words such as "forthwith" and "immediately." This is accomplished by repeatedly applying two Greek adverbs: *eutheos* meaning "directly," and *euthus* meaning "at once." How are these adverbs applied in the other Gospels? Here is the breakdown. Keep in mind that Mark has only sixteen chapters compared to Matthew's twenty-eight.

Adverb	Matthew	Mark	Luke	John
Eutheos	*15*	*40*	*8*	*4*
Euthus	*4*	*6*	*2*	*3*
Total	**19**	**46**	**10**	**7**

The frequency of usage in Mark is unmistakably distinctive! Those of the Lord's servants who are involved in various "full-time" ministries understand, in a measure, non-stop ministry exhaustion. (Many elders and other saints know this all too well also.) Can you imagine the life of the Lord Jesus? Day in and day out, at any time of day or night, people were coming to Him with their problems and ailments. Those rejecting His message confronted Him continuously. No wonder He fell asleep in the stern of a boat and did not wake up when the boat was being tossed to and fro in a violent storm. Add to this His fervent prayer life. Even though His life was marked by a constant state of physical exhaustion, He still arose early, often while it was yet dark, to spend time conversing with His Father. Mark presents to us not just a serving Savior, but One that incessantly, steadily, and promptly served others. The Lord Jesus poured His life out to satisfy the needs of others and in so doing left us a lowly example to follow.

February 21 – How Did Christ Serve? – Part 1
(Mark Observation)

In depicting the Servant of Jehovah, Mark provides the perfect character sketch of a godly servant. The Lord Jesus teaches us through His selfless example what true servanthood is all about. Just prior to his death, Paul's final exhortation to his spiritual son Timothy was to fulfill his ministry: *"Preach the word! Be ready in season and out of season"* (2 Tim. 4:2). Christ knew all about "in season" and "out of season" ministry; He was on duty at all times! How might the Lord's service to others be described? Mark provides a complete character sketch.

The Lord's service was motivated by love. *"Then Jesus, moved with compassion"* (Mark 1:41). The Lord teaches us that the only true motive for Christian service to God is love and, nonetheless, that the only reason to serve others is love. Biblical love initiates sacrificial giving! *"For God **so loved** the world that **He gave** His only begotten Son."* Mark notes the Lord's self-sacrificing example throughout his Gospel (Mark 3:20, 4:35-36, 4:38, 6:31, 7:34, and 8:12). Love is discerning and understands what is best for those who need help. Love, not pity, must be our reason to serve others, or we may unknowingly enable their sin or interfere with God's chastening hand in their lives.

The Lord served others before Himself. *"Then the multitude came together again, so that they could not so much as eat bread"* (Mark 3:20). *"For there were many coming and going, and they did not even have time to eat"* (Mark 6:31). The Lord was so busy serving others, so disposed to mankind, so available to the distressed, that He often had no time to properly care for Himself. On one occasion, we find the Lord asleep in the stern of a boat, during daytime and while in the midst of a raging storm – physical exhaustion and emotional fatigue frequented His body, yet we never read of Him complaining once.

The Lord served with tenacity. *"Then He healed many who were sick with various diseases, and cast out many demons; and He did not allow the demons to speak, because they knew Him"* (Mark 1:34, also 3:10). The disciples said to the Lord, *"Everyone is looking for You"* (Mark 1:37). This statement highlights the immensity of Christ's counseling and healing ministry. Who wouldn't want to go to a physician who had a one hundred percent success rate of curing patients and mending families?

February 22 – How Did Christ Serve? – Part 2
(Mark Observation)

The Lord did not seek popularity. What was the Lord's response when His disciples informed Him that *"everyone is looking for You?"* The Lord replied, *"Let us go into the next towns"* (Mark 1:38). He could have used the opportunity to promote Himself and gain a fan club, but He was more interested in the quality of His disciples than the quantity of the followers. Mark reveals Christ's progressing humility in response to his instant fame. At first, He tolerated the popularity, then He shunned it, and finally He avoided it altogether: *"And immediately His fame spread throughout all the region around Galilee"* (Mark 1:28). *"But Jesus withdrew with His disciples to the sea. And a great multitude from Galilee followed Him"* (Mark 3:7). Later, the Lord even requested of those that He had healed to keep quiet about it (Mark 7:35-36, 8:25-26, 9:30). It is evident from Mark's various healing accounts that the Lord did not desire fame or popularity, but rather that He desired to demonstrate that genuine service is veiled in secrecy. May each of us learn of Christ and pursue His meek and lowly example.

The Lord served compassionately. The Lord Jesus had His eyes open to the needs of others; He was discerning – *"He looked upon them."* What do a leper, four blind men, and three disciples have in common? They were all touched by Christ to satisfy a need. The leper was a social outcast and longed to be embraced. For the blind, every clumsy step ventured into the unknown, but the Lord lifted this darkness and gave their souls security. At His transfiguration, the fearful disciples were comforted in a time of panic: *"But Jesus came and touched them and said, 'Arise, and do not be afraid.' When they had lifted up their eyes, they saw no one but Jesus only"* (Matt. 17:7-8). Why didn't the Lord just speak a good word to these individuals? He understood that a loving touch could convey what words couldn't. Let us not fear to reach out and touch those in need, so they, too, might see *no man save Jesus!* The Lord cared about the possessed, the sick, the blind, the deaf, the mute, the paralyzed, the diseased, the suffering, and the dead. He often touched those He healed (Mark 1:30-31). There is a whole world of needy people, and Christ teaches us to open our eyes to see them and not to be afraid to share some skin with those in need. Listening and touching are important gestures of love.

February 23 – How Did Christ Serve? – Part 3
(Mark Observation)

The Lord continued serving despite constant opposition. Before the events of Calvary, nearly twenty references of the Lord doing ministry in the face of challenges, disdain, and rejection are found in Mark (2:6-7, 2:16, 2:24, 3:2, 3:6, 3:22, 5:17, 5:40, 6:3, 6:5, 7:1-2, 8:11, 10:2, 11:27-28, 12:13, 12:18, 12:28, 14:4, …). Christ shows us that if we are doing anything for the Lord, we will be criticized and suffer for it, so expect it. The same pharisaical attitude that existed during Christ's first advent still continues unto this day. The Lord Jesus left us a self-sacrificing example to follow. A true servant cares nothing for himself, about what he is asked to do, or about what others think of him; the only focus must be to do the Master's bidding.

For this is commendable, if because of conscience toward God one endures grief, suffering wrongfully. For what credit is it if, when you are beaten for your faults, you take it patiently? But when you do good and suffer, if you take it patiently, this is commendable before God. For to this you were called, because Christ also suffered for us, leaving us an example, that you should follow His steps (1 Pet. 2:19-21).

The Lord was a good administrator. The Lord redeemed the most out of His time on earth and showed good managerial skills while serving. Concerning evangelism, the Lord sent His disciples *"forth two by two"* (Mark 6:7). In accomplishing the miracle of feeding the 5000 (plus women and children), the Lord had the people sit down in ranks of hundreds and fifties (Mark 6:39-40).

In application, might we, before taking on new ministries and responsibilities, learn discipline, good organizational skills, and efficient and frugal means of accomplishing God-directed ministry. Why would the Lord give us more to do for the kingdom of God, if we have not learned to be efficient in accomplishing what He has already requested of us? Many of the Lord's people today cannot respond with their time or finances to the urgent needs of the mission field because they are strapped with debt and, thus, enslaved to an employer or business. May we all learn from the Lord's example of managing every task to an efficient and profitable conclusion. He did all things well!

February 24 – How Did Christ Serve? – Part 4

(Mark Observation)

The Lord prayed before serving. *"Now in the morning, having risen a long while before daylight, He went out and departed to a solitary place; and there He prayed"* (Mark 1:35). *"And when He had sent them away, He departed to the mountain to pray"* (Mark 6:46). Matthew records Christ praying on only three separate occasions, but Mark and Luke often refer to the Lord's prayer life. This difference is in keeping with the Gospel themes, as the exalted King would be less dependent upon help from above than the lowly human Servant.

How often do we surge ahead of the perfect plan of God? Waiting is often harder than working, for we feel compelled to do something, but often it is not to pray. Prayer demonstrates complete faith in the Lord to initiate, direct, and complete each matter of our lives according to His will (1 Jn. 5:14). Besides moving the hand of God to affect His glory, prayer transforms our hearts by conforming our thinking to the mind of Christ.

Hudson Taylor, who labored for the kingdom in China, had three important principles concerning prayer: "You can work without praying, but it is a bad plan. You cannot pray in earnest without working. Do not be so busy with work for Christ that you have no strength left for praying. True praying requires strength."[9]

Warren Wiersbe writes, "Prayer is not an escape from responsibility; it is our *response* to God's *ability*. True prayer energizes us for service and battle."[10]

Before choosing His disciples, the Lord spent an entire night in prayer (Luke 6:12). The Lord prayed before feeding the 5000, just prior to Peter's pronouncement that He was *"the Christ the Son of the living God,"* and before raising Lazarus from the dead. The Lord's final hours before Calvary were spent in prayer. The prayer life of the Lord Jesus was so intense and so fruitful that on one occasion the disciples asked the Savior to teach them how to pray. They wanted in on the blessings of prayer. How about you? How is your prayer life? We should follow the Lord's example: prayer preceded service and followed accomplishments – prayer preceded crisis and followed achievements. The Lord Jesus exhorted *"that men always ought to pray and not lose heart"* (Luke 18:1).

February 25 – *"The Way of the Lord"*
(Mark 1)

"The voice of one crying in the wilderness: 'Prepare the way of the Lord; make His paths straight'" (Mark 1:3). The Gospel of John is packed with *sevens*, a number speaking of perfection and completeness. It is used in John to declare the perfections of Christ's work and person. However, the Holy Spirit saw fit to include a sevenfold witness in the first thirteen verses of Mark's Gospel for the same purpose. Before beginning His lowly service to humanity in verse 14, *"the way of the Lord"* was well prepared. Mark ensured that his audience knew that the One who was in the form of a Servant was none other than God Himself. Hamilton Smith summarizes the seven testimonies of the divine glory of Christ:

v. 1   The first witness is the writer of the Gospel – Mark, by reminding us that He is *"Jesus Christ, the Son of God."*

vv. 2-3   Second, the prophets are quoted, as being witness of the glory of His Person.

vv. 4-8   Third, we have the witness of John, the Forerunner, to the glory of the perfect Servant.

vv. 9-11   Fourth, we have the witness of the voice from Heaven to the glory of Christ.

vv. 12-13   Fifth, we have a brief allusion to the temptation in the wilderness. The temptation of our Lord in the wilderness became a witness to His infinite perfection whereby He overcame Satan.

v. 13   Sixth, creation itself bears witness to the glory of His Person, for we read He was *"with the wild beasts."* However much the beasts may fear men, they have no fear of this blessed Man, for He, indeed, is their Creator.

v. 13   Last, we read, *"the Angels ministered unto Him."* The One who came to be the Servant is, Himself, served by angelic hosts. He is none less than *"the Son,"* *"the First Begotten,"* of whom, when He comes into the world, it is said, *"Let all the angels of God worship Him."*[11]

64

February 26 – The Traditions of Men
(Mark 6)

Mark 6 records that the Lord Jesus was doing ministry in the land of Gennesaret with His disciples. Those in need throughout the region were coming to Him to be healed *"and as many as touched Him were made well"* (Mark 6:56). The scribes and Pharisees in Jerusalem heard about what was happening in Gennesaret and journeyed there to question the Lord. They had no excitement over His performed miracles or any interest in His message; instead they challenged Him with a question: *"Why do Your disciples not walk according to the tradition of the elders, but eat bread with unwashed hands?"* (Mark 7:1). All sorts of disabilities were healed and illnesses cured but what interested the Pharisees most was the disciples were not ceremonially washing their hands before they ate bread as required by the rabbinical tradition. The Lord's response condemned their cold hearts; they valued their vain traditions over the welfare of their countrymen:

> *Well did Isaiah prophesy of you hypocrites, as it is written: "This people honors Me with their lips, but their heart is far from Me. And in vain they worship Me, teaching as doctrines the commandments of men." For laying aside the commandment of God, you hold the tradition of men"* (Mark 7:6-8).

The Lord then offered them an example of their hypocrisy. They taught the people that it was permissible to *gift to God* (Corban), instead of caring for their parents, thus voiding the fifth of God's Ten Commandments (i.e., the temple received the funds needed to properly care for one's aging parents). The Law required the Jews to wear a blue tassel/cord on the fringes of their garments to publicly identify them as Jehovah-worshippers and remind of them of their covenant with Him (Num. 15). The Pharisees had enlarged the borders of their garments and set aside this law (Matt. 23:5). When human traditions replace God's commands, it is not superior spirituality that is exhibited, but vain piety. Likewise, we should remember that while particulars of our church meetings may change over time, we should never set aside Christ's order for His Church for what seems more profitable or spiritual to us. We are creatures of rote, so let us guard against making our worship a mindless activity; rather, let us refresh the heart of God.

February 27 – The Ascension and More
(Mark 16)

In just fourteen verses, Mark introduces the Lord Jesus as the Son of God and expedites Him into active ministry as the Servant of Jehovah. *And* Jesus steadily worked until they nailed His worn out and beaten body to a cross. On resurrection day, the Lord issued, to His stunned disciples, the Great Commission decree. Mark then concludes His Gospel by upholding the central theme he has focused on:

> *So then, after the Lord had spoken to them, He was received up into heaven, and sat down at the right hand of God. And they went out and preached everywhere,* **the Lord working with them** *and confirming the word through the accompanying signs. Amen* (Mark 16:19-20).

Verse 19 records the ascension of the Lord Jesus back into heaven, thus, a splendid climax to conclude Mark's story. However, that was not all that the Holy Spirit had in mind, for He inspired Mark to add one more verse. In doing so, every disciple since that day understands that Christ labors with them. In Matthew, Christ's authority in directing the disciples is prominent throughout: *"Jesus sent them forth." "He commanded them," "go not,"* and *"but go."* Mark, however, alludes to an aspect of the Commission which Matthew does not: *"the Lord working with them."* We do not labor for the kingdom alone or in vain, for it is His work, and He labors with us to accomplish it – we are His eyes to discern the needs of others and His hands to serve them. Paul enlightened the believers at Corinth that *"we are laborers together with God"* (1 Cor. 3:9; KJV). Christ labored with His disciples after commissioning them, and He still labors with His saints today.

With earnest gratefulness and loving appreciation, God the Father proclaimed to the far reaches of creation itself, "Behold My Servant!" His meek and humble character, His compassion for the suffering, and His resolute spirit in the face of opposition invite us to follow His example and to be true "servants of God." True love needs no title to serve, just the power of humility to do so.

> There are many of us that are willing to do great things for the Lord, but few of us are willing to do little things.
>
> — D. L. Moody

February 28 – Christ's Parables – Part 1
(Luke Observation)

The Lord's parables are one of the most mystifying aspects of the His ministry. He told some forty parables in all. These parables are often perplexing, cryptic, and hard to understand. The Lord told parables in response to questions, self-righteous attitudes, pious murmurings, or as a means of engaging an audience to think about spiritual matters more deeply. On some occasions, the subject matter was so vast that the Lord strung several parables together in addressing His listeners, but at other times, a single allegory sufficed.

If studied individually, these forty parables seem to address a wide range of subjects and have an equally vast intended purpose. Yet, stepping back from the intrinsic value of each story to a panoramic view, the Lord's parable ministry reveals some interesting patterns. For example, it can be surmised from the collective gospel accounts that the Lord told no parables for perhaps a year and a half after His baptism. Furthermore, the Lord spoke only fourteen parables by the close of the Galilean Ministry and eight of these were told on the same day. It was not uncommon for several months to pass without any parables being communicated or for several to be spoken all at once. Viewing the Gospels collectively, all the parables seem to be spoken on only fifteen different occasions, with fifteen parables spoken on two occasions. It is also observed that nearly two-thirds of the parables were disclosed in the final eight months of the Lord's earthly ministry.

What is a parable? The word "parable" means to "cast along side." The Lord used a story format to align a spiritual truth beside a common everyday activity the people could relate to, such as sowing seed, using a dragnet for fishing, or watching birds feed in a mustard tree.

Why did the Lord speak in parables? The Lord Jesus intentionally spoke in parables to reveal truth, yet in a partially-veiled manner. The parables were not just enjoyable stories but served as a test to the hearers. The casual onlooker, the "window shopper," would hear and not understand, nor would he or she desire any more understanding – "thanks for the good story." But those longing to understand the spiritual significance of the parable would seek the Lord for further instruction – this was often just the disciples. The Lord Jesus is a perfect Gentleman – He never forces Himself on anyone.

February 29 – Christ's Parables – Part 2
(Luke Observation)

As the Lord approached the cross, the parable veil thinned, and the meaning of His stories became more obvious, even to the dissident. While speaking parables in Jerusalem on the Tuesday before His death, even the Pharisees understood that He was speaking of them. In general, the parables can be organized into four main subjects, with each compilation of parables leading to the next in a nearly chronological fashion. These are: The "Mystery of the Kingdom" parables, Salvation and the Fruit Thereof parables, Second Advent and Jewish Attitudes parables, and Rewarding the Faithful parables.

In the eight "Mystery of the Kingdom" parables, the Lord reveals a chronology of events that would characterize the "kingdom of heaven" from His first advent (a seed-sowing mission) until His return to rule the world in peace. Satan is busy in the first four parables undermining the kingdom of heaven. In these parables, Satan is seen attacking the gospel message, trying to neutralize the influence of believers on earth, corrupting church leadership, order, and structure, and finally, promoting false doctrine within the Church. However, in the last three parables, Satan is absent, and God demonstrates His fathomless grace in saving sinners. Christ paid the great price for the hidden treasure (yet unrestored Israel) and the pearl (the Church) and also effects blessing for those Gentiles not bowing to the Antichrist during the Tribulation.

In the second group of parables, the Lord focuses on important aspects of salvation such as not mixing the law with grace and the necessity of repentance to receive salvation. Then several parables reinforce the "practice" of the believer once his "position" in Christ is secure (forgiving, giving, obeying, and loving each other and the Lord).

The remaining parables largely focus on the Lord's Second Advent and were mainly told in the final three or four months of the Lord's ministry on earth. Part of these parables focus on religious pride and Jewish rejection of the Lord and the consequences of that rejection, while others emphasize rewards for the faithful when the Lord comes into His Kingdom, including: faithfulness to the opportunities we are given to serve (the parable of the Laborers), abilities given to serve (the parable of the Talents), and using what God makes available to us to serve (the parable of the Pounds).

March 1 – Christ's Miracles
(Luke Observation)

Apparently, only a fraction of Christ's total number of miracles were written down for our appreciation. Mark notes, *"For He healed many, so that as many as had afflictions pressed about Him to touch Him"* (Mark 3:10). What types of miracles did the Lord perform?

Miracles of Physical Healing. Included are healings of fever (2), blindness (4), hemorrhage (1), dropsy (1), leprosy (2), paralysis (4), deaf-mute (1), and severed body parts (1).

Miracles of Resurrection. Only three resurrections were recorded in the Old Testament; Elijah and Elisha are associated with these. The Lord raised three people from the dead during His ministry on earth, then effected His own resurrection also (John 10:17-18). The Lord Jesus was the seventh and, thus, the perfect resurrection of the Bible.

Miracles Removing Demon Possession. The Lord is recorded seven different times as driving out demons from the host they possessed. This always resulted in emotional and physical healing.

Miracles Defying Earthly Physics. Besides miracles that brought personal healing, the Lord Jesus performed supernatural feats to demonstrate His power over creation. Twice He calmed a raging storm by a simple command (Matt. 8:27). Water became His sidewalk for crossing the Sea of Galilee and for Peter's brief excursion as well. Directly after this event, the Lord instantaneously moved their boat a great distance across the sea to arrive at Capernaum (John 6:15-21).

Miracles Related to Plant and Animal Life. Though the Lord had no tax liability, He graciously agreed to pay taxes so as to not stumble the unsaved. For this reason, and for this purpose only, Peter received the money via the mouth of a fish (Matt. 17:27). On two different occasions, the Lord commanded fishermen to drop their nets for a great draught of fish (Luke 5; John 21). Near the end of the Lord's ministry, to demonstrate His disgust for fruitless Israel, He cursed a fig tree. The disciples noted how quickly it was completely withered (Matt. 21:20).

Miracles Related to Food and Drink. On two different occasions, the Lord took a few fish and loaves of bread and multiplied them to feed thousands of people to their fill. In so doing, He demonstrated that He was the Master of quantity. The Lord's first miracle, turning water into the best wine, also confirmed that He is the Master of quality also.

March 2 – God Manifest in the Flesh
(Luke 1)

One night on a lonely hillside, some 2000 years ago, shepherds were dazzled by the sudden appearance of an angel, and then a whole host of angels praising God. The message was profound:

Then the angel said to them, "Do not be afraid, for behold, I bring you good tidings of great joy which will be to all people. For there is born to you this day in the city of David a Savior, who is Christ the Lord" (Luke 2:10-11).

Through the birthing process, Jesus Christ became connected with all people as the Savior. Man could not make Him a Savior; He was born Savior of the world. Through birth, Christ's humanity was established – a link *"to all people."* As a man, He would likewise experience all the pangs of living upon a cursed planet and, before dying, feel the very condemnations He, Himself, had imputed to humanity in the Garden of Eden. Luke skillfully captures the anguish of these aspects of the Lord's life.

Luke, as Andrew Jukes puts it, is the writer who "sees Christ as the Son of Adam or the Son of Man, not so much connected with a kingdom, or the Servant of God, [but] as the One whose sympathies as a Man linked Him with Adam's fallen and ruined children."[12]

Gabriel had informed Mary months earlier: *"Behold, you will conceive in your womb and bring forth a Son, and shall call His name Jesus. He will be great, and will be called the Son of the Highest"* (Luke 1:31-32). "Jesus" is translated from *Iesous* in the Greek which is derived from two Hebrew words: *Yehovah* and *yasha`* which means "to deliver or to save." Literally, *Jesus* is "Jehovah's salvation." To utter the name "Jesus" is to refer to the sacred covenant name of God in the English language. "Jesus" is a special name. It was by that name God declared His gift to the World, His Son, who was born of a peasant maiden, swaddled in grave clothes and laid in a cattle feeding trough. He was *"the Son of the Highest,"* yet born in connection with fallen humanity. He was and still is God's Messenger and Message of peace and goodwill to all people (Luke 2:14).

70

March 3 – "The Son of Man"
(Luke 1)

Who better than a physician to speak of the humanity of Christ? Not only does Luke show us the moral beauty and perfection of Christ, but he also reveals to us the frailties of His humanness. Luke presents to us a touchable Savior, who desires to touch others with compassion and kindness.

"The Son of Man" is an Old Testament term to express human association and, thus, links Christ to earth as a man. As stated in the previous section, Luke applies the title to the Lord Jesus twenty-five times in his gospel, while, in contrast, John, whose theme is the deity of Christ, only refers to the Lord as the Son of Man twelve times. The Lord Jesus spoke more often of Himself as "the Son of Man" than as "the Son of God," for the title identified His mission and not His essence. It is noted that only the Lord Jesus speaks of Himself as "the Son of Man" in the Gospels, some eighty-four times; yet, there are fourteen references to "others" identifying the Lord Jesus as the "Son of God," a title He applies to Himself only five times (all occurrences are rightly placed in John). The Lord normally spoke of His humble station and ministry, while others were privileged to acknowledge His divine rule and essence.

One of the early references in the Bible to the "Son of Man" is found in Psalm 8. This Psalm is then quoted in the epistle to the Hebrews and applied to speak of the incarnation of Christ. The title "Son of Man" is not found in any New Testament epistle, except for the one reference in Hebrews 2:6-9, which refers to Psalm 8.

The Epistles are books of wisdom given to the church to understand the great mysteries of God, which were before hidden in the recesses of God's mind. The Church, in Christ, has a heavenly, not an earthly, calling. The Lord Jesus will always be a man, but now He is highly exalted and at the right hand of God in heaven. It would now be inappropriate to address Him personally as the "Son of Man." This is why the expression is not found in the Epistles, save once in Hebrews as an explanation of Psalm 8. Christ finished that mission to earth, and consequently, at the pleasure of the Father, now has a name above all names.

March 4 – The Unique Conception
(Luke 1)

What are miracles? Everything mankind has observed in creation he has sought to characterize by rules of order. Conservation of energy and motion, laws of gravity and thermodynamics and the like represent our knowledge of creation based on observation. Therefore, God has to cause some non-regularities in our ordered world in order to call our attention to the fact that there is an outside influence to be reckoned with – the Creator.

Such were the births of Isaac, John the Baptist, and Jesus Christ. Before each miracle (an irregularity in an ordered system) occurred, Scripture records that the people understood the natural order that was in place. These were not ignorant people. They knew how babies were made and when procreation could no longer happen. If they had not known these things, no miracle would have been recognized, and God would have received no glory in doing it. In the case of Sarah and Elizabeth, they both were post-menopause and physically incapable of bearing children (Gen. 18:11; Luke 1:18, 36). In the case of Mary, the mother of Jesus, she was a virgin (Luke 1:34). So, it is really thanks to science that we have the wherewithal to actually recognize the hand of God in our lives! Without the understanding of natural order, we would not be able to recognize a miracle when one occurs. Luke is very careful to document the "order" of things, so we might better recognize the divine miracle of the incarnation of Christ.

The conception of the Lord Jesus was "unique." There is no patient confidentiality in this matter; Luke provides a full medical report for all to appreciate:

1. The conception of Christ was through the power of the Holy Spirit (Luke 1:35).
2. The conception of Christ did not involve any man (Luke 1:34).
3. The conception of Christ took place in the womb, an embryo normally attaches to the womb after conception (Luke 1:31).
4. The conception of Christ would never be repeated again, for the Last Adam need only suffer once for sin (Heb. 10:10-18), and He would rule over the house of Israel *forever* (Luke 1:33).
5. The conception of Christ resulted in a virgin giving birth to *"the Son of the Highest"* (Luke 1:27, 1:32, 1:34).

March 5 – God's Lampstand
(Luke 1)

The only source of light in the tabernacle was a *Lampstand* made from a single piece of beaten gold. In type, the Lampstand represented Christ and its light – the Holy Spirit's testimony of truth centered in Christ (2 Cor. 1:20; Rev. 19:10). The flowing olive oil supplied to each of the seven burning wicks represents the perfect enabling power of the Holy Spirit to accomplish the will of God (Zech. 4:6). The Lampstand typifies the Person and work of Christ. The Holy Spirit's work in the Church now, as in Israel then, was and is completely dependent on Christ. Every ray of light that radiates God's glory in the life of believers today flows from Christ as empowered by the Holy Spirit.

The sole light of the Lampstand existed prior to the Levites being dedicated to the Lord for priestly service (Num. 8:1-4). Likewise, spiritual darkness today is dispelled only by the illuminating testimony of Christ in Spirit-filled believers (2 Cor. 4:2-6; Eph. 5:18). Only that service which God enables to reflect His Son's glory will please Him.

This is why the Lord Jesus taught His disciples, before commissioning them, that they must shine out life-changing truth for others to see: *"Let your light so shine before men, that they may see your good works and glorify your Father in heaven"* (Matt. 5:16). They were to imitate Christ's own Spirit-enabled ministry. The Lord had been previously anointed and empowered by the Holy Spirit to accomplish His appointed ministry: *"The Spirit of the Lord is upon Me"* (Luke 4:18) and *"Jesus returned in the power of the Spirit to Galilee"* (Luke 4:14). Hence, Zacharias' prophetic announcement concerning Christ just prior to His birth has been fulfilled. Through Christ, God promised *"to give light to those who sit in darkness and the shadow of death, to guide our feet into the way of peace"* (Luke 1:79). Simeon also foretold Christ's illuminating message just eight days after His birth: *"A light to bring revelation to the Gentiles, and the glory of Your people Israel"* (Luke 2:32). Years later, the Lord declared, *"I am the light of the world"* (John 8:12). He was *"the true Light which gives light to every man coming into the world"* (John 1:9). The Lord Jesus was God's perfect Lampstand, casting His light before fallen humanity in the power of the Holy Spirit. All those who desire to serve the Lord must follow His example and be His light in a dark world also.

March 6 – Rejoicing in God My Savior
(Luke 1)

After Gabriel finished explaining all that was about to happen to her, Mary visited her aunt Elizabeth, who was six months pregnant with John. Mary shared a song of rejoicing with Elizabeth; this is the opening line: *"My soul magnifies the Lord, and my spirit has rejoiced in God my Savior"* (Luke 1:46-47). Mary had been told that she would give birth to *Immanuel*, meaning "God with us," and that her son's name would be Jesus, meaning "Jehovah's Salvation." She therefore joyfully ascribed deity to her unborn child, who she declared was her own Savior also!

There are many Old Testament passages which speak of the deity of the coming Redeemer and Savior of the World: *"For I am the Lord your God, the Holy One of Israel, your Savior"* (Isa. 43:3). *"I, even I, am the Lord, and besides Me there is no savior"* (Isa. 43:11). *"There is no other God besides Me, a just God and a Savior; there is none besides Me"* (Isa. 45:21). *"That I, the Lord, am your Savior, and your Redeemer, the Mighty one of Jacob"* (Isa. 49:26). God saw that there was no intercessor from among men, so *"His own arm"* brought salvation (Isa. 59:16). Clearly, God is the Holy One of Israel, and the only Intercessor and the only Savior for the nation of Israel.

When we compare the above passages with the illumination of New Testament truth, there is only one inescapable conclusion – Jesus Christ is the Son of God, fully divine in essence and hence the only true Savior. Besides Mary's declaration of Christ's deity also consider that believers are to look for His coming: *"the appearing of our great God and Savior"* (Tit. 2:13). Jesus Christ is the only Savior for humanity (1 Tim. 4:10). The Father has sent His Son as Savior of the world (1 Jn. 4:14). Christ is the only wise God, our Savior (Jude 21, 25).

We conclude that Jesus Christ, God manifested in flesh, is the only Savior that will ever be offered to the world: *"Christ is head of the church; and He is the Savior of the body"* (Eph. 5:23).

George Mueller is nothing. The Lord Jesus is everything. In myself, I am worse than nothing; by grace, in Christ, the son of the King.

— George Mueller

March 7 – The Unique Birth
(Luke 1)

Twice in the opening sentence, Luke announces that he is declaring, in an "orderly" means, what he knows to be truth from the testimonies of multiple eyewitnesses. (He does not specifically refer to Matthew and Mark.) Luke's personal compulsion to proclaim what he knew to be true would then be guided, arranged, and constrained by the Holy Spirit to present an "orderly" account of the humanity of Christ *"from the very first."* This focus is why Luke provides such an in-depth account of the conception and birth of Christ – his foundation of the humanity of Christ is like no other.

The angel Gabriel personally spoke with Mary in the privacy of her own home concerning the conception and birth of the Messiah (Luke 1:26-38). Mary was a virgin betrothed to a man from Nazareth named Joseph, who was of the house of David. Gabriel told her to rejoice, for she was highly favored, and because the Lord was with her, she would be called blessed among women – she would have the honor of giving birth to Israel's Messiah. Furthermore, Gabriel said:

> *Do not be afraid, Mary, for you have found favor with God. And behold, you will conceive in your womb and bring forth a Son, and shall call His name Jesus. He will be great, and will be called the Son of the Highest; and the Lord God will give Him the throne of His father David. And He will reign over the house of Jacob forever, and of His kingdom there will be no end* (Luke 1:30-33).

A decreed census, near the time of Christ's birth, forced Joseph and Mary to travel to Bethlehem. Christ was born there and the events surrounding his birth well picture the world's condescending attitude towards Him. He was born in a stable because there was *"no room in the inn."* He was *"wrapped in swaddling clothes"* which depicted the clear purpose of His birth – to suffer and to die. He was *"laid in a manger"* which declares His human poverty. Yet, the manger provided accessibility to all. If the Lord had been born in a palace, only the "well-to-do" and the nobility would have seen Him. Yes, access to Him would have been limited in a palace, but not so lying in the manger of a stable; any inquisitive soul who wanted to behold the Savior was welcome. Even lowly shepherds took advantage of the opportunity.

75

March 8 – Little Bethlehem (Part 1)
(Luke 2)

The prophet Micah, writing in the eighth century B.C., shifts his focus from revealing Kingdom Age events to foretelling the birth of Israel's future Deliverer and His work. The Messiah's birthplace would be the same as David's, Bethlehem, located just south of Jerusalem: *"But you, Bethlehem Ephrathah, though you are little among the thousands of Judah, yet out of you shall come forth to Me the one to be Ruler in Israel, whose goings forth are from of old, from everlasting"* (Micah 5:2). Israel's Messiah would be the eternal God incarnate – the One who literally stepped out of "the days of immeasurable time" into time! At that time, God's Son would take on flesh to become the world's Savior (John 1:14). Micah affirms the deity of Christ, who would be born of a virgin (Isa. 7:14) in the small town of Bethlehem of Judah.

The phrase *"little among the thousands"* literally means, "too small to be among." Each tribe was divided into its thousands of soldiers. Places too small to form a thousand by themselves were united with others to do so. So lowly was Bethlehem that it was not counted among the possessions of Judah when Joshua divided the land.

As there was a Bethlehem in Galilee, naming the county, Ephrathah, ensured that there would be no confusion as to which town Micah was speaking of. Luke records the story of Joseph and Mary venturing from Nazareth to Bethlehem for a census, and that Mary gave birth to the Lord Jesus in a stable in Bethlehem (Luke 2:4-11). Bethlehem means the "house of bread" and wonderfully represents the work of Christ to save sinners: *"For the bread of God is He who comes down from heaven and gives life to the world"* (John 6:33).

When the Magi came to Jerusalem seeking the one born king of the Jews, the scribes rightly identified the birthplace of the Messiah as Bethlehem (Matt. 2:3-6). When the Magi did not return to tell Herod that they had found the Messiah, the king had all baby boys two and under in the region slaughtered to remove any rivals to his throne. However, Joseph was warned in a dream to escape into Egypt with his family, which he did (Matt. 2:15).

March 9 – Little Bethlehem (Part 2)
(Luke 2)

Micah was not the only prophet to write about the early years of Israel's future Messiah. For example, Hosea wrote: *"When Israel was a child, I loved him, and out of Egypt I called My son"* (Hos. 11:1). While primarily Hosea is reminding Israel of God's past goodness and calling them to repentance, Matthew quotes Hosea to affirm its messianic fulfillment. For after Herod's death, Joseph returned safely to Nazareth from Egypt and that was where the child Jesus was raised. This created confusion for some because Jesus claimed to be the Messiah, yet He was from Nazareth, not Bethlehem.

Additionally, Isaiah identifies the tribal lands from which the promised Deliverer would come, Zebulun and Naphtali (Isa. 9:1). Christ's hometown of Nazareth was in Zebulun's territory, and Naphtali composed much of Galilee where the Lord spent most of His earthly sojourn. Clearly, a great light was afforded to those residing in Zebulun and Naphtali (Isa. 9:2; Matt. 2:2). Because Matthew directly applies Isaiah's prophecy to Christ's ministry in Galilee, we can be assured of its meaning (Matt. 4:13-17).

Through the prophets, God painted a predictive portrait, so that Israel would recognize their Messiah when He arrived. He would be born of a virgin (Isa. 7:14), from the tribe of Judah (Gen. 49:10), the seed of David (2 Sam. 7:12-13), and in Bethlehem of Ephrathah (Mic. 5:2), but would live in Egypt for a time (Hos. 11:1), before being raised in Nazareth in Zebulun (Isa. 9:1; Matt. 2:23). Jesus Christ did fulfill each of those prophecies, and dozens more, to emphatically prove that He was Israel's Messiah and the Savior of the world.

Little Bethlehem wonderfully foreshadows both of Christ's advents. In Genesis 35 and Micah 5, a **Son** is born. In Ruth 2, a **Savior** (i.e., a Kinsman Redeemer) and the Lord of the harvest appears. In 1 Samuel 16, a **Sovereign** is anointed (the Shepherd and King of Israel). While the Son, the Savior, has already come to seek and save the lost, the latter aspect of Christ's rule is yet future. May all humanity rejoice in God's life-giving message and Messenger from "little Bethlehem"!

More astonishing than a baby in the manger is the truth that this promised baby is the omnipotent Creator of the heavens and the earth!

— John MacArthur

March 10 – Christ's Childhood
(Luke 2)

Only in Luke do we get a glimpse of Christ's childhood. The Lord is shown to us at the age of twelve in the temple: *"**sitting** in the midst of the teachers, both **listening** to them and **asking** them questions"* (Luke 2:46). Notice Luke's prevalent depiction of human exercise in this account. When his parents inquired about His three-day disappearance, the Lord calmly replied, *"Why did you seek Me? Did you not know that I must be about My Father's business?"* (Luke 2:49). Even at this early age the Lord Jesus was aware of and intent on doing the Father's will.

Concerning the Lord's submission to parental authority, Luke informs us that *"He went down with them* [His parents], *and...was subject to them"* (Luke 2:51). Until the Lord received new marching orders, He remained under the God-ordained authority He was placed under. This serves as a good example for all to follow. Godly authority is like a funnel; if we remain in proper relationship to it, God's blessings flow down to us through that funnel. If we rebel against it, we place ourselves under Satan's authority and lose the communion and blessings of God.

Christ experienced human growth and maturity: *"And Jesus increased in wisdom and stature, and in favor with God and men"* (Luke 2:52). The Lord learned to eat, crawl, walk, talk, etc. in the same way you and I did. Perhaps the angels gasped when the Lord stumbled while learning to walk or wondered when He jabbered as a baby. How could we fully identify with Him in our human frailty if He did not experience all these things and more, as we do?

The Lord's home, until called to ministry, was Nazareth. Only Luke records that the Lord was "brought up" in Nazareth; Matthew merely states He returned there from Egypt.

Patience; kindness; generosity; humility; courtesy; unselfishness; good-temper; guilelessness; sincerity – these make up the supreme gift, the stature of the perfect man.

— Henry Drummond

March 11 – "The Son of Adam"
(Luke 3)

Christ entered into a season of prayer promptly after His baptism. At that time, the Holy Spirit descended upon Him in the form of a dove, and the Father Himself declared from heaven, *"You are My beloved Son; in You I am well pleased"* (Luke 3:22). Luke then injects the lineage of Christ to show that, though He came from a "seed of the woman," He was a representative of Adam on earth. The genealogy ends with who was *"the son of Adam, the son of God."* Where the first Adam failed, the Last Adam would not.

Immediately after this divine proclamation, the evil tempter assaulted the Lord for forty days. The Last Adam, the Son of God, triumphed over Satan – His righteous and holy character had been thoroughly proven. Luke waits two chapters to introduce the genealogy of Christ so that He might introduce his audience to the Last Adam, who was not human in the same way we are, but was proven to be sinless and perfect. Jesus Christ was God's replacement representative for the first Adam (Rom. 5:12-21).

Not only is Luke the only Gentile writer in Scripture, but he also addresses both of his written works, Acts being the other, to his Greek friend Theophilus. Luke's personalized salutation acquaints us immediately with a strong appeal to "human affection" which will characterize his Gospel. Theophilus means "beloved of God," and Luke's salutation serves as a testimony that the Gentiles are beloved of God. Mark wrote to the Romans, but Luke is setting forth an appeal to the Greeks concerning Christ. The Greeks prided themselves on intellectual observations and sought to apply knowledge and improve themselves (1 Cor. 1:22). They would be very interested in Luke's orderly presentation of the "perfect" man, the Last Adam.

Adam's righteousness was ours so long as he maintained it, and his sin was ours the moment that he committed it; and in the same manner, all that the [Last] Adam is or does, is ours as well as His, seeing that He is our representative. Here is the … gracious system of representation and substitution.[13]

— C. H. Spurgeon

March 12 – Unresponsive to Temptation
(Luke 4)

We understand that Christ, as *holy humanity*, could not sin, for there was nothing in His members that would respond to sin; His very essence repulses sin and loathes its working. Some have suggested that Satan's forty days of external solicitations caused an internal moral struggle within Christ (Luke 4:1-3). This was not the case. How could the Father, looking down from heaven, declare, *"This is My beloved Son, in whom I am well pleased"* (Matt. 3:17), if the Lord was struggling internally with thoughts of sin? As John declared, the Lord Jesus **was**, not might be, *"the Lamb of God who takes away the sin of the world"* (John 1:29). The Father never questioned the impeccability of Christ – only Satan and men do that – He was blameless and perfect, the only acceptable substitutional sacrifice for man's sin.

The Lord Jesus knows all about being tested through sufferings; in fact, the writer of Hebrews states His full maturity was demonstrated in this manner (Heb. 2:10). He also is quite familiar with the latter form of testing, for on one occasion Satan externally solicited Him to do evil for forty days straight (Mark 1:13). He did not respond to Satan's temptations or falter in character through life's difficulties.

The second form of temptation the Lord Jesus knows nothing about (drawn away by internal desires, Jas. 1:14)! This is the pragmatic lusting of our fallen members. John tells us that sin was an intruder into humanity; it was not inherent in Adam, but it entered in from the world and then passed down to the next generation. *"For all that is in the world – the lust of the flesh, the lust of the eyes, and the pride of life – is not of the Father but is of the world"* (1 Jn. 2:16). The ungodly lusting of our members originally came from the world.

The basis of lusting is dissatisfaction. Ever since Satan told Eve that she could be more than what God had created her to be and have more than what God had given her, humanity has been dissatisfied. Dissatisfaction advocates that "God is unfairly limiting me, and I desire more." Is it possible for Christ to have been dissatisified? No, Christ, being God, is perfectly satisfied – He is self-sufficient. Lusting "in the flesh" is not of God, but of the world. Lucifer and Adam sinned because of dissatisfaction with being what God created them to be. But as the Creator, no such evil desire was a part of Christ's humanity.

80

March 13 – The Forty-Day Test
(Luke 4)

Then Jesus, being filled with the Holy Spirit, returned from the Jordan and was led by the Spirit into the wilderness, being tempted for forty days by the devil. And in those days He ate nothing, and afterward, when they had ended, He was hungry (Luke 4:1-2).

Luke's record tells us that the Lord was tempted (tested) by Satan for the entire forty days that He was in the wilderness, not just the final day, which both Luke and Matthew record. But why was the Lord Jesus subjected to forty days of testing and not thirty or fifty?

The number forty is used in Scripture to represent *probation* and *testing*, which explains its frequent occurrence. At times, God extended the nation of Israel forty-year probationary periods to test or prove them: the Israelites were tested in the wilderness forty years, delivered and had rest during the forty years that Othniel, Barak, and Gideon judged Israel and enjoyed dominion during the forty-year reigns of five kings: David, Solomon, Jeroboam, Jehoash, and Joash. Another example of forty as the number of probationary testing is found in God's dealings with Nineveh; Jonah preached that, unless the inhabitants repented, God's judgment would fall on them in forty days.

The Bible also records a few occasions when individuals went forty days without food or drink through the supernatural care of God: Elijah during his wilderness experience (1 Kgs. 19:8), Moses before Jehovah on Mount Horeb (Ex. 34:28), and Christ in the wilderness. How was this possible? Once, the disciples observed that the Lord Jesus had not eaten for an extended period of time, and they encouraged Him to eat something. He responded: *"'I have food to eat of which you do not know.' Therefore the disciples said to one another, 'Has anyone brought Him anything to eat?' Jesus said to them, 'My food is to do the will of Him who sent Me, and to finish His work'"* (John 4:32-34).

Clearly, there are times in which God supernaturally sustains an individual's body for the purpose of accomplishing His work. The Lord Jesus was led into the wilderness by the Holy Spirit; He was where God wanted Him and God sustained the Lord's body during that time. The Lord teaches us that doing God's will should be the primary objective of one's life and though the temporal facets of life, such as food and drink are necessary, one should not be ruled by them.

81

March 14 – Christ's Two-Day Ministry
(Luke 4)

Only Luke provides the age of the Lord when He entered His public ministry after His baptism and anointing (Luke 3:23). He was about 30 years old, the same age in which a priest could sacrifice in the temple and a Jewish man could publicly read Scripture in the synagogue. The Lord did both, but the former was done outside the camp of Judaism (Heb. 13:12-14) at a place called Golgotha.

Christ maintained every aspect of Jewish Law, including keeping the feasts of Jehovah and keeping the Sabbath day holy. It was His custom to visit the local synagogue on the Sabbath (Luke 4:16). Only Luke records the details of one particular Sabbath day in His hometown synagogue of Nazareth.

> *And He was handed the book of the prophet Isaiah. And when **He had opened the book, He found the place** where it was written: "The Spirit of the Lord is upon Me, because He has anointed Me to preach the gospel to the poor; He has sent Me to heal the brokenhearted, to proclaim liberty to the captives and recovery of sight to the blind, to set at liberty those who are oppressed; to proclaim the acceptable year of the Lord." Then He closed the book, and gave it back to the attendant and sat down. And the eyes of all who were in the synagogue were fixed on Him. And He began to say to them, "**Today this Scripture is fulfilled in your hearing**"* (Luke 4:17-21).

Notice that the Lord Jesus had to open the book and find the portion of Scripture to be read. The Lord had to expend effort to locate the portion of sacred text, just as you and I must turn pages in our Bibles.

The Lord Jesus discontinued His reading of Isaiah's prophecy in the middle of a sentence to highlight His two advents to the earth. The remainder of Isaiah 61:1-2 reads, *"**and the day of vengeance of our God**; to comfort all that mourn."* In His incarnation, the Son of God had come to *"seek and to save,"* not to judge the wicked. When Christ was born, He brought God's offer of peace to the earth, as the angels declared on the night of His birth and He Himself declared to His disciples on resurrection day. Praise God that the Lord Jesus abruptly stopped when He did, or all humanity would have received God's retribution for sin. Thankfully, that has been reserved for another day!

March 15 – Under Authority
(Luke 7)

It was an awkward situation for the Jewish leaders in Capernaum; they did not believe in Jesus, yet the centurion who had been kind to them requested them to ask Jesus to heal his ill servant, who was very dear to him. The Lord agreed to go with the Jewish leaders, but as they neared the centurion's home, he sent friends to them with a message:

Lord, do not trouble Yourself, for I am not worthy that You should enter under my roof. Therefore I did not even think myself worthy to come to You. But say the word, and my servant will be healed. For I also am a man placed under authority, having soldiers under me. And I say to one, "Go," and he goes; and to another, "Come," and he comes; and to my servant, "Do this," and he does it (Luke 7:6-8).

The centurion's humility was evident; he did not ask Christ to come into his Gentile home. The Lord commended the centurion's grasp of authority and responsibility: *"I say to you, I have not found such great faith, not even in Israel!"* (Luke 7:9). When the messengers returned to the centurion, they found that his servant was completely healed. The Lord had been honored by the centurion and He responded by granting the centurion's request – he knew little truth, but had great faith!

The centurion, speaking to the Lord Jesus on behalf of his sick servant, understood that one must be under authority to have authority. Since the Lord Jesus had divine authority over diseases, the centurion knew that the Lord Jesus was under authority and could therefore heal his servant, which the Lord did. What is the lesson for us? We too must be under God-ordained authority to honor God and serve others in His name. The only other system of authority is satanic and the believer cannot honor God while under Satan's rule. It is good to remain under authority in whatever station God has put us, until God clearly repositions us under new authority.

This is one of two miracles that the Lord performed from a distance, and both were the only two recorded miracles of Gentiles (the healing of the Syro-Phoenician woman's demon-possessed daughter is the other; Mark 15:21-28). This dispensational distinction is maintained because the message Christ and His disciples were preaching at this time was *"to the lost sheep of the house of Israel"* (Matt. 10:6).

March 16 – Christ's Compassionate Ministry
(Luke 7-9)

Mark portrays the busy ministry of the Lord, whereas Luke adds more detailed information about the miracles Christ performed to better highlight Christ's compassion for others. The following three miracles serve as an example:

Only Luke records the resurrection of the widow of Nain's **only** son from the dead (Luke 7:12).

Only Luke states that Jairus' daughter, also raised from the dead, was his **only** daughter (Luke 8:42).

Only Luke mentions that the demon possessed boy, whom the Lord healed, was his father's **only** child (Luke 9:38).

It is evident from Luke's writings that the Lord feels the loss of children; He understands the home's need for children and was moved to alleviate each family's distress.

Likewise, only Luke affords the story of Lazarus and the rich man (Luke 16) to fully manifest the state of the lost after death. What Hebrews 9:27 states in a sentence, *"It is appointed for men to die once, but after this the judgment,"* is vividly depicted with real-life characters in this story. The Lord confirmed His love for those listening by solemnly warning them of the eternal reality of hell – *"the wages of sin is death."* The frank dialogue between Abraham and the rich man and his unbearable situation in torturous hades should cause every unrepentant soul sleepless nights; the rich man would never rest again.

Although it usually provoked the pious Pharisees to anger, the Lord often "rubbed shoulders" with the "socially unacceptable." Only Luke refers to the Lord as *"a friend of tax collectors and sinners"* (Luke 7:34). The Lord often visited them in their homes to speak of spiritual matters. The Lord was available to anyone who was concerned about his or her soul. He spoke to the vile, the demon possessed, the immoral, the distressed, and the brokenhearted – and met each one of their needs. The Lord loves sinners, but still hates their sin. We should follow the Lord's example and not be afraid to socially interact with the lost.

March 17 – Woe to Capernaum, Bethsaida, Chorazin
(Luke 10)

Towards the end of His earthly sojourn, the Lord sent seventy disciples two by two throughout Judea to preach the kingdom message. The Lord's instructions to them included how to respond to rejection:

> *But whatever city you enter, and they do not receive you, go out into its streets and say, "The very dust of your city which clings to us we wipe off against you. Nevertheless know this, that the kingdom of God has come near you." But I say to you that it will be more tolerable in that Day for Sodom than for that city. "Woe to you, Chorazin! Woe to you, Bethsaida! For if the mighty works which were done in you had been done in Tyre and Sidon, they would have repented long ago, sitting in sackcloth and ashes. But it will be more tolerable for Tyre and Sidon at the judgment than for you. And you, Capernaum, who are exalted to heaven, will be brought down to Hades. He who hears you hears Me, he who rejects you rejects Me, and he who rejects Me rejects Him who sent Me"* (Luke 10:8-16).

When the disciples returned, they reported that many had believed Christ's word and that many miracles had been done in His name. But Christ's curse remained on those cities rejecting His message, namely, Capernaum, Bethsaida, and Chorazin. Only a few ancient ruins remain of those Jewish cities today. However, this sad ending has a more thrilling meaning, given one of Ezekiel's prophecies: although ancient Israel would be destroyed by Babylon, many of Israel's destroyed cities would, in fact, be rebuilt and resettled in the exact same locations after the Jewish exile was complete (Ezek. 36:11).

There are many cities in Israel today that still bear their ancient names: Cana, Nazareth, Jericho, Nain, Bethany, Bethlehem, Hebron, Gaza, etc. Ezekiel's prophecy has been fulfilled. But while many cities are still known by their ancient names, those cursed by Christ do not exist today. The Lord honored both His promises: one to restore a faithful remnant and the other to judge those rejecting His truth. Ezekiel then says that not only will the Lord restore the Jews to their homeland and make it abundantly prosperous, but He will also remove the reproach of His people (Ezek. 36:13-15). The Jewish people have been hated for centuries, but during Christ's rule on earth, they will be greatly honored and appreciated by the nations (Zech. 8:20-23).

March 18 – Beware of Leaven
(Luke 12)

Leaven, in Scripture, speaks of sin, corruption, or evil doctrine (Matt. 13:33; 1 Cor. 5:8). The first mention of leaven in the Bible describes the simple meal Lot's wife prepared for the two visiting angels (Gen. 19:3). The unleavened bread stood in sharp contrast to Lot's "leavened" life (speaking of his failure to separate from worldliness). The next mention of leaven in Scripture is connected with the unleavened bread at the Passover Feast (Ex. 12). Through the Feast of Unleavened Bread that followed the Passover, the Israelites, who had been immersed in a pagan culture, were taught that leaven (the filth and corruption of Egypt) should not be in their homes. Though they were in the world, they were not to be of the world. In a later tradition, Jewish parents actually hid leaven in their homes so that their children could search it out and sweep it out of the house before the feast began.

The leaven to be avoided in the believer's life comes in diverse varieties. The Lord Jesus warned His disciples against the influence of humanized traditions that oppose sound doctrine: *"Beware of the leaven of the Pharisees, which is hypocrisy"* (Luke 12:1). He also warned them concerning *"the leaven ... of the Sadducees"* (Matt. 16:6). The Sadducees were materialists who denied the existence of the supernatural, the spiritual nature of man, and the idea of a future resurrection. In our present day, the ideologies of the Sadducees live on in intellectualism, humanism, higher criticism, post-modernism, and naturalism. Lastly, the Lord Jesus warned His disciples not to be influenced by *"the leaven of Herod"* (Mark 8:15). Herod, a Jew, was in cahoots with the Roman Empire, and was, therefore, a friend of the world (Jas. 4:4). In the case of Herod and those like him, love for God and His Word have been supplanted by the love for materialism, fame, and political ambition. Little in one's life has value to God after he or she has become socially mesmerized by God-hating ideologies.

Paul instructed the Church at Corinth to remove the leaven (those who continue in sin) out of their assembly (1 Cor. 5). Leaven within one Christian household negatively influences the entire House of God (1 Tim. 3:15). Whether symbolizing vain philosophies of men, false doctrine, worldliness, or sin, leaven has no place in the believer's life. May we heed the Lord's warning and avoid the ills of a leavened life.

March 19 – Fear the Lord Only
(Luke 12)

Jehovah is not an angry God poised to instantly crush those who stray from righteousness. Rather, He is a longsuffering, merciful, gracious, loving God who is slow to anger and quick to forgive. The more we know of God, the more we will reverently fear Him and appreciate Him, but there is no reason for His children walking with Him to fear anything else but Him. Israel in the Old Testament was repeatedly promised by God's prophets that He would severely chasten them if they departed from Him and His Law. So, if they revered God as they should, then they did not need to be anxious about His wrath.

From God's perspective, any fear other than towards Him indicates faithlessness. That is why believers are to *"be anxious for nothing, but in everything by prayer and supplication, with thanksgiving, let your requests be made known to God; and the peace of God, which surpasses all understanding, will guard your hearts and minds through Christ Jesus"* (Phil. 4:6-7). One day the Lord spoke plainly to a large crowd about what, or better whom, they should fear: *"My friends, do not be afraid of those who kill the body, and after that have no more that they can do. But I will show you whom you should fear: Fear Him who, after He has killed, has power to cast into hell; yes, I say to you, fear Him!"* (Luke 12:4-5).

Indeed, the enemy can harass believers during their lives, and if permitted by God, end their natural lives, but the devil has no hold on the hereafter and does not possess eternal life as God does. For those who have trusted Christ as Savior, and have been forgiven and placed in God's family, there is no reason to fear God's judicial wrath over sin. We are to realize that God's anger against us fell on Christ at Calvary once for all and, because that judgment is past, we are liberated to wholly love God. John puts the matter this way: *"There is no fear in love; but perfect love casts out fear, because fear involves torment. But he who fears has not been made perfect in love. We love Him because He first loved us"* (1 Jn. 4:18-19). Believers should not be distracted by needless worry, such as whether they are heaven-bound or not. Knowing the claims of God's Word, we realize by faith that the entire matter is eternally settled (John 5:24): Oh that we might all have God's holy fear before us and the infinite love of Christ flowing through us.

March 20 – The Cost of Discipleship
(Luke 14)

Our desire to be a disciple of Christ is a direct measure of how much we truly love Christ and believe His message. The reason we hold back from being fools for Christ, and thus, from seeing the mighty hand of God in our lives, is disbelief – we don't trust God. Through disbelief, the One who was offended for us becomes an offense to us. Those associating with Christ superficially will ultimately find Him offensive. The Lord Jesus didn't teach a middle ground concerning discipleship; consequently, following the Lord is an all-or-nothing venture:

> *If anyone desires to come after Me, let him deny himself, and take up his cross daily, and follow Me. For whoever desires to save his life will lose it, but whoever loses his life for My sake will save it* (Luke 9:23-34).

> *If anyone comes to Me and does not hate his father and mother, wife and children, brothers and sisters, yes, and his own life also, he cannot be My disciple* (Luke 14:26).

> *And whoever does not bear his cross and come after Me cannot be My disciple* (Luke 14:27).

> *So likewise, whoever of you does not forsake all that he has cannot be My disciple* (Luke 14:33).

The Lord never spoke of "becoming" His disciple, but what it meant to "be" His disciple, which implies an active, ongoing commitment. Consequently, He tells us not to call Him Lord, if we are not willing to do what He commands (Luke 6:46). He must be Lord of all, or He is not Lord at all. Christianity is more than coming to the Lord for salvation; it is also going on with Him to live out His spiritual life before others. We come to His cross and leave with our own cross.

The Gospel message pleads for the hell-bound sinner to embrace the cross of Christ, and no less so for the heaven-bound saint to take up his or her cross that he or she might enjoy life now. The Lord does not want us to only believe upon Him to evade judgment; He wants us to become like Him through exercising obedient faith. If we truly believe the gospel message, we will yield to Him and experience His abundant life now (John 10:10). We validate what we believe by what we do!

88

March 21 – Tormented in Hades
(Luke 16)

God's offer to be one with Him through Christ is rescinded when physical death occurs (Heb. 9:27). The Lord's teaching in Luke 16 confirms that if someone dies apart from trusting Him for salvation, the spiritual essence of that person will await final judgment in a place of torment called Hades (their final destiny being the Lake of Fire). There was a certain rich man who died and was taken to Hades by angels. Being in torment, he begged Abraham, who was in paradise, to send a poor beggar named Lazarus to his aid. This was Abraham's reply:

> *"Son, remember that in your lifetime you received your good things, and likewise Lazarus evil things; but now he is comforted and you are tormented. And besides all this, between us and you there is a great gulf fixed, so that those who want to pass from here to you cannot, nor can those from there pass to us." Then he said, "I beg you therefore, father, that you would send him to my father's house, for I have five brothers, that he may testify to them, lest they also come to this place of torment." Abraham said to him, "They have Moses and the prophets; let them hear them"* (Luke 16:25-29).

Because the rich man only requested one drop of water to cool his tongue, it seems he knew his chances of obtaining any relief was not likely. Abraham affirmed that there was a barrier between their realms of habitation to ensure that the wicked remain in their prison. These disembodied souls are completely conscious of their surroundings and are able to communicate, meaning that there is no such thing as *soul sleep* after death, nor does the human soul cease to exist after death.

The rich man seeing his wretched state became an instant evangelist – he did not want other family members to die and end up with him in Hades. He pleaded with Abraham that Lazarus return to the physical realm to warn his brothers about the terrible place awaiting them after death. Abraham explained that true faith is not based on sight, and even if his brothers witnessed someone returning from the dead to warn them, they would not believe in the miracle (Luke 16:30-32). God's word was sufficient to show them what God expected of them. The same is true today; when individuals choose to trust God's Word alone for salvation, they do not need to ever be afraid of going to Hades.

March 22 – "Whose Son Is He?"
(Luke 20)

The Herodians, the Sadducees, the Pharisees, and various scribes and lawyers took turns challenging the Lord's authority on the Tuesday before His crucifixion. A group of scribes, observing that the Lord Jesus answered all their inquiries well, decided not to ask Him any more questions, so the Lord decided to ask them one:

> *How can they say that the Christ is the Son of David? Now David himself said in the Book of Psalms: "The Lord said to my Lord, 'Sit at My right hand, till I make Your enemies Your footstool.'" Therefore David calls Him "Lord"; how is He then his Son?* (Luke 20:41-44).

Matthew's account of the dialogue records the Lord asking, *"What do you think about the Christ? Whose Son is He?"* (Matt. 22:42). The Gospel of Mark also records the conversation. The Lord is referencing the Messianic text of Psalm 110, the most quoted Old Testament passage in the New Testament. In all, fourteen quotations from this psalm are directly applied to the Lord Jesus in the New Testament. The Lord Jesus quoted Psalm 110:1 to confront the Pharisees' ignorance. In doing so, He both proved the psalm's authorship by David and acknowledged its divine inspiration.

The point of the Lord's question was this: David prophesied that Jehovah would cause one of David's descendants to be enthroned with God as David's "Lord" (*Adonai*). The Lord Jesus was showing the religious leaders of His day that the Messiah must be a man (i.e. a descendant of David), but also God incarnate for the great King David to revere Him as Lord.

Because they refused to reply, the Pharisees showed that they understood the point of the Lord's question. The implications of the only logical answer to the Lord's question were obvious (Matt. 22:46). The Lord Jesus is God incarnate – the Word of God became flesh (John 1:14). He is the Son of God and the Son of David. W. Wiersbe writes:

> The only explanation is that Messiah must be both God and man. As eternal God, Messiah is David's Lord, but as man, He is David's son (Rom. 1:3; 9:4–5; Acts 2:32–36; 13:22–23).[14]

March 23 – The Garden of Gethsemane
(Luke 22)

In comparing Luke's and John's accounts of the events in the Garden of Gethsemane the night Christ was arrested, you might think the writers were speaking of two different instances. John describes a band of men approaching the Garden with *"lanterns and torches and weapons"* to seek out and arrest Jesus. Why were so many needed? Was Jesus a violent man? Was He leading a political rebellion? The answer to the latter questions is "No." In response to the first question, apparently Christ's arresters thought that a large number would be needed to search out and find a "hiding" Jesus on the Mount of Olives in the dark. Remember that it was the Pascal Feast and, thus, a full moon. But, to their surprise, they did not have to find a hiding Jesus:

> *Jesus therefore, knowing all things that would come upon Him, went forward and said to them, "Whom are you seeking?" They answered Him, "Jesus of Nazareth." Jesus said to them, "I am [He]." And Judas, who betrayed Him, also stood with them. Now when He said to them, "I am [He]," they drew back and fell to the ground. Then He asked them again, "Whom are you seeking?" And they said, "Jesus of Nazareth." Jesus answered, "I have told you that I am [He]. Therefore, if you seek Me, let these go their way,"* that the saying might be fulfilled which He spoke, *"Of those whom You gave Me I have lost none"* (John 18:4-9). Note: "He" in the above brackets is not within the Greek text.

In John, the Lord is shown to be the great I AM by referring to Himself by that name three times in response to His arresters. Peter, attempting to protect the Lord, struck a man's head with a sword, yet the soldiers did not arrest him (John 18:10). Why? Because the Lord told them to let His disciples go, and that is exactly what they did (John 18:8). John declares once again that the Savior is God in flesh, the Great I AM who is in full control of the situation. Conversely, Luke upholds the Lord's humanity in Gethsemane. In Luke alone do we read of the Lord's anguish in prayer; *"His sweat was, as it were, great drops of blood falling"* (Luke 22:44). Only in Luke do we read of angels ministering to Christ in the garden and that the Lord healed Malchus' ear after Peter severed it. The same event from two perspectives!

March 24 – The Crucifixion
(Luke 23)

Both Luke and John document that the superscription hanging above the Lord's head at Calvary was in Greek, Latin, and Hebrew. As Luke is an appeal to humanity and John is writing to the whole world, it makes sense that the use of all three languages was recorded by these two evangelists. If Matthew had written concerning this detail, perhaps he would have only focused on the Hebrew language. Likewise, Mark would have likely referred to the language of the Roman Empire, Latin.

Only Luke describes the Lord's conversations with the dying thief during the crucifixion account and then the thief's conversion prior to the Lord's death. The thief, quite familiar with suffering for wrongdoing, saw in the Lord's sufferings a purity and righteousness that both convicted him of his sinful state and caused him to look to the Savior for salvation. How the words of the Savior have encouraged and given hope to every saved sinner since: *"Assuredly, I say to you, today you will be with Me in Paradise"* (Luke 23:43). Paul would later declare this plainly, *"We are confident, yes, well pleased rather to be absent from the body and to be present with the Lord"* (2 Cor. 5:8).

The Lord had three civil and three religious trials in less than 12 hours. During the Lord's civil examination, Matthew's two witnesses to the righteousness of Christ were figures of aristocratic influence (Pilate and his wife), but in Luke, the additional testimonies of two common folk are offered to declare the Lord's innocence. The repentant thief proclaimed, *"This Man has done nothing wrong"* (Luke 23:41). Having watched the way in which the Lord suffered on the cross, a Roman centurion declared after the Lord expired, *"Certainly this was a righteous Man"* (Luke 23:47). Even in the matter of witnesses, the writers maintain their vantage points of Christ: Matthew, Christ's royalty; Luke, Christ's humanity, but grace abounds in both.

Look at that Roman soldier as he pushed his spear into the very heart of the God-man. What a hellish deed! But what was the next thing that took place? Blood covered the spear! Oh! thank God, the blood covers sin. There was the blood covering that spear – the very point of it. The very crowning act of sin brought out the crowning act of love; the crowning act of wickedness was the crowning act of grace.

— D. L. Moody

March 25 – My God, Why Have You Forsaken Me?
(Luke 23)

Even while the Lord Jesus was hanging from a cross, He was fully aware and in control of His situation. He astutely fulfilled every Old Testament prophecy so there would be no question that He was Israel's promised Messiah. At the end of the three hours of darkness, and just before His death at 3:00 PM, the Lord quoted Psalm 22:1 with a shrill cry: *"My God, My God, why have You forsaken Me?"* (Matt. 27:45-46). The Lord affirmed that while He was being our Sin-bearer, fellowship with His Father was severed. The Lord also wanted to ensure that Psalm 22 would be associated with His redemptive work. The Lord fulfilled dozens of Old Testament prophecies at His first advent, but ten specific Psalm 22 prophecies can be identified as being fulfilled by Christ at Calvary; clearly, these do not apply to David.

Psalm 22 Prophecies Pertaining to Calvary	OT Reference/NT Fulfillment
"My God, My God, why have You forsaken Me?"	Ps. 22:1/ Mark 15:34
Time of darkness	Ps. 22:2; Amos 8:9/ Matt. 27:45
Mocked and insulted	Ps. 22:7-8/ Matt. 27:39-43, 45
Scoffers to mock: "He trusted in God, let Him deliver Him"	Ps. 22:8; Ps. 31:14-15/ Matt. 27:43
Be thirsty during execution	Ps. 22:15/ John 19:28
Hands and feet pierced	Ps. 22:16/ Matt. 27:31, 35
Stripped of clothes	Ps. 22:18/ Luke 23:34
Soldiers cast lots for outer coat	Ps. 22:18/ Matt. 27:35; Mark 15:24
Soldiers divided inner garment	Ps. 22:18/ Matt. 27:35; Mark 15:24
Committed Himself to God before dying	Ps. 22:20-21/ Luke 23:46

Christ was made *"the reproach of men and despised by the people"* and *"a worm"* (Ps. 22:6). "Worm" is rendered from the Hebrew word *tolaath*. The *tola* worm was smashed to yield a scarlet-colored dye; this pictures the humble servant nature of Christ and how He was crushed to produce the blood of our redemption. Praise the all-wise Lamb!

March 26– Christ's Resurrected Body
(Luke 24)

The Lord Jesus remained on earth to encourage and instruct His disciples for forty days after His resurrection. His first appearance to them was quite a shocker. The disciples, for fear of the Jews, had gathered together in secret behind locked doors when, suddenly, the Lord stood in their midst (John 20:19). Not only could He pass through solid objects prior to His appearance, but He also knew right where the disciples were. After examining the Lord's hands and His side, the disciples were completely convinced that the One before them was He that had been crucified three days earlier. This was one of five separate eye-witness accounts on the very day He was raised from the dead. Scripture contains five more personal testimonies of the Lord's physical presence before His ascension into heaven. Paul states that on one such occasion more than 500 believers saw Him (1 Cor. 15:6).

The Lord Jesus prophesied His own resurrection (John 2:19-21; Acts 2:26-27) and showed His disciples His resurrected body (Luke 24:40; John 20:27). When He first met with the disciples after His resurrection, the Lord told them He was not a spirit, but flesh and bone (Luke 24:37-39). He then ate some fish and honeycomb in their presence (Luke 24:42). By showing the nail prints in His body to the disciples, the Lord Jesus demonstrated that the body He now had was the same body which had been nailed to a cross.

While it is true that the Lord kept some of His disciples from immediately recognizing Him after His resurrection (this was for teaching purposes), most of them recognized Him immediately. This meant that the Lord's glorified body was much like His pre-resurrection body in appearance, though it was flesh and bone without blood (Luke 24:39). His resurrected body could taste food, could be touched, and could be seen and heard; it also could instantly vanish and reappear elsewhere. So, while His body exhibited some properties of natural law, it also had supernatural qualities. Same body, but different.

The Lord's body was flesh and bone. His glorified body did not require natural metabolic operations to sustain it as our bodies do. In fact, Paul says *"that flesh and blood cannot inherit the kingdom of God"* (1 Cor. 15:50). Obviously, we too need resurrected bodies because our present ones are not fit for heaven.

March 27 – After Resurrection and Ascension
(Luke 24)

Only Luke acknowledges certain astonishing details of Christ's human behavior after His resurrection. Luke alone informs us of the long **walk** on the Emmaus Road while fellowshipping with two disciples. Only in the book of Luke do we read that the Lord **ate** food after His resurrection. Walking with and eating with those He loved further demonstrates the approachability of the risen, glorified Savior.

Luke also is the only Gospel to recount the Lord leading His disciples out of Jerusalem and blessing them before He departed back to heaven:

> *And He led them out as far as Bethany, and He lifted up His hands and blessed them. Now it came to pass, while He blessed them, that He was parted from them and carried up into heaven. And they worshiped Him, and returned to Jerusalem with great joy, and were continually in the temple praising and blessing God. Amen* (Luke 24:50-53).

The Lord did not have to, but He lifted His hands to bless His disciples, thereby identifying with them and showing His divine care of them. In Luke's Gospel, the hands of the Lord are repeatedly touching and blessing those in need.

Each Gospel writer concludes his account in a unique manner to climax his theme of Christ's glory. Matthew presents Christ in His kingdom on earth, while Mark records the ascension of Christ, then notes that He is still working with His disciples. Luke concludes his Gospel in no less a remarkable manner: *"He was parted from them and **carried up** into heaven"* (Luke 24:51). The Son of Man did not ascend back to heaven, but was "carried up" to heaven. The choice of words conveys a connotation of human frailty and the consequential necessity of God's helping hand.

Throughout his Gospel, Luke focuses his audience's attention to human events surrounding Christ's life, the humanity of the Lord Jesus, and the human appeal of His ministry. Luke presents a touchable Savior who is more than willing to demonstrate the love of God by touching and blessing all that will come to Him.

March 28 – Why John?
(John Introduction)

Have you ever wondered why John was entrusted with the privilege of presenting Christ's deity? John seems to answer this quandary in John 14:21: *"He who has My commandments and keeps them, it is he who loves Me. And he who loves Me will be loved by My Father, and **I will love him and manifest Myself to him**."* Five times the night before the Lord was crucified, He told His disciples of the intimate tie between their love for Him and practical obedience: *"If you love Me, keep My commandments"* (John 14:15). He would demonstrate this truth Himself the next day: *"But that the world may know that I love the Father, and as the Father gave Me commandment, so I do. Arise, let us go from here"* (John 14:31). There was no question of the love of the Father for the Son, or of the Son for the Father, but the Son was going to show the world how much He loved the Father through obedience.

John 14:21 contains a promise for all those who will likewise demonstrate love for God by simply obeying His Word: The Lord said He would *"manifest Myself to him."* John was the beloved disciple and, apparently, the least inhibited in expressing his love for the Lord – it was to him, the disciple who loved much, that a fuller manifestation of Christ was granted. It was John, and only John, who was an eye witness to the Apocalypse, *"the Revelation of Jesus Christ"* (Rev. 1:1). The divine disclosure of Christ's glory to John is a direct testimony of the immensity of John's love for the Lord Jesus. Those who have been forgiven much love Christ more, those who love much obey Christ more, and those who obey Christ are enabled to comprehend Him more. Thus, our highest aspiration each day should be to be drawn more deeply into the secret recesses of infinite love through obedience.

During Christ's ministry on earth, the seventy disciples were empowered and sent forth to preach (Luke 10). Twelve disciples received specialized ministry. Three (Peter, James and John) were permitted to see a maiden's resurrection, to witness the Lord's transfiguration, and invited to pray with the Lord at Gethsemane. But then there was the one: John, the beloved disciple, who laid his head on the Lord's breast just hours before His death. Others could have done the same, but only John was willing to express his affection for the Lord. Each of us is as near to the Lord Jesus as we desire to be!

March 29 – The "Only Begotten Son" (Part 1)
(John Observation)

The term "begotten" means "unique." The writer of Hebrews refers to Isaac being Abraham's *"only begotten son"* (Heb. 11:17), but Abraham obviously had other sons. Ishmael was born 13 years before Isaac, and several sons were born to Abraham through Keturah after the death of Abraham's first wife, Sarah (Gen. 25:1-4). But Isaac was Abraham's *only son* of promise; through Isaac, and him alone, would the Messiah come, and God's covenant with Abraham be fulfilled.

The term "begotten" is specifically connected with the Lord Jesus in three ways in Scripture to declare some facet of "uniqueness." He is the only begotten of the Father (John 1:14, 1:18, 3:16, 3:18), which speaks of the Son's unique position and eternal relationship as the Son of God, the One who was with the Father in glory from the beginning (John 1:1, 17:5). Then, in Hebrews 1:6, the term "begotten" is applied to the Son's incarnation. J. N. Darby, commenting on this verse, suggests that the divine glories associated with Christ's incarnation are twofold:

> This glory is twofold, and in connection with the twofold office of Christ. It is the divine glory of the Person of the Messiah, the Son of God. The solemn authority of His word is connected with this glory. And then there is the glory with which His humanity is invested according to the counsels of God – the glory of the Son of man; a glory connected with His sufferings and in all the temptations to which the saints, whose nature He had assumed, are subjected.[15]

> *"Thou art My Son, this day have I begotten Thee."* It is this character of Sonship, proper to the Messiah, which, as a real relationship, distinguishes Him. He was from eternity the Son of the Father, but it is not precisely in this point of view that He is here considered. The name expresses the same relationship, but it is to the Messiah born on earth that this title is here applied.[16]

"Begotten" is also used to speak of Christ's unique resurrection and ascent back to glory in Hebrews 1:5 and Acts 13:33. Paul declares that Christ is *"the firstfruits"* from the dead (1 Cor. 15:20) – the first to experience glorification. Christ is merely the wave sheaf; the full harvest is yet to come, which is the Church's "blessed hope" (Tit. 2:13). The Son of God is "unique" in His eternality, incarnation, and resurrection.

March 30 – "The Only Begotten Son" (Part 2)
(John Observation)

John is bestowed with the honor of presenting the Lord Jesus as the "Son of God." It is a divine title appearing more times in John than in any of the other Gospels. John does not introduce "a son of God," but *"the only begotten Son"* and *"the only begotten of the Father."* These expressions are found nowhere else in all of Scripture, save the one time John also declares this divine solidarity in his first epistle (1 Jn. 4:9). Hence, John proclaims Jesus Christ as the unique Son of God to the whole world. In response, the world should "honor the Son," an exhortation found six times in John's Gospel. In fact, of the twenty-two times the word "honor" is found in the four Gospels, thirteen reside in John. "Honor" is a key word pertaining to the fourth Gospel account. The Son of God is to be respected, revered, and worshiped.

The special relationship of the Eternal Son of God with God the Father is exhibited in the Lord's frequent use of the expression "My Father." The phrase is found in John thirty-two times, compared to fifteen times in Matthew, not at all in Mark, and five in Luke. The Jews understood perfectly what the Lord was implying by the use of the term: *"Therefore the Jews sought all the more to kill Him, because He not only broke the Sabbath, but also said that God was His Father, making Himself equal with God"* (John 5:18). The Jews sought to kill Jesus for claiming equality with God, a fact that He repeatedly stated.

By using the expression "My Father," Christ was claiming a unique relationship with God that no one else possessed and enjoyed. It is ironic that the religious Jews of Christ's day perfectly understood the Lord's claim of deity, but the skeptics of our day allow their heads to swell with intellectual reasoning to avoid the clear facts of the matter. The discussion boils down to this: either Christ is who He said He was, the Son of God and the Savior of the world, or a lunatic, or the most notable liar that ever lived. The latter option is impossible, for the Lamb of God would not have been a sacrifice without blemish; consequently, we would still be dead in our trespasses and sin. There is absolutely no middle ground on this matter – Jesus Christ is God incarnate. He claimed to be God and that was the blasphemous charge that the Sanhedrin determined He deserved death for (Mark 14:63-64; Luke 22:66-71). Each person must decide if the Lord spoke the truth.

John:
Honor = 13X out of 24 in the gospels
My Father - 38X (John) 15X (matthew) 0 (Mark) 5x (Luke)

March 31 – John's Omissions – Part 1
(John Observation)

No parables in John. Parables both revealed and concealed divine truth. For the seeker, the parable presented an opportunity to learn more, but for those who were rejecting Christ, the fuller truth would never be known (Matt. 13:10-13). The word "parable" is found thirty-two times in the Gospels, but only once in John. The Greek word rendered "parable" in John 10:6 is *paroimia*, literally meaning "a proverb" or a "figure of speech." The normal Greek word used thirty-one times in the synoptic Gospels is *parabole*, meaning "a similitude implied by a fictitious narrative." The Lord articulated the importance of Himself as the Good Shepherd in John 10; the passage is not an application-enriched story aimed at the listener.

No genealogies. In keeping with the priestly type of Christ presented in Melchizedek, the Lord is *"without descent, having neither beginning of days, nor end of life"* (Heb. 7:3). Because God is eternal, there just is no genealogy that could establish "The Ancient of Days."

No details of Christ's baptism. From the synoptic Gospels we learn that John the Baptist did not want to baptize Christ, for he understood that he was unholy and that the Messiah needed no repentance. Christ, however, insisted that John baptize Him, for in His baptism Christ demonstrated His condescension to identify with those He came to save. John records none of these details, but does highlight God's own emblematic recognition of Christ as the Son of God. John (the baptizer) states the matter plainly just after Christ's baptism:

> *And John bore witness, saying, "I saw the Spirit descending from heaven like a dove, and He remained upon Him. I did not know Him, but He who sent me to baptize with water said to me, 'Upon whom you see the Spirit descending, and remaining on Him, this is He who baptizes with the Holy Spirit.' And I have seen and testified that this is the Son of God"* (John 1:32-34).

No record of the temptation. John presents Christ as God made flesh (John 1:14), and as James insists, *"God cannot be tempted"* (Jas. 1:13). This fact should put to death any degrading doctrines that pertain to the Lord's ability to sin or to His members having the capacity to be enticed to sin.

April 1 – John's Omissions – Part 2
(John Observation)

No transfiguration. This omission may seem puzzling, for didn't the transfiguration declare the inherent glory of Christ? Doesn't this fit John's theme? Yes, but where did the glory of Christ shine forth? On earth. John presents Christ from the heavenly view, not in an earthly relationship. Matthew gave prominence to Christ's kingly glory on earth; John speaks of the embedded glory that only heaven has witnessed and can fully comprehend. In the transfiguration, it is not the man who is God that is paramount, but that God became an earthly man. Samuel Ridout comments on the practical side of this truth:

> Our Lord is transfigured throughout the entire Gospel of John, but it is only to faith: *"We beheld His glory, the glory as of the Only Begotten of the Father."* No need for Him to manifest that glory visibly. His one great object throughout the Gospel is to bear witness to the truth of who He was and who had sent Him.[17]

No appointed apostles. In John, all ministry and work are designated for the hands of the Son of God (see John 2:23-25 as an example). In this way, Christ is ensured the preeminence among all those with whom He comes in contact. No sharing of ministry or glory is seen in John's Gospel; that would come after Christ's resurrection (John 17:22).

No "repent" or "forgive." Matthew proclaims the earthly kingdom message of repentance and acceptance of the Messiah. Matthew, three times, applies the term "believe" in association with Christ's interaction with individuals. This term is never publicly proclaimed as part of the gospel of the kingdom; repentance is stressed instead. John, however, stresses the heavenly perspective of mankind's spiritual condition and the ultimate solution – rebirth. In God is all life, and apart from God is death. John reckons all men spiritually dead and, thus, needing to be spiritually reborn (John 3:7) and quickened or made alive (John 5:21). It is necessary to repent to truly believe, but only by believing the Gospel can one be made alive.

April 2 – John's Omissions – Part 3
(John Observation)

No "prayers" by Jesus. The most common Greek word associated with "praying" in the Gospels is *proseuchomai* (pros-yoo'-khom-ahee), which means "to pray to God either in supplication or worship." It is found forty-seven times in Matthew, Mark, and Luke but not once in John. The root word *proseuche,* also translated "prayer," occurs eight times in the synoptic Gospels but not at all in John. Another Greek word *deomai*, translated "beseech," "pray," or "make request," is found nine times in the synoptic accounts, but again not in John. One more Greek word that is translated as "prayer," *erotao,* when added with the preceding three Greek words, accounts for nearly all references to prayer in the Gospels. *Erotao*, a verb that denotes "to ask from an equal," is translated "pray" or "prayed" only four times in Matthew, Mark, and Luke and is used to show equality in human speech, not to petition the throne of heaven for help. If we were enjoying a meal together at our dining room table, I might ask you to "please pass the salt." I am speaking to you as an equal (*erotao*); it would be unbefitting for me to drop to my knees and beg you for the salt.

Erotao is associated with prayer seven times in John. Once it is used to illustrate the literal meaning of "asking" in John 4:31: *"In the meantime His disciples urged ["prayed" in KJV] Him, saying, "Rabbi, eat."* This was clearly not a petition to God for something, but an expression of their concern for their leader. The remaining six occurrences are related to Christ "praying" to His Father or, literally, "talking to His Father as an equal." In all, *erotao* is translated "pray" six times in John (seven in the KJV). Why is this significant?

The Lord Jesus explained the answer publicly, *"I and My Father are one"* (John 10:30). The response of the Jews in the next verse showed that they understood that He was asserting divine equality: *"Then the Jews took up stones **again** to stone Him"* (John 10:31). Christ, being self-existing Himself, "spoke with" the Father as an equal, not as a subordinate. John employs *erotao* to show the Lord's equality with His Father in normal speech. In essence, they are equal and speak as equals. In the other Gospels, the Lord prays to His Father as a subordinate, because as the Son of Man, He took on the form of a servant and, thus, lowered Himself in "position," but not in essence.

April 3 – John's Omissions – Part 4
(John Observation)

No apprehensions of the Cross. As the "Son of God," Christ stood above His sorrow and grief, whereas the other Gospels record His apprehensions of the cross. What Luke records would be completely out of place in John: *"Father, if Thou be willing, remove this cup from Me,"* or *"being in an agony, He prayed more earnestly."* Not one word in John describes Christ's perspiration while praying in Gethsemane, but Luke writes, *"His sweat was, as it were, great drops of blood falling down to the ground."* These statements describe the "Son of Man" as the "man of sorrows." John is the only one to present the heavenly view that night and, thus, highlights Christ's great expectation of being received into heaven, obtaining His glory again and being with His Father forevermore:

> *When Jesus knew that His hour had come* **that He should depart from this world to the Father**, *having loved His own who were in the world, He loved them to the end* (John 13:1).

> *Jesus spoke these words, lifted up His eyes to heaven, and said: "Father, the hour has come.* **Glorify Your Son, that Your Son also may glorify You"** (John 17:1).

> *I have glorified You on the earth.* **I have finished the work which You have given Me to do. And now, O Father, glorify Me together with Yourself,** *with the glory which I had with You before the world was* (John 17:4-5).

No ascension. Each Gospel writer superbly concluded their account in a means which crescendoed their presentation of the Lord Jesus. In concluding his Gospel, John upholds the theme of the Lord's deity through the omission of the ascension of Christ to heaven. Why? Because the Son of God is omnipresent. The Lord avowed: *"No one has ascended to heaven but He who came down from heaven, that is, the Son of Man who is in heaven"* (John 3:13). God the Father and the Holy Spirit are visibly seen in God's heavenly throne room (Rev. 4:2-3, 5, 5:1), but yet are omnipresent. The Lord Jesus throughout eternity will be viewed in human form, but likewise is omnipresent. Hence, there was no need for John to record His bodily ascension to heaven.

April 4 – Light, Love, and Life
(John Observation)

John abounds with key words and phrases that distinctly highlight his theme of the Lord's deity. These would include: "Son of God," "My Father," "I AM," "world," "believe," "eternal life," "honor," "verily, verily," "love(d)," "light," and "life." John stresses that when one believes in the light of God, they experience the love of God and receive eternal life. Note the distribution of these Gospel-related words (in their various forms of speech) among the four writers:

Key Words	Matthew	Mark	Luke	John
Light	14	1	13	24
Love	13	7	15	57
Life, Live	17	9	19	54
Believe	10	17	11	99

Whereas Matthew stresses "righteousness" in association with the kingdom, John focuses on "eternal life." Both are connected and form one divine truth: Without life in Christ, one cannot display the righteousness of God. Why will the kingdom of God be full of righteousness? Righteousness is what emanates from a Holy God. All those who are born of God will radiate His righteous and holy life.

The words "repent" and "forgive" are not found in John because John conveys the gospel message from a precise heavenly perspective. Spiritually speaking, the plain truth is shrouded in a sincere warning that is often introduced by the phrase "truly, truly." This phrase is not found in the other Gospels. From the onset, John wants his audience to understand the basics of spiritual life and death. There is nothing like death to bring life into focus. *"All things were made through Him, and without Him nothing was made that was made. In Him was life, and the life was the light of men"* (John 1:3-4).

To Nicodemus, the inquisitive Pharisee, the Lord invited and warned: *"He who believes in the Son has everlasting life; and he who does not believe the Son shall not see life, but the wrath of God abides on him"* (John 3:36). To beloved Martha, the Lord Jesus inquired, *"I am the resurrection and the life. He who believes in Me, though he may die, he shall live. And whoever lives and believes in Me shall never die. **Do you believe this?**"* (John 11:25-26).

April 5 – The Sevens of John – Part 1
(John Observation)

The number seven is God's number throughout the Bible. Seven represents perfection and completeness; it is God's holy number. For this purpose, the number seven is employed at least twenty times in John's gospel account.

Seven different people confess the Deity of Christ: John the Baptist, Nathanael, the Samaritan woman, Peter, the healed blind man, Martha, and Thomas.

Seven "I AM" titles are ascribed by Christ to Himself: "The Bread of Life," "The Light of the World," "The Door," "The Good Shepherd," "The Resurrection and the Life," "The Way, the Truth, and the Life," and "The True Vine."

Seven public miracles are recorded: He turned water to wine; He healed a nobleman's son who was near death; He healed the impotent man at the Pool of Bethesda; He fed 5000 men, plus women and children, from a boy's sack lunch; He calmed a raging storm while in the midst of it; He healed the man born blind; and He raised Lazarus from the dead.

Seven private manifestations of His deity: He knew Nathanael while he was still under the fig tree; He did not commit Himself to the people because He knew the thoughts of all men; He knew the sins of the Samaritan woman; He moved the disciples' boat instantaneously to Capernaum; He knew of Lazarus' sickness and death without being told; He declared the details of Calvary to His disciples beforehand; and He provided a catch of 153 fish for His disciples.

Seven times *"These things have I spoken unto you"* appears in John.

Seven times Christ references His Father's "will."

Seven times Christ addressed the woman at the well (John 4).

Seven times Christ spoke of Himself as *"The Bread of Life"* (John 6).

Seven things the *Good Shepherd* does (John 10).

Seven times Christ made reference to "the hour" in which He would accomplish His Father's work.

April 6 – The Sevens of John – Part 2
(John Observation)

As noted in the previous devotion, the number seven is God's number of perfection and completeness in Scripture. We continue to recognize the groupings of seven in John to highlight the perfections of the Lord Jesus' divine essence:

Seven discourses: The New Birth (3:1-36), The Water of Life (4:1-42), The Divine Son (5:19-47), The Bread of Life (6:22-66), The Life-Giving Spirit (7:1-52), The Light of the World (8:12-59), and The Good Shepherd (10:1-42).

Seven feasts or holy convocations: First Passover (2:13, 23), Feast of the Jews – Second Passover (5:1), Third Passover (6:4), Tabernacles (7:2), The Great Day of Convocation (7:37; Lev. 23:36), Dedication (10:22), and Fourth Passover (11:55).

Seven witnesses of Christ's deity: John the Baptizer (1:29-34), Nathaniel (1:43-51), Peter (6:66-69), the Lord Jesus (10:22-30), Martha (11:27), Thomas (20:28), and John (1:14, 20:30-31).

Seven times Christ instructed His disciples to pray in His name.

Seven times the word "hate" is found in John 15.

Seven ministries of the Holy Spirit to the believer are noted (John 16).

Seven times Christ referred to believers as the Father's "gift" to Him (John 17).

Seven times John recorded that Christ spoke only the Word of the Father.

Seven times the writer of John (John) referred to himself but not by name.

Seven important events pertaining to Christ's ministry appear in all four Gospels: The ministry of John the Baptist as the forerunner of Christ, the feeding of the 5000, Peter's confession of Jesus being the Christ, the Triumphal Entry presentation of Messiah, and the crucifixion, burial and resurrection of the Lord.

April 7 – The Divinity of Christ – Part 1
(John Observation)

Christ is Holy; the following are the divine attributes of Christ which John upholds to his audience:

Creator: *"All things were made through Him, and without Him nothing was made that was made"* (John 1:3). Paul declares: *"For by Him all things were created that are in heaven and that are on earth, visible and invisible, whether thrones or dominions or principalities or powers. All things were created through Him and for Him. And He is before all things, and in Him all things consist"* (Col. 1:16-17). The Lord Jesus is the Creator and the Sustainer of all. He then must be Lord and sovereign over all; thus, Paul refers to Him as the "firstborn" of creation to speak of His preeminence and authority over all things. He is not Michael the archangel, as some cults teach, or any created being, for that matter, for how can one create themselves, be before themselves or maintain themselves – He created all things, and nothing was made without Him.

Omnipresent: John spoke of the Lord Jesus, while He walked upon the earth: *"The only begotten Son, **who is in the bosom of the Father**, He has declared Him"* (John 1:18). The Lord Himself declared, *"No one has ascended to heaven but He who came down from heaven, that is, **the Son of Man who is in heaven**"* (John 3:13). Some Christians have a problem with the thought of the Lord being omnipresent and human. How can I see God in one place, and yet He dwells everywhere? It is simply beyond human comprehension but not human observation. John wrote of the visible manifestation of all three persons of the Godhead in Revelation 4 and 5. He described the brilliant and majestic glory of the Father (Rev. 4:2-3) and then of the Father's hand (Rev. 5:1). He noted the representation of the Holy Spirit in seven fires before the throne of God (Rev. 4:5) and of the Lamb (the Lord Jesus) standing in the midst of the heavenly multitude (Rev. 5:6). All three persons of the Godhead are omnipresent but may choose to display their divine glory in just one particular location. The visible manifestation of Christ is fixed – glorified humanity forever. This attribute allows Christ to literally fulfill His promise to believers, *"I will never leave you nor forsake you"* (Heb. 13:5).

April 8 – The Divinity of Christ – Part 2
(John Observation)

Omniscience: The Lord said to Nathanael, *"Before Philip called you, when you were under the fig tree, I saw you"* (John 1:48). Though many people sought Christ, most were half-hearted followers or just interested in a good story or seeing a supernatural wonder. Speaking of these, John writes, *"But Jesus did not commit Himself to them, because **He knew all men**, and had no need that anyone should testify of man, for **He knew what was in man**"* (John 2:24). How astounded the Samaritan woman at the well must have been to hear the Lord's response to her denial of having a husband: *"You have well said, 'I have no husband,' for you have had five husbands, and the one whom you now have is not your husband; in that you spoke truly"* (John 4:18). How is it possible for the Lord to know and to do anything that we ask in His name (John 14:14)? We understand that the asking is in accordance to His will (1 Jn. 5:14), but how is He to know our needs and hear our requests if He is not omniscient?

Omnipotent: The Lord, referring to Himself, said, *"Destroy this temple, and in three days I will raise it up"* (John 2:19). In Himself He had the power to lay down His life and raise it up again (John 10:17-18). He demonstrated His sovereign authority and power over creation by walking upon water, calming storms, feeding multitudes from a boy's sack lunch, moving a boat instantaneously across the Sea of Galilee, and raising the dead. The demons feared His presence and yielded to His instruction (Luke 4:41, 8:28). Satan was rebuked by Christ and submitted to His command (Matt. 4:10-11).

Eternal: *"In the beginning was the Word, and the Word was with God, and the Word was God. **He was in the beginning with God**"* (John 1:1-2). *"**Before** Abraham was I Am"* (John 8:58). The fact that He created all things is solid evidence that He is God, the pre-existent One (John 1:3-4). *"And now, O Father, glorify Me together with Yourself, with the glory which I had with You before the world was"* (John 17:5). The Lord Jesus is the eternal Son of God, the *"Alpha and Omega, the first and the last"* (Rev. 1:11).

April 9 – The Divinity of Christ – Part 3

(John Observation)

Equality with the Father: *"I and My Father **are one"*** (John 10:30). The Jews fully understood the Lord's claim: *"Therefore the Jews sought all the more to kill Him, because He not only broke the Sabbath, but also said that God was His Father, making Himself equal with God"* (John 5:18). Albert Barnes comments to the vast weight of the Lord's statement – His affirmation of deity:

The word translated "one" is not in the *masculine*, but in the *neuter* gender. It expresses *union*, but not the precise nature of the union. It may express any union, and the particular kind intended is to be inferred from the connection. In the previous verse He had said that He and His Father were united in the same object – that is, in redeeming and preserving His people. It was this that gave occasion for this remark. Most of the Christian fathers understood [this verse] … as referring to the oneness or unity of nature between the Father and the Son, and that this was the design of Christ appears probable from the following considerations:

First. The question in debate was not about His being united with the Father in plan and counsel, but in power. He affirmed that He was able to rescue and keep His people from all enemies, or that He had power superior to men and devils – that is, that He had supreme power over all creation. He affirmed the same of His Father. In this, therefore, they were united.

Second. The Jews understood Him as affirming His equality with God, for they took up stones to punish Him for blasphemy (John 10:31, 33), and they said to Him that they understood Him as affirming that He was God.

Third. Jesus did not deny that it was His intention to be so understood.

Fourth. He immediately made another declaration implying the same thing, leaving the same impression, and which they attempted to punish in the same manner (John 10:37-39). If Jesus had not intended so to be understood, it cannot be easily reconciled with moral honesty that He did not distinctly disavow that such was His intention. The Jews were well acquainted with their own language. They understood Him in this manner, and He left this impression on their minds.[18]

April 10 – The Divinity of Christ – Part 4
(John Observation)

True: *"Jesus said to him, 'I am the way, the truth, and the life. No one comes to the Father except through Me'"* (John 14:6). There is no other way to enjoy eternal paradise with God than through the Lord Jesus Christ. Thomas A Kempis wrote of the Lord Jesus: "I am the Way unchangeable; the Truth infallible; the Life everlasting."[19] His blood alone washes away sin, and only through His sacrifice can a repentant, believing sinner be justified – receive a righteous standing before God.

Just: *"My judgment is righteous* [or, *just*; KJV]" (John 5:30). *"For the Father judges no one, but has committed all judgment to the Son"* (John 5:22). Speaking of the just Judge, Paul declares: *"For it is written: 'As I live, says the Lord, every knee shall bow to Me, and every tongue shall confess to God.' So then each of us shall give account of himself to God"* (Rom. 14:11-12). *"Therefore God also has highly exalted Him and given Him the name which is above every name, that at the name of Jesus every knee should bow, of those in heaven, and of those on earth, and of those under the earth"* (Phil. 2:9-10).

Holy and Sinless: When the Lord Jesus asked, *"Which of you convicts Me of sin?"* (John 8:46), no one could reply; not a word! Albert Barnes comments to the significance of the Lord's question:

The word sin here evidently means error, falsehood, or imposture. It stands opposed to truth. The argument of the Savior is this: A doctrine might be rejected if it could be proved that he that delivered it was an impostor, but as you cannot prove this of Me, you are bound to receive My words.[20]

Perfect Love: *"Greater love has no one than this, than to lay down one's life for his friends"* (John 15:13). The Lord is love, displayed sacrificial love for others, and exhorted His disciples to do the same:

Beloved, let us love one another, for love is of God; and everyone who loves is born of God and knows God. He who does not love does not know God, for God is love. In this the love of God was manifested toward us, that God has sent His only begotten Son into the world, that we might live through Him. In this is love, not that we loved God, but that He loved us and sent His Son to be the propitiation for our sins" (1 Jn. 4:7-10).

April 11 – The Divinity of Christ – Part 5
(John Observation)

Grace: *"And the Word became flesh and dwelt among us, and we beheld His glory, the glory as of the only begotten of the Father, full of grace and truth"* (John 1:14). The Lord's example should be followed by all those who name Him as Savior – let us not be just balanced, but full of both grace and truth. Paul puts it this way: *"Let your speech always be with grace, seasoned with salt, that you may know how you ought to answer each one"* (Col. 4:6). If it was not necessary to say, could not be said in love, and was not true, the Lord Jesus did not say it. May the Lord's people follow the same threefold rule before speaking to others.

Unique Son of God: Concerning Christ, God the Father revealed to John the Baptist, *"This is the Son of God"* (John 1:34), and *"The only begotten of the Father"* (John 1:14). The Lord affirmed: *"He who has seen Me has seen the Father"* (John 14:9). Only the Lord has such a special relationship with the Eternal Father as evidenced by the frequent use of the phrase "My Father," which is found in John thirty-two times. The Jews understood perfectly what the Lord was implying by the use of the term and sought to kill him for *"making Himself equal with God"* (John 5:18). Even though the Jews desired to kill Him for this assertion, the Lord Jesus continued to proclaim that He was the unique, eternal Son of God.

Controls Time and Events: *"Therefore they sought to take Him; but no one laid a hand on Him, because His hour had not yet come"* (John 7:30). In the Garden of Gethsemane, the Lord commanded the very soldiers that were arresting Him to take only Him and let His disciples go – this after Peter tried to kill a man (John 18:8-12). And let us remember the divine dignity of our Lord's words about being in control of His own death:

> *Therefore My Father loves Me, because I lay down My life that I may take it again. No one takes it* [speaking of His own life] *from Me, but I lay it down of Myself. I have power to lay it down, and I have power to take it again. This command I have received from My Father* (John 10:17-18).

April 12 – The Divinity of Christ – Part 6
(John Observation)

Laid Aside His Glory: While speaking to His Father, the Lord Jesus said: *"I have glorified You on the earth. I have finished the work which You have given Me to do. And now, O Father, glorify Me together with Yourself, with the glory which I had with You before the world was"* (John 17:4-5). Paul explains precisely what the Son of God did to effect propitiation for sin (i.e., the means in which God's anger over human sin is forever satisfied):

> *Let this mind be in you which was also in Christ Jesus, who, being in the form of God, did not consider it robbery to be equal with God, but made Himself of no reputation, taking the form of a bondservant, and coming in the likeness of men. And being found in appearance as a man, He humbled Himself and became obedient to the point of death, even the death of the cross. Therefore God also has highly exalted Him and given Him the name which is above every name, that at the name of Jesus every knee should bow, of those in heaven, and of those on earth, and of those under the earth, and that every tongue should confess that Jesus Christ is Lord, to the glory of God the Father* (Phil. 2:5-11).

The Lord's utter humility and sacrificial behavior in serving others is an example for all to follow. To the extent that He was despised and disgraced by mankind, God has highly exalted Him above all power and principalities, to be esteemed, worshipped, and appreciated.

Presently, the Lord Jesus sits at the right hand of the Majesty on high (Heb. 1:13), on His Father's throne (Rev. 3:21). This is a position of highest honor and privilege and acknowledges that the Lord perfectly completed the work of redemption that the Father gave Him to accomplish. Sitting at the right hand of God symbolizes a position of power (Matt. 26:24) and identifies who God delights in (Ps. 16:11). The outcome of Christ's selflessness is majestic honor and glory!

Just as water ever seeks and fills the lowest place, so the moment God finds you abased and empty, His glory and power flow in.

— Andrew Murry

April 13 – The Divinity of Christ – Part 7
(John Observation)

The Light of the World: *"Then Jesus spoke to them again, saying, 'I am the light of the world. He who follows Me shall not walk in darkness, but have the light of life'"* (John 8:12). He was God's Light from heaven so that all on the earth could witness real and eternal life. *"In Him was life, and the life was the light of men. And the light shines in the darkness, and the darkness did not comprehend it"* (John 1:4-5). Concerning this truth, Andrew Jukes notes:

> There stood One, in a servant's form, in the likeness of sinful flesh, whose life, even while others judged Him, was judging everything, and showing, by its holy contrast, what was in men and what was not, according to God's mind. "The Life was the light."[21]

The first Adam was originally created in the "likeness" and "image" of God, but, after the fall, moral "likeness" was lost, and man would bear God's "image" with diminished capacity. Man was still God's representative on earth, but not a very good one. Genesis 5:3 states that Adam begot children *"in his own likeness, after his image."* Image is not likeness; these are distinctly different ideas. Likeness is similitude, being like; image is representation, whether alike or not. The Lord Jesus, *the last Adam,* is never spoken of as "being in the likeness of God." He cannot be "like" God since He is God. Adam's descendants, though still representing God, would be like their father Adam in moral likeness.

The Lord Jesus Christ, being fully God, revealed the glory of God on earth as only a Holy God could. Though the first Adam failed to represent God and show forth God's moral glory, the last Adam displayed perfect representation. *"And the Word became flesh and dwelt among us, **and we beheld His glory, the glory as of the only begotten of the Father**, full of grace and truth"* (John 1:14).

> We must have the glory sink into us before it can be reflected from us. In deep inward beholding we must have Christ in our hearts, that He may shine forth from our lives.

— Alexander MacLaren

April 14 – Holy, Holy, Holy
(John 1)

Just as Luke presents the life of Christ more uniquely than any other Gospel, John acclaims the deity of Christ like no other. Only God is perfect, self-sufficient, and self-existing – there is none like Him; He is thrice holy! *"For I am the Lord your God, the Holy One of Israel, your Savior"* (Isa. 43:3). *"I, even I, am the Lord, and besides Me there is no savior"* (Isa. 43:11). *"For I am God, and there is no other; I am God, and there is none like Me"* (Isa. 46:9). The prophet Isaiah clearly teaches that the Savior of mankind is none other than Holy God Himself. As God is triune, Isaiah highlights the roles of God the Father, God the Son, and of the Holy Spirit in His salvation plan for humanity (Isa. 48:16-17). These truths are then expounded in the New Testament.

John uses plain language, Old Testament types and symbols, and numerical imagery to show that Jesus Christ is God in flesh – *holy humanity.* John expediently and emphatically introduces the Lord Jesus as being truly God, the Creator, in the opening verses of his account:

> *In the beginning was the Word, and the Word was with God, and **the Word was God**. He was **in the beginning with God**. **All things were made through Him**, and without Him nothing was made that was made. **In Him was life**, and the life was the light of men. And the light shines in the darkness, and the darkness did not comprehend it* (John 1:1-5).

The Lord Jesus is holy! He was acknowledged as being holy in the womb by the angel Gabriel (Luke 1:35). Demons, while fearing premature judgment, asserted, *"Let us alone! What have we to do with You, Jesus of Nazareth? Did You come to destroy us? I know who You are – the Holy One of God"* (Mark 1:24)! Peter proclaimed, *"We have believed and have come to know that You are the Holy [hagios] One of God"* (John 6:69; NASB). The early church declared that Christ was holy (Acts 4:27, 30).

Holy, Holy, Holy is our God. John not only refers to the holiness of Christ, but also to the "Holy Father" (John 17:11) and to the ongoing work of the Holy Spirit related to believers. He is our Comforter (literally, the advocate) of the believer. He is our Helper, our Teacher, our Reprover, and our Guide into deeper truth (John 16:7-14).

April 15 – Christ's Forerunner
(John 1)

The prophet Isaiah was a voice crying in the spiritual wilderness of Israel's apostasy, so God used him to speak of one that would come in a future day in the same spirit of ministry to announce the Lord's coming: *"Prepare the way of the Lord; make straight in the desert a highway for our God"* (Isa. 40:3). All four of the Gospel writers apply this verse to John the baptizer (Matt. 3:1-4; Mark 1:1-4; Luke 1:76-78; John 1:23). Though John dwelt in the desert, his preaching made a highway for the Lord Jesus through the spiritual wilderness of Israel. As a result, some, like His disciples, did believe on Christ, and did witness the glory of God. John said, *"And the Word became flesh and dwelt among us, and we beheld His glory, the glory as of the only begotten of the Father, full of grace and truth"* (John 1:14).

But as in Isaiah's day, the majority of the Jewish nation rejected John's introduction of their Messiah: *"He was in the world, and the world was made through Him, and the world did not know Him. He came to His own, and His own did not receive Him"* (John 1:10). Many in Israel were moved by John's ministry at the first, some even believed his message and followed Christ, but the majority did not. The Lord Jesus, speaking to the Pharisees said that John *"was the burning and shining lamp, and you were willing for a time to rejoice in his light"* (John 5:35). Later, the Lord reminded the Pharisees of their rejection of John's message: *"For John came to you in the way of righteousness, and you did not believe him"* (Matt. 21:32).

Indeed, many witnessed the glory of God in Christ during His first advent, but the entire world did not see it, for Christ was sent to find the lost sheep of Israel (Matt. 15:24). In the Kingdom Age, however, the remainder of Isaiah's prophecy will be fulfilled: *"All flesh shall see it together; for the mouth of the Lord has spoken"* (Isa. 40:5). The Jewish nation will need to embrace the Lord in faith and in truth before the glory and the blessings of the Lord will be witnessed by all men. The process will begin when Israel exercises genuine faith in revealed truth and it will be completed in the Kingdom Age when Israel receives the Holy Spirit and is able to exhibit the character of Christ. John bravely completed his mission as Christ's forerunner and was martyred. He understood that he must decrease and Christ must increase (John 3:30).

April 16 – We Beheld His Glory
(John 1)

Long ago, the fine flour of the *meal* offering (Lev. 2) symbolized our Lord's perfect moral character – His sinless perfection in all His doings. John wrote of Christ's demonstrated perfect character: *"And the Word became flesh and dwelt among us, and we beheld His glory, the glory as of the only begotten of the Father, **full of grace and truth**"* (John 1:14). The Lord's flesh concealed the outshining glory of God but allowed His divine moral excellence to be viewed by all. Of all the men who have ever walked on this earth, only the Lord Jesus Christ could say:

> *My judgment is righteous, because I do not seek My own will but the will of the Father who sent Me* (John 5:30).

> *I always do those things that please Him [His Father]* (John 8:29).

> *Whatever I speak, just as the Father has told Me, so I speak* (John 12:50).

> *If you had known Me, you would have known My Father also* (John 14:7).

> *I have manifested Your name to the men* (John 17:6).

In every respect of moral nature and divine character the Son was a perfect representation of the Father: *"The Son can do nothing of Himself, but what He sees the Father do; for whatever He does, the Son also does in like manner"* (John 5:19). This is why the Lord Jesus could adamantly declare to Philip on the eve of His death: *"He that has seen Me has seen the Father"* (John 14:9). He was perfect in all His doings, in every circumstance, in each word spoken, and in every thought mentally conceived – all to the glory of God and thus achieving in His life the full appreciation of His Father. In application, the Lord's pattern of behavior should be followed by all those who name Him as Savior – let us not be just balanced in what we do, but strive to be full of grace and truth, that we too can manifest His name among men.

April 17 – A Prophet Like Moses (Part 1)
(John 1)

After seeing Jehovah's awesome display of power on Mount Sinai, the Israelites asked Moses to be their mediator. The Lord was pleased with their understanding of His holiness and their need of an intercessor to approach Him. Moses then uttered this prophecy to them:

The Lord your God will raise up for you a Prophet like me from your midst, from your brethren. Him you shall hear, according to all you desired of the Lord your God in Horeb in the day of the assembly, saying, "Let me not hear again the voice of the Lord my God, nor let me see this great fire anymore, lest I die" (Deut. 18:15-16).

This meant that Moses would serve as Jehovah's prophet to communicate crucial messages to His people. Though God would send a long line of prophets to converse with Israel in the unfolding centuries, Moses' prophetic ministry was unique in comparison (Deut. 34:10). He had enjoyed extended intimate fellowship with God, he spoke for God to the people, and he was a mediator representing the people to God. In this sense, Moses pictured the special Prophet (speaking of Christ) that God would send in a future day to bring His ultimate message of hope to Israel. Those not heeding His Prophet's message would be judged appropriately by God (Deut. 18:18-19).

The role of a prophet was an important ministry in Israel; the prophet had to bravely stand before the people and be a mouthpiece for God. Prophetic exercise occurred mostly when there was spiritual decline among God's people. At such times, God sent prophets to make people aware of their sin, to call them to repentance, and to warn them of forthcoming judgment if they did not repent. Such was the situation in Israel when the Lord Jesus, the Living Word of God, was sent to the earth and was born of a virgin to testify for God (John 1:1-2).

During the Lord's first advent to the earth, He entered into the office of prophet after being anointed by the Holy Spirit at thirty years of age (Luke 3:21-23). After being tested forty days in the wilderness by Satan, the Lord Jesus began His prophetic ministry of declaring God's message to the nation of Israel, the gospel of the kingdom (Matt. 4:17).

April 18 – A Prophet Like Moses (Part 2)
(John 1)

The Jews remembered the words of Moses who foretold the coming of a special prophet that would behave like God and would speak for God perfectly. They inquired of John whether he was this particular prophet. John said he was not, but then pointed them to Christ as the One they should be looking for (John 1:21-23). Luke agrees, and makes it abundantly clear that the words of Moses pertaining to the special prophet were fulfilled by Christ (Acts 3:22-26). Christ came to be the Great Revealer of the mind of God to the lost sheep of Israel. He continued this prophetic ministry among the Jews for over three years before giving Himself as a ransom for humanity at Calvary. The Lord ended His prophetic ministry on earth when He ascended into heaven.

It was important that Israel receive accurate communication from Jehovah. Under the Mosaic Law there was to be no tolerance for anyone posing as a spokesman for false deities. Those uttering prophesies in Jehovah's name which He did not speak or in the name of false gods were to be put to death. Whatever a true prophet of God said would happen, always did happen (Deut. 18:22). A true prophet spoke for God and not of himself. The New Testament confirms that the ministry of the Lord Jesus completely fulfilled Moses' prophecy in Deuteronomy 18:18: *"I will raise up for them a Prophet like you from among their brethren, and will put My words in His mouth, and He shall speak to them all that I command Him."* The Lord Jesus perfectly conveyed the message of God to Israel, and indeed to all humanity. He confirmed many times that this was the essence of His earthly ministry:

As I hear, I judge; and My judgment is righteous, because I do not seek My own will but the will of the Father who sent Me (John 5:30).

Then Jesus said to them, "When you lift up the Son of Man, then you will know that I am He, and that I do nothing of Myself; but as My Father taught Me, I speak these things. And He who sent Me is with Me. The Father has not left Me alone, for I always do those things that please Him" (John 8:28-29).

Do you not believe that I am in the Father, and the Father in Me? The words that I speak to you I do not speak on My own authority; but the Father who dwells in Me does the works (John 14:10).

April 19 – The Lamb of God

(John 1)

The Gospel of John swells with unique content, planned omissions, key words, "types" of Christ, and declarations of deity. Christ is revealed as the "Word of God" and the "Bread from Heaven." Matthew presents Christ as fulfilling Old Testament prophecy, but John shows Christ as the literal fulfillment of Old Testament "types."

John the Baptist declared that Christ was *"the Lamb of God which takes away the sin of the world"* (John 1:29). Paul agrees that Christ was the literal fulfillment of the Passover Lamb (Ex. 12): *"For even Christ our Passover is sacrificed for us"* (1 Cor. 5:7). On the eve of the Exodus, God gave instructions concerning the Passover lamb. On the tenth day of the first month, the head of each Hebrew home was to choose a male lamb, a yearling without any blemishes. Once chosen, it was separated and was watched closely for four days to ensure its fit condition. Four days later, the young, tested, unblemished lamb was to be killed in the evening. For the initial Passover, the lamb's blood was to be applied to the doorpost and lintel of the offerer's home in order to spare the life of the firstborn living there. The millions of lambs slaughtered up until the time of Christ were a testimony that the blood of animals could never fully atone for man's sin; it was necessary for the perfect, unblemished, fully-tested Man, the Lamb of God, to shed His blood.

Some four hundred years prior to the first Passover, another prelude to Christ's sacrifice took place. In obedience to God's command, Abraham went to the land of Moriah and upon the mount that God showed him Abraham built an altar to sacrifice his beloved son Isaac. God was testing and refining the quality of Abraham's faith through the ordeal. During this trial, Abraham uttered two prophetic statements which preface the events of Exodus 12 and have their final fulfillment in the sacrifice of Christ at Calvary. First, *"God will provide Himself a Lamb for a burnt offering"* (Gen. 22:8). Second, *"In the mount of the Lord it shall be seen* [provided]*"* (Gen. 22:14). Both speak of the future sacrifice of Christ at Jerusalem; the Lord Himself declared this to the Pharisees, saying, *"Abraham rejoiced to see My day: and he saw it, and was glad"* (John 8:56). God did provide His Lamb and He was sacrificed in the mount of the Lord. Jesus Christ is God's Lamb for us, but we each must receive Him as our Passover Lamb to be saved.

April 20– You Must Be Born Again
(John 3)

The only way to personally beat death is to receive eternal life in Christ; while those in Christ may experience physical death, they will never experience spiritual death. While speaking to Martha, the Lord affirmed, *"I am the resurrection and the life. He who believes in Me, though he may die, he shall live. And whoever lives and believes in Me shall never die. Do you believe this?"* (John 11:25-26).

The Lord Jesus likened the receiving of His life to being born again. He told an inquiring Pharisee named Nicodemus, *"Most assuredly, I say to you, unless one is born again, he cannot see the kingdom of God"* (John 3:3). In other words, no one can make it to heaven without receiving spiritual life in Christ. Those trusting Christ for salvation are born again and have become God's spiritual children: *"But as many as received Him, to them He gave the right to become children of God, to those who believe in His name: who were born, not of blood, nor of the will of the flesh, nor of the will of man, but of God"* (John 1:12-13).

Logically then, without being born again (receiving Christ's life), one cannot become a child of God, and one cannot be born again without trusting the Lord Jesus alone for salvation. Through being born again, the Christian can enjoy the resurrection life of Christ now (Phil. 3:10) and have the hope of bodily resurrection into His presence later (1 Cor. 15:51-52).

God's personal offer to be one with Him is rescinded when physical death occurs (Heb. 9:27). If a person dies without Christ, he or she will spend eternity without Him in a spiritual abode called the Lake of Fire, commonly referred to as Hell. Hell is a place without grace, mercy, second chances, love, light, and most importantly God. All that enter Hell's gate will spend eternity in utter agony. Thankfully, we need not suffer in Hell, because the Lord Jesus has already suffered God's wrath for every sin we have committed. But we must be born again to receive His pardon and be with Him forever.

It comes to my having the mind of God; do I want to be like Christ in everything? If born of God, I have power to overcome all that is not of God, and to walk according to God.

— G. V. Wigram

April 21 – The Serpent on the Pole
(John 3)

We read in Numbers 20 that the Israelites had become completely dissatisfied with God's provision of manna. Whenever God's provision of spiritual sustenance is loathed, a believer's inner man (i.e., his or her spirit) quickly withers. This permits the carnal nature within the believer to have its way without restraint. This is why Paul identifies a spiritually healthy person as one whose *"inward man is being renewed day by day"* (1 Cor. 4:16). The enjoyment and satisfaction of reading and meditating on God's word as one engages in spontaneous prayer and personal reflection is the same as feasting on God's manna.

Jehovah brought fiery serpents among the people of Israel because of their murmuring and disbelief; those bitten died (Num. 20:4-6). Understanding their desperate need, the Israelites came to Moses and acknowledged: *"We have sinned, for we have spoken against the Lord and against you; pray to the Lord that He take away the serpents from us"* (Num. 20:7). Moses immediately interceded on behalf of the people and God responded with a solution to avoid death: *"Make a fiery serpent, and set it on a pole; and it shall be that everyone who is bitten, when he looks at it, shall live"* (Num. 20:8). Moses did as the Lord said and explained the "look and live" provision to the people. No one forced anyone to take advantage of this life-saving provision. Those bitten, who wanted to live, looked by faith at the bronze serpent and those who refused were responsible for their own demise.

In Scripture, bronze speaks of "fiery" judgments, while the serpent itself is a symbol of sin and rebellion (Rev. 12:9), and the lofty pole prefigures Christ's cross. The typological imagery is astounding and the Lord Jesus wanted to ensure that Nicodemus understood the pattern put in place centuries before: *"And as Moses lifted up the serpent in the wilderness, even so must the Son of Man be lifted up, that whoever believes in Him should not perish but have eternal life"* (John 3:14-16). At Calvary, Christ became sin for us and took our place. Everyone who looks by faith to the Savior's completed work on the cross shall not experience spiritual death, but shall live forever with Christ. Because Christ rose from the grave, those trusting in Him receive eternal life in Him. All of us were born snake-bitten (i.e., spiritually dead in Adam; Rom. 5:12), meaning that we too must look to Christ to live with Him.

April 22 – Two Resurrections
(John 5)

Though Job is one of the oldest books in our Bibles, ironically it is the first to speak of resurrection. Job was a God-fearing, righteous man who God permitted to suffer greatly for personal refinement and for God's glory. Even after the loss of all his wealth, his children, and his health, Job would not blaspheme God, but instead anticipated being with Him in the afterlife: *"For I know that my Redeemer lives, and He shall stand at last on the earth; and after my skin is destroyed, this I know, that in my flesh I shall see God, whom I shall see for myself, and my eyes shall behold, and not another. How my heart yearns within me!* (Job 19:25-27).

Even if God took Job's life, he understood that ultimately he would be resurrected and that he would dwell with his Redeemer. Though Job suffered much, God did restore and bless him later in his life. What was his hope during those difficult days? He knew that his resurrected body would not be covered with sores, but be suitable to live with God.

Whether one spends eternity in heaven or in hell, everyone will undergo a spiritual resurrection. This ensures that all individuals will have a body suited for their final destination. The Lord Jesus taught that He, as the Son of God, created all life and that all life was in Him (John 1:3-4), and at His command all the deceased would be resurrected (i.e. every disembodied soul would be joined to an immortal body):

> *Most assuredly, I say to you, the hour is coming, and now is, when the dead will hear the voice of the Son of God; and those who hear will live. ... For the hour is coming in which all who are in the graves will hear His voice and come forth – those who have done good, to the resurrection of life, and those who have done evil, to the resurrection of condemnation* (John 5:24-29).

Two types of resurrection are identified: a resurrection of the just to enable eternal residence in heaven and a resurrection of the condemned to be punished for eternity in the Lake of Fire (Rev. 20:10, 15). The Lord Jesus has received authority from His Father to initiate both of these resurrections, but Scripture informs us that the first resurrection (i.e. of the just) occurs in several stages, while the resurrection of the condemned happens all at once. In either case, Christ will be honored!

April 23 – Four Witnesses
(John 5)

Under the constraints of the Mosaic Law, there had to be at least two witnesses to validate a matter as true, thus the Lord says, *"If I bear witness of Myself, My witness is not true"* (John 5:31). To address this legitimate point of the Law, the Lord Jesus supplies four witnesses that could authenticate His Messianic credentials (John 5:33-47).

The first witness was Christ's forerunner John the baptizer (John 5:33-35). The people believed that John was a prophet sent by God, a perception that the Pharisees were quite aware of (Luke 20:6). John had declared that Jesus was the Messiah, *"the Lamb of God who takes away the sin of the world"* (John 1:29). Why would anyone want to reject what a prophet of God had declared to them?

The second witness was the works that He had done (John 5:36). Though the Lord knew that the Jews would not believe in Him through signs alone, He understood the need to fulfill Scripture and work wonders before them to prove He was the Messiah. Later, He pled with those who had rejected His claims: *"If I do not do the works of My Father, do not believe Me; but if I do, though you do not believe Me, believe the works, that you may know and believe that the Father is in Me, and I in Him."* (John 10:37-38). Only God could cleanse lepers, cure diseases, heal blindness, and raise the dead, and if He was only pretending to be God, why would God do such miracles through Him?

The third witness was God the Father (John 5:37-38) who on three separate occasions had spoken from heaven to express His pleasure in His Son, Israel's Messiah. The first was directly after Christ's baptism, *"This is My beloved Son, in whom I am well pleased"* (Matt. 3:17). A similar statement was uttered from heaven at Christ's transfiguration (Matt. 17:5). The third time is after the Lord foretold His death and asked His Father to glorify His name. God affirmed that He would do so again through Christ's work at Calvary (John 12:28).

The fourth witness was Old Testament Scripture, which provided hundreds of predictive prophesies concerning both His first and second advents (John 5:39-47). He suggested that if they believed in the Law of Moses, then they should believe His message for Moses foretold of His coming: *"But if you do not believe his writings, how will you believe My words?"* (John 5:47). To reject Christ is to reject Scripture!

April 24 – The Well of Living Water (Part 1)
(John 4)

After God rested from His work of creation, a river flowed out of Eden to provide the whole land with blessing and refreshment. Symbolically speaking, water is often connected with God's rest and blessing (Gen. 2:10; Rev. 22:1) – He being the fountainhead of both.

Centuries after Eden, the Lord would meet a runaway bondservant named Hagar in the wilderness by *"a fountain of water"* (Gen. 16:7), commonly referred to as *"a well"* (Gen. 16:14). This is the first mention of a well in Scripture. How fitting for the all-sustaining Lord to meet a distressed woman in a life-threatening situation by a well in a desert place! Interestingly, the first occurrence of a well in the New Testament is when the Lord went out of His way to meet a Samaritan woman with a sin-devastated life at Jacob's well (John 4:6). The Lord Jesus said to her, *"If you knew the gift of God, and who it is who says to you, 'Give Me a drink,' you would have asked Him, and He would have given you living water"* (John 4:10). He offered her "living water" (Himself) to satisfy her spiritually-parched life. Like Hagar, she believed and obeyed the Lord, and received a great blessing from Him.

The prophet Isaiah writes, *"Therefore with joy you will draw water from the wells of salvation"* (Isa. 12:3). A fountain of lasting joy springs up from the believer's spirit when Christ dwells within. For Hagar, this refreshment was not found in Egypt (the world); it was received on the way to Shur (Gen. 16:7). The world's entangling circumstances work to lead us into despair, but direct communion with the Lord during our wilderness experiences results in satisfaction!

Peter mentions a well, for the final time in Scripture, when he warns against false teachers: *"These are wells without water, clouds carried by a tempest, for whom is reserved the blackness of darkness forever"* (2 Pet. 2:17). False teachers offer falsehoods, which culminate in false hopes. No bubbling fountain of refreshment is there; only a deep, dry hole waiting for its next victim to fall into it. In contrast, the Lord Jesus is God's messenger of truth, and offers an abundant life of joy despite circumstances (John 10:10). When one embraces the Savior, a jubilant fountain of refreshing spiritual drink is enjoyed and blessings of the abundant life are obtained. Like Israel in the wilderness, we too can sing to the Fountain of Life, *"Spring up, O well"* (Num. 21:17).

April 25 – The Well of Living Water (Part 2)
(John 4)

The Lord's dialogue with the Samaritan woman at Jacob's well in John 4 is fascinating – it is His longest recorded personal conversation. The Lord chose to return to Galilee through Samaria. Being weary and towards late afternoon, He chose to sit down by the well and wait for a specific woman that He desired to talk to (the disciples had departed to buy provisions). Because of her ignoble reputation, she came to the well at about 6:00 PM in order to avoid other women drawing water later at dusk; nobody wanted to talk to her.

Ignoring the ethnic bias of that day, the Lord, being thirsty, asked her to draw water for Him. The Savior used His own human need to introduce Himself to her as the source of living water for her soul's need. The Samaritan woman was surprised that a Jew would speak to her, let alone ask her for something. Her response showed that she did not understand what the Lord was offering her. The Lord then asked her to get her husband, but the unnamed woman replied by saying that she was not married. The Lord affirmed that she had told the truth, but then filled in the details of her life's story: she had been married five times before and was now living with a man that was not her husband.

She knew that there was no way a Jewish stranger could have known her past; so she said, *"Sir, I perceive that You are a prophet."* Being uneasy that her past sins were exposed, she abruptly changed the subject to their differing customs in worshipping God. The Lord did not ignore her diversion, but responded to it to teach her of Himself: *"Woman, believe Me, the hour is coming when you will neither on this mountain, nor in Jerusalem, worship the Father.... The hour is coming, and now is, when the true worshipers will worship the Father in spirit and truth"* (John 4:21-23). The woman replied, *"I know that Messiah is coming (who is called Christ). When He comes, He will tell us all things"* (John 5:25). The Lord's answer was concise, *"I who speak to you am He"* (John 4:26). The One offering eternal, living water to her was none other than the promised Messiah. The woman departed, without her water pot, to tell others of the One who knew about her past but still offered Himself to her! Many believed her testimony and came to hear Christ's message and many trusted in Him. In only seven brief statements the Lord masterfully led a poor destitute sinner to salvation.

April 26 – True Worshippers
(John 4)

After conquering the Northern Kingdom in eighth century B.C, the Assyrians resettled various conquered people groups in central Israel. These foreigners intermarried with surviving Jews and became known as the Samaritans. Because of their mixed pedigree, they were not permitted access to the temple in Jerusalem and a harsh distain for Samaritans became the cultural norm. Over time, they developed their own religious system of worship on Mount Gerizim near Jacob's well. During the Lord's conversation with the Samaritan women at this well, He revealed an important truth concerning true worship and the change that would occur in the Church Age after Judaism was abolished:

Jesus said to her, "Woman, believe Me, the hour is coming when you will neither on this mountain, nor in Jerusalem, worship the Father. You worship what you do not know; we know what we worship, for salvation is of the Jews. But the hour is coming, and now is, when the true worshipers will worship the Father in spirit and truth; for the Father is seeking such to worship Him. God is Spirit, and those who worship Him must worship in spirit and truth" (John 4:21-24).

The human spirit is God conscious and the deepest part of our being. Christians are indwelt by the Holy Spirit after conversion and are thus equipped as believer-priests to worship Him anywhere and anytime. The Lord said that true worshippers of God must do so through their spirit, as properly enabled by the Holy Spirit to both learn and express truth (John 16:13-14). This means that we labor in God's Word to understand what He has revealed about Himself (i.e., His character, nature, attributes, and what He has done and what He promises to do). What God does is always an extension of who He is!

The value of our priestly service relates directly to having fellowship with God in spirit and in truth. Only through Spirit-led worship which expresses divine truth can the believer offer any acceptable sacrifice of praise to God. If we become satisfied with the goodness of Christ and yet lose sight of who He is and what He desires for us, we will become feeble and powerless. God strengthens those who want to be guided into the knowledge of Himself and the purposes of His grace by experiencing His Son.

April 27 – "I AM"
(John 6)

Moses' second question to God at the burning bush was, *"What is your name?"* or by implication, Who are you? God's response to Moses' question was, *"I AM WHO I AM"* (Ex. 3:13-15). In preparation for their deliverance from Egypt and the wilderness experience to follow, God wanted His covenant people to know Him as "I AM." The Hebrew word *hayah* is used here to mean "I will be," and is a wordplay on *Yahweh* (Jehovah) in Exodus 3:15, which means "to be." Moses was to tell the children of Israel that I AM, the self-existing One, had sent him to deliver them from bondage and out of Egypt.

It is of no surprise then that the New Testament reveals the Lord Jesus Christ as the great I AM of Exodus; He is the only One who can satisfy all human need. Seven is the number of perfection and completeness and John presents in his gospel account the seven I AM statements of Christ: "The Bread of Life," "The Light of the World," "The Door," "The Good Shepherd," "The Resurrection and the Life," "The Way, the Truth, and the Life," and "The True Vine." The perfect, self-existent One declared in His own words the fullness of I AM. The Lord Jesus also warned His audience: *"I said to you that you will die in your sins; for if you do not believe that **I am** ["He" is not in the text], you will die in your sins"* (John 8:24). This means that those who call on a Jesus who is less than God incarnate cannot be saved; they would be seeking help from a different Jesus than God presents in Scripture.

Regrettably, many today fail to know and appreciate the fullness of who Christ really is. God has supplied everything He wants us to know about His Son presently in Scripture (Heb. 1:2-3). God has revealed Himself to us through His Son. If we want to know the Father, we must first know the Son, and then the Spirit of God will assist us every step of the way (John 16:13-15). We have no excuses for neglecting I AM.

Not only was Moses to go to Egypt in the name of *Yahweh,* the Self-Existing One, but he was to inform the Israelites that this was God's name forever and it was to be remembered by them forever. The Self-Existing One was eternal, thus, His name would remain the same. God told the prophet Malachi, *"I change not"* (Mal. 3:6). Likewise, the writer of Hebrews proclaims, *"Jesus Christ the same yesterday, and today, and forever"* (Heb. 13:8). Jesus Christ is the great I AM!

April 28 – The Bread of Life (Part 1)
(John 6)

John combines three "wilderness images" that the Lord used in His final months of ministry to speak of Himself as the only way of salvation: The manna from heaven (John 6), the water from a rock (John 7), and the pillar of fire at night (John 8). Specific Jewish rituals during the Feast of Tabernacles celebrated the latter two.

Seven times in John 6, the Lord Jesus refers to Himself as the "Bread of Life" which came down from heaven. He likens the Israelites feeding upon the manna in the wilderness in order to live to a believer feeding on Him now to obtain eternal life and be able to live for Him.

> *Then Jesus said to them, "Most assuredly, I say to you, Moses did not give you the bread from heaven, but My Father gives you the true bread from heaven. For the bread of God is He who comes down from heaven and gives life to the world." Then they said to Him, "Lord, give us this bread always." And Jesus said to them, "I am the bread of life.* **He who comes to Me shall never hunger, and he who believes in Me shall never thirst***" (John 6:32-35).*

Appropriating the finished work of Christ to one's account by faith is the only means of receiving eternal life, and applying His Words for life is the only way to live for Him. His Word is our spiritual food! God would use manna to teach the Israelites this lesson, immediately after delivering them from Pharaoh at the Red Sea. How would God feed two million people in a wilderness? His food provision was something that had never been seen before; the people called it manna, which literally means, "What is it?" Manna was small in size, white in color, round in shape, and tasted like a wafer made with honey (Ex. 16:14, 31). God's plan was to furnish a normal portion of manna five days each week, plus a double portion on Friday to supply Saturday's needs.

The Israelites quickly learned that though the manna was God's provision for them, it had to be personally gathered in the morning (it spoiled by the afternoon). Likewise, believers today must continually feed on the Lord Jesus (i.e., to mediate on His Word) to receive help and guidance for each day. Christ speaks to us in the quietness of His presence and provides all that we need. We need a fresh, daily portion of manna because we cannot live on yesterday's enjoyment of Christ!

April 29 – The Bread of Life (Part 2)
(John 6)

Eating of the Bread of Life from Heaven confers eternal salvation, and continuing to feed on Him is the only spiritual food which satisfies the human soul and strengthens the inner man for spiritual conflict. The Lord Jesus said, *"He who comes to Me shall never hunger, and he who believes in Me shall never thirst"* (John 6:35). Just as the Israelites had to eat manna in the wilderness to live, the believer in the Church Age will be destitute of spiritual vigor unless he or she consistently feeds on the Bread of Life. The manna of Exodus and the Bread of Life of John 6 have a number of specific typological correlations. Both the manna to the Israelites and Christ to those trusting Him:

(1) Were a supernatural gift from God (rained down from heaven vs. directly from heaven's throne).
(2) Were supplied where the people were (in the wilderness vs. in the world).
(3) Were to be eaten (to sustain physical life vs. to gain spiritual life).
(4) Were to be gathered daily (each morning vs. throughout each day).
(5) Were obtained by labor (going out to gather vs. meditation on God's Word).
(6) Were not to be neglected (turned to worms vs. lost opportunities to know and serve).
(7) Were incomprehensible to the natural man (not natural vs. obviously supernatural).
(8) Were despised by the mixed multitude (hated by the Egyptians vs. despised by the world).
(9) Were preserved for future generations (placed in the ark vs. the eternal Word).
(10) Were supplied until the destination was reached (ceased at Canaan vs. grace received by faith no longer needed in heaven).

Personally appropriating the finished work of Christ by faith is the only means of gaining Christ's life, and obeying His Word the only means of living it out for Him. His Word is our spiritual food for each and every day! No believer can gather another's manna; each one must personally meditate on the Word of God to obtain his or her provision of grace for each day. Starving our spiritual man of what God provides to maintain our spiritual vitality can only end badly for the believer.

April 30 – The Water-Supplying Rock
(John 7)

After delivering the Israelites from their bondage in Egypt, the Lord brought them to Rephidim, but there was no water in that desolate place (Ex. 17:1-7). It was not long before the people complained to Moses, and Moses brought the matter to the Lord. God's solution was an unusual one; he was to strike a specific rock at Horeb with the rod of God. Moses did so, and an abundant flow of water came gushing out of the rock. Though the Israelites strove with God at Rephidim, they were not chastened, for God's judgment fell on the Rock in one stroke. The Rock, of course, pictures Christ, who was crucified and suffered divine wrath for our sin (1 Cor. 10:4). Because of Christ's work at Calvary, the blessings of God can freely flow out to humanity through Christ.

Forty years after this, Moses received the rebuke of God for striking another rock in the same manner when he had been instructed to speak to the rock to receive God's provision of water (Num. 20:7-13). Moses' disobedience mattered to God, because it broke the "type" of Christ that He wanted to present to Israel. Christ was to suffer only once for sin, then the blessing of His priestly work would be received through speaking to Him as High Priest (Heb. 10:10-18).

The Lord often used Jewish traditions to speak of Himself. He did so twice at the Feast of Tabernacles a few months before Calvary:

On the last day, that great day of the feast, Jesus stood and cried out, saying, "If anyone thirsts, let him come to Me and drink. He who believes in Me, as the Scripture has said, out of his heart will flow rivers of living water." But this He spoke concerning the Spirit, whom those believing in Him would receive; for the Holy Spirit was not yet given, because Jesus was not yet glorified (John 7:37-39).

A Jewish ritual practiced at the Feast of Tabernacles celebrated God's provision of water in the wilderness. Each day for seven days, a solemn procession of priests traveled from the temple to the spring of Gihon to fill a gold pitcher with water. They then returned to the temple and poured out the water before the Bronze Altar to symbolize the water gushing from the rock Moses struck in the wilderness. This was not done the last day of the feast, and that is when the Lord Jesus stood up and gave a gospel invitation to come to Him and drink abundantly.

May 1 – Appealing to the Human Conscience
(John 8)

John is the only Gospel writer to record the encounter of the Lord Jesus with a group of self-righteous, religious zealots who were demanding the death of a woman caught in the act of adultery (John 8:2-11). It was early in the morning and apparently the Lord had just arrived at the temple Himself. Their demands were hypocritical; the fact that the guilty man had been set free demonstrated their lack of reverence for God's Law (Deut. 22:22-24). The Lord told them, *"He who is without sin among you, let him throw a stone at her first"* (John 8:7). He successfully appealed to their consciences (oldest to the youngest), and they all departed from the guilty woman without casting one stone. As it is unbiblical to declare forgiveness without repentance, the Lord did not do so (she did not ask to be). But He did appeal to her conscience through a warning, *"Neither do I condemn you; go and sin no more"* (John 8:11). Christ came to seek and save sinners His first advent; His second advent would result in harsh consequences. The Lord could not condone her sin, she was guilty and deserved death, but He extended her mercy – some more time to find salvation in Him.

For believers in the Church Age, it is relatively easy for us to think or speak condescendingly of Israel's stubborn and foolish behavior in the scene before us. But would not the Lord feel the pain of misplaced devotion and allegiance within the Church, who is spiritually one with Him, even more keenly than He did centuries ago with His covenant people that did not have the Holy Spirit indwelling them?

It would be pharisaical for us in the Church Age to fling a stone at the hardhearted Jewish elders and ignore the application of the story. Do we allow idols in our hearts to displace our love for the Lord Jesus? Do we flirt with the world and feast on immoral things, and then draw near to our Lord with vile filth still on our breath as we pray sweet nothings into His ear? Are we superficially pretending to be a chaste virgin awaiting her wedding day? Is our bridal attire stained with unconfessed sin and religious pride? The application of Israel's error is still pertinent today. In Christ, all true Christians enjoy security, though the enjoyment of our relationship with Christ is dependent on good behavior and an uncontaminated thought-life. The abiding presence of the Lord Jesus Christ is a great defense against entering into sin.

May 2 – The Light of the World
(John 8)

God had marvelously delivered His people from Egypt and their brutal captivity, but now they were trekking through an unknown desert to a place that they had never been before. The Lord had a solution to soothe their apprehension: *"And the Lord went before them by day in a pillar of cloud to lead the way, and by night in a pillar of fire to give them light, so as to go by day and night. He did not take away the pillar of cloud by day or the pillar of fire by night from before the people"* (Ex. 13:21-22). The ever-present cloud was a kind token of Jehovah's parental care and His abiding presence among His people. Additionally, the cloud would illuminate their camp at night and its shadow would protect them from excess solar radiation during the day.

Even during times of rebellion, the pillar of God's presence would never depart from the children of Israel. God would accompany His covenant people through the best of times and the worst of times to ensure that they entered into the Promised Land. Centuries later, David, understanding the blessing of God's abiding presence in his life, would write: *"Yea, though I walk through the valley of the shadow of death, I will fear no evil; for You are with me"* (Ps. 23:4).

Approximately six months prior to His crucifixion, the Lord Jesus used this familiar icon from Hebrew history to teach of Himself. He was teaching at the temple during the Feast of Tabernacles when He declared the second of seven "I AM" statements recorded in John's Gospel: *"I am the light of the world. He who follows Me shall not walk in darkness, but have the light of life"* (John 8:12). During the Feast of Tabernacles, a huge candelabra was lit in the temple at night to remind the people of the pillar of fire that guided the Israelites through the wilderness (i.e., God was in the pillar). The wicks of the lamps in the candelabra were made from the priests' worn-out garments. Hanging the lamps over the women's court at the temple ensured that *all* would be able to see the spectacular sight. Christ utilized this traditional ceremony to declare to the whole congregation that He was God's light shining forth to mankind; its illumination had no prejudice to gender, ethnic origin, or social status. Christ came into the world and He died for the whole world (1 Jn. 2:2; Heb. 2:9), that "whosoever will" may step into the light and have fellowship with God through Him.

131

May 3 – Loving the Light
(John 8)

At the end of the Feast of Tabernacles, the Lord Jesus said, *"I AM the light of the world"* (John 8:12). The Lord Jesus was God's abiding presence in the world and through Him God would guide blind sinners into life-transforming truth. Earlier in His earthly ministry, He taught:

> *And this is the condemnation, that the light has come into the world, and men loved darkness rather than light, because their deeds were evil. For everyone practicing evil hates the light and does not come to the light, lest his deeds should be exposed. But he who does the truth comes to the light, that his deeds may be clearly seen, that they have been done in God* (John 3:19-21).

The ultimate test of whether someone has truly trusted Christ for salvation is whether or not they continue practicing evil. A true child of God does not persist in sin (1 Jn. 3:9); a child of light does not blatantly keep walking in darkness because he or she yearns for God's abiding presence and fellowship. Not only are there deep longings to be with God, but profound remorse when under the conviction of the Holy Spirit that should lead a true child of God to repentance and restoration.

The Lord also explained to His disciples why the world hated Him and why it would hate them also: *"If I had not come and spoken to them, they would have no sin, but now they have no excuse for their sin"* (John 15:22). The Lord's sinless presence among sinners was a convicting testimony of God's holiness and His words left no doubt in the sinner's mind as to their sinful state and need for righteousness. They had been exposed to soul-penetrating light, and instead of coming to the Light, they had scurried back into satanic darkness.

The Light of the World even told the Pharisees what they were going to do to Him because they were determined to walk in darkness:

> *"When you lift up the Son of Man, then you will know that I am He, and that I do nothing of Myself; but as My Father taught Me, I speak these things. And He who sent Me is with Me." ... As He spoke these words, many believed in Him. Then Jesus said to those Jews who believed Him, "If you abide in My word, you are My disciples indeed. And you shall know the truth, and the truth shall make you free"* (John 8:28-32).

No one is forced into God's light, but those who come find freedom!

May 4 – The Darkness of Disbelief (Part 1)
(John 9)

John 6 demonstrates that the unrighteous long to see a "sign or a wonder" in order to believe (John 6:30), while the righteous believe in order to see and understand (John 6:68-69). "Light," symbolizing divine truth, and "believing," an action of faith not based on sight, are paramount topics throughout John's Gospel. The antitype of each of these is strongly tied together in the behavior of the spiritually blind Pharisees. They were blind because they chose to ignore the truth and continued in the darkness of self-righteousness.

> *And Jesus said, "For judgment I have come into this world, that those who do not see may see, and that those who see may be made blind." Then some of the Pharisees who were with Him heard these words, and said to Him, "Are we blind also?" Jesus said to them, "If you were blind, you would have no sin; but now you say, 'We see.' Therefore your sin remains"* (John 9:39-41).

Spiritual blindness ignores the true reality of things and instead embraces what is often an obvious perversion of the truth. Mark the utter stupidity of the Pharisees' statements while speaking with the Lord Jesus: (1) These strict, self-righteous, Law-keepers had to be reminded by Christ that their plans to murder Him would, in fact, break the Mosaic Law (John 7:19, 8:59). (2) Speaking to the Lord Jesus, the Pharisees said, *"Are You also from Galilee? Search and look, for no prophet has arisen out of Galilee"* (John 7:52). Perhaps they had forgotten that Jonah was of Galilee. (3) The Pharisees brought a woman caught in the act of adultery before the Lord to be judged, but where was the man? The Law was no respecter of persons – adultery demanded the death of both parties (John 8:1-11; Lev. 20:10). (4) The Pharisees proclaimed to Christ, *"We are Abraham's descendants, and have never been in bondage to anyone. How can You say, 'You will be made free'?"* (John 8:33). But, in fact, they had been ruled relentlessly by four world empires over the last 600 years.

God has offered mankind a choice – to hide in the calamity of darkness and experience eternal death, or to step into and abide in divine light and experience life in and with God.

May 5 – The Darkness of Disbelief (Part 2)
(John 9)

Spiritual blindness clouds human reasoning, perverts logic and distorts our perception of reality. This is why, in spiritual matters, man must ignore sight-based faith, our mutable feelings, and simply trust God at His word – this is true faith. God rewards true faith by opening our understanding of spiritual truth; naturally speaking, we cannot understand the things of God (1 Cor. 2:9-13).

Previously, the Lord Jesus told those Jews who had just believed on Him, *"Know the truth, and the truth shall make you free"* (John 8:32). On the eve of His crucifixion, He told His disciples (less Judas) that He was leaving them to prepare a place for them, and He would be coming back at a future time to receive them to Himself.

After Thomas expressed concern about not knowing the way He was going, the Lord told His disciples that He was the way to the Father: *"I am the way, the truth, and the life. No one comes to the Father except through Me"* (John 14:6). He would be just like the pillar of light that illuminated the way of the Israelites through the Red Sea during the darkness of night. Those who believe in Him as God's truth and light can have confidence of eternal life with God; those who hide from the light and choose to walk in darkness, prove to themselves that they are foolishly blind.

Christ, the Light of the world, challenges saint (1 Jn. 1:5-7) and sinner alike to step out from darkness and to walk in accordance with divine truth. In so doing, the unregenerate sinner will find salvation of his or her soul and the saint will learn more of the peace of God which surpasses all understanding. Accordingly, God's light without God's grace would be a miserable existence indeed, and thankfully God does not offer either exclusively from the other.

Darkness is my point of view, my right to myself; light is God's point of view.

— Oswald Chambers

Where, except in uncreated light, can the darkness be drowned?

— C. S. Lewis

May 6 – The Good Shepherd
(John 10)

The shepherd imagery of John 10 is actually only a portion of a New Testament trilogy. First, John presents Christ as the "Good Shepherd" who lays His life down for the sheep. Then the writer of Hebrews highlights the sanctifying work of the Lord Jesus as the Great Shepherd (Heb. 13:20-21). Finally, Peter proclaims Christ as the Chief Shepherd who will return and gather His sheep to Himself (1 Pet. 5:4). The latter reference speaks of Christ's return to the air to "snatch away" from the earth those who have truly believed on Him. May we contemplate the kindhearted words of our Lord, the Good Shepherd:

> *I am the door. If anyone enters by Me, he will be saved, and will go in and out and find pasture. The thief does not come except to steal, and to kill, and to destroy. I have come that they may have life, and that they may have it more abundantly. I am the good shepherd. The good shepherd gives His life for the sheep. But a hireling, he who is not the shepherd, one who does not own the sheep, sees the wolf coming and leaves the sheep and flees; and the wolf catches the sheep and scatters them. The hireling flees because he is a hireling and does not care about the sheep. I am the good shepherd; and I know My sheep, and am known by My own. As the Father knows Me, even so I know the Father; and I lay down My life for the sheep* (John 10:9-15).

Christ's sacrificial love for the sheep stands in sharp contrast to the hireling shepherds of Israel, who led God's sheep astray, neglected their care, and deserted them in times of danger (Ezek. 34). Therefore, those who have been charged with the care of God's sheep must attend to His flock. Those who neglect this ministry should consider the Lord's decree of judgment against the base shepherds of Israel (Ezek. 34:10). Peter learned a valuable lesson after he had denied the Lord – it was easier to die for the Lord than to live for Him. Peter was later called to be one of many shepherds (elders) of God's sheep (1 Pet. 5:1-2), and although he could only be martyred once for the Lord, he would die a hundred times in caring for God's sheep. *"Simon, son of Jonah, do you love Me?"* (John 21:16). Let us heed the warning and selflessly tend to the Lord's own because we love the Lord. The Lord willingly gave up His life to care for His sheep (John 10:17) and so should we.

May 7 – The First Liar Is Cast Down
(John 12)

Paul identifies Satan as *"the god of this age"* (2 Cor. 4:4) and *"the prince of the power of the air"* (Eph. 2:2). On three occasions near the end of His earthly ministry, the Lord Jesus said that Satan is *"the ruler of this world"* (John 12:31, 14:30, 16:11). The world is Satan's delegated domain, but he must function within divine boundaries. God is holy, and He cannot tempt anyone to sin (Jas. 1:13), but Satan is allowed to test man's resolve to obey God's expressed will.

Satan exercises his delegated authority to promote the corruption of truth. The Lord Jesus plainly acknowledged this fact while speaking to the Pharisees, the leaders of religious corruption in Israel at that time:

You are of your father the devil, and the desires of your father you want to do. He was a murderer from the beginning, and does not stand in the truth, because there is no truth in him. When he speaks a lie, he speaks from his own resources, for he is a liar and the father of it (John 8:44).

Notice that the enemy of our souls never speaks the truth; he always distorts the truth to deceive those who devalue God's Word. The devil is never more dangerous than when he has a Bible in his hands.

Just a few days before His crucifixion, Christ again told His disciples what He was about to suffer in Jerusalem (John 12:23-27). He did not want them to be disheartened when they saw Him nailed to a cross; rather, He wanted them to understand that He was God and in full control of the situation: *"Now I tell you before it comes, that when it does come to pass, you may believe that I am"* (John 13:19). After foretelling His crucifixion to His disciples, the Lord asked the Father to glorify His name. A voice from heaven immediately responded, *"I have glorified it and will glorify it again"* (John 12:28). The Lord then said:

"This voice did not come because of Me, but for your sake. Now is the judgment of this world; now the ruler ["the prince"; KJV) of this world will be cast out. And I, if I am lifted up from the earth, will draw all peoples to Myself." This He said, signifying by what death He would die (John 12:30-33).

The cross was no accident; Christ was in full control. He was resolute to honor His Father and destined to defeat "the father of lies."

May 8 – The Angel of the Lord (Part 1)
(John 12)

There are about two dozen separate visitations of "the Angel of the Lord" in the Old Testament. When God appeared to someone in the Old Testament, the event is referred to as a *theophany,* which means "God appearance." At such times, the Lord usually appeared as a normal-looking man, but on certain occasions He took other forms to accentuate His message. For example, the Lord spoke to Moses from a bush that appeared to be burning (Ex. 3), and to the Israelites from within a pillar of cloud (Ex. 13). The Israelites watched Mount Sinai visibly burn and quake at God's presence, though He Himself was concealed by thick, ominous clouds.

In addition to the title of "the Angel of the Lord," the context of Scripture can be used to identify a theophany, which has the following characteristics. The Angel of the Lord is rightly worshipped as God by others (Josh. 5:14; Judg. 6:18-20). The Angel of the Lord initiates covenants and promises that only God can keep (Gen. 16:10, 22:16-17). In most occurrences, the Angel of the Lord clearly identifies Himself as God (Gen. 31:11-13; Ex. 3:2-6).

Whether in human form or in some unusual depiction, the One appearing was normally referred to as "the Angel of the Lord." The title is unique and should not be confused with the expression "an angel of the Lord," which may refer to the appearances of one of many holy angels. Specifically, a theophany is a pre-incarnate visit of the second Person of the Godhead to the earth as His Father's messenger. The Lord Jesus stated that no one had ever personally seen God the Father (John 6:46). The Lord also said, *"He who has seen Me has seen the Father"* (John 14:9). This means that God the Father did not appear to anyone previously, but rather the only One who could perfectly represent Him did, the Lord Jesus pre-incarnate. Hence, some refer to these appearances as *Christophanies*, or literally, "Christ appearances."

Angel means "messenger" in both the Hebrew and Greek texts. In the Old Testament, the Son of God brought the message of God to those who needed to hear it. In the New Testament, the Messenger was God's Message – *"the Word became flesh and dwelt among us, and we beheld His glory"* (John 1:14). Now, as a Man in the glory, the Living Word continues to represent the holiness of God to every creature.

May 9 – The Angel of the Lord (Part 2)
(John 12)

As previously mentioned, when the Son of God appears in the Old Testament, He is referred to as "the Messenger (Angel) of the Lord." Perhaps this is why Jacob referred to the Lord as "the Redeeming Angel" (Gen. 48:16). Similarly, in the New Testament, the Son of God is called the Word (John 1:1; 1 Jn. 1:1); the Son became a man to bring the ultimate message of God to humanity. The Lord Jesus was a living message sojourning on the earth; He was both the message and the Messenger of God.

In addition to the title of "the Angel of the Lord," the context of Scripture can be used to identify a theophany, which has the following characteristics. The Angel of the Lord is rightly worshipped as God by others (Judg. 6:18-20). The Angel of the Lord initiates covenants and promises that only God can keep (Gen. 16:10, 22:16-17). In most occurrences, the Angel of the Lord clearly identifies Himself as God (Gen. 31:11-13; Ex. 3:2-6).

There are also New Testament passages which refer to Old Testament appearances in such a way as to verify that the Person of Christ was the one witnessed. For example, Isaiah writes: *"In the year that King Uzziah died, I saw the Lord sitting on a throne, high and lifted up, and the train of His robe filled the temple"* (Isa. 6:1). In the New Testament, John refers to Isaiah's vision while explaining that Christ was fulfilling his prophecies:

> *Therefore they could not believe, because Isaiah said again: "He has blinded their eyes and hardened their hearts, lest they should see with their eyes, lest they should understand with their hearts and turn, so that I should heal them." These things Isaiah said when he saw His glory and spoke of Him* (John 12:39-41).

John confirms that the Lord Jesus fulfilled Isaiah's prophecies and that the prominent One that Isaiah saw in his glorious vision of God upon His throne was the same One (now in the flesh) that John loved and served – the Lord Jesus Christ.

May 10 – One Bath, but Many Washings
(John 13)

The disciples gathered in an upper room with the Lord to eat the Passover together. Before the feast began, the Lord girded Himself as a slave, poured water in a basin, picked up a towel, and began washing the dirty feet of His disciples. Normally, this was the task of a household servant to refresh visitors, but since the Lord was the host and the disciples were His guests, He humbled Himself to serve them.

Peter did not appreciate the Lord's act of kindness and refused to have his feed washed. The Lord told Peter that in a future day he would understand what He was doing and then replied, *"If I do not wash you, you have no part with Me"* (John 13:8). This statement caused Peter to reverse his position, *"Lord, not my feet only, but also my hands and my head!"* (John 13:9). The Lord's answer is remarkable: *"'He who is bathed needs only to wash his feet, but is completely clean; and you are clean, but not all of you.' For He knew who would betray Him; therefore He said, 'You are not all clean'"* (John 13:10-11). Besides setting an example of service He expected His disciples to follow, the Lord was revealing important doctrinal truth about regeneration.

The symbolic meaning of the scene before us was first typified during the consecration process of the first High Priest. Moses bathed Aaron once at the Bronze Laver (Lev. 8:6), but afterwards Aaron would have to stop at the Laver and wash his hands and feet before entering the tabernacle (i.e., into God's presence; Ex. 30:17-21). The full bath pictures spiritual regeneration, which was never repeated. This is why the Lord told Peter (a true believer) that he was already clean and did not need to be spiritually bathed again, and also why Judas, a phony, was not clean (he had not undergone the washing of regeneration).

Paul writes: *"Not by works of righteousness which we have done, but according to His mercy He saved us, through the washing of regeneration and renewing of the Holy Spirit"* (Tit. 3:5). The Holy Spirit works to convict the lost of their sinful state, their need of righteousness, and that God must judge their sin (John 16:8-10). At conversion, the Holy Spirit implants a desire for holiness and works to cleanse the new believer from polluted things. The act of regeneration occurs at conversion and implants new life and a new order of living within the believer; what was dead is now spiritually alive (Eph. 2:1-3)!

139

May 11 – "Lord and Teacher"
(John 13)

On the eve of His crucifixion, the Lord hosted the Passover meal for His disciples. Normally, the host provided a servant to wash the feet of his guests before enjoying the feast together. Not having a servant, the Lord Jesus *"rose from supper and laid aside His garments, took a towel and girded Himself. After that, He poured water into a basin and began to wash the disciples' feet, and to wipe them with the towel with which He was girded"* (John 13:4-5). Afterwards He explained the meaning of His actions:

> *You call Me **Teacher and Lord**, and you say well, for so I am. If I then, your **Lord and Teacher**, have washed your feet, you also ought to wash one another's feet. For I have given you an example, that you should do as I have done to you. Most assuredly, I say to you, a servant is not greater than his master; nor is he who is sent greater than he who sent him* (John 13:13-16).

The Lord was the perfect Teacher (Master; KJV) because He was first a selfless servant of others. The disciples rightly referred to Jesus Christ as their "Teacher and Lord," but notice Christ switched the order of these titles to "Lord and Teacher" to declare the right priority in which His disciples should relate to Him. True authority serves others instead of being served. If the disciples did not relate to Him as Lord above all else, they would fail to represent Him properly in ministry.

Because He was Lord, He willingly served those He loved. He was their Lord and Teacher. Just a few days earlier the Lord had taught His disciples: *"But you, do not be called 'Rabbi'; for one is your Teacher, the Christ, and you are all brethren. ... But he who is greatest among you shall be your servant. And whoever exalts himself will be humbled, and he who humbles himself will be exalted"* (Matt. 23:8-12). This was the example of Christ; although He was Lord, He was willing to humble Himself to serve others. This is our example to follow also and if we do, we will have the Lord's blessing: *"If you know these things, blessed are you if you do them"* (John 13:17).

May 12 – The Comforter Is Coming (Part 1)
(John 14)

It is through the Gospel of John that we obtain the fuller relation of the Holy Spirit's work concerning believers. He is the Comforter (literally, the advocate) of the believer. He is the Helper, the Teacher, the Convicter, and the Guide into deeper truth.

The matter of preparing His disciples for the arduous task ahead was very much on the mind of the Lord Jesus the night before He died. Much of the Lord's discourse with His disciples, as recorded in John 14 through 16, centers on this topic. After telling the disciples in John 13 that one of them was a betrayer, that Peter was going to deny Him, and that He was leaving them, the Lord provides a message of comfort in John 14. He informed them that after His departure the Comforter, speaking of the Holy Spirit, would be coming to them:

> *And I will pray the Father, and He will give you another Helper, that He may abide with you forever – the Spirit of truth, whom the world cannot receive, because it neither sees Him nor knows Him; but you know Him, for He dwells with you and will be in you. ... These things I have spoken to you while being present with you. But the Helper, the Holy Spirit, whom the Father will send in My name, He will teach you all things, and bring to your remembrance all things that I said to you* (John 14:16-17, 25-26).

After His resurrection, the Lord commissioned His disciples and opened their understanding of Scripture. He then instructed them to wait in Jerusalem for the coming of the Holy Spirit. He, the Comforter, would infuse them with divine power to enable their ministry. Knowledge of their divine calling and their new understanding of Scripture would be of no avail without God's facilitating power.

The same is true for us today. To be strong in the Lord means that we must read God's Word, meditate on it, and obey it. Only then will we be able to fulfill the Lord's calling for our lives. It is through God's Word that the Holy Spirit manifests His fullness as the mighty occupant of our inner man. We should not think that we possess Him; He resides within to possess and control us for the glory of the Lord Jesus Christ!

May 13 – The Comforter Is Coming (Part 2)
(John 14)

The deity of the Holy Spirit is expressed in various ways in Scripture, but one of the most obvious is through His direct association with the other Persons of the Godhead. The Holy Spirit is directly associated with the other members of the Trinity some sixteen times in the New Testament. For example, He is called "the Spirit of God" (1 Cor. 6:11), and "the Spirit of Jesus" (Acts 16:7). Clearly, the Spirit of God has full association with the other members of the Godhead (Matt. 28:19; 2 Cor. 13:14). While forgiven sinners can obtain a position of holiness in Christ through justification, individual believers are never called "Holy" by name. However, "Holy" is a personal name for God, speaking of His uniqueness (Ps. 111:9; Isa. 57:15). There are approximately eighty references to "the Holy Spirit" or "Spirit Holy" in Scripture. God does not attribute His name to others, so it is evident that His Spirit is a Person within the Godhead.

The Holy Spirit has divine attributes clearly consistent with each member of the Godhead:

- Omniscience: the Holy Spirit knows the things of God (1 Cor. 2:11-12).
- Omnipresence: we cannot flee from the Spirit's presence (Ps. 139:7).
- Eternal Existence: He is the "Eternal Spirit" (Heb. 9:14).
- Omnipotence: the Holy Spirit was involved in creation (Job 33:4; Ps. 104:30).
- Without error: the Holy Spirit is "the Spirit of Truth" (1 Jn. 5:6).
- Divine Wisdom: no one can counsel God's Spirit (Isa. 40:13).
- Immutable: The Holy Spirit does not change (Isa. 11:2).

The Holy Spirit is divine; in essence He has the same attributes and character qualities as the other members of the Godhead. As God, the Holy Spirit is a Person who unmistakably disapproves of sin, is deeply grieved by it, and works to save sinners from its deadly influence. As Isaiah alludes to, the Holy Spirit works to convict sinners of their need for a Savior by impressing them with the truth and the fearful consequences of rejecting God's offer. The Lord said the Holy Spirit would be about the same type of work during the Church Age: *"He will convict the world of sin, and of righteousness, and of judgment"* (John 16:8). The Holy Spirit's ministry is essential to the revelation of God's Son to the world!

May 14 – To Pray in His Name
(John 14)

As previously mentioned, the Gospel of John upholds the theme of the Lord Jesus in His deity and includes several occurrences of the number *seven* to further symbolize that theme. John presents a strong connection between prayer and knowing and doing the will of God through "sevens." In John, the Lord refers to His Father's "will" *seven* times, speaking only His Father's words *seven* times, and that His disciples should pray only in His name on *seven* different instances. Hence, perfect praying centers in the will and the Word of God; it is not selfish. Of course, John speaks of this in a literal fashion also: *"And whatever you ask in My name, that I will do, that the Father may be glorified in the Son. If you ask anything in My name, I will do it. If you love Me, keep My commandments"* (John 14:13-15). *"Now this is the confidence that we have in Him, that if we ask anything according to His will, He hears us"* (1 Jn. 5:14). We must know God's Word to know how to pray in a way that would honor Christ's name.

The 19th century evangelist Charles Finney summarizes what it means to pray in Christ's name:

> To use this name acceptably implies a realizing sense of our character and relations, and of His character and relations; God's character and governmental position – our character and governmental position. Now, unless the mind has a realizing sense, so as really to mean what it ought to mean in using Christ's name, it does not do so acceptably. … To pray in His name, we must ask the thing not for ourselves, because we are not our own; we do not own ourselves, and of course, therefore, we can own nothing else. The fact is, we are Christ's, and when we seek anything in Christ's name, we seek it for Him. We are Christ's servants, and as children we belong to Christ.[22]

Prayer is not a "name it and claim it" formula for success. Righteous praying centers in God's will and is motivated by love for the Savior's name. The Lord was a man of prayer and proved that prayer should precede service. Prayer shows faith and dependence in God to initiate, direct, and complete each matter of our lives according to His will. Prayer transforms our hearts by conforming our thinking to the mind of Christ. For those who love the name of Jesus Christ and His will, prayer is a great blessing which moves the hand of God!

May 15 – "My Friends"
(John 15)

The phrase "My friends" as spoken by the Lord to His disciples conveys an important distinction of association which is often overlooked. Is Jesus our Friend, or are we His friends? Scripture always conveys the thought of us being the Lord's friends and not the opposite association. The Holy Spirit has been completely specific for a reason!

The only person in the entire Bible to be directly called "a friend of God" is Abraham (2 Chron. 20:7; Isa. 41:8; Jas. 2:23). In Exodus 33:11 we read, *"So the Lord spoke to Moses face to face, as a man speaks to his friend"* (Ex. 33:11). John the baptizer spoke of *"the friend of the Bridegroom"* (John 3:29) or "the Bridegroom's friend." Speaking to His disciples, the Lord Jesus referred to Lazarus as *"our friend"* (John 11:11). Later, He said, *"You are My friends if you do whatever I command you"* (John 15:14). Friendship involves selfless ministry, and Christ demonstrated at Calvary His sacrificial love for His friends (John 13:1, 15:13). As far as distorting the proper focus, it was the Pharisees, not believers, which said of the Lord, *"Behold a man gluttonous, and a winebibber, a friend of publicans and sinners"* (Matt. 11:19). The Holy Spirit was completely specific for a reason.

It is Christ's connection with us that ensures fellowship, not our familiarity with Him. The receipt of His love consequently prompts our allegiance and devotion to Him (1 Jn. 4:19); we prove we are His through obedience. Referring to Christ as our friend is an innocent expression, but in effect unintentionally lowers Christ to our station. Which sounds better: "I am a friend of the President," or "the President is my friend?" The answer is the former. By being his friend, I relate to him in his position of authority, whereas if he were just my friend, I would lower him to my common social position as a "nobody."

There is no desire to legalize this scriptural distinction in our terminology, but rather that we would better appreciate all that Christ has accomplished for us. While the old hymns *What a Friend We Have in Jesus* and *I've Found a Friend* may not be technically correct, they do contain lovely lyrics that express the truth of Proverbs 18:24: *"But there is a friend who sticks closer than a brother."* Certainly, the Lord has proven Himself friendly, but His exalted position and our responsibility to Him in thought and deed are vitally important also.

May 16 – "I Have Chosen You"
(John 15)

God's message to His people throughout the ages has been consistent concerning their separation from the world's ungodliness. He told His covenant people at the time of the Egyptian Exodus: *"I will bring you out from under the burdens of the Egyptians"* (Ex. 6:6), *"come to Me"* (Ex. 32:26), and *"separate yourselves"* (Num. 16:21). Correspondingly, the Lord Jesus said to His disciples, *"I chose you out of the world, therefore the world hates you"* (John 15:19). The cross of Christ has carved out of the world a group of people Christ calls His own. These compose the Church, literally the "called-out company." Accordingly, the Church is consecrated to Him and is to ignore worldly philosophies (Col. 2:8); as a result, the world hates godliness, and God hates worldliness in the believer's life (Jas. 4:4).

The believer must counterbalance the call to holy separation with the call of the Great Commission – *"Go therefore and make disciples of all the nations…"* (Matt. 28:19). Where is the symmetry between the Lord's commands to "separate" from the world and to "go" into the world? It is being in the world, but not of the world. A ship is designed to operate in water, but when water floods into the ship, it ceases to behave as intended – it sinks. It is the same with the believer's vessel. It is designed to be in the world as a testimony for God, but when the world gets into the Christian's life, he or she is sunk. The children of darkness are then quite eager to make an open spectacle of the fallen comrade who is thus a "castaway" in Christian service (1 Cor. 9:27). Although failures are not final with God, the consequences of lusting for earthly things to a Christian's testimony can be so devastating that recovery to full ministry is nearly impossible.

Likewise, Scripture speaks of two contrasting means that call the believer's heart out of the world. The first is to set one's mind on things above (Col. 3:2), and the second is to realize that the things of the earth are temporary. God has promised, *"'Yet once more I shake not only the earth, but also heaven.' Now this, 'Yet once more,' indicates the removal of those things that are being shaken, as of things that are made, that the things which cannot be shaken may remain"* (Heb. 12:26-27). The world is nasty and temporal, but heaven is wonderful and eternal. Let us not lust after or be satisfied with passing things.

May 17 – The Vine
(John 15)

Some have made this passage (John 15:1-17) say what it does not – the analogy does not teach that true believers can lose their salvation. The subject matter is not salvation, but fruit bearing. Having just departed the upper room, the Lord is speaking only to His disciples (i.e., true believers, as Judas has already departed the group). The fact that Christ refers to "a man" and not "them" in verse 6 affirms that Christ knew the eleven were branches (true believers) in the Vine (in Him). The key words in this text are: "love" (ten occurrences), "abide" (nine times mentioned), and fruit (found eight times). The Lord's desire for every believer is that they abide in Him, experience the love and joy of God, and yield spiritual fruit. Those who do not choose to abide in the goodness of Christ will be incapable of bearing spiritual fruit.

Two applications are offered from John 15:1-6. First, some may say that they are true branches, but their mimicked fruit-bearing will be proven to be counterfeit in time. True faith has a lasting reality (Jas. 2:17). You can fake it for a while, but not without zapping yourself dry; only Christ's resources can prompt fruit-bearing in believers: *"I am the vine, you are the branches. He who abides in Me, and I in him, bears much fruit; for without Me you can do nothing"* (John 15:5).

Second, the Greek verb *airo*, translated "takes away" in verse 2, is better rendered as "lift up." *Airo* has vast implications depending upon the context of the passage. In the New Testament, *airo* is rendered as some form of "taking away" twenty-two times or of "lifting up" thirty-six times. So what does our kind Lord do when true believers (branches in Him) do not bear fruit? He cleans the sinful muck off them through His Word (John 15:3) and "lifts" them up out of it in order to obtain better conditions for bearing fruit (John 15:2). The Lord does not cast away believers the moment they become unfruitful because of sin.

However, we see that those in the world are more than ready to burn up a believer's testimony when failure occurs (John 15:6). Please notice that this is not the Lord or angels, but men who gather and burn the fruitless branches. This teaching addresses the *practice* of the believer and not his or her *position* in Christ. John upholds both the Lord's desire (fruitfulness of His branches) and His ministry as the Vine and caretaker of His branches to promote fruitfulness.

146

May 18 – The Washing of the Word
(John 15)

In the Vine illustration the Lord reminded His disciples (less Judas) of several important facts concerning their cleansing and fruitfulness:

You are already clean because of the word which I have spoken to you. Abide in Me, and I in you. As the branch cannot bear fruit of itself, unless it abides in the vine, neither can you, unless you abide in Me. I am the vine, you are the branches. He who abides in Me, and I in him, bears much fruit; for without Me you can do nothing (John 15:3-5).

First, it is through the cleansing of (i.e., knowing and yielding to) God's Word that believers become more Christ-like. Second, without this cleansing it is impossible to abide in Christ. Third, without abiding in Christ believers can do absolutely nothing to please Him. The disciples had been made clean because they had believed on the message of salvation Christ brought, but continued cleansing by the Word would be necessary to maintain fruitfulness. Branches need light and nourishment from the vine to bear fruit. Branches covered in sinful muck will not be fruitful; the hindering filth must be removed first.

The difficulty for us is that we live in a world of sinful muck and that we are adversely affected by it every day. The influence of secular philosophies, amusements, and ensnaring associations is nonstop. This means that we must learn to recognize and think of filth as God does. This is possible through the ongoing sanctifying ministry of Christ:

Christ also loved the church and gave Himself for her, that He might sanctify and cleanse her with the washing of water by the word, that He might present her to Himself a glorious church, not having spot or wrinkle or any such thing, but that she should be holy and without blemish (Eph. 5:25-27).

The washing of the Word enables believers to identify and repudiate thoughts, motives, and behavior which do not have the Lord's approval. Paul tells us that *"to be carnally minded is death ... the carnal mind is enmity against God. ... So then, those who are in the flesh cannot please God"* (Rom. 8:6-8). What exposes the depravity of our carnal thinking? The answer is the conviction of the Holy Spirit through exposure to God's Word and we all need this ministry daily.

May 19 – The Glories of Christ
(John 17)

The glories of the Lord Jesus are threefold: Intrinsic, Official, and Moral. His intrinsic glory is that which is essential to Him as the Son of God – He is fully divine and an equal to the Father: *"And now, O Father, glorify Me together with Yourself, with the glory which I had with You before the world was"* (John 17:5). Christ's official glory is that which pertains to Him as the Mediator of the New Covenant – He is the Great High Priest. The Lord acquired His official glory – His reward and promotion for finishing the immeasurable work of redemption assigned to Him: *"Father, I desire that they also whom You gave Me may be with Me where I am, that they may behold My glory which You have given Me; for You loved Me before the foundation of the world"* (John 17:24).

The Lord's moral glory consists of the perfections which characterize His earthly life and ministry: *"And the Word became flesh and dwelt among us, and we beheld His glory, the glory as of the only begotten of the Father, full of grace and truth"* (John 1:14). He was perfect in all His doings, in every circumstance, in each word spoken, and in every thought mentally conceived.

During His earthly sojourn, His intrinsic glory was veiled and His official glory not yet received. Yet, His moral glory could not be hidden; His character shined forth the integrity and perfections of His divine essence. Of this glory A. W. Tozer wrote, "Christ is God acting like God in the lowly raiments of human flesh."[23] It is His moral glory which was witnessed by man and illuminates every page of the Gospel accounts.

William G. Moorehead speaks to the moral glory evident in the Lord's humanity:

> The moral glory of Jesus appears in His development as Son of Man. The nature which He assumed was our nature, sin and sinful propensities only excepted. His was a real and a true humanity, one which must pass through the various stages of growth like any other member of the race. From infancy to youth, from youth to manhood, there was steady increase both of His bodily powers and mental faculties, but the progress was orderly. "No unhealthy precocity marked the holiest of infancies." He was first a child, and afterwards a man, not a man in child's years. … At every stage of His development, in every relation of life, in every part of His service, He is absolutely perfect.[24]

May 20 – I Will Sanctify My Great Name
(John 17)

Just before His crucifixion, the Lord Jesus told His Father: *"I have manifested Your name to the men"* (John 17:6). What does it mean to manifest God's name? Attributes of *name* and *person* are inseparable; the Lord Jesus, in living flesh, had put God on display. God entered the realm of space and time in human form to declare His moral excellence, the power of His greatness, and the rich essence of His life. Consequently, man has been summoned to appreciate the goodness of God and thankfully some have responded to the drawing effect of God's love and have received and experienced eternal life in Christ.

That which was from the beginning, which we have heard, which we have seen with our eyes, which we have looked upon, and our hands have handled, concerning the Word of life – the life was manifested, and we have seen, and bear witness, and declare to you that eternal life which was with the Father and was manifested to us (1 Jn. 1:1-2).

All those who knew the Lord Jesus witnessed in His life the declaration of "Holy be Your name." The believer must follow Christ's example (1 Pet. 2:21); to exhale in one breath "Holy be Your name," and inhale human traditions, secular philosophies, and the rudiments of the world in the next is hypocrisy and dishonors God's name.

The prophet Ezekiel delivered a powerful rebuke against the nation of Israel. He informed his countrymen of God's anger concerning their ungodly behavior. Their insolence and idolatry had caused God's name to be blasphemed among the nations and His retribution was coming:

*"I do not do this for your sake, O house of Israel, but **for My holy name's sake**, which you have profaned among the nations wherever you went. And **I will sanctify My great name**, which has been profaned among the nations, which you have profaned in their midst; and the nations shall know that I am the Lord,"* says the Lord God, *"when I am hallowed in you before their eyes"* (Ezek. 36:22-23).

When the heathen say, "These Christians are so repulsive that their God must be even worse," a terrible blasphemy of God's name occurs. God will sanctify His name one way or another, even if we choose not to! May our godly behavior make others aware of God's greatness.

May 21 – A Prayer for Unity and Glory
(John 17)

While speaking to His Father the night before His crucifixion, the Lord prayed that those who would believe on His message would be one, just as He and the Father were one (John 17:20-22):

> *I do not pray for these* [His disciples] *alone, but also for those who will believe in Me through their word; that they all may be one, as You, Father, are in Me, and I in You; that they also may be one in Us, that the world may believe that You sent Me. And the glory which You gave Me I have given them, that they may be one just as We are one.*

The unity of God's people displays God's glory – the unity of the Godhead. *Unity* is spiritual and reflects God's essence, but *uniformity* is carnal and ultimately divides the Church (1 Cor. 3:1-4). Christ desires that there be no divisions in the Church, but rather that all believers enjoy fellowship to the fullest degree possible in reference to their understanding of scriptural truth – unity rests on this foundation.

The teaching and understanding of truth is vital to the building up of the Church: *"He who prophesies* (i.e., declares divine truth) *speaks edification and exhortation and comfort to men"* (1 Cor. 14:3). We also recognize that Scripture is the tool God uses to remove from us what is not sound in life and doctrine and to establish that which pleases Him.

Yet, doctrine alone is insufficient to guide believers in proper conduct; we need a work of grace in our hearts also: *"Knowledge puffs up, but love edifies"* (1 Cor. 8:1). Love and grace must temper our actions to ensure the edification of others (1 Cor. 8:1; Eph. 4:15-16). Separation among believers will occur when divine truth is embraced and false doctrine is shunned (2 Thess. 3:6). Yet, not all division is profitable. If love does not guide one's activities, isolation of the members within the body of Christ will occur over minute points of disagreement, the result of which will hinder the Church's working and growth. Just as grace and truth are inseparable aspects of Christ's character (John 1:14), the believer should not invoke one quality without the other. On this point, Paul commands, *"But, speaking the truth in love, may grow up in all things into Him who is the head – Christ"* (Eph. 4:15). The challenge, then, is to have fellowship with all believers to the degree that doctrine allows.

May 22 – A Prayer to Be in Glory
(John 17)

As in Mark, Luke portrays the Lord as a "man of prayer." Though He prayed often, Christ is only recorded as having prayed fifteen specific times in the Gospels. Luke records more of these incidents than any other writer – ten times in all. The Lord often sought the face of His Father early each day. Humanly speaking, the Lord was dependent on His Father. He received daily instruction and strength from heaven.

Although the Lord Jesus spent much time in prayer, precious few details of His prayers are recorded. He presented a model prayer to His disciples in order to teach them how to pray; this was done at their request. He prayed before certain miracles, that the people might know of His Father in heaven. He prayed before eating, as shown in the "feeding of 5000," and at the "Last Supper."

What is the "Lord's Prayer"? Sadly, it is not what is often repeated in churches today, which is in direct disobedience to Christ's command to exclude vain repetitions in our prayers (Matt. 6:7). The Lord's Prayer is what is recorded in John 17 the night before His crucifixion. This is one of the longest prayers in the entire Bible, yet it only takes two or three minutes to read. In this tender petition of heaven, the Lord prays for Himself (John 17:1-5), for His disciples (John 17:6-19), and for all those who would believe after them (John 17:20-26). How wonderful it is to know that long ago the Lord Jesus prayed for you and me:

> *Father,* **I desire that they also whom You gave Me may be with Me where I am,** *that they may behold My glory which You have given Me; for You loved Me before the foundation of the world. O righteous Father! The world has not known You, but I have known You; and these have known that You sent Me. And I have declared to them Your name, and will declare it, that the love with which You loved Me may be in them, and I in them* (John 17:24-26).

This prayer reveals that Christ earnestly desires us to be with Him. Although as God, the Lord Jesus is self-sufficient, from a relationship standpoint, He does not enjoy completeness until His beloved bride is with Him (Eph. 1:23). Hence, we can have confidence that our Beloved, our Great Shepherd and Great High Priest, is still praying for us until we all are home in His presence (Heb. 4:14-16; 13:20-21)!

May 23 – The Great Exchange Is Finished
(John 19)

Before the sin offering was killed in Levitical days, the offerer placed his hands upon the head of the animal and confessed his sins to symbolize the transfer of the offense to the animal. The sacrifice was then killed and completely burned. This indicated the sin had been fully atoned for and forgiven. The picture of the sin offering is clear; Christ identified with us by becoming a man, took our sin upon Himself at Calvary as God's Lamb, and was judged by God in our place:

> *For Christ also suffered once for sins, the just for the unjust, that He might bring us to God, being put to death in the flesh but made alive by the Spirit* (1 Pet. 3:18-19).

The sin offering was completely consumed by fire and the Lord Jesus was completely consumed in the judgment for our sin. David prophesied that the billows and waves of God's wrath would break upon the Sin-bearer, the Messiah (Ps. 42:7). During those three hours of darkness, while hanging between heaven and earth nailed to a cross, the Lord Jesus was forsaken by God the Father (Matt. 27:45-46). He was stripped of His clothing and His dignity – as a public spectacle He endured the persistent insults, the demeaning jeers, and the blatant blasphemy. Having completed His task as the sin offering, the Lord declared with a loud voice, *"It is finished."* He then offered up His spirit to the Father (John 19:30). This fulfilled His prophetic words:

> *Therefore My Father loves Me, because I lay down My life that I may take it again. No one takes it from Me, but I lay it down of Myself. I have power to lay it down, and I have power to take it again. This command I have received from My Father* (John 10:17-18).

The Lord Jesus was both the Mediator of a New Covenant (Heb. 8:7-9) and the ransom that established it: *"For there is one God and one Mediator between God and men, the Man Christ Jesus, who gave Himself a ransom for all, to be testified in due time"* (1 Tim. 2:5-6). The priest who presided over the sin offering was innocent of the offerer's sin, but yet became connected with it in order to apply the blood of the sacrifice to make atonement for the sinner – this pictures Christ's ministry as the Mediator between God and men.

May 24 – My Lord and My God
(John 20)

Because Thomas was not gathered with the disciples on the day of Christ's resurrection, he did not see or talk with Him. Thomas was reluctant to believe the testimony of his brethren; he wanted to see and feel the living Savior for himself (John 20:24-27). The Lord suddenly afforded Him the opportunity and Thomas wasted no time in declaring what he then knew to be truth: *"My Lord and my God!"* (John 20:28). It was a profound declaration, but the Lord responded to it by admonishing His disciple: *"Thomas, because you have seen Me, you have believed. Blessed are those who have not seen and yet have believed"* (John 20:29). In other words, blessed are those who read God's Word and believe that Jesus Christ is Lord and God:

- Paul identified Jesus Christ as our Great God and Savior (Tit. 2:13).
- Paul and James stated that the Lord Jesus is the Lord of Glory (1 Cor. 2:8; Jas. 2:1).
- Referring to Christ, John and Paul said that God was made manifest in the flesh (John 1:14, 18; 1 Tim. 3:16).
- The Lord Jesus said that He was the divine Shepherd who was smitten of God (Zech. 13:7; Matt. 26:31).
- Isaiah proclaimed that the Savior to be born was the Almighty: the everlasting God (Isa. 9:6-7).
- The apostles preached that Jesus Christ was the Son of God (Acts 9:20).
- Paul taught that God was in Christ reconciling the world (2 Cor. 5:19).
- The Lord Jesus forgave sins and only God has the right to do that (Isa. 42:24; Mark 2:5-7; Luke 7:48-50, 5:18-26).
- God and the Lamb are one in divine glory and are worshipped by all (Rev. 7:17, 15:4, 21:23).
- The demons recognized Jesus as God and feared Him (Luke 4:24, 4:41, 8:28).
- The Lord Jesus is the wisdom of God (Matt. 23:24; Luke 11:49).
- The Lord Jesus knows the thoughts of men (John 6:64).
- Speaking of Christ, Paul states that *"in Him dwells the fullness of the Godhead bodily"* (Col. 2:9).

The Lord Jesus Christ is the eternal Son of God in whom all the fullness of God dwells bodily. His divinity is recognized throughout Scripture. Blessed are you if you believe He is Lord and God.

May 25 – Did Christ's Resurrection Really Happen?
(John 21)

Jesus declared to the Pharisees that His resurrection would be a sign to them. It would set Him apart from anyone else who had ever lived and would prove that He was the Son of God (Matt. 12:39-40; Rom. 1:4). Paul claims that the Christian faith stands or falls on the resurrection of Jesus Christ (1 Cor. 15:12-19). His resurrection gives us hope for the future (our glorification) and once baptized into His resurrected life we have spiritual power to live for Him today. So what is the evidence for proving that the resurrection of Christ did occurred?

Eyewitness accounts. The Bible records five eyewitness accounts of seeing Jesus Christ on resurrection day and then at least five more over the next 40 days before His ascension into Heaven. Paul states that at least 500 people saw Him on one of these occurrences (1 Cor. 15:6).

Logically who would steal the body of Christ? The Romans would not want to take the body of Jesus as they desired to keep crowded Jerusalem calm and orderly during the Jewish feasts. The Jews would not want to steal His body because the last thing they wanted was His disciples to publicly proclaim His resurrection. This was the reason they asked Pilate for guards to be posted at Jesus' tomb. The disciples of Jesus had no reason to steal the body; otherwise they would be risking their lives for what they knew was not true – a fake religion. Clearly, the power of the Holy Spirit would not have been powerfully shown in them if they were grieving Him by lying (Eph. 4:29-30).

Radically changed lives. The disciples were transformed from common laborers to zealous men willing to hazard their lives for Christ; all were eventually martyred for Christ, excluding John who was imprisoned on Patmos. James, the half brother of Christ, had resisted Jesus' claims (John 7), but after Christ personally met with him, that all changed (1 Cor. 15:7). As a result, we see Mary and Jesus' half siblings with other believers in Jerusalem waiting for the Holy Spirit (Acts 1:14). Both James and Jude, Christ's half brothers, wrote epistles. Paul, a prominent Jewish leader, who had Christians murdered, saw Christ and became a believer and an Apostle of Christ (Acts 9).

Signs at Pentecost. Peter told the Jews that the signs they were seeing were a continuation of Jesus' ministry. This proved that Jesus Christ was approved by God and had experienced resurrection (Acts 2).

May 26 – A Hyperbolic Ending?
(John 21)

The apostle John posed a notable hyperbole at the conclusion of his gospel account in speaking of the Lord's ministry:

This is the disciple who testifies of these things, and wrote these things; and we know that his testimony is true. And there are also many other things that Jesus did, which if they were written one by one, I suppose that even the world itself could not contain the books that would be written. Amen (John 21:24-25).

John had wonderfully revealed the splendor of the Lord's deity throughout his record. In closing, it seemed only fitting to say that the One who was so much bigger than the world obviously had done and could do much more than the world could ever be aware of, let alone understand.

Paul expresses a similar truth in his epistle to the Ephesians: *"That in the ages to come He might show the exceeding riches of His grace in His kindness toward us in Christ Jesus"* (Eph. 2:7). The implication is that believers will need all of eternity to fully comprehend the grace of God shown us in Christ! This means that there is so much more of the Savior to learn than what has been already revealed to us in God's Word about Him. Indeed, there is much more truth to come, but we simply cannot comprehend it presently in our present situation; however, we are to learn what we can of Him now. This is possible by meditating on what God has revealed about Christ in Scripture and what the Holy Spirit reveals of Him to us through obedience and experience.

Moses said long ago: *"The secret things belong to the Lord our God, but those things which are revealed belong to us and to our children forever, that we may do all the words of this law"* (Deut. 29:29). There is much about the Lord that has not yet been revealed to us, but we are not responsible to understand such mysteries. We are, however, to value what God has and is showing us of Christ now. Our spiritual appetite should be to know more of Him and obey what we know to be true. For those who do, Christ promises to manifest more of Himself to them (John 14:21).

May 27 – The Aspiration of the Gospels
(Gospel Overview)

We have briefly viewed the unfathomable mind of God in the four Gospels. The literary design, the theme development, the different writing styles, the diverse human agents, the omissions, the inclusions, the variations, the key words and phrases, the embellished details, and much more speak of one Supreme Mind. May we praise God for both His effort in portraying His Son to us in such a unique fashion and for the One in whom all Scripture centers – the Lord Jesus Christ.

What is the main aspiration of the Gospel message? John affords a vital summary: *"And truly Jesus did many other signs in the presence of His disciples, which are not written in this book; but these are written **that you may believe that Jesus is the Christ**, the Son of God, and **that believing you may have life in His name**"* (John 20:30-31). Did you notice the two "believes" in this passage? In the Greek language, the first verb "believe" is in the "aorist" tense, while the second verb is in the "present" tense. John wrote his record of Christ for two reasons. First, that we might believe, speaking of a unique action in the past, which has a continuing effect – this relates to trusting the Gospel message for salvation and being regenerated. After receiving eternal life, the second "believe" becomes most important. This believing should be continuous and progressing in maturity such that the believer displays and enjoys the life of Christ more and more and, no less, learns to love the Lord more and more.

Many Christians today are retaining doctrinal purity, maintaining a blameless life, and serving the Church continuously, yet they lack a deep devotion to Christ. The Church today must heed the same warning that Christ issued to the church at Ephesus: *"Nevertheless I have this against you, that you have left your first love. Remember therefore from where you have fallen; repent and do the first works, or else I will come to you quickly and remove your lampstand from its place – unless you repent"* (Rev. 2:4-5). The Lord does not want just followers; He wants disciples that will die to self and live for Him. Orthodoxy and ministry are not enough; Christ demands the believer's heart, as well as his or her mind, hands, and feet. Those believers who deny Christ as their first love will ultimately lose their testimony for Him. Our deficient love hinders us from experiencing His abundant life!

May 28 – The Threefold Ministries of the Church
(Acts Introduction)

The Lord expects the Church to be engaging in three key ministries during His absence: an upward ministry, an inward ministry, and an outward ministry. A stool which can safely support a person's weight must have at least three legs with each supporting its share of weight. A local church will suffer if any of these three ministries are neglected!

The "upward ministry" is for the *exaltation* of God in worship. The scriptural imagery associated with a believer engaging in this ministry is that of a priest (Heb. 13:15; 1 Pet. 2:5, 9; Rev. 1:6). The Lord commanded His disciples to regularly remember Him and to proclaim the value of His death through the keeping of the Lord's Supper (Luke 22:10-20). The Lord's Supper, also called *"the breaking of bread,"* was a regular practice of the early Church each Sunday (Acts 20:7). Paul explained to the believers at Corinth that it was important for them to remember the Lord regularly by keeping the Lord's Supper and warned them not to partake of it unworthily (1 Cor. 11:23-32).

The "inward ministry" centers in the *edification* of all believers. The Bible likens this ministry to that of a shepherd (John 21:15-17; Acts 20:28-31; 1 Pet. 5:1-3). The Lord commissioned His disciples to teach those responding to the gospel message all the things that they had been taught by Him (Matt. 28:20). Believers in the early Church readily taught new disciples what they knew to be true, by referring them to His Word (Acts 2:42, 4:2, 5:42). The apostles also instructed believers to engage in this important ministry to *"grow up in all things"* (Eph. 4:14-15). God's Word was to be preached and used to *"convince, rebuke, exhort, with all longsuffering and teaching"* (2 Tim. 4:2). Teaching, reproof, instruction, and correction by God's Word is necessary to make believers profitable for good works (2 Tim. 3:17).

The "outward ministry" is to *evangelize* all nations (Matt. 28:19). Two separate images are used in Scripture to speak of this ministry. First, the fisherman ventures to the water (where the fish are) and casts in a line and works to land one fish at a time. This pictures one-on-one evangelism (e.g., Paul to Lydia in Acts 10). Second, the farmer scatters seed over a wide range of soils. In Ephesus, Paul shared the gospel from house to house (Acts 20:20), in schools (Acts 19:9), in synagogues (Acts 19:8), and wherever else he could (Acts 20:25).

157

May 29 – Be My Witnesses
(Acts 1)

Forty days after His resurrection the Lord Jesus was gathered with a company of His followers on the Mount of Olives near Jerusalem. He told them to wait in Jerusalem, for they would *"be baptized with the Holy Spirit not many days from now"* (Acts 1:4). Then some of them inquired if He was going to immediately restore the kingdom to Israel. He told them not to be concerned about the timing of such things. Instead, He asked them to be dedicated to another cause: *"But you shall receive power when the Holy Spirit has come upon you; and you shall be witnesses to Me in Jerusalem, and in all Judea and Samaria, and to the end of the earth"* (Acts 1:8). The gospel commission was received.

Ten days later, at the Feast of Pentecost, the Holy Spirit came, and has been indwelling believers and equipping them to be witnesses for Christ ever since. The original disciples were to begin where they lived and then move outward until all nations had heard the Good News message. To properly edify His Church, the Lord gave some individuals, such as evangelists and teachers, as gifts to the Church for a particular reason: *"for the equipping of the saints for the work of ministry, for the edifying of the body of Christ"* (Eph. 4:12). Every believer in the body of Christ has a work of ministry, the benefit of which will bless the entire body. For example, though the evangelist is skillful in reaching the lost for Christ, his or her main ministry to the Church is to equip and to stir up others within the Body to evangelize wherever God has placed them as a testimony to the lost. The result of this is that, in a collective sense, the Church is stimulated and equipped to obey the Great Commission (Matt. 28:19-20).

Consequently, one may *"do the work of an evangelist"* (2 Tim. 4:5) without being an evangelist, or *"be apt to teach"* without being a gifted teacher, or *"feed the flock of God"* without having received the pastoring gift. The Lord's program for evangelizing the world started with a handful of spiritually motivated and enabled believers that would simply tell others what they knew and then teach those who believed their testimony what Christ had taught them. One-to-one witnessing and discipleship is Christ's method for reaching the nations with the gospel message. Not all saints are evangelists, but all saints are to be witnesses. *"He that wins souls is wise"* (Prov. 11:30).

May 30 – The Mount of Hope
(Acts 2)

God's departing glory in Ezekiel's day (leaving the temple eastward and returning to heaven) signaled Jerusalem's doom a few years later by the Babylonians. A similar scene occurred six centuries later on the Mount of Olives when the Lord gloriously ascended into Heaven (Acts 1:9-12). Jehovah permitted the Jews several years to repent and receive His Son, their Messiah, whom they had crucified, but they would not, and in 70 A.D. the temple and portions of Jerusalem were destroyed.

Foreknowing this catastrophe, God sent two angels to convey a message of hope to the Jewish nation, as the disciples observed the Lord ascending into heaven: *"This same Jesus, who was taken up from you into heaven, will so come in like manner as you saw Him go into heaven"* (Acts 1:11). Zechariah informs us that the Lord Jesus will return to the Mount of Olives to deliver Jerusalem from the Antichrist:

> *For I will gather all the nations to battle against Jerusalem; the city shall be taken. ... Then the Lord will go forth and fight against those nations, as He fights in the day of battle. And in that day His feet will stand on the Mount of Olives, which faces Jerusalem on the east. And the Mount of Olives shall be split in two, from east to west, making a very large valley; half of the mountain shall move toward the north and half of it toward the south. ... And in that day it shall be that living waters shall flow from Jerusalem, half of them toward the eastern sea and half of them toward the western sea; in both summer and winter it shall occur* (Zech. 13:2-8).

At that time, the nations will have gathered against Jerusalem under the authority of the Antichrist. The city will be conquered and half of its inhabitants will be enslaved when Christ suddenly appears, descends on, and splits the Mount of Olives. The initial attack by Israel's enemies on Jerusalem will be successful. Feeling confident of total victory, these barbaric invaders pause to plunder homes, to rape Jewish women, and to enslave survivors. However, just when Jerusalem seems doomed, the Lord Jesus will return to the Mount of Olives and will intervene to save the city, and also empower the Jews to overcome their enemies. Given the prominence of the Mount of Olives in relationship to Jerusalem, everyone in the vicinity will be able to see the Lord's magnificent return and to witness what happens afterwards.

May 31 – The Holy Spirit Comes (Part 1)
(Acts 2)

As prophesied by several prophets, God instituted a New Covenant with His people that would give them eternal salvation, a new and clean heart, and allow the Holy Spirit to indwell them forever (Isa. 45:17-19; Jer. 31:31-40; Ezek. 34:23-28). With His own blood, Christ, as High Priest, sealed the New Covenant with the house of Judah and the house of Israel (Luke 22:20; Heb. 8:8). Hence, there is only one individual who can be Israel's Shepherd and King-Priest forever, the Lord Jesus Christ. In anticipation of His finished work at Calvary, God then could promise Israel through Ezekiel, *"A new heart also will I give you, and a new Spirit will I put within you"* (Ezek. 36:26).

The prophet Joel foretold that the Jewish nation would receive the Holy Spirit, and a new heart (Joel 2:28-29). By His coming, God would put His Law deep inside His people forever and they would intimately know Jehovah as *"The Lord of Hosts"* (Jer. 31:33-35). Joel also stated that the Holy Spirit would supernaturally equip the Jewish nation to both know and reveal the Lord to the nations:

And it shall come to pass afterward that I will pour out My Spirit on all flesh; your sons and your daughters shall prophesy, your old men shall dream dreams, your young men shall see visions. And also on My menservants and on My maidservants I will pour out My Spirit in those days (Joel 2:28-29).

After ten days of waiting in Jerusalem, the Holy Spirit was poured out on the disciples and the Church Age began with wonderful signs. Peter quoted the above passage on the day of Pentecost to acknowledge that Joel's prophecy had been partially fulfilled (i.e., when Jewish believers were suddenly able to speak in various languages; Acts 2:17-21). Prophesying, dreaming dreams, seeing visions, speaking tongues, etc., are evidences that the Holy Spirit had been received by Israel. The Holy Spirit enables direct communication with God and the ability to express His will to others. There are important implications of Peter's statements, which pertain both to the Apostolic Age (at the beginning of the Church Age) and the Tribulation Period, when refined Israel will be restored to God after receiving the Holy Spirit at Christ's second advent. At that time Joel's prophecy will be completely fulfilled.

June 1 – The Holy Spirit Comes – Part 2
(Acts 2)

According to Acts 2:9-11, ten specific languages were heard in Jerusalem at the Feast of Pentecost, just after Christ's ascension into Heaven. This was the day the Church Age began (Acts 2:4; 1 Cor. 12:13). The Holy Spirit came to the waiting believers as promised by the Lord Jesus. He baptized them into the body of Christ, bestowed spiritual gifts to them, and enabled them to powerfully serve the Lord and speak for Him. This event served two main purposes. First, it verified in the sight of the Jews that the apostles were continuing the ministry of Christ and were doing so by His power (Acts 2:22). Second, the sign of the unknown tongue (see next devotion) was a final warning to the nation of Israel to repent and turn to God through Christ.

These supernatural sign gifts (e.g., tongues) apparently diminished in normalcy during the Apostolic Age, as there is no mention of them in Scripture after 60 A.D. It is significant that over half the New Testament was written after this timeframe. Although the New Testament does record the names of many Jews who did turn from Judaism to Christ, Israel, as a nation, rejected Him and will continue to do so until His second advent (Joel 2:18-3:21; Zech. 12:10).

This explains why Peter, inspired by the Holy Spirit, slightly modified the Hebrew text of Joel 2 when quoting it to his countrymen:

And it shall come to pass in the last days, says God, that I will pour out of My Spirit on all flesh; your sons and your daughters shall prophesy, your young men shall see visions, your old men shall dream dreams. And on My menservants and on My maidservants I will pour out My Spirit in those days; and they shall prophesy. I will show wonders in heaven above and signs in the earth beneath: blood and fire and vapor of smoke. The sun shall be turned into darkness, and the moon into blood, before the coming of the great and awesome day of the Lord. And it shall come to pass that whoever calls on the name of the Lord shall be saved (Acts 2:16-21).

When explaining the timing of God's pouring out of the Holy Spirit, Peter exchanged "afterward" to "in the last days," thus denoting that Messiah would return to the earth to reestablish Israel at a future time. Hence, Pentecost was only a foretaste of better things to come for the Jewish nation in the Kingdom age. At that time, supernatural signs in the heavens, which did not happen at Pentecost, would occur.

June 2 – The Sign of the Unknown Tongue
(Acts 2)

The sign of the unknown tongue is used throughout Scripture as a warning to Israel of imminent judgment. Moses told the people that if they rebelled against the Lord, He would punish them through a nation whose language they did not know (Deut. 28:49). This meant that God would use an army from a distant land to punish them. Isaiah warned Israel of this sign just prior to the invasion of Assyria (Isa. 28:11-12). Jeremiah referred to the same sign as a final warning to Judah of imminent judgment (Jer. 5:15). The Jews ignored Jeremiah's messages and the sign of the unknown tongue came (Babylon decimated Judah). Yet, this was not the last time God would use the sign of an unknown tongue to alert the Jews of impending judgment for their unfaithfulness.

Several specific languages were heard in Jerusalem during Pentecost (Acts 2:9-11). These served as a final warning to the nation of Israel to repent and turn to God through Christ. As a nation, they had rejected and crucified their Messiah, but as individuals, they now had the opportunity to be saved – unavoidable judgment was coming to Israel and trusting Christ was the only way for them to obtain God's forgiveness.

The Jewish people had a natural propensity to be guided by sight rather than faith, *"for the Jews require a sign, and the Greeks seek after wisdom"* (1 Cor. 1:22). The Lord said, *"This is an evil generation. It seeks a sign, and no sign will be given to it except the sign of Jonah the prophet"* (Luke 11:29). The Lord performed ample miracles while on earth, yet the Jews did not believe that He was the Messiah and, in fact, crucified Him. At Pentecost, Peter reminded the Jews that God had shown His approval of Jesus of Nazareth by the miracles, wonders, and signs that He did (Acts 2:22-24). God had now provided them their final sign before judgment would come. In 70 A.D. judgment did come.

A large Roman army led by the future Emperor Titus besieged and conquered Jerusalem. The temple that had been built towards the end of the sixth century B.C., and that had then been renovated by Herod the Great five centuries later, was destroyed. There were to be no more offerings, sacrifices, Levitical priesthood, or stench of humanized religion in the nostrils of Jehovah. To this day, although the Jews are back in their land and are a self-governing nation, they have no temple or priesthood to reinstate because God put it away in the Church Age.

June 3 – In One Accord
(Acts 4)

Paul exhorts the believers at Philippi to *"be like-minded, having the same love, being of one accord, of one mind"* (Phil. 2:2). How is it possible for believers from different cultural and ethnic backgrounds, with unique problems and difficulties, to have one mind? The answer is revealed, *"Let this mind be in you, which was also in Christ Jesus"* (Phil. 2:5). When all believers have the lowly mind of Christ, we will be of one mind. It is a mindset that is not puffed up in vain glory, but is focused on the needs of others. Christ was the Servant of servants before He was the King of kings – let this mind be in us!

The early church seems to have enjoyed this oneness. *"And the multitude of them that believed were of **one heart** and of **one soul***: *neither said any of them that ought of the things which he possessed was his own; but they had all things common"* (Acts 4:32). Only when believers have surrendered their minds, hearts, and souls can complete unity be achieved. Individual and selfish ambitions are foreign objects that adversely affect Body-life. God has revealed to us in His triune nature that where godliness resides, individuality and unity will exist in harmony. Acts verifies that the early Church enjoyed this type of unification and thus was blessed with miraculous evangelical results:

First Example: *"These all continued with one accord in prayer and supplication"* (Acts 1:14). *"When the day of Pentecost was fully come, they were all with one accord in one place"* (Acts 2:1). The result: Spirit filling (Acts 2:4) and 3,000 souls are saved (Acts 2:41).

Second Example: *"They continuing daily with one accord"* (Acts 2:46). The result: *"The Lord added to the church daily"* (Acts 2:47).

Third Example: *"Now Peter and John went up together to the temple"* (Acts 3:1). The result: A lame man was healed (Acts 3:8), and about 5,000 souls were saved (Acts 4:4).

Fourth Example: *"They raised their voice to God with one accord"* (Acts 4:24) and *"Those that believed were of one heart and of one soul"* (Acts 4:32). The result: *"They were all filled with the Holy Spirit, and they spoke the word of God with boldness"* (Acts 4:31).

Fifth Example: *"They were all with one accord in Solomon's Porch"* (Acts 5:12). The result: *"Believers were increasingly added to the Lord, multitudes both of men and women"* (Acts 5:14).

What might happen today if your local church enjoyed such unity?

June 4 – Only Christ Can Satisfy
(Acts 4)

Unlike other creatures, when God created Adam, He breathed into him an eternal spirit, which gave Adam consciousness of God (Gen. 2:7; Job 27:3, 32:8). As descendants of Adam, this spirit resides in us also and awakens our minds to the reality of God's existence and that there is life after death. During a nighttime stroll, man will invariably gaze heavenward, and while beholding the starry host immersed in a canopy of blackness, a voice deep within him whispers, "There is Someone responsible for this – there is a Creator." The Psalmist writes, *"You will light my lamp; the Lord my God will enlighten my darkness"* (Ps. 18:28). God is seeking the rebel and calling him back to Himself. God's Spirit pleads through our own human spirit to draw near and be restored to our Creator. The Lord Jesus said that it is impossible for man to worship God except through his human spirit and in divine truth; this necessitates trusting the truth of Christ's message in order to be spiritually restored to God (John 4:24).

Our human spirit desperately needs God and communion with Him to be satisfied. It is only through man's spirit that worship can be rendered to God (Phil. 3:3). Consequently, at the spirit level of man resides his most intense need – to be one with his Creator. Many will try to fill this void with religiosity, others with momentary thrills that satisfy base lusts (e.g. drugs, amusements, unlawful sex); others, with more sophisticated fascinations (e.g. fame, power, intellect, and wealth). What temporal stimulus could ever satisfy man's deepest spiritual need to be one with his Creator? None. My spirit has a deep longing that only God can satisfy.

Peter, speaking of Jesus Christ, said, *"Nor is there salvation in any other, for there is no other name under heaven given among men by which we must be saved"* (Acts 4:12). The Lord conveyed to Paul what must be believed to receive His salvation: *"that Christ died for our sins according to the Scriptures, and that He was buried, and that He rose again the third day according to the Scriptures"* (1 Cor. 15:3-4). So if, by faith, one believes and receives Christ for the forgiveness of his or her sins, he or she is then born again and begins a new, eternal, and abundant life with God (John 3:3; 1 Pet. 1:23). Only Christ can satisfy our deepest longings, because He is the One who put them within us.

June 5 – The Place Was Shaken
(Acts 4)

After having been arrested for preaching Christ, the apostles gathered with a company of believers in Jerusalem to pray. All that were gathered in that place were of one accord and lifting up one voice to the Lord Jesus Christ in prayer (Acts 4:24, 32):

> *"Now, Lord, look on their threats, and grant to Your servants that with all boldness they may speak Your word, by stretching out Your hand to heal, and that signs and wonders may be done through the name of Your holy Servant Jesus." And when they had prayed, the place where they were assembled together was shaken; and they were all filled with the Holy Spirit, and they spoke the word of God with boldness* (Acts 4:29-31).

The Lord Jesus had charged His disciples to preach the gospel in Jerusalem initially and that was what they were doing. In the scene before us we have a great example of what happens when God's people are obedient, in unity, want to honor Christ's name, and desire enablement to obey His Word – God answered their prayer by again filling them with the Holy Spirit. This enabled them to do the very thing they had prayed for – to preach the Word of God with boldness.

Luke says that the place where the saints gathered (not the people) was shaken by the presence of the Lord. The early Church experienced the thrill of ongoing revival. They knew of God's presence among them and an atmosphere of joy and power pervaded that place. Christ longs to renew and revitalize His people to experience the wonder of Himself and to empower them to go on with Him; this is what revival is.

What happened in Jerusalem afterwards is what normally occurs when the Church experiences ongoing reviving: Many souls were won to Christ. Sometimes entire communities have been transformed from bastions of sin to beacons for heaven. It is estimated that approximately 100,000 people turned from sin and confessed Christ as Savior during the Welsh Revival of 1904-1905. Crime ceased. Taverns closed. In the wee morning hours, people were holding hands and singing hymns together. The people sensed God's presence among them and the entire region was permeated with joy. May we too experience such vibrant fellowship with God, that our communities cannot avoid seeing Christ.

June 6 – Maintaining Holy Hands
(Acts 5)

In Acts 5, we read of an astounding judgment of God against two believers in the early days of the Church Age:

> *But a certain man named Ananias, with Sapphira his wife, sold a possession. And he kept back part of the proceeds, his wife also being aware of it, and brought a certain part and laid it at the apostles' feet. But Peter said, "Ananias, why has Satan filled your heart to lie to the Holy Spirit and keep back part of the price of the land for yourself? While it remained, was it not your own? And after it was sold, was it not in your own control? Why have you conceived this thing in your heart? You have not lied to men but to God." Then Ananias, hearing these words, fell down and breathed his last. So great fear came upon all those who heard these things. And the young men arose and wrapped him up, carried him out, and buried him. Now it was about three hours later when his wife came in, not knowing what had happened. And Peter answered her, "Tell me whether you sold the land for so much?" She said, "Yes, for so much." Then Peter said to her, "How is it that you have agreed together to test the Spirit of the Lord? Look, the feet of those who have buried your husband are at the door, and they will carry you out." Then immediately she fell down at his feet and breathed her last. And the young men came in and found her dead, and carrying her out, buried her by her husband. **So great fear came upon all the church and upon all who heard these things** (Acts 5:1-11).*

Ananias and Sapphira were struck dead for lying to the Holy Spirit about the price that they had sold their property for. They did not have to sell their property or donate the proceeds to the Lord, but having done so, they kept back a portion of the money after publicly dedicating it all to God. God's justice had a purifying effect on God's people. Remembering the holiness of God and His stern judgment of sin should dissuade His people from putting their hands on what is forbidden. This narrative confirms that the sin of one member in the Church affects the whole body, for each believer is vitally connected to Christ and to each other in Him. Undealt with corruption within the Body will spread its unholy influence to ruin the holy testimony that the Church is to have of Christ. So for His honor and to bless our fellow believers, may we have holy hands that do not clutch what is filthy or what is the Lord's.

166

June 7– Resist the Devil, Draw Near to God
(Acts 5)

James suggests that there is one ultimate remedy to resolve satanic attacks against us – be holy and draw near to God through Christ:

Therefore submit to God. Resist the devil and he will flee from you. Draw near to God and He will draw near to you. Cleanse your hands, you sinners; and purify your hearts, you double-minded. Lament and mourn and weep! ... Humble yourselves in the sight of the Lord, and He will lift you up (Jas. 4:7-10).

The enemy of our souls is ruthless. He labors to tempt and to deceive us from staying near to Christ and resting in His truth. Besides this ongoing strategy, there are a variety of ways that Satan can negatively affect us. For example, Satan is able to directly inject evil thoughts into the human mind – this act is called *demonic obsession*. Paul declares that there is a *"spirit that is now at work in the sons of disobedience"* (Eph. 2:2) and can affect the thinking of believers also, as in the case of Ananias and Sapphira (Acts 5:3). This is distinguished from *demonic possession* of the unregenerate (Acts 16:16-19) and external *demonic oppression* that Paul suffered (2 Cor. 12:7-9). Obsession is a tool used by Satan to mentally torment believers. The enemy may plant luring thoughts to entice strongholds in our flesh (e.g., pornography), or he may observe a self-erected stronghold in the heart, such as bitterness, and seek to stir up unforgiving thoughts. Satan then can stimulate these carnal mindsets with ungodly thoughts to inflict anxiety, distress, and depression. Without the mental citadels (e.g., envy, greed, bitterness) Satan's efforts of obsessing the believer's mind would be ineffective and he would soon conclude the attack.

Apparently, Ananias had a stronghold of greed or pride in his heart and became susceptible to satanic obsession. Peter confronted Ananias with the sin of withholding what he had given to the Lord: *"Satan filled your heart to lie"* (Acts 5:3). Because Ananias had not drawn near to the Lord in repentance previously, the devil was able to gain a victory over him by exciting the ungodly bent. In this case, the offense to God resulted in the deaths of him and his wife. The only way to withstand such attacks is to pull down strongholds in our hearts, maintain purity, and then stay near to the Lord Jesus who has already defeated the devil.

June 8 – Scattered Abroad and Enjoying Rest
(Acts 8-9)

During Israel's wilderness journey, two silver trumpets were blown by the priests to direct the affairs of the nation. Although Christians today are not under Law, they also enjoy priestly communion with God, which means they should not move or act apart from the divine testimony of God's Word and the prompting of His Spirit. God's Word shows the Church how we should assemble together, and how to walk, to war, and to worship effectively. God is no less concerned today about the movements of His people and also the rest of His people than He was during the Israelites' wilderness journey. Luke writes:

*At that time a great persecution arose against the church which was at Jerusalem; and they **were all scattered** throughout the regions of Judea and Samaria, except the apostles (Acts 8:1-2).*

*Then the churches throughout all Judea, Galilee, and Samaria **had peace** and were edified. And walking in the fear of the Lord and in the comfort of the Holy Spirit, they were multiplied (Acts 9:31).*

Through persecution the Lord repositioned His people on the gospel battlefront and they were also comforted by the Holy Spirit to enjoy His rest ("peace"; KJV). Both the movements of His people and the rest He gives them are within His full control. When the Lord seems to be silent, we must wait for His marching orders, and when He clearly says "go," we must rise up and move forward with Him. He puts His people in proper order to be a testimony of Himself to others. God puts His people under orders that He might accomplish all His purposes for them. May we always value God's order for the Church – it is a testimony to others of His wisdom and greatness (Eph. 3:10)!

It is a great privilege to go on with the Lord, and to face the unknowns and the challenges of the next day with confidence. The believer's union with Christ means that He meets every trial His redeemed encounter. This is why the Lord keenly felt Saul's attack on His Church (Acts 9:4). In Christ, we have all we need to overcome whatever challenge we face: *"For as the sufferings of Christ abound in us, so our consolation also abounds through Christ"* (2 Cor. 1:5). We can have confidence then: Wherever I am – the Lord is there with me.

168

June 9 – Clean and Unclean
(Acts 10)

Leviticus showed the Jews both the way to approach God (chps. 1-16) and then how to walk in holiness before God (chps. 17-27). Hence, much of that book taught God's covenant people the difference between the *holy* and the *profane* and between *clean* and *unclean*.

Peter was still distinguishing the latter qualities per the dictates of the Law, so God provided an object lesson to help him adopt God's perspective on the matter. One day while Peter was staying in Joppa, he ascended to the housetop to pray. Peter received a vision there. He saw a great sheet bound by its four corners coming down from heaven; it contained an assortment of unclean creatures. The Lord commanded, *"Rise, Peter; kill and eat"* (Acts 10:13). Peter refused because the edicts of Leviticus 11 forbade it. The Lord responded: *"What God has cleansed you must not call common"* (Acts 10:15). Peter learned through this thrice-repeated vision that what God calls clean is clean, and that all men, not just Jews, could be cleansed by Christ's blood.

Later, Peter explained what he had learned to Cornelius, a Gentile who feared and honored the Lord: *"You know how unlawful it is for a Jewish man to keep company with or go to one of another nation. But God has shown me that I should not call any man common or unclean"* (Acts 10:28). The Law prohibited the Jews from having any contact with Gentiles lest the Jews be defiled, but in the Church Age, the gospel message is for everyone, Jew and Gentile (Rom. 1:16).

Peter seemingly understood that some "unclean" precepts of the Law no longer applied, for he was staying with Simon, a Jew, who made his living by skinning and tanning animal hides. By the Law he would be unclean, yet Peter stayed in his home many days (Acts 9:43).

In the vision, the Lord not only affirmed that the Levitical dietary laws were no longer in effect for the Jews, but also that the wall of partition between Jew and Gentile had been broken down; the two could become one in Christ (Eph. 2:11-18). The Jews were no longer to think of any people as "clean" or "unclean"; the important distinction is whether a person is "saved" or "lost." Those justified in Christ are saved; those who are not are lost. While we tend to think of others in terms of social and economic classes, spiritually speaking, there are only two groups of people in the world today: "saints" and "ain'ts."

June 10 – First Called "Christians"
(Acts 11)

We read in Acts 11:26 that *"the disciples were first called Christians in Antioch."* "Christian" simply means "Christ-one." Although the Bible refers to believers by various names, the term "Christian" specifically relates the *identity* of all believers in Christ to their *calling* to serve Christ. Unfortunately, this term has come to mean something quite different from its original meaning found in Scripture. Today, many think that they are Christians because they have Christian parents or grandparents, or because they went to a church once in their life, or because they were baptized as a baby, or because they know something about Christ. The Lord Jesus makes it clear that it is not by knowing about Him, or doing things for Him, that one becomes a Christian, but rather by knowing Him personally as Savior-Lord (Matt. 7:21-23). Accordingly, the Christian Life is not a mere imitation of Christ (i.e. doing what Jesus would do), but rather the realizing of who Christ is, the understanding of what He has accomplished, and then allowing Him to control all my thoughts, words, and deeds (Gal. 2:20).

The word "disciple" in Acts 11:26 is derived from the Greek word *mathetes*, meaning "a learner." What is a Christian to learn? The Lord Jesus answers this question: *"Come to Me, all you who labor and are heavy laden, and I will give you rest. Take My yoke upon you and **learn from Me**, for I am gentle and lowly in heart, and you will find rest for your souls. For My yoke is easy and My burden is light"* (Matt. 11:28-30). This is the only passage in the New Testament where the Lord personally informs us of what He is like and that we should learn of Him. By being yoked with Him, believers learn of the Lord's gentle and humble spirit, enjoy fruitfulness, and gain His peace.

The disciple of Christ is to learn Him, and by doing so they become better equipped to be "Christ-ones." As we learn of Him, we better know how to live for Him. *"A disciple is not above his teacher, nor a servant above his master. It is enough for a disciple that he be like his teacher, and a servant like his master"* (Matt. 10:24-25). Consequently, doing things in the name of Christ without honoring His name is hypocrisy; that is not biblical discipleship. Not only does the believer learn Christ by spending time in His Word, but the believer is also increasingly transformed into Christ-likeness by doing so (2 Cor. 3:18).

June 11 – The Power of Corporate Prayer (Part 1)
(Acts 12)

The power of believers collectively praying in unity is witnessed several times in the book of Acts (e.g. 1:14, 4:24-31), as in the story of Peter's miraculous escape from prison recorded in Acts 12:

> *Peter was therefore kept in prison, but constant prayer was offered to God for him by the church. ... So, when he had considered this, he came to the house of Mary, the mother of John whose surname was Mark, where many were gathered together praying* (Acts 12:5, 12).

Herod had Peter bound in chains between two soldiers and securely tucked away in an inner prison cell. He intended to have the apostle publicly executed the next day, but the Lord had different plans and sent an angel to rescue Peter from prison. The fact that the angel had to wake Peter up to lead him out of the fortification shows us that Peter was enjoying God's peace; he was not fretting about his future. Peter's chains fell off, locked doors and gates opened on their own, guards were kept unaware of his escape, and a few moments later Peter was walking the streets of Jerusalem alone. He came to a house where he knew the saints would be gathered to pray and indeed they were. The apostle was then able to inform everyone how God had wonderfully answered their prayers (Acts 12:6-11). This exciting outcome of humble, unified prayer is exactly what the Lord promised His disciples:

> *Again I say to you that if two of you agree on earth concerning anything that they ask, it will be done for them by My Father in heaven. For where two or three are gathered together in My name, I am there in the midst of them* (Matt. 18:19-20).

Indeed, the Lord has promised to answer those prayers asked of the Father in His name, when two or more are in agreement on those requests that will honor His name (Matt. 18:19-20; John 14:13, 15:16, 16:23). Believers in the Church Age have a glorious and protected entrance before the Lord at all times; in fact, they are invited to come boldly to the throne of grace to receive mercy in any time of need (Heb. 4:14-16). Having immediate access to God should prompt Christians to labor together in prayer, wherever and whenever they can.

June 12 – The Power of Corporate Prayer (Part 2)
(Acts 12)

While the scene in Acts 12:5-11 is a great example of impromptu corporate prayer, we should not think that such effective praying merely occurred in the Church Age. Daniel 2 provides an example of spontaneous corporate prayer in the Old Testament. Daniel gathered with three other consecrated Jewish men to pray that God would reveal the secret of King Nebuchadnezzar's reoccurring dream. After the Lord revealed the entire matter to Daniel, his first response was to pause and praise God. While Daniel did receive the revelation that would preserve their lives, he knew it was provided in response to their collective prayers: *"what **we** asked for"* … *"made known to **us**"* (Dan. 2:23).

Daniel shows us a wonderful pattern to follow when facing dire situations in life: First, seek the Lord in united prayer with those who are likewise committed to purity. Second, pause and praise the Lord for answers to prayer before relishing the outcome personally. Third, share what the Lord has accomplished with others who can also benefit from knowing God's will and faithfulness. Fourth, ensure that God alone is honored in the matter. Let us be careful not to rob the Lord of what is to be only His, for it is written, *"He who glories, let him glory in the Lord"* (1 Cor. 1:31). We are to be glory-reflectors, not glory-robbers!

Clearly, what believers have in Christ today transcends all Old Testament types and figures. Christians do not have to travel to temples, shrines, mosques, synagogues, or even church buildings to have immediate access to God. As children of God, we are invited to come boldly to God's throne and to receive from our Father the bounty of His love. Oh that the unregenerate today might be in awe and even envious of our direct access to God through Christ. May the lost witness the power of the Church who is in full communion with Christ.

We are too busy to pray, and so we are too busy to have power. We have a great deal of activity, but we accomplish little; many services but few conversions; much machinery but few results. …Oh, men and women, pray through; pray through! Do not just begin to pray and pray a little while and throw up your hands and quit, but pray and pray and pray until God rends the heavens and comes down.

— R. A. Torrey

June 13 – The Noble Bereans
(Acts 17)

Luke highlights the behavior of the "fair-minded" Bereans after hearing Paul and Silas preach Christ in the synagogue of the Jews:

These were more fair-minded ["more noble"; KJV] *than those in Thessalonica, in that they received the word with all readiness, and searched the Scriptures daily to find out whether these things were so. Therefore many of them believed, and also not a few of the Greeks, prominent women as well as men* (Acts 17:11-12).

Why were the Bereans praised? Because they diligently searched the Scriptures to know what was true – they did not want to be deceived. After being confronted with the gospel message, they sought to verify or disprove it by investigating Old Testament Scripture. Similarly, every child of God should be like the Bereans, proving matters out to determine what is true and false by rightly dividing all of Scripture. We should be discerning! Paul exhorted Timothy:

*Be diligent to present yourself approved to God, a worker who does not need to be ashamed, **rightly dividing the word of truth**. But shun profane and idle babblings, for they will increase to more ungodliness* (2 Tim. 2:15-16).

Our present culture is besieged by blatant wickedness and sadly the devil often uses subtle deception to ensnare complacent believers who are not willing to study Scripture diligently. Deceit is often forged with something acceptable. Accordingly, much discernment is required in daily conduct, or the believer will certainly fall prey to the enemy's trickery and craftiness. Many self-promoting preachers today are using the gospel for profit. The cults are advertising strong pro-family and pro-morality themes. They often entangle individuals by promoting good intentions at the cost of sound doctrine. Media aimed at ensnaring children often disguises pantheism, animism, reincarnation, and necromancy within carefully arranged humor, special effects, and exhilarating music to create a palatable message for children to digest and often under the eye of undiscerning Christian parents. May we all be like the noble Bereans and search Scripture to affirm the truth.

June 14– Seek the Lord
(Acts 17)

As Paul was entering the city of Athens, he noticed an inscription on a pagan altar "TO THE UNKNOWN GOD." Having come to Mars Hill, he was quite eager to tell the religious people of Athens about *"the One whom you worship without knowing"* (Acts 17:23). Paul told them about their Creator who made everything and was Lord over heaven and earth and did not reside in human erected temples. Furthermore, since the one true God gives life and breath to all things, He is not honored by those who worship what He has created. Paul's message then concluded with this personal challenge:

> *And He has made from one blood every nation of men to dwell on all the face of the earth, and has determined their preappointed times and the boundaries of their dwellings,* **so that they should seek the Lord,** *in the hope that they might grope for Him and find Him, though He is not far from each one of us; for in Him we live and move and have our being* (Acts 17:26-28).

Paul's challenge to seek the Lord, who was near to them, echoes the words of the prophets down through the centuries. Although Moses is speaking of a future time in Israel, his promise wonderfully shows God's desire to be one with those who will seek Him: *"You will seek the Lord your God, and you will find Him if you seek Him with all your heart and with all your soul"* (Deut. 4:29). Those who seek God – will find Him! Scripture repeatedly offers man an opportunity to search out and commune with God, if man will yield to what God wants him to understand and obey: *"You will seek Me and find Me, when you search for Me with all your heart"* (Jer. 29:13). *"Now set your heart and your soul to seek the Lord your God"* (1 Chron. 22:19). *"The Lord is near to all who call upon Him, to all who call upon Him in truth"* (Ps. 145:18). God provides abundant mercy to those who humbly seek Him with empty hands, which He promises to fill with heaven's blessings.

Thus, the Lord Jesus could offer Himself as the means of receiving God's blessing: *"Come to Me, all you who labor and are heavy laden, and I will give you rest. Take My yoke upon you and learn from Me, for I am gentle and lowly in heart, and you will find rest for your souls"* (Matt. 11:28-39). A seeking sinner will always find the seeking Savior.

June 15 – Gathering on the Lord's Day
(Acts 20)

God honors those who obey His commandments. In the Old Testament, the Sabbath day ordinance provided a simple test as to what God's people really valued – their own private affairs or what the Lord deemed important. The Lord is honored when His people remember and honor Him as requested, instead of doing what they are inclined to do for themselves on the day set aside for God.

Today, the Church is not under the Law (Gal. 4:19-5:1) and the Jews are no longer under the Law either (2 Cor. 3:6-18; Heb. 13:12-13), but the Ten Commandments still reflect God's moral standard to be lived out in His people. The Law is not dead, but we are dead to it; that is, it has no judicial hold on Christians (Rom. 7:4-6). Christians are not commanded to keep the Sabbath, but there is a principle throughout Scripture of setting aside one day in seven to honor God (Gen. 2:1-3), and the early Church set a precedent for gathering for this purpose on Sunday.

To draw a distinction between Christianity and the Law (and the system of Judaism derived from it), the early Church met on Sunday, rather than Saturday. Christians continued to gather corporately on one day in seven to worship the Lord, but they did so on the first day of the week, the day of Christ's resurrection (1 Cor. 16:2). Luke records that Paul's ministry at Troas was timed such that he would not leave until he had broken bread with the disciples, who gathered on Sunday:

> *But we sailed away from Philippi after the Days of Unleavened Bread, and in five days joined them at Troas, where we stayed seven days. Now on the first day of the week, when the disciples came together to break bread, Paul, ready to depart the next day, spoke to them and continued his message until midnight* (Acts 20:6-8).

The first day of the week is also referred to as "the Lord's Day" by the apostle John (Rev. 1:10). Let us seek to make the Lord's Day a special day for the Lord. Saints should put aside their own personal ambitions and gather to hear the preaching of the Word, to break bread, to pray, and to encourage each other (Acts 2:42). The Lord's Day should be a special day for all spiritually-minded Christians – a day set aside to remember and honor the Lord with other believers.

June 16– All Spiritual Blessings
(Overview of Epistles)

Why does God bless believers today? Because the Father loves His Son, and we, being "in Christ," will then be the object of God's love and favor. These blessings in Christ can be identified by scanning the Epistles for such phrases as "in Christ," "in Jesus Christ," or "in Christ Jesus." These expressions are not found in the Gospel accounts and are only found once in the book of Acts. However, the Epistles, which unveil the manifold wisdom and mysteries of God concerning Christ's accomplishments, have over eighty references to these phrases. It is noted that the phrase "with Christ" speaks of positional or identification truths, while the phrase "in Christ" normally speaks of blessing resulting from our spiritual union with the Son of God.

What do we have "in Christ"? We have…
- Redemption (Rom. 3:24)
- No condemnation (Rom. 8:1)
- Spirit of life (power over sin) (Rom. 8:2)
- The love of God (Rom. 8:39)
- Oneness in the body of Christ (Rom. 12:5)
- Sanctification (1 Cor. 1:2)
- Hope (1 Cor. 15:19)
- Life (1 Cor. 15:22)
- Triumph, by God's grace (2 Cor. 2:14)
- Been made a new creation (2 Cor. 5:17)
- Liberty (Gal. 2:4)
- Been made children of God (Gal. 3:26)
- Equality (Gal. 3:28)
- All spiritual blessings in heavenly places (Eph. 1:3)
- Been created unto good works (Eph. 2:10)
- Salvation (2 Tim. 2:10)
- Preservation (Jude 1)

As the believer maintains an impassioned focus on the Lord and recalls to mind all that we have "in Him," life's circumstances do not seem so overwhelming. What we have spiritually in Christ forever is not comparable with the temporary trinkets we often overvalue.

June 17 – They Called Him "Jesus"

(Overview of Epistles)

The Gospels introduce the man Jesus as God's Savior of humanity, while the Epistles, written after Christ's glorification, declare more fully His exalted position over all creation. This transition of tone can be observed in how the Lord's given name, Jesus, is used in Scripture: The Gospels contain only one mention of any title preceding the name of "Jesus" (*"Lord Jesus"*; Luke 24:3). He is addressed as "Jesus Christ" only five times. In all, only six of the 625 references to the name "Jesus" in the Gospels connect a title of exaltation to His name.

In the same way, the Gospels record the message of Christ before the crucifixion to the lost house of Israel, and the book of Acts recounts the preaching of Jesus to a lost Gentile world. However, the exaltation of Jesus Christ is quite evident in the Epistles, which explain the glorious mysteries of God concerning salvation, and in the Revelation, which declares Christ's authority over all things. Of the 290 times the proper name "Jesus" is found in the epistles and Revelation, 263 references are associated with a dignified title. Here is the breakdown:

Name/Title	Occurrences in Epistles and Revelation
Jesus Christ (only)	82
Lord Jesus Christ	78
Christ Jesus (only)	55
Lord Jesus (only)	20
Jesus our Lord	7
Jesus Christ our Lord	9
Savior Jesus Christ	6
Christ Jesus the Lord	2
Jesus is the Christ	2
Jesus the Son of God	1
Jesus is the Lord	1 (for a total of 263)

Of the twenty-seven remaining references to "Jesus," ten have direct connection with God the Father and two with the Holy Spirit, seven exalt Christ within the same sentence and two occurrences do so within the same thought, and six are miscellaneous references. All this to say that after Christ's exaltation, the apostles were quite careful to bestow honor to the Lord when speaking His name and so should we.

177

June 18 – *"The Just Shall Live by Faith"*
(Romans 1)

At first the prophet Habakkuk was bothered that God seemed to be indifferent, even tolerating, the ungodly and idolatrous behavior of His covenant people in Judah. The Lord informed His prophet that He was fully aware of the moral and spiritual decline of His covenant people and was going to use the Babylonians to chasten them. This caused Habakkuk further consternation, as he could not understand how a holy God could use a people more wicked than His own to discipline them. The prophet knew his thinking was not right and even asked the Lord to correct him. God's answer was: *"The just shall live by faith"* (Hab. 2:4). This principle is valid and vital to God's people in all ages.

This verse is quoted three times in the New Testament to explain enjoying spiritual life in Christ through faith (Rom. 1:17; Gal. 3:11; Heb. 10:38). This principle in Romans emphasizes that those justified in Christ should be characterized by "just" behavior. The Galatian reference focuses on pleasing God by "living" in the resurrection power of Christ's life. The writer of Hebrews reminds us of the necessity of genuine "faith" to progress in the work of the Lord.

The message to Habakkuk (and to us too) is that trusting God and obeying His Word results in life (communion with Him), while pride and rebellion lead to death (separation from Him; Rom. 6:23). The greatest good is accomplished when man lives by faith and trusts God with his fate. While the main thrust of Habakkuk's prophecy concerned the future chastening of Israel by Babylon, its ultimate fulfillment relates to the second advent of Christ and Israel's final restoration. The writer of Hebrews quotes Habakkuk 2:3-4 with a slight modification: *"For yet a little while, and He who is coming will come and will not tarry. Now the just shall live by faith; but if anyone draws back, My soul has no pleasure in him"* (Heb. 10:37-38). The apostle switches the neuter pronouns in the prophecy to the masculine to speak of Christ's future coming. At the time Hebrews was written, Christ had already suffered the terror of Calvary and been exalted to the Father's throne in Heaven. But Christ must return in power and majesty to rid the earth of evil, to obliterate Israel's enemies, and to restore and bless the Jewish nation in the Promised Land. The writer says that all this will happen in *"a little while,"* and *the just shall live by faith* in the meantime!

178

June 19 – Altogether Foolish
(Romans 1)

In Romans 1, Paul provides the first of three arguments that mankind is inherently sinful and deserves judgment: creation demands a Creator. Romans 2 contains the remaining two arguments: the guilty conscience and disobedience to God's Law. The premise for prosecuting humanity is expressed in Romans 1:18: *"For the wrath of God is revealed from heaven against all ungodliness and unrighteousness of men, who suppress the truth in unrighteousness."* When God reveals something of Himself to man, He then holds man accountable for obeying it; if dismissed, then His judgment is deserved.

The first particular revelation of God is identified in Romans 1:20: *"For since the creation of the world His invisible attributes are clearly seen, being understood by the things that are made, even His eternal power and Godhead, so that they are without excuse."* To look at the order and sophistication of life and say there is no Designer is to reject what God has displayed about Himself. But natural man has not only rejected the notion that he is accountable to a Creator, but he also made and worshipped images of the very creatures that God offered as evidence of His intellect: *"Professing to be wise, they became fools, and changed the glory of the incorruptible God into an image made like corruptible man – and birds and four-footed animals and creeping things"* (Rom. 1:22-23). Sadly, many in our modern culture view themselves as the ones in control of their own destinies, thus revering themselves above God. An idol is anything that displaces our proper reverence for God – it does not necessarily have to be an image of gold.

We then learn that those who affront God in this fashion are given over to a reprobate mind: *"Therefore God also gave them up to uncleanness, in the lusts of their hearts, to dishonor their bodies among themselves"* (Rom. 1:24-25). Without the Holy Spirit's conviction and enlightenment, the worst of man's depraved condition becomes apparent; these idolaters indulged in homosexual activities (Rom. 1:27-31). Such behavior is an abomination to God (Lev. 20:13); it is rebellion against His creation order for the genders and for marriage. Without God, the darkened conscience will never understand its need for Christ. May believers remember that any idolatry (what causes thoughts unworthy of God or misplaced affections) is insulting to God.

June 20 – The Circumcised Heart

(Romans 2)

The Lord required male circumcision of 99-year-old Abraham as His sign to Abraham of His covenant with him and his descendants (Gen. 17:1-14). So Abraham and all the males of his house were circumcised the very day God had commanded it (Gen. 17:26-27). Then, his descendants for ongoing centuries would continue this symbolic ritual to honor God and to acknowledge His covenant with them. Paul tells us that circumcision was a "token" of Abraham's righteous standing gained by faith in God's promise (Gen. 15:6), not by the act of circumcision: Circumcision was *"a seal of the righteousness of the faith which he had while still uncircumcised"* (Rom. 4:11).

Why was male circumcision given as a sign? By stripping away the foreskin from the organ that best identified an individual as a male, God was symbolizing the stripping away of an old identity and the reliance on God for a new one. The act of circumcision in Genesis 17 complements beautifully the name changes given Abram and Sarai. God was about to enact His covenant with them by giving them a son. It was only fitting that they realize their new identity as God's chosen people and as human instruments to bless the entire world. Abraham was already declared just by God before circumcision was instituted (Rom. 4:11). The "circumcised life" was the lifestyle Abraham was living before God.

It is the same for believers today. When sinners humble themselves before God and confess their need for a Savior, God responds by cleansing and regenerating them (Tit. 3:5), sealing them with the Holy Spirit (Eph. 1:13), and declaring them righteous (imputing divine righteousness to their account – Rom. 4:4-5; 2 Cor. 5:21). *"If anyone is in Christ, he is a new creation; old things have passed away; behold, all things have become new"* (2 Cor. 5:17). However, our new identity in Christ demands that we live the "circumcised life," which is the "cutting off" or "putting to death" of the desires and the will of our flesh. Paul summarizes in Romans 2:29 that it is the circumcision of the heart God wants in a believer's life, not just an outward show. This is what Moses meant when he commanded Israel (men and women) to *"circumcise the foreskin of your heart."*

June 21 – Justified by Grace
(Romans 3)

The New Testament epistles provide further details about how justification is accomplished. Paul informs us that a believer is justified by God's grace (Rom. 3:24), by Christ's blood (Rom. 5:9), and by faith (Rom. 5:1). James declares another astounding fact pertaining to justification: *"You see then that a man is justified by works, and not by faith only"* (Jas. 2:24). Humanly speaking, this may seem confusing. How can justification be so complicated if God simply accredited Abraham a righteous standing based on his faith (Jas. 2:23)?

Using your God-given imagination for a moment, in your mind's eye envision a huge reservoir in the upper elevations of a mountain range. Water from melting snow from mountain grandeurs gently streams down into bubbling brooks, which, in turn, fill this reservoir to full capacity. An enormous dam holds back the vast resource except for what water is rushing out from its base into a deep channel. This channel conveys the water a great distance to a collection pool in the flat plains below. As individual headgates about this collection pool are opened, the vital blessing of the reservoir is applied to parched fields already sown with seed. Thus, the immense reservoir so far above in the mountains is responsible and necessary for an abundant harvest to follow below. Justification is, from a biblical sense, depicted in this imaginary scene. The reservoir pictures God's vast grace waiting to be bestowed from heavenly realms above. The channel represents the means in which God's grace is conveyed to mankind – through the blood of Jesus Christ. The act of opening the headgates symbolizes an individual trusting in the gospel message and, thus, receiving God's manifold grace through the blood of Christ. The harvest of good works that follows is the practical demonstration of a justified soul. It is the proof of a changed life or as James concludes, *"Faith by itself, if it does not have works, is dead"* (Jas. 2:17).

Thus, a believer is justified by grace, through Christ's blood, by personal faith, and is evidenced by good works. True faith produces good deeds, including obedience. A soul that has been declared righteous by God should seek to live righteously. Those who have been justified in Christ should live to show others Christ in their actions. What God redeems through Christ has been sanctified to honor Him.

June 22 – God Demonstrates His Own Love
(Romans 5)

The prophet Isaiah foretold that God's offer of salvation would be available for all men, not just for Israel. Consequently, the prophet implores the wicked to repent of their evil deeds and turn to the Lord:

> *Seek the Lord while He may be found, call upon Him while He is near. Let the wicked forsake his way, and the unrighteous man his thoughts; let him return to the Lord, and He will have mercy on him; and to our God, for He will abundantly pardon* (Isa. 55:6-7).

This promise advises the sinner what to do and supplies the assurance of God's mercy if the sinner complies. This message will be proclaimed to the nations during the Tribulation Period by Jewish evangelists and angels alike: Do not worship the beast or take his mark – worship God, for His judgment is coming (Rev. 14:6-12). God's abundant mercy being extended freely to repentant sinners (who have done nothing to please God) seems illogical. What does God get out of such a proposition? The answer is redeemed souls. God judged His only Son in order to bless His vile enemies: *"But God demonstrates His own love toward us, in that while we were still sinners, Christ died for us. Much more then, having now been justified by His blood, we shall be saved from wrath through Him"* (Rom. 5:8-9).

Our sense of fairness cannot reconcile why God would exhibit such love, especially when it cost Him the death of His Son, but in this truth is where we must rest. Isaiah explained that we cannot rationalize God's love or His ways, nor does He expect us to: *"For My thoughts are not your thoughts, nor are your ways My ways. For as the heavens are higher than the Earth, so are My ways higher than your ways, and My thoughts than your thoughts"* (Isa. 50:8-9). Lord, we are so thankful that your thoughts and ways are so far above ours; otherwise we would still be condemned sinners with no hope. Amen. Believers are not to ignore, doubt, subtract, or add to God's Word just because they do not understand what it means or cannot fathom how God could possibly do what He says He will do. The Lord Jesus said: *"For assuredly, I say to you, till heaven and earth pass away, one jot or one tittle will by no means pass from the law till all is fulfilled"* (Matt. 5:18). We have God's Word and His love in Christ – what else really matters in life?

182

June 23 – Justified by His Blood
(Romans 5)

The blood of Christ is the foundation of the believer's acceptance with God. Through the blood of Christ, God can righteously justify condemned sinners who believe on His Son's name for salvation (Rom. 3:22-24). Likewise, the applied blood of Christ is the basis of the sinner's confidence that he or she can draw near to a holy God:

> *But God demonstrates His own love toward us, in that while we were still sinners, Christ died for us. Much more then, **having now been justified by His blood**, we shall be saved from wrath through Him* (Rom. 5:8-9).

The righteousness of God beyond what was revealed in the Law was fully displayed at Calvary; it was here God judged His Son for all the offenses humanity had committed against Him (Rom. 3:21). This means that He can, through the blood of Christ, extend forgiveness to those who are dead in trespasses and sins. Through this righteous transaction, God is demonstrating the harmony of all aspects of His holy character in the matter of saving sinners: He is just, righteous, merciful, gracious, loving, compassionate, longsuffering, sovereign, all-knowing, all-powerful, unchanging, etc. C. H. Mackintosh warns believers not to let justification through Christ's blood alone slip from our doctrinal foundation:

> *It is all through the blood of Jesus* – nothing less – nothing more – nothing different. *"It is the blood that makes an atonement for the soul."* This is conclusive. This is God's simple plan of justification. ... From Genesis 3 to the close of Revelation, I find the blood of Christ put forward as the alone ground of righteousness. We get pardon, peace, life, righteousness, all by the blood, and nothing but the blood. The entire book of Leviticus, and particularly the chapter upon which we have just been meditating, is a commentary upon the doctrine of the blood.[25]

If it were not for the cross and the shed blood of Christ, God would be constrained by His holy character to commit the guilty (humanity) to the judgment of eternal death. May the believer never forget the tremendous significance God the Father ascribes to His own Son's blood – we are redeemed and cleansed by the blood of Christ alone!

183

June 24 – God's Wrath Is Redirected
(Romans 5)

The Bible shows us that the Lord's anger is always perfect and in agreement with His divine character. God is not motivated to action by one particular emotion in such a way that any part of His perfect character is compromised. Love, grace, mercy, justice, righteousness, long-suffering, purity, etc. are always satisfied in every divine action. This is why Paul speaks of the *"fruit of the Spirit"* in Galatians 5:22-23 and not the "fruits of the Spirit." All God's character is homogeneous in reflecting His holiness.

Yes, God is a God of love (1 Jn. 4:8), but He could not justly save mankind by His love alone – His justice demanded judgment for sin:

> *Having now been justified by His* [Christ's] *blood,* **we shall be saved from wrath through Him.** *For if when we were enemies* **we were reconciled to God** *through the death of His Son, much more, having been reconciled, we shall be saved by His life* (Rom. 5:9-11).

Thankfully, God's love found a way to righteously offer salvation through judging His Son for human sin. He can legally offer the gift of eternal salvation to *"whosoever will."* Those who reject His gracious offer will spend an eternity in hell; *"the wages of sin is death"* (Rom. 6:23). "The eternity of punishment is a thought which crushes the heart," said C. H. Spurgeon. "The Lord God is slow to anger, but when He is once aroused to it, as He will be against those who finally reject His Son, He will put forth all His omnipotence to crush His enemies."[26]

Nearly six centuries before the events of Calvary occurred, the prophet Daniel foretold the timetable of God's future dealings with the nation of Israel. This *Seventy-week* prophecy began from the command to rebuild Jerusalem in the fifth century B.C. until Israel is restored to Christ in the Kingdom Age. But the prophecy begins with the basis for why God could accomplish what Daniel was foretelling (Dan. 9:24). Only Calvary could be referred to by the phrases *"to make an end of sin"* and *"to make reconciliation for iniquity"* and only Jesus Christ can *"bring in everlasting righteousness"* as the anointed *"Most Holy."* The Lord Jesus is God's great Reconciler! And thankfully, we have life in Him and therefore will never experience God's wrath.

June 25 – The "Old Man" Is Dead
(Romans 6)

Positionally speaking, co-crucifixion took place at the cross and became effectual for a believer at his or her conversion. Paul explains, *"Knowing this, that our old man was crucified with Him, that the body of sin might be done away with, that we should no longer be slaves of sin"* (Rom. 6:6). At the cross, the old man, the man in Adam, the man that we once were before salvation, the man who was dominated and controlled by the flesh – that man died with Christ. Paul conveys the practical aspects of this positional truth to the believers at Galatia: *"Those who are Christ's have crucified the flesh with its passions and desires"* (Gal. 5:24). The believer has been positionally crucified with Christ so that his or her flesh nature will lose its controlling influence as he or she matures in Christ. It is not that the flesh nature diminishes in strength, but rather that the Holy Spirit within the believer overpowers it. What originated in the world cannot compete with that which is supernatural; thus, a yielded life cannot be overcome by the flesh nature.

> Some sins we have committed,
> Some we have contemplated,
> Some we have desired,
> Some we have encouraged;
> In the case of some we are innocent only because we did not
>   succeed.

> — Lucius Annaeus Seneca

Practical sanctification occurs in the believer as his or her flesh nature loses its influence (its control dies out) and the likeness of Christ becomes apparent; this process will be complete at glorification. Accordingly, Paul commands believers in Colossians 3:5 to "mortify" (or put to death) the deeds of the body (i.e. the flesh) and in Romans 13:14 to starve the lusts of the flesh. The goal of these activities is that Christ and not the *nature* of the Old Man is witnessed in the believer's life. All believers were crucified with Christ in order to declare the power of His resurrection in daily life.

June 26 – The "New Man" Is Alive
(Romans 6)

In John 3, the Lord Jesus likened Himself to the bronze serpent lifted up on a pole by Moses to provide healing for those who had been bitten by God's fiery serpents. The bronze speaks of "fiery" judgments, while the serpent itself is a symbol of sin, and the lofty pole prefigures Christ's cross. God positionally condemned sin in the flesh (the energy of lawlessness) through the death of His Son on the cross. As a result, Paul tells us that "the Old Man" (i.e., what we were in Adam by nature) was crucified and died when Christ died, so that we are no longer slaves to sin (Rom. 6:6). Because Christ rose from the grave, those trusting in Him receive eternal life in Him and the ability to overcome sin through the power of the Holy Spirit (John 3:16; Rom. 8:13).

From a practical standpoint, all of us were born snake-bitten (i.e., spiritually dead in Adam; Rom. 5:12). Although many will never admit that they are dying because of sin, those who do realize their hopeless condition can escape eternal condemnation and experience the full love of God by trusting in Christ for healing. As C. H. Mackintosh explains, God has much more for us than just escaping death; He wants us to experience His love and newness of life – and live as a "New Man":

> It is a very common error to view the Lord Jesus rather as the averter of God's wrath, than as the channel of His love. That He endured the wrath of God against sin is most preciously true. But there is more than this. He has come down into this wretched world to die upon the cursed tree, in order that, by dying, He might open up the everlasting springs of the love of God to the heart of poor rebellious man.[27]

Paul told the believers at Ephesus that because they had heard and learned Christ (i.e., believed His Message), they had the ability to put off the former conduct of the *Old Man* and live as a *New Man* in Christ: *"that you put off, concerning your former conduct, the old man which grows corrupt according to the deceitful lusts, and be renewed in the spirit of your mind, and that you put on the new man which was created according to God, in true righteousness and holiness"* (Eph. 4:22-24). Positionally speaking, the Old Man is what we were in Adam and the New Man what we are in Christ; let us live Christ and not like a dead man.

June 27 – The "Inward Man" Is Renewed

(Romans 7)

In Romans 7, Paul describes his personal struggles to obey God's Law apart from divine power. *"For I delight in the law of God according to the inward man, but I see another law in my members, warring against the law of my mind, and bringing me into captivity to the law of sin which is in my members"* (Rom. 7:22-23). Though Paul's inner man (i.e. his spirit) desired to obey God, he found no natural wherewithal to do so. Yet, as a believer, it is this spiritual part of our essence which must govern our thinking and our actions: *"Even though our outward man is perishing, yet the inward man is being renewed day by day"* (2 Cor. 4:16). But what is the inward and outward man?

God, who is triune, created man in His image. Man is not God, nor triune, but is tripartite. God is three distinct persons (Father, Son and Spirit), while man is one person with three parts (spirit, soul, and body). The Holy Spirit acknowledges that each of us possesses a spirit, a soul, and a body (1 Thess. 5:23). These human components are interrelated, but are exclusive in their properties. The body is "world-conscious," the soul is "self-conscious," and the spirit of man is "God-conscious." The spirit is the noblest part of man and refers to the innermost area of our being – the "inner man." The body is the lowest portion of our existence and forms the outermost being. Between these two components dwells the soul. The soul comprises our intellect, our emotions, our personality, and our will. The soul links with the physical realm through the five senses, and through the spirit the soul connects with God. The soul is a bridge between the body and the spirit. When a believer is in fellowship with God, the Holy Spirit has the freedom to commune with man's spirit, which transmits godly thoughts to the soul. This in turn exercises the body to conform to the Spirit's rule to become a vessel fit for the infusing power and goodness of the Spirit.

Before the fall of man, Adam's soul was completely under the control of his spirit. But the spirit cannot act directly on the body; it cannot bypass the soul. Thus, man has the will to choose to ignore his spirit and follow the desires of the flesh. God created the soul of man to stand between the body and the spirit in order to exercise power over the whole of man. It has the ability to consider spiritual things and render decisions other than what natural reason would endorse.

June 28 – No Good Thing (Part 1)
(Romans 7)

Each believer must learn to recognize their behavior for what it is – either controlled by the flesh nature or by his or her *inner man* as yielded to the Spirit of God. What nature rules the mind will determine the body's behavior. Hence, a believer should desire that their inner man be under the control of the Holy Spirit and God's Word. In the Christian life, no matter how small a temptation or trial may be, it cannot be overcome in our own strength, for within each of us is a foul nature that opposes the things of God (Gal. 5:17). All the resolution in the world cannot cause what is pitifully weak (our flesh) to master what originated with the devil (a spirit of rebellion).

For this reason, it is important for a believer to remember what God says about his or her flesh nature. Everything God says about the flesh is negative. In the flesh there is *"no good thing"* (Rom. 7:18). The flesh profits *"nothing"* (John 6:63). A Christian is to put *"no confidence"* in the flesh (Phil. 3:3). He is to make *"no provision"* for the flesh (Rom. 13:14). A person who lives for the flesh is living a negative life, as Charles Ryrie observes:

> It [the flesh] refers to our disposition to sin and to oppose or omit God in our lives. The flesh is characterized by works that include lusts and passions (Gal. 5:19-24; 1 Jn. 2:16); it can enslave (Rom. 7:25); and in it is nothing good (Rom. 7:18). Based on this meaning of the word "flesh," to be carnal means to be characterized by things that belong to the unsaved life (Eph. 2:3).[28]

Consequently, Paul reminds us that our flesh wants to do what our conscience knows is wrong to do: *"For when we were in the flesh, the sinful passions which were aroused by the law were at work in our members to bear fruit to death"* (Rom. 7:5-6). The flesh, governed by the fallen nature, is never satisfied; it wants more than what is reasonable or lawful. Solomon put it this way: *"The eye is not satisfied with seeing, nor the ear filled with hearing"* (Eccl. 1:8). Instead of drinking *"a little wine for [one's] stomach's sake"* (1 Tim. 5:23), the flesh longs to be drunk with wine (Eph. 5:18). This is because when a person is drunk, the restraining influence of reason is lost and it becomes easier for the flesh to rule the moment.

June 29 – No Good Thing (Part 2)
(Romans 7)

Instead of eating what is necessary to maintain a fit body, the flesh engages in gluttony (Prov. 23:21, 28:7). Scripture exhorts us to dress modestly to avert flaunting our bodies before others (1 Tim. 2:9; 1 Pet. 3:3), and not to seek to be the center of attention (Luke 14:8), but the flesh wants to be noticed and admired by others. The marriage covenant protects the sexual relationship between a husband and a wife, but unchecked cravings lead to fornication, which is a great offense against God (1 Thess. 4:3; Eph. 5:5) and against one's own body (1 Cor. 6:18).

Paul spoke of a law within his members (Rom. 7:23) which continued to oppose the law of God in his mind (i.e., his understanding of what God demanded of him). He referred to this nature as the law of sin (Rom. 7:25) and he knew it was an abiding evil presence within himself. There is no need to put a pre-conversion or post-conversion label to the latter portion of Romans 7; an unregenerate person or a believer not walking in the Spirit will both struggle as Paul describes. He knew that this ongoing battle cannot be won through natural means:

For I know that in me (that is, in my flesh) nothing good dwells; for to will is present with me, but how to perform what is good I do not find. For the good that I will to do, I do not do; but the evil I will not to do, that I practice. Now if I do what I will not to do, it is no longer I who do it, but sin that dwells in me (Rom. 7:18-20).

However, after conversion Christians should be governed, not by the law of sin within them, but rather by the Spirit of God (Rom. 8:13). Moderation and self-control are a testimony to others that God is the One controlling a believer's actions (Phil. 4:5). Apparently, many in the church at Corinth did not have such a testimony because they were being controlled by their lusting flesh. In the opening verses of 1 Corinthians 3 Paul tells them three times that they are "*carnal*." The normal Greek word translated "flesh" in the New Testament is *sarx*, and Paul uses this word as a modifier (*sarkikos*) to describe their carnal behavior; they were "fleshly." Their flesh was governing their behavior within the assembly, and, as a result, the testimony of the church was suffering because their communion with Christ was being hindered.

June 30 – No Good Thing (Part 3)
(Romans 7)

To summarize, though the phrase "the flesh" sometimes refers to the human body, it is normally applied in the New Testament Epistles to refer to the fallen, independent nature which allows sin its opportunity within us. Paul states that through the fall of Adam, sin and spiritual death entered the world (Rom. 5:12). Every individual coming from Adam's line is born with Adam's inherited fallen nature (Ps. 51:5, 58:3); that is, we are born sinners and separated from God. This is why John states that those who reject Christ's offer for salvation are already condemned (John 3:17); we are all conceived and born into this lost spiritual condition. John further explains that the *"lusts of the flesh"* within us are not found in God, but are of the world – a system apart from God and under Satan's delegated control (1 Jn. 2:16).

Thankfully, God's work of sanctification begins in the believer's life immediately after he or she answers the call of salvation. God begins to fashion the new believer into a holy vessel and each believer is exhorted to cooperate in the working out of what God is working into his or her life (1 Thess. 5:23; Heb. 13:21). All believers will ultimately be conformed to the moral image of Christ (Rom. 8:29); there is no human choice of involvement in that aspect of sanctification – it is God's will and power that accomplishes this.

Yet, there is an ongoing call to each believer to not resist God's working in his or her life, but instead to yield to it by surrendering to Him. God promises to chasten those who choose not to submit to Him in order that they may become broken in disposition before Him and experience sanctification (Heb. 12:6). Consequently, sanctification in a practical sense is happening to every believer, but some are more serious about it than others and, accordingly, will reap the greater blessing of being further refined here and now. The limiting factor in this process is how much we allow our flesh to stand in the way of our progress onward to Christ-likeness.

The Lord Jesus loves us too much to leave us the way we are, so He is fashioning each believer into a magnificent trophy of His grace, which will eternally beam with His holy character. While in the sanctification process, we must remember that there is absolutely nothing in our flesh that can please God; it is totally putrid to Him.

July 1 – "In the Likeness of Sinful Flesh"
(Romans 8)

Paul writes: *"For what the law could not do in that it was weak through **the flesh**, God did by sending His own Son **in the likeness of sinful flesh**"* (Rom. 8:3). The same Greek word *homoioma*, translated as "likeness" in this verse, is also used in Philippians 2:7, which states that Christ *"was made in the likeness of men."* The word "likeness" in both verses means "resemblance" or "form." Humanly speaking, Christ's form was that of a man, but He was more; He also possessed a divine nature. The Lord looked like everyone else, but He did not act like them. His life was unique for *"in Him is no sin"* (1 Jn. 3:5), He *"knew no sin"* (2 Cor. 5:21), and He *"did no sin"* (1 Pet. 2:22).

Speaking of Christ, the writer of Hebrews declares the matter frankly, *"who **being the brightness of His** [God's] **glory** and **the express image of His** [God's] **person**, and upholding all things by the word of His power, when He had by Himself purged our sins, sat down at the right hand of the Majesty on high"* (Heb. 1:3). It was needful for Christ to be veiled in flesh, or mankind would have been consumed by the direct presence of Almighty God. The veil of flesh allowed Christ to directly outshine God's moral glory to the world. When you looked on the Lord Jesus, you would see the form of a man, with the character of God shining through. Mark the words of Christ to Philip:

Have I been with you so long, and yet you have not known Me, Philip? He who has seen Me has seen the Father; so how can you say, "Show us the Father"? Do you not believe that I am in the Father, and the Father in Me? (John 14:9-10).

Christ was fully human but had a different spiritual nature than Adam. Adam was made "innocent" (Eccl. 7:29) and bore God's image and likeness (Gen. 1:26) until he fell; then he bore his own likeness (Gen. 5:3). The Last Adam, Christ, was not just *innocent humanity,* as Adam was; He was *holy humanity* (Luke 1:35). *"For in Him dwells all the fullness of the Godhead bodily"* (Col. 2:9). Nowhere in Scripture do we read of Adam being "holy." God was not in Adam, but *"God was in Christ, reconciling the world to Himself"* (2 Cor. 5:19).

July 2 – The New Nature (Part 1)
(Romans 8)

Prior to trusting Christ as Lord and Savior, people do not have the ability to please God; in fact, their old nature directly opposes God in thought and in deed (Rom. 5:10, 8:7). Paul minces no words on this important point: *"For those who live according to the flesh set their minds on the things of the flesh, but those who live according to the Spirit, the things of the Spirit. For to be carnally minded is death, but to be spiritually minded is life and peace"* (Rom. 8:5-6). The believer needs a new nature that longs to please God and will perform His will.

This new nature is received from God at conversion through an act of the Holy Spirit called regeneration: *"But when the kindness and the love of God our Savior toward man appeared, not by works of righteousness which we have done, but according to His mercy He saved us, through the washing of regeneration and renewing of the Holy Spirit"* (Tit. 3:4-5). The Holy Spirit washes us by bringing us to see the wrong in our sinful attitudes and desires. He makes us feel their uncleanness, and leads us to repent of and repudiate them. Peter refers to the new nature received as a divine nature: *"By which have been given to us exceedingly great and precious promises, that through these you may be partakers of the divine nature, having escaped the corruption that is in the world through lust"* (2 Pet. 1:4). Regeneration is the implantation of a new life and a new order of living. This is why a regenerated person is referred to as a "new man" in Colossians 3:10; he or she received a new disposition which is to govern his or her thinking and behavior. This new disposition is God's own nature, which cannot sin (1 Jn. 3:9), though the believer may still sin by ignoring its moral reckoning (1 Jn. 1:9-2:1).

Before the one-time act of regeneration, the believer was spiritually dead, but through rebirth he or she is made spiritually alive! Imagine for a moment a peach seed placed within a coffin containing a rotting corpse. The seed contains life, while the coffin contains nothing but death. In time, the seed will sprout and grow into a fruit-bearing tree. Through the power of the Holy Spirit, God implants life within a repentant sinner; that which was once dead now lives to bear fruit to God (John 15:1-5).

July 3 – The New Nature (Part 2)
(Romans 8)

John refers to the new nature as a righteous seed implanted within a new believer. This seed cannot invoke sin or lead the believer away from what pleases God: *"No one who is born of God practices sin, because His seed abides in him; and he cannot sin, because he is born of God"* (1 Jn. 3:9; NASV). "Born of God" and "born again" are equivalent terms with regeneration.

The Lord Jesus said that no one would enter heaven without being born again (John 3:3). The only way to be born again is by trusting Jesus Christ alone for salvation: *"But as many as received Him, to them He gave the right to become children of God, to those who believe in His name: who were born, not of blood, nor of the will of the flesh, nor of the will of man, but of God"* (John 1:12-13). Without being born again, a human soul will remain spiritually dead and without the capacity to please God. In this state, every individual will act as a child of the devil and be controlled by the lusts and desires of his or her flesh (Eph. 2:1-3). Consequently, if we are going to live for God we must be born again and yield to that new and holy nature received from Him.

It is only by the conviction of the Holy Spirit and the power of God's Word resounding in our minds that we are enabled to repent, choose Christ, and receive eternal life in Him. Until then we are simply dead corpses marching in cadence with Satan, performing his rebel agenda, and coming ever nearer to his final destination – hell (Eph. 2:1-3). Once we trust Christ, we become a New Man in Him, and receive His nature through the Holy Spirit; what we positionally were in Adam (the Old Man) is gone, but we still have his old nature within us.

Peter highlights that great privilege believers have in being new creatures in Christ and thus partakers of God's nature. May we long to think, speak, and act as God would…He makes it possible to do so! May the children of light never march again in Satan's zombie band.

His divine power has given to us all things that pertain to life and godliness, through the knowledge of Him who called us by glory and virtue, by which have been given to us exceedingly great and precious promises, that through these you may be partakers of the divine nature, having escaped the corruption that is in the world through lust (2 Pet. 1:3-4).

July 4 – The Carnal Mind is Death – Part 1
(Romans 8)

There are many things for which our flesh can lust: social status, fame, food, vices, sexual pleasures, money, beauty, etc. It is impossible to allow our flesh to lust for what it wants and not to expect our behavior to adversely affect our spiritual vitality. Peter acknowledges that a believer cannot simultaneously live according to the flesh and be in the will of God (1 Pet. 4:2). Paul emphasizes the same truth when writing to the Christians at Rome:

> *For those who live according to the flesh set their minds on the things of the flesh, but those who live according to the Spirit, the things of the Spirit. For to be carnally minded is death, but to be spiritually minded is life and peace. Because the carnal mind is enmity against God; for it is not subject to the law of God, nor indeed can be. So then, those who are in the flesh cannot please God* (Rom. 8:5-8).

Clearly, when the believer is in the flesh, he or she cannot please God; this is a practical truth. God's solution for us in overcoming the flesh's impulses begins by understanding a positional truth. Positionally speaking, co-crucifixion took place at the cross and became effectual for a believer at his or her conversion (Rom. 6:6). In Adam, we were *"made subject to vanity"* (Rom. 8:20). At the cross, the Old Man, the man in Adam, the man that we once were, the man who was dominated and controlled by the flesh died with Christ. Paul conveys the practical aspects of this positional truth to the Galatian believers: *"Those who are Christ's have crucified the flesh with its passions and desires"* (Gal. 5:24). The purpose of crucifixion was to end the life of someone, though death itself would occur sometime later. From God's perspective, believers have been crucified with Christ so that their craving flesh will eventually die (i.e. there should be a diminishing influence of the old nature in believers as they mature in Christ).

When a believer thinks on what is corrupt, it must lead to a legitimate harvest of corruption (Gal. 6:7-8). Consequently, believers must desire to be controlled by the Holy Spirit instead of their lusting flesh – only then are the deeds of the flesh mortified and fellowship with God maintained: *"If by the Spirit you put to death the deeds of the body, you will live"* (Rom. 8:13). As soon as you see your flesh raise its ugly head, do not pamper it, do not justify it, just blast it – no mercy!

July 5 – The Carnal Mind Is Death – Part 2
(Romans 8)

Furthermore, Paul commanded the saints at Colosse to *"put to death your members which are on the earth: fornication, uncleanness, passion, evil desire, and covetousness, which is idolatry"* (Col. 3:5). In addition to the believer being on high alert and being willing to instantly mortify any fleshly thoughts or impulses whenever observed (Rom. 8:13), Paul told the believers at Colosse not to feed (strengthen) the nature of the Old Man, but rather to put him off (Col. 3:9).

The ungodly longings of the flesh (some of which are listed in Col. 3:5) should not be strengthened through sinful behavior or by wrong thinking, but rather these should be starved so that they lose their influence and can be "put off" from the believer's conduct completely. If not fed, these ungodly longings lose their hold on the believer's life and die out more quickly – although ultimate freedom will not be achieved until glorification. Paul conveys this same fundamental truth to the believers at Rome:

> *Likewise you also, reckon yourselves to be dead indeed to sin, but alive to God in Christ Jesus our Lord. Therefore do not let sin reign in your mortal body, that you should obey it in its lusts* (Rom. 6:11-12).

Mortification or gratification are the only two things the flesh understands, but if we choose to gratify the flesh, even a little, it will want more the next day because the flesh is never satisfied (Eccl. 1:8). The only spiritual recourse in dealing with the lusting of the flesh is to extend it a deadly blow and to keep on mortifying it day after day – this is God's will for every believer. Consistent mortification of the flesh ends the sway of the carnal mind to cause death (separation) – for the believer this is the loss of spiritual fellowship with the Savior.

Scripture presents the solution to sin and death: *"For the wages of sin is death, but the gift of God is eternal life in Christ Jesus our Lord"* (Rom. 6:23). We choose our sin, but it is God who chooses the consequences of our sin and offers consoling grace for those who regret and repent of their sin (1 Jn. 1:9). God's infinite grace and forgiving heart ensure that failures are never final unless we choose to wallow in self-pity rather than find refuge in His grace.

July 6 – My People, Who Were Not My People
(Romans 9)

Despite Israel's unfaithfulness to Jehovah, Paul (and many Old Testament prophets) tells us that the Lord will be moved with compassion and mercy to restore Israel to a place of special intimacy with Him in a future day. God has not abandoned His adulterous wife, His covenant people of old (Ezek. 16:32, 38); He has an agenda for restoring the nation of Israel to a position of honor and blessing. Isaiah foretold that God's Servant-Messiah would accomplish this feat in two ways: First, He would *"bring Jacob back to Him, so that Israel is gathered to Him"* (Isa. 49:5). Second, He would also be *"a light to the Gentiles, that You should be My salvation to the ends of the earth"* (Isa. 49:6). Hosea confirms that same twofold plan:

> *Then I will sow her* [Israel] *for Myself in the earth, and I will have mercy on her who had not obtained mercy; then I will say to those who were not My people* [Gentiles], *"You are My people!" And they shall say, "You are my God!"* (Hosea 2:23).

The Gentiles were not His people by covenant and therefore were without hope (Eph. 2:11). Yet, Paul explains how God would restore Israel to Himself and also extend mercy to the Gentiles:

> *That He might make known the riches of His glory on the vessels of mercy, which He had prepared beforehand for glory, even us whom He called, not of the Jews only, but also of the Gentiles. As He says also in Hosea: "I will call them My people, who were not My people, and her beloved, who was not beloved." "And it shall come to pass in the place where it was said to them, 'You are not My people,' there they shall be called sons of the living God"* (Rom. 9:23-26).

Paul quotes Isaiah once and Hosea twice in this passage to further explain that it was always God's intention to offer salvation to both Jews and Gentiles. In fact, God would use believing and blessed Gentiles to provoke Israel to jealousy and draw them back to Himself (Rom. 11:11). Jehovah would call a people His children that were not His people, and then He would rebuild the Jewish nation to become a beacon of divine truth among the nations (Amos 9:11-12). Thankfully through Christ, all men can experience the wonders of God personally.

July 7 – Lord of All or Not at All
(Romans 9)

Although a new believer would not fully understand what Christ's Lordship personally entails, there certainly could be no rejection of His Lordship where the matter of salvation is concerned: *"If you confess with your mouth the Lord Jesus and believe in your heart that God has raised Him from the dead, you will be saved"* (Rom. 10:9). *"Believe on the Lord Jesus Christ, and you will be saved, you and your household"* (Acts 16:31). Jesus Christ is the Lord of Glory (1 Cor. 2:8), the Lord of both the Living and the Dead (Rom. 14:9), the Lord of the Harvest (Luke 10:2), and the Lord of Sabaoth (Rom. 9:29), who encourages, strengthens, and rewards His afflicted saints (Jas. 5:4).

The title "Lord," in reference to God, has three scriptural senses: First, it conveys the *position* that God has over all things. As the high and lifted-up One, He is holy and separate from all else, thus, He alone deserves our reverence (Isa. 6:1). Second, "Lord" declares God's *ownership*. He created all things, so obviously He possesses what He has formed (1 Cor. 10:26). Third, "Lord" acknowledges God's *rule* over all that He has created. Given who God is and what He has done, we should willfully submit to His sovereign rule over our lives (Luke 5:5). Who He is intrinsically should cause us to bow before Him, what He has accomplished warrants our devotion, and what He says must be obeyed because He is Lord! As God, the Lord Jesus has position, ownership, and rule over all creation, including His followers.

Though these three senses of Lordship are confirmed in the Gospels through the Lord's miracles and statements, by the declarations of both holy and evil angelic beings, and by the response of those who believed on His name, each sense of Lordship is more thoroughly developed in the Epistles. Likewise, a progression of the concept of Christ being more than the disciples' teacher (He was their Lord first; Luke 5:5, 9:49) is clearly observed from the Gospels to the Epistles: In the Gospels, the Lord Jesus was known as a teacher, guide, instructor, and even by the more official title of Rabbi, but after His exaltation the Holy Spirit refers to Him as the One in supreme authority – He is Lord of all (e.g., Col. 4:1; 2 Tim. 2:21). If Christ is not Lord of all in our thinking, our behavior will reflect that ideology. We must want all of Christ, including His Lordship, or none of Him – He cannot be divided.

July 8 – The Blessed Olive Tree (Part 1)
(Romans 11)

Paul employs two similar analogies in Romans 11 to reveal God's plan to restore the Jewish nation, to bless the Gentiles, and also to warn Gentile believers to learn from God's dealing with Israel and avoid repeating their mistakes (1 Cor. 10:6, 11):

First, Paul notes that though Israel stumbled over Christ, the Jewish nation had not fallen from God's favor forever. Second, that through the failure of Israel, God brought salvation to the nations. Third, God would abundantly bless the Gentiles in Christ to make His covenant people jealous and draw them back to Himself (Rom. 11:11-15).

Next, Paul gives two analogies to illustrate what he wants the believers at Rome to understand.

For if the firstfruit is holy, the lump is also holy; and if the root is holy, so are the branches. And if some of the branches were broken off, and you, being a wild olive tree, were grafted in among them, and with them became a partaker of the root and fatness of the olive tree ... And they also, if they do not continue in unbelief, will be grafted in, for God is able to graft them in again. For if you were cut out of the olive tree which is wild by nature, and were grafted contrary to nature into a cultivated olive tree, how much more will these, who are natural branches, be grafted into their own olive tree? For I do not desire, brethren, that you should be ignorant of this mystery, lest you should be wise in your own opinion, that blindness in part has happened to Israel until the fullness of the Gentiles has come in. And so all Israel will be saved (Rom. 11:16-17, 23-26).

God's covenant with Abraham which promised blessing to all families of the earth is both the firstfruit offering and the root of the olive tree. Christ is represented in the lump taken from the firstfruit offering and the olive tree that draws up blessing from its root. It would be natural for the blessings of the root to pass through the tree to nourish its branches (picturing the two houses of Israel), but these were cut off by disbelief. God then grafted in a wild olive branch, the Gentiles, into Christ's blessings; this pictures the Church Age. Later, God will graft back into the tree the original branches, as the Jewish nation will come to faith at the conclusion of the Church Age (when the fullness of the Gentiles occurs; Rom. 11:25). All the goodness God intends for us and Israel comes through Christ – our blessed Olive Tree.

July 9 – The Blessed Olive Tree (Part 2)
(Romans 11)

A line of Old Testament prophets expressed God's disgust for the nation that was to declare His holy name among the nations, but had instead polluted it. Disbelief leads to rebellion and the loss of God's blessings and fellowship. Willful sin and rebellion draws down God's chastening hand. God did to Israel exactly what He told them He would do if His people erred from the Law and abandoned Him (Deut. 28).

Yet, the analogy shows us that God will restore Israel to Himself. The fact that the Jews (the natural branches) could be, and indeed will be, grafted back into the olive tree indicates that the focus of the illustration is not eternal salvation per se, but rather the blessings that God desires to share with those who exercise faith in Him. Gentile believers (the wild branch) are a second benefactor of the New Covenant and thus are permitted to share in the blessings promised Israel (Eph. 2:11-3:7). Gentiles are grafted into the olive tree, indicating the blessings of Christ rooted in God's covenant with Abraham. The New Covenant permits individual Jews to be saved now and the Jewish nation to be reconciled to God after the Church Age ends.

Since Christ's rejection, the Jewish nation remains in spiritual blindness (Rom. 11:7) and cut off from the blessings God desired for them in Christ. If the Lord so severely judged His covenant people (the natural branches) for their willful idolatry and wickedness, why would He not hesitate to chasten those committing the same offenses who were not natural branches (the Gentiles). This is the essence of Paul's warning to believers: willful sin and pride result in a loss of blessing:

> *For if God did not spare the natural branches* [the Jews], *He may not spare you* [the wild branches grafted in] *either. Therefore consider the goodness and severity of God: on those who fell, severity; but toward you, goodness, if you continue in His goodness. Otherwise you also will be cut off* (Rom. 11:21-22).

Paul and John foretold that the spiritual condition of the professing Church would be apostate, materialistic, fruitless, and loveless just before the Antichrist is revealed and the Tribulation Period begins (2 Thess. 2:3; Rev. 3:15-18). Let us have no part in it! May the Lord enable His true Church to hold fast to Him and His Word.

July 10 – How Unsearchable Are His Judgments
(Romans 11)

God is honored when His people trust His character and promises even when they do not understand what He is doing. If we fully understood the mind of God, we would naturally revere Him less! It is right for us, then, during the storms of life, to acknowledge that God is God, and to count on Him to accomplish what is beyond reason and is outside of our control.

This is why Paul did not boast in what he suffered while serving Christ, but rather in the manifestation of His grace in his difficulties. *"Therefore most gladly I will rather boast in my infirmities, that the power of Christ may rest upon me"* (2 Cor. 12:9). This focus caused him to highly extol the Lord, instead of complain:

> *Oh, the depth of the riches both of the wisdom and knowledge of God! How unsearchable are His judgments and His ways past finding out! "For who has known the mind of the Lord? Or who has become His counselor?" 'Or who has first given to Him and it shall be repaid to him?" For of Him and through Him and to Him are all things, to whom be glory forever. Amen* (Rom. 11:33-36).

Because all the wisdom, the knowledge, and the judgments of God are infallible and that all things are under His control and for His glory, Paul had great hope for the future. In Christ, believers are secure to the praise of God's glory forever (Rom. 8:31-39):

> *If God is for us, who can be against us? He who did not spare His own Son, but delivered Him up for us all, how shall He not with Him also freely give us all things? Who shall bring a charge against God's elect? It is God who justifies. Who is he who condemns? It is Christ who died, and furthermore is also risen, who is even at the right hand of God, who also makes intercession for us. Who shall separate us from the love of Christ? Shall tribulation, or distress, or persecution, or famine, or nakedness, or peril, or sword? ... For I am persuaded that neither death nor life, nor angels nor principalities nor powers, nor things present nor things to come, nor height nor depth, nor any other created thing, shall be able to separate us from the love of God which is in Christ Jesus our Lord.*

Though the world is a dark place, the believer's future in Christ is very bright, for nothing can separate us from the love of God in Christ.

July 11 – Present Your Bodies
(Romans 12)

In Leviticus, God had prescribed a specific way that Israel could approach Him in worship, this being through explicit atoning blood sacrifices as offered by the priests. In the Church Age we also are to be occupied with the way we can approach God in worship, only for us it is through Christ and in the power of the Holy Spirit. Each Christian is a believer-priest and is called on to be a continual, living sacrifice. This is accomplished through a variety of ways, such as: offering up praise to God (Heb. 13:15), yielding to God's Word to avoid conformity to the world (Rom. 12:1-2), supporting the Lord's work through gifts (1 Cor. 16:2), and by frequently remembering the Lord Jesus by observing the Lord's Supper (1 Cor. 11:22-33).

One of the ways that believers worship the Lord is to reject the world's philosophies and attractions by renewing our minds on what is true and spiritual. Paul writes:

I beseech you therefore, brethren, by the mercies of God, that you present your bodies a living sacrifice, holy, acceptable to God, which is your reasonable service. And do not be conformed to this world, but be transformed by the renewing of your mind, that you may prove what is that good and acceptable and perfect will of God (Rom. 12:1-2).

Scripture speaks of two complementary means that call the believer's heart out of the world. The first is to set one's mind on things above (Col. 3:1-2), and the second is to come to realize that the things below are temporary and shakable. As the writer of Hebrews reminds us, in a coming day, all that does not honor the Lord will be removed:

...removal of those things that are being shaken, as of things that are made, that the things which cannot be shaken may remain. Therefore, since we are receiving a kingdom which cannot be shaken, let us have grace, by which we may serve God acceptably with reverence and godly fear. For our God is a consuming fire (Heb. 12:27-29).

The world is evil and temporal, but heaven is wonderful and eternal. This is why we should devote not just ourselves to the Lord, but all our resources also. What is not for Him will ultimately burn up anyway.

201

July 12 – "Own No Man Anything, But…"
(Romans 13)

Paul instructed the Christians in Rome to *"owe no one anything except to love one another, for he who loves another has fulfilled the law"* (Rom. 13:8). Earlier, he told the believers that the purpose of the Law was to show man's sinfulness and need for a Savior (Rom. 3:20-25). If someone stole something, it proved that they were a sinner – he or she did not "keep" the law. The purpose of the Mosaic Law was to declare God's holiness and man's depraved state. However, once someone trusted Christ, they would be indwelt by the Holy Spirit and he or she would be able to "fulfill" the Law. When one chooses not to steal, that is keeping the law. But fulfilling the law is not "not stealing" from another; it is giving to that person. Giving expresses love. God's holiness is reflected in *keeping the law*, but His gracious character is represented in *fulfilling the law*. Through the power of the Holy Spirit, believers convey the love of God to others in a supernatural way. It is not natural to love our enemies, to do good to those who persecute us, to bless those who curse us, or to withhold vengeance when it is just.

Believers should never be satisfied with their outward projection of God's love. Can a husband love his wife too much? No, he will never love his wife as Christ loves the Church (Eph. 5:25). Thus there will always be room to abound more and more. The church at Thessalonica was thriving in the midst of persecution; yet, Paul exhorts, *"And may the Lord make you increase and abound in love to one another and to all, just as we do to you"* (1 Thess. 3:12). The Lord is honored and we receive His joy when we permit the Holy Spirit to love others in only the way He can. If you have people problems, the first weapon to use is genuine love…Christ's love will soften even the hardest of hearts.

How does one "put on" love (1 Thess. 5:8)? Paul gives further instruction: *"See that no one renders evil for evil to anyone, but always pursue what is good both for yourselves and for all"* (1 Thess. 5:15). Yes, we should rejoice in the Lord and be engaged in prayer, but when people problems are overwhelming you, resort to demonstrating Christ's love. The more you are hated – the more you should love. Usually, in God's time, the oppressor will break down because God's love is irresistible.

July 13 – "Put On the Lord Jesus Christ"
(Romans 13)

The Old Testament is full of portraits of God's substitutionary sacrifice of His Son for sinners and the imputation of divine righteousness to those trusting in His justification alone. Christ is the believer's righteousness, in both the practical and positional sense of the word (1 Cor. 1:30; 2 Cor. 5:21). When the offerer put his hand on the head of his sacrifice, he was identifying himself with it and so was God. This identification is further extended to the offering priest who received the skin of the animal offered in a burnt sacrifice (Lev. 7:8).

The priest would likely fashion coverings for himself with the skin, such as shoes, clothes, or a hat. While the priest was in the tabernacle, his priestly service required him to be clothed with priestly garments. However, during his routine apart from the tabernacle, his clothing derived from the skins would be a constant reminder of the offering previously sacrificed. When observed by others, it would be the burnt offering sacrifice (the priest's covering) that would be noticed, not the priest himself. What is the application for the believer today?

Paul writes, *"Put on the Lord Jesus Christ, and make no provision for the flesh, to fulfill its lusts* (Rom. 13:14). The position of righteousness we have in Christ should cause us to "shine out" Christ practically during daily priestly service to Him. In our day-to-day life, others should not see us, but the "sacrifice" – the Lord Jesus. The inherent beauty of the bride of Christ in Revelation 19:7-9 is the glory of Christ seen in the bride. Not only does she have a position of righteousness, but the works of righteousness Christ has done through her are spectacular.

When God looks at a believer, He sees the perfection of Christ. Thus, in Christ, there is nothing for the believer to fear, except to disappoint the One for whom he or she is to live. John put the matter this way: *"There is no fear in love; but perfect love casts out fear, because fear involves torment. But he who fears has not been made perfect in love. We love Him because He first loved us"* (1 Jn. 4:18-19). Just as the burnt offering was voluntary in Moses' day, so is our service to Christ today. Having understood our complete acceptance in Christ and our opportunity to declare His righteousness in word and deed, may we all wear the *skin* of His sacrifice with honor.

July 14 – The Branch and Root of Jesse (Part 1)
(Romans 15)

Paul quotes the prophecy of Isaiah to not only show that Jesus Christ was its literal fulfillment, but that all people, not just the Jews, would be able to have hope in Him:

And again, Isaiah says: "There shall be a root of Jesse; and He who shall rise to reign over the Gentiles, in Him the Gentiles shall hope." Now may the God of hope fill you with all joy and peace in believing, that you may abound in hope by the power of the Holy Spirit (Rom. 15:12-13).

Isaiah prophesied that the coming Jewish Messiah would be both a "stem" ("shoot") and the "Root of Jesse": *"There shall come forth a Rod from the stem of Jesse, and a Branch shall grow out of his roots"* (Isa. 11:1). J. A. Motyer explains the striking features of the dual titles relating to Christ in this prophecy:

The reference to Jesse indicates that the *shoot* is not just another king in David's line but rather another David. In the books of Kings, successive kings were assessed by comparison with "their father David" (e.g., 2 Kgs. 18:3) but no king is called "David" or "son of Jesse." Among the kings, David alone was "the son of Jesse" (e.g., 1 Sam. 20:27-33; 1 Kgs. 12:16), and the unexpected reference to Jesse here has tremendous force: when Jesse produces a shoot, it must be David. But to call the expected king *the Root of Jesse* is altogether another matter, for this means that Jesse sprang from him; he is the root support and origin of the Messianic family in which he would be born. ... In the same way, here, the Messiah is the root cause of his own family tree pending the day when, within that family, he will shoot forth.[29]

Isaiah predicted that the house of David would be in spiritual decline, but suddenly, out of this decaying branch, a fresh shoot of promise springs out. Hence, the Messiah, the *Rod* or *Branch* of David, will spring up from the *stem of Jesse*, but He will also be the *root cause* of this new life. Paul's point is that Christ, the root cause of life, can be experienced through the Holy Spirit in the here and now. Thankfully, those rooted in Christ can abound in His power and hope every day!

July 15 – The Branch and Root of Jesse (Part 2)
(Romans 15)

There are other aspects of Isaiah's prophecy that Paul quotes in Romans 15:12 that speak of the sovereignty and power of God at work in the incarnation of His Son. Christ would be the Righteous Branch of David, but yet He would not be tainted by sin or curse.

The prophet Samuel anointed David, the eighth son of Jesse, as the king of Israel (1 Sam. 17:12). In David's autumn years the Lord promised him, through the prophet Nathan, that a new and everlasting dynasty would be established and one of David's descendants would sit on his throne forever (2 Sam. 7:12-16).

Although the Messiah must be in the royal line of David, we also know that He could not be a descendant of evil King Jeconiah, on whom Jeremiah pronounced a curse (Jer. 22:30). Jeremiah's prophecy then magnifies the incarnation of the Lord Jesus Christ as Messiah. Joseph, the husband of Mary (the mother of the Lord Jesus), was a descendant of Shealtiel who was the son of Jehoiachin or Jeconiah (Matt. 1:12; 1 Chron. 3:17). Therefore, no son of Joseph could sit upon David's throne. Mary, however, was also a descendant of David through Nathan (Luke 3:24-38). Thus, the son of Mary could fulfill both prophecies if she conceived supernaturally through the power of the Holy Spirit and not by Joseph her husband.

In summary, Isaiah predicted that a David-like Jewish Messiah would originate His own birth as a descendant of David in such a remarkable way that He would avoid the curse of Jeconiah. Therefore, He would not be corrupted by the fallen nature inherited from Adam, but would be the rightful heir to the throne of David forever. All this explains why there are fifty-eight references to David in the New Testament; he was an esteemed patriarch greatly respected by the Jewish nation and a wonderful type of the coming Messiah, who was both David's Lord and his Son (Luke 20:41-44).

Indeed, the Lord Jesus Christ is the Branch of David and the Root of Jesse. Only God could be both the cause and effect of this prophecy and that is why Paul tells us that the outcome of it is life and hope!

July 16 – Crushed Under Your Feet

(Romans 16)

Paul invokes unusual imagery borrowed from a story in the book of Joshua to encourage believers to stand strong in the Lord against evil and false teachers:

> *I want you to be wise in what is good, and simple concerning evil. And the God of peace will crush Satan under your feet shortly* (Rom. 16:19-20).

Joshua is a strong type of Jesus Christ. Even the meaning of both their names is the same – "Jehovah's salvation." After a spectacular military victory over the five armies of southern Canaan, it was time for their leaders to be judged. Joshua commanded that the five kings be brought out of the cave prison; then He addressed his captains: *"'Come near, put your feet on the necks of these kings.' And they drew near and put their feet on their necks. Then Joshua said to them, 'Do not be afraid, nor be dismayed; be strong and of good courage, for thus the Lord will do to all your enemies against whom you fight'"* (Josh. 10:24-25). After Joshua's captains stepped on the necks of the kings, Joshua slew all five kings with a sword and had their bodies hung on five trees as a public testimony of their defeat. The pressing of one's foot on the neck of an enemy was an Eastern custom to demonstrate complete victory. Spiritually speaking, Christ allows His followers to share in the victory that is only possible through Him. It was not the captains who actually slew the enemy, but Joshua, representing Christ.

The overall picture before us has its prophetic origin in Genesis 3:15, which foretold that Christ would bruise the serpent's head. The Lord Jesus fulfilled this prophecy at Calvary (John 12:31-33). In Eden, God had said to the serpent (Satan), *"And I will put enmity between you and the woman, and between your seed and her Seed* [Christ]; *He shall bruise your head, and you shall bruise His heel"* (Gen. 3:15). At Calvary, Satan was defeated by the seed of the woman.

Paul may be referring to Christ's future victory over Satan and the wicked at his second advent to the earth (Rev. 19:17-20:3) or he may be speaking of the victory that a believer can have over evil today in Christ. As a believer relies on God's grace to accomplish holy living, the victory is won through Christ, and the devices of Satan are spoiled.

206

July 17 – "Our Lord Jesus Christ"
(1 Corinthians 1)

If you were an apostle in the early days of the Church Age and you wanted to transform a group of believers that were carnal, divided, and out of order into a Christ-honoring gathering how would you go about doing it? This was Paul's challenge with the church at Corinth. Instead of immediately tackling issues and problems, He chose to uphold the Head of the Church, the Lord Jesus Christ, before the Corinthians. Paul knew that if believers held Him in utmost esteem, most of their problems would be resolved:

> *To the church of God which is at Corinth, to those who are sanctified in Christ Jesus, called to be saints, with all who in every place call on the name of **Jesus Christ our Lord**, both theirs and ours: Grace to you and peace from God our Father and the **Lord Jesus Christ**. I thank my God always concerning you for the grace of God which was given to you by Christ Jesus, that you were enriched in everything by Him in all utterance and all knowledge, even as the testimony of Christ was confirmed in you, so that you come short in no gift, eagerly waiting for the revelation of our **Lord Jesus Christ**, who will also confirm you to the end, that you may be blameless in the day of our **Lord Jesus Christ**. God is faithful, by whom you were called into the fellowship of His Son, **Jesus Christ our Lord**. Now I plead with you, brethren, by the name of our **Lord Jesus Christ**, that you all speak the same thing, and that there be no divisions among you, but that you be perfectly joined together in the same mind and in the same judgment* (1 Cor. 1:2-10).

Paul uses the Greek word *kurios*, which is normally translated as "Lord" in the New Testament, six times in ten verses to speak of Christ's supremacy over them. In fact, this is the highest concentration of *kurios* in any equivalent passage in the New Testament. Its linguistic root *kuros* means "supreme in authority," and normally refers to God the Father or God the Son, as in this text. Some might think that Paul went a little overboard with his usage of *kurios*, but that is not the case. When God's people let divine headship slip, they soon devalue God's order and conduct for them to follow. The result is carnality and the loss of God's blessing. The Holy Spirit used Paul to affirm this warning to the church at Corinth and to us too!

July 18 – He Who Glories, Glory in the Lord
(1 Corinthians 1)

The believers were glorying in all sorts of things besides Christ, which was causing disunity and division in the assembly. Paul reminds them of a truth witnessed throughout Scripture:

*But God has chosen the foolish things of the world to put to shame the wise, and God has chosen the weak things of the world to put to shame the things which are mighty; and the base things of the world and the things which are despised God has chosen, and the things which are not, to bring to nothing the things that are, that no flesh should glory in His presence. But of Him you are in Christ Jesus, who became for us wisdom from God – and righteousness and sanctification and redemption – that, as it is written, "**He who glories, let him glory in the Lord**" (1 Cor. 1:27-31).*

God continues to prompt our admiration and worship by using weak and foolish things (including people) to confound what is powerful and wise by secular standards. Understanding that without Christ we can do nothing (John 15:5), but in Christ we can do all things (Phil. 4:13) should keep believers from glorying in themselves. Any and all praise must be the Lord's. When we glory in ourselves, we follow Lucifer's example and act like his children, which God is determined to bring to nothing. Scripture is full of timeless reminders as to whom we should glory in:

Give to the Lord, O families of the peoples, give to the Lord glory and strength. **Give to the Lord the glory** due His name; bring an offering, and come into His courts (Ps. 96:8).

Not unto us, O Lord, not unto us, but to Your name **give glory**, because of Your mercy, because of Your truth (Ps. 115:1).

Everyone who is called by My name, **whom I have created for My glory**; I have formed him, yes, I have made him (Isa. 43:7).

Therefore, whether you eat or drink, or whatever you do, **do all to the glory of God** (1 Cor. 10:31).

But he who glories, **let him glory in the Lord** (2 Cor. 10:17).

July 19 – Eye Has Not Seen
(1 Corinthians 2)

Many have thought that Paul was speaking of heaven when he wrote: *"Eye has not seen, nor ear heard, nor have entered into the heart of man the things which God has prepared for those who love Him"* (1 Cor. 2:9). While it is true that God's heavenly abode will be more spectacular than we could ever imagine, that is not what Paul is referring to. Please notice that Paul then says, *"But God **has revealed them** to us through His Spirit. For the Spirit searches all things, yes, the deep things of God"* (1 Cor. 2:10). This means that the very thing that we could have never understood, naturally speaking, has been revealed to us by the Holy Spirit. We call this divine *revelation*.

The *revelation* of God was conveyed to us through the divine *inspiration* given to the apostles by the Holy Spirit: *"These things we also speak, not in words which man's wisdom teaches but which the Holy Spirit teaches"* (1 Cor. 2:13). Then as we read Scripture (that which has been inspired by God), the Holy Spirit gives us *illumination* to understand what we read: *"But the natural man does not receive the things of the Spirit of God, for they are foolishness to him; nor can he know them, because they are spiritually discerned"* (1 Cor. 2:14).

Hence, we can approach God, not through human knowledge or wisdom, but rather through divine revelation, which the Holy Spirit enables us to understand. Man's knowledge is based on comparison, observation, and demonstration. God is unique, eternal, and spiritual; He cannot be compared to anything else in creation. As Paul has just told us, God cannot be understood through science or human reasoning.

The pre-conversion ministry of the Holy Spirit gives illumination to the carnal mind as to the meaning of God's Word and then causes that individual to feel the weight of their rebellion against it. Feelings of guilt, the need to be right with God, and the fear of impending judgment are what a sinner experiences before trusting Christ as Savior (Rom. 2:15; Heb. 9:14). It is only the Spirit of God who can accomplish this type of ministry in the unregenerate heart (John 16:8).

For believers, the divine agencies of the Word of God and the Spirit of God continue to work in us to both reveal and accomplish God's purposes. May the Holy Spirit continue to illuminate our minds that we might discover the vast riches of Christ, God's Truth, in Scripture!

209

July 20 – Laboring With God
(1 Corinthians 3)

The believers at Corinth were carnally touting their favorite preachers in a divisive way; they had forgotten the bigger picture of ministry altogether. It is not the particular laborer that matters in the work of the Lord, but rather that the Lord is laboring with His people. To confront this dangerous sectarianism Paul reminds them:

*So then neither he who plants is anything, nor he who waters, but God who gives the increase. Now he who plants and he who waters are one, and each one will receive his own reward according to his own labor. For **we are God's fellow workers**; you are God's field, you are God's building* (1 Cor. 3:7-9).

The Jews had discovered many times throughout their history that without the Lord they were helpless, but with the Lord, even giants could not stand against them. Paul uses a horticulture illustration to acknowledge this same condition of service in Church Age. While God uses some to till, others to plant, others to water, and others to reap, it is He who gives the harvest; the laborers alone cannot produce anything.

It is natural for us to boast of our temporal accomplishments, but this is not profitable for eternity. May we remember that if the Lord is not in the work – we are wasting our time and resources! Conversely, when we are in the will and strength of God, we *"can do all things through Christ"* (Phil. 4:13). Also, let us remember that *isms* tend to create *schisms* in the Body of Christ, so let us not be followers of men, lest the work of God suffer through needless disunity.

The Lord Jesus reminded His disciples at His ascension that though He was departing them, He would still continue laboring with them:

So then, after the Lord had spoken to them, He was received up into heaven, and sat down at the right hand of God. And they went out and preached everywhere, the Lord working with them and confirming the word through the accompanying signs (Mark 16:19-20).

We do not labor for the kingdom alone or in vain, for it is Christ's work, and He labors with us to achieve it. We are His eyes to discern the needs of others and His hands to serve them, but *"we are God's fellow workers"* and being yoked with Christ ensures all is doable!

July 21 – The Judgment Seat of Christ
(1 Corinthians 3)

Paul tells us two important facts about the Judgment Seat of Christ. First, all believers will undergo this judgment shortly after their glorification: *"For we shall all stand before the judgment seat of Christ. ... So then each of us shall give account of himself to God"* (Rom. 14:10-12). Second, he reminds believers that only what is built on the foundation of Christ and for His glory has value in eternity:

> *For no other foundation can anyone lay than that which is laid, which is Jesus Christ. Now if anyone builds on this foundation with gold, silver, precious stones, wood, hay, straw, each one's work will become clear; for the Day will declare it, because it will be revealed by fire; and the fire will test each one's work, of what sort it is. If anyone's work which he has built on it endures, he will receive a reward. If anyone's work is burned, he will suffer loss; but he himself will be saved, yet so as through fire* (1 Cor. 3:11-15).

Thankfully, the Judgment Seat of Christ is not a determination of salvation (those in Christ are eternally His), but it is an investigation of works that believers have done in Christ's name. Each believer will be examined and rewarded for faithful service done with pure motives and in the power of the Holy Spirit, for what is of the flesh cannot please God. Foundations on personal glory, false doctrine, and humanism will crumble away (Luke 6:46-49). Only what is invested for eternity has value to the Lord; all that is shown to be worthless will be incinerated by the brilliance of Christ's holy presence and we will be delighted to see it go up in smoke! At the Judgment Seat of Christ, the Lord Jesus will honor all who have honored Him with their lives (2 Cor. 5:10).

Paul wrote the Thessalonian believers shortly after being forced to depart from them. They were suffering for their new faith, so he wrote them about the *Day of Christ* (i.e., the rapture of the Church and the Judgment Seat of Christ). This transforming event would give them glorified bodies so that they could be with Christ in heaven (1 Cor. 15:51-52). An individual's soul is saved when he or she trusts in Christ alone for salvation, but at the rapture, the believer's body will be saved from the presence of sin. May we also long for the Day of Christ, but in the meantime serve Christ in a way that will remind others of Him now.

July 22 – You Have Only What You Received
(1 Corinthians 4)

One of David's greatest psalms is recorded in 1 Chronicles 29:10-11. In that poem, he publicly declares God's majesty, omnipotence, and generosity to Israel. Then he affirms that no earthly position or possession should distract God's people from honoring the Lord, because all things come from Him: *"Both riches and honor come from You, and You reign over all. In Your hand is power and might; in Your hand it is to make great and to give strength to all"* (1 Chron. 29:12).

Paul reminds the carnal Corinthians of the same truth:

Now these things, brethren, I have figuratively transferred to myself and Apollos for your sakes, that you may learn in us not to think beyond what is written, that none of you may be puffed up on behalf of one against the other. For who makes you differ from another? And what do you have that you did not receive? Now if you did indeed receive it, why do you boast as if you had not received it? (1 Cor. 4:6-7).

The Corinthian believers had a tendency to hero-ize certain teachers within the assembly and also itinerant preachers (1 Cor. 1:10-13). This practice of favoring certain ministers and being critical of others was fostered in pride, so the result was division in the church. What is of the flesh will always work to undermine God's best for His people! He transferred the issue to a simplified illustration involving him and Apollos to ensure the Corinthians understood his point. Paul then reminded them that he and Apollos, and indeed every minister of Christ, received their ability and calling from God. Since different teachers were given various abilities and ministries according to God's will, why should we compare God's servants, especially to their detriment? If all we have comes from God, who are we to question what He gives or why He gives it? Be thankful for what He does give!

Without Christ, the believer is nothing, has nothing, and can do nothing for God. But in Him we inherit all things (Rom. 8:17), rule over all things (2 Tim. 2:12), and can do all things that God endorses (Phil. 4:13). Let us maintain this big picture reality and not squabble about distinctions that have no bearing on furthering the cause of Christ. Both David and Paul affirm that believers have no boast, but in the Lord: *"He who glories, let him glory in the Lord"* (1 Cor. 1:31).

July 23– To Gather in His Name
(1 Corinthians 5)

The early Church met to hear God's Word, to pray together, to keep the Lord's Supper and for fellowship (Acts 2:42). Believers gathered in the name of the Lord Jesus, hence, in the authority of that Name. Paul ensured that the church at Corinth understood this fact: *"In the name of our Lord Jesus Christ, when you are gathered together"* (1 Cor. 5:4). Whenever God's people meet together, they do so in Christ's name and to be with Him. It is the Lord's presence alone that draws us to every meeting of the church – because He is there, I want to be there. When a believer justifies careless absenteeism, in effect he or she is casting a vote to close down the assembly and remove Christ's name from the community! On this matter, C. H. Mackintosh writes:

> Of the many favors conferred upon us by our ever-gracious Lord, one of the very highest is the privilege of being present in the assembly of His beloved people, where He has recorded His name. We may assert with all possible confidence that every true lover of Christ will delight to be found where He has promised to be. We may rest assured that anyone who willfully neglects the assembly is in a cold, dead, dangerous state of soul. To neglect the assembling of ourselves is to take the first step on the inclined plane that leads down to the total abandonment of Christ and His precious interests.[30]

The Lord extended this promise to His disciples: *"For where two or three are gathered together in My name, there am I in the midst of them"* (Matt. 18:19-20). The Lord told the thief on the cross, *"Today you will be with Me in paradise"* (Luke 23:43). Paradise is wherever the Lord is, meaning that the closest experience of heaven itself on this side of glory is to be gathered together with other believers in the presence of the Lord Jesus. The gathering of the local assembly should be loved, for it is a visible reminder to the world that Christ has a record of Himself here – a testimony (a lampstand) in the world.

The purpose of our church meetings is not to gather to gifted men, particular ministries, schooling preferences, occupational ranks, civil status, ethnic orientations, or political causes. We gather to be with the Lord, to worship Him, to honor Him, to ask Him for help in learning His mind and to refresh and encourage His people.

July 24 – God's Holy Temple
(1 Corinthians 6)

David understood from God's covenant with him (2 Sam. 7) that he was to clear the way so that his son could build the Lord's house. In God's providential purposes, He called David to be a fighter and Solomon to be a builder – both are essential in the triumphal work of God and represent both advents of Christ. This is why King Solomon could say: *"The Lord my God has given me rest on every side; there is neither adversary nor evil occurrence"* (1 Kgs. 5:4). Solomon had established the most glorious kingdom in Israel's history. For as long as the earth exists, Jerusalem will be the formal place of worship, except in the Church Age. At present, all believer-priests compose the temple of God and lift up worship and living sacrifices to God wherever and whenever they desire (Rom. 12:1; 1 Pet. 2:5, 9; Rev. 1:6).

Paul reminds the saints at Corinth of this beautiful truth to exhort them to holy living: *"Do you not know that your body is the temple of the Holy Spirit who is in you, whom you have from God, and you are not your own? For you were bought at a price; therefore glorify God in your body and in your spirit, which are God's"* (1 Cor. 6:19-20). Sometimes all true believers, the Body of Christ, are spoken of as His living temple on earth – the Church (1 Tim. 3:15; 1 Pet. 2:5). Sometimes the temple of the Lord relates to the testimony of believers gathered at one location – the local church (1 Cor. 3:16-17), which is to be a lampstand of God to a lost world (Rev. 2:5). However, in 1 Corinthians 6:19-20, Paul exhorts individual believers to understand that their bodies are temples of the Holy Spirit and that they should render their whole self in consecrated service for the glory of God.

After hearing of the ruin of Jerusalem, the place God had chosen to place His name, Nehemiah showed great concern for the Lord's work and His people; he fasted and prayed for four months (Neh. 1). Do we feel the same sense of desperation today that Nehemiah felt long ago? Today, the Church is God's temple and is to display Christ's character while declaring His salvation message to the world. Do we mourn over the Church's indifference, moral failures, and lack of commitment to the Lord Jesus and His Word? What might God do today if believers, like Nehemiah, were broken over the Church's ruined testimony, and in fasting and prayer pleaded with the Lord to revive His Church?

July 25 – The Lord's Table
(1 Corinthians 10)

Paul exhorts the believers at Corinth not to remove themselves from the Lord's Table to feed on humanism and worldly trifles; to do so is to fellowship with demons and that would be offensive to the Lord Jesus:

> *I do not want you to have fellowship with demons. You cannot drink the cup of the Lord and the cup of demons; you cannot partake of the Lord's table and of the table of demons. Or do we provoke the Lord to jealousy? Are we stronger than He?* (1 Cor. 10:20-22).

The Lord's Table is an expression that is used in both the Old and New Testaments to convey this concept of divine provision and fellowship (Ps. 23:5, 78:19; Mal. 1:7, 12; 1 Cor. 9:13, 10:18). Both the Levitical priests (through the provisions gained at the Altar; Lev. 6:16, 26, 7:6, 31-32) and believer-priests under the new covenant of grace (1 Cor. 10:20-21) have been invited to abide at the Lord's Table.

In the New Testament, the biblical expression "the Lord's Table" (i.e., the spiritual abode where believers receive blessing and commune with Christ; 1 Cor. 10:1-22) is often confused with the biblical term "the Lord's Supper" (which refers to a physical remembrance meeting of the local church; 1 Cor. 11:17-34). Many in Christendom often refer to the Lord's Supper with the non-scriptural term "the communion service." There is *communion with Christ* at the Lord's Table, but more specifically, there is a *remembrance of Christ* at every Lord's Supper – the value of His death is proclaimed afresh. The Lord's Table is spiritual and is set by Him, whereas the table at the Lord's Supper is physical and is set by us; at the former we receive provisions from the Lord, but at the latter we remember Him and render worship to Him.

The Lord's Table speaks of the sum total of the spiritual blessings we have in Christ, while the Lord's Supper refers to the remembrance meeting of the Church. In the sense that the souls of believers are refreshed through Spirit-led worship, the Lord's Table would include the Lord's Supper, but the distinct terminology and significance of each should not be lost. It is a great privilege to remember the Savior and refresh the heart of God during the Lord's Supper. Likewise, it is a blessing to the heart of all believers to commune with and receive from the Savior at His Table. May we never choose to leave His presence!

July 26 – Sanctity of the Genders
(1 Corinthians 11)

God instituted His order for the genders when He fashioned the first man and then created the first woman from that man (Gen. 1:27, 2:24). Genesis 2 informs us that the woman came from the man, was made for the man, and was brought to the man by God to be his helper. The general principle in creation is that men are to lead and women are to support. God's creation order is further depicted in biblical authority structures for other spheres such as home order, civil order, and church order. In marriage, husbands are to love and care for their wives and wives are to submit to and respect their husbands (Eph. 5:22-33). In the realm of civil authority, it is notable that nowhere in the Bible do we find any example of God appointing a woman to lead His people. Although Deborah was a wise prophetess who gave counsel to others from her home (Judg. 4:4), she did not lead Israel's army into battle, for she knew that would be inappropriate (Judg. 4:6). The same pattern of gender roles is also witnessed in Church order; only men were called to be apostles of the early Church, only men served as church elders (Titus 1:6; 1 Tim. 3:1-2), only men are to be appointed as church deacons (1 Tim. 3:11-12), and only the men were to lead in prayer and teach publicly (1 Cor. 14:34-35; 1 Tim. 2:8-9).

Likewise, there are also ministries reserved for women, into which men cannot intrude. The Bible is full of examples of godly women who served and assisted others through various means and methods. For example, the sisters, like the Kohathites of old, have been entrusted with the ministry of the coverings within the house of God. They are to cover and conceal all glories that compete with God's glory (1 Cor. 11:2-16). As the assembly gathers in the presence of the Lord Jesus, each woman who covers her head ensures that she (the glory of man; 1 Cor. 11:7) and her long hair (her own personal glory; 1 Cor. 11:15) do not compete with God's glory, as symbolically portrayed in the man's uncovered head (1 Cor. 11:7). This earthly scene patterns the heavenly reality where only God's glory is observed and where the cherubim and the seraphim use their wings to cover their own intrinsic glories in His presence. As the covering cherub Lucifer learned, God does not tolerate any competing glories in His presence (Ezek. 28:12-17). God created the genders and has uniquely sanctified both to reveal His glory!

July 27 – Remembering the Lord Together
(1 Corinthians 11)

We read of four times that the Lord Jesus personally met with Paul to convey vital doctrine; one such event was to ensure that the Lord's Supper was not changed into something that He did not institute:

> *For I received from the Lord that which I also delivered to you: that the Lord Jesus on the same night in which He was betrayed took bread; and when He had given thanks, He broke it and said, "Take, eat; this is My body which is broken for you; do this in remembrance of Me." In the same manner He also took the cup after supper, saying, "This cup is the new covenant in My blood. This do, as often as you drink it, in remembrance of Me"* (1 Cor. 11:23-26).

While it is true that the Lord Jesus invites all believers to participate in the Lord's Supper, a local assembly of God's people should not welcome just anyone into their midst to break bread. It is not that the Lord's Supper needs to be protected per se, but rather that we do not want to grieve the Holy Spirit by allowing the unregenerate, those in sin, or those who are embracing false doctrines to participate as if they were sanctified believer-priests fit for worship (1 Pet. 2:5, 9).

Who should participate in the Lord's Supper? First, only those who have a sound profession of Christ should participate; the Lord's Supper was given by the Lord to His disciples as a memorial feast (Luke 22:19). Second, those who partake must be doctrinally sound (2 Thess. 2:6, 3:14; 2 Jn. 9-10) and, third, morally sound (1 Cor. 5:1-5, 11, 13). If these aspects are not met, those individuals are welcome to observe, but they should not partake of the bread and wine, nor participate audibly.

Letters were used to validate these priestly qualities in believers journeying from one church to another (Acts 18:26-27; Rom. 16:1; Col. 4:7-8). These letters enabled visiting believers to be received into another local church fellowship with joy and all the privileges and responsibilities of a believer-priest (Rom. 15:7). To preclude the Lord's discipline, only believer-priests who exhibit His life should partake of the wine and the bread. This is why all believers are commanded to examine themselves before partaking of the emblems (1 Cor. 11:27). Believer-priests who come together to remember the Lord in the beauty of His holiness with hearts full of adoration should always be welcome.

July 28 – Anointed Priests Are Equipped
(1 Corinthians 12)

Just as the Levitical priests were anointed with oil at their consecration, the Holy Spirit anoints believers at their conversion (1 Jn. 2:20). Old Testament priests, prophets, and kings were often anointed with oil when they were consecrated (set apart) for the Lord's use. Likewise, each believer is anointed and called to serve the Body of Christ. Not only does this separate out the believer for God's purpose, but this anointing actually provides divine discernment of the truth, which enables the believer to follow after God's will in his or her ministry. It is through this provision of the Holy Spirit a new believer becomes part of a holy priesthood which is *"to offer up spiritual sacrifices, acceptable to God by Jesus Christ"* (1 Pet. 2:5) forever.

Levitical priests were also completely equipped by the Lord with all the necessary implements and clothing to fulfill the office of priest. Similarly, the Holy Spirit distributes spiritual gifts to believer-priests in the Church Age *"as He wills"* (1 Cor. 12:11). Paul writes:

There are diversities of gifts, but the same Spirit. There are differences of ministries, but the same Lord. And there are diversities of activities, but it is the same God who works all in all. But the manifestation of the Spirit is given to each one for the profit of all (1 Cor. 12:4-8).

The number of these spiritual gifts per believer will vary (1 Cor. 12:4), but each will receive at least one spiritual gift (1 Cor. 12:7). Also, the manner in which these gifts will be used will differ (1 Cor. 12:5), and the beneficiaries (those who receive the spiritual ministry) will vary (1 Cor. 12:6). Thankfully, the Lord fully equips us for the service to which He calls us. It is a joy to honor Him in priestly service.

In many ways, the pattern of the Levitical priesthood typifies with astonishing foreknowledge the eternal realities now accomplished by the Holy Spirit on the believer's behalf. As each believer-priest is infused by the power of the Holy Spirit and serves with pure motives, the Lord Jesus is honored and God Himself is refreshed. What was freely offered in sacrifice on earth through Christ fills the throne room of heaven with a sweet aroma. In this spiritual sense, Christ is our Golden Altar of Incense in which we can offer to God what He appreciates and we can do so at any time on any day.

July 29 – The God of Order and Peace
(1 Corinthians 14)

The church meetings at Corinth were chaotic, so Paul labored to bring the assembly back into God's order so that they would enjoy God's peace, and the Gentiles would not think that they were all wacky (1 Cor. 14:23). Proper order in the affairs of life, including our worship, is exceedingly important to God, *"for God is not the author of confusion but of peace"* (1 Cor. 14:33) and He desires that *"all things be done decently and in order"* (1 Cor. 14:40). Satan is the author of deception and confusion (John 8:44), but God sets in place standards of proper order to confound his attempts to pervert divine truth.

We witness this same revelation of truth in the Old Testament. Isaiah wrote: *"Woe to those who call evil good, and good evil; who put darkness for light, and light for darkness; who put bitter for sweet, and sweet for bitter!"* (Isa. 5:20). Solomon confirmed God's revulsion for those calling evil – good: *"He who justifies the wicked, and he who condemns the just, both of them alike are an abomination to the Lord"* (Prov. 17:15). Satan rarely presents outright lies; rather, he depends upon a series of blurred deceptions to gain his footing and to wreak havoc within the Church. I will illustrate this point: "Despite what you might have thought previously, black really means white." You say, "No, black is the opposite of white." But then I pick up a reliable dictionary, perhaps *The American Heritage Dictionary*,[31] and show you that the meaning of "black" is "dark," and then I confirm that one of the meanings of "dark" is "dim." Finding the entry for "dim" I prove to you that "dim" can denote "pale." And finally I look up the word "pale" and verify that one of the connotations of "pale" is "white." I have proven to you using a series of only four imprecise meanings (variations of the best meaning, if you will) that black is equal to white.

If the devil can deceive the believer into compromising even a small portion of the truth, be sure that he will return again to do the same. He may wait until we are comfortable in our complacency, but he will be back! Thus, we must stand fast with the belt of truth securely fastened to resist Satan's attempts to lure us into compromise through lies and deception. Let us stand fast in the light of divine revelation and not be moved into his darkness by his trickery! We are to reflect the God of peace and of order in all that we do, not the chaos of the devil.

July 30 – If No Resurrection, Then No Hope
(1 Corinthians 15)

Paul understood that the resurrection of the dead was more than just an "I hope so" crutch to get the believer through tough times; it was an essential part of the believer's salvation. He stated that if there was no resurrection of the dead, *"then also those who have fallen asleep in Christ have perished. If in this life only we have hope in Christ, we are of all men the most pitiable"* (1 Cor. 15:18-19). Without resurrection there is no salvation! *"For if the dead do not rise, then Christ is not risen. And if Christ is not risen, your faith is futile; you are still in your sins!"* (1 Cor. 15:16-17). Paul stated that if the resurrection of Christ did not occur, then we would still be spiritually dead even though we had trusted in Christ. We would just be forgiven dead people!

Picture yourself visiting a terminally ill friend in a hospital. While you are talking to your friend, she gets drowsy, closes her eyes, stops breathing, and a few moments later quietly passes into eternity. If you could raise your friend from the dead, would she be any better off? No, she has a deadly disease and would just die again. If you could somehow instantly heal her disease, would she be any better off? No, she would just be a healthy dead person. Your friend needs both life and to be healed from her disease. The Lord Jesus dealt with the deadly disease called sin at Calvary, and because He was raised from the dead, believers can not only be forgiven of their sins, but they in Him receive His life. The Lord Jesus gave up His life that we might live out His life now. This is why the Lord could say, *"I give them eternal life, and they shall never perish; neither shall anyone snatch them out of My hand"* (John 10:28). In Christ there is life; outside Christ there is only death!

Paul adamantly states that those in Christ have salvation and will never experience divine wrath: *"But God demonstrates His own love toward us, in that while we were still sinners, Christ died for us. Much more then, having now been justified by His blood, we shall be saved from wrath through Him"* (Rom. 5:8-9). Why could Paul be so sure that believers would never suffer God's wrath? Because God would be unjust to punish believers for crimes He had already punished His Son for on their behalf. To do so would mean that Christ did not satisfy God's judicial wrath for sin. But Christ's resurrection proves that God was satisfied, meaning that we can have God's forgiveness and life.

July 31 – The Glorified Body
(1 Corinthians 15)

Have you ever wondered what kind of body believers will have in heaven? Some in Paul's day were pondering this question, but others were challenging the teaching of resurrection because they could not understand how a physical body could exist in heaven. Paul uses a horticultural example to explain this difficulty. Just as a seed must fall into the ground and die in order to bring forth life, we must die to experience resurrection. Our future resurrected bodies will draw characteristics from our earthly bodies, in the same way a corn plant acquires its characteristics from the kernel of corn that was sown (1 Cor. 15:36-38). The plant is not the seed per se, but what it is was drawn from the seed. Accordingly, individuality of our human soul will be maintained in heaven, though our visible form will be different.

Paul says that our present bodies are perishable, weak, and are natural; however, our glorified bodies will never perish, will be powerful, and spiritual (1 Cor. 15:51-53). The former often dishonors the Lord, while that would be impossible with the latter body – there is no flesh nature within it to cause the glorified body to rebel against the Lord. John states that believers will have a body like the Lord Jesus' body, which obviously cannot commit sin (1 Jn. 3:2). Paul describes the same truth: *"For our citizenship is in heaven, from which we also eagerly wait for the Savior, the Lord Jesus Christ, who will transform our lowly body that it may be conformed to His glorious body, according to the working by which He is able even to subdue all things to Himself"* (Phil. 3:20-21). Having a Christlike body in heaven means that everyone will morally act like God forever. There will be no ill thoughts about other people, no crippling bents, no temptations, nor will there be any addictions with which to grapple. God is a holy God and to dwell in His presence we will have to be holy too.

Paul states that the appearing of the Lord Jesus is the blessed hope of the Church (Tit. 2:11) and that those who love the Lord's appearing will be rewarded (2 Tim. 4:8). John says that those who live expectant of Christ's return will live purely, because the Lord is pure and because a believer would not want to be ashamed when He does suddenly come for His people (1 Jn. 2:28, 3:3). So although believers have not received their resurrection bodies yet, they are to live as though they have!

August 1 – The Influence of Companions
(1 Corinthians 15)

It has often been stated that you become like those you spend time with. The book of Proverbs certainly upholds this point of view:

He who walks with wise men will be wise, but the companion of fools will be destroyed (Prov. 13:20).

Make no friendship with an angry man, and with a furious man do not go, lest you learn his ways and set a snare for your soul (Prov. 22:24-25).

Fools mock at sin, but among the upright there is favor (Prov. 14:9)

Likewise, Paul warns the believers at Corinth: *"Do not be deceived: 'Evil company corrupts good habits'"* (1 Cor. 15:33). Bad companions will corrupt good character. If we closely associate with an angry person – we will become angry also. Spending time with foolish people does not increase our wisdom, but rather prompts more folly.

The marks of a disciple of Christ are to learn the Master (Matt. 11:29) and to become like Him (Matt. 10:25). This means that if we have close fellowship with the blessed Savior, we will be more like Him. Time in Christ's presence as we meditate on Him through His Word enables us to learn His mind and gain His moral likeness (Phil. 2:1-5).

The Sanhedrin, the Jewish judicial body, had nothing kind to say about the Lord Jesus or His disciples, but after arresting the disciples for preaching Christ, they inadvertently gave them a compliment:

Now when they saw the boldness of Peter and John, and perceived that they were uneducated and untrained men, they marveled. And they realized that they had been with Jesus (Acts 4:13).

How did the Jewish leaders come to this conclusion? After hearing Peter's speech and observing the bold but gracious, Christlike behavior of the disciples, the elders knew who the disciples had been with – Jesus! Because they had spent much time with the Lord, the character of their words and behavior reminded others of Christ. This same spiritual testimony is possible today; may others know that we have been with Jesus Christ also.

222

August 2 – You Cannot Outgive the Lord
(1 Corinthians 16)

Paul exhorts the church at Corinth, *"On the first day of the week let each one of you lay something aside, storing up as he may prosper, that there be no collections when I come"* (1 Cor. 16:2). First, all believers are to regularly give to the work of the Lord (giving weekly is implied). Second, *"Let each one of you"* means that our giving is a personal matter and should not be publicized (Matt. 6:3). Third, "storing up" means that there must be prayerful preparation in deciding how much should be given to the Lord. Fourth, our giving should be proportionate to how God has prospered us.

Under the Law there were rigid tithes and gifts that were demanded of the Jews, but during the Church Age, believers are not told how much to return to the Lord. Clearly, from Paul's instructions to the believers at Corinth, the Lord does not expect us to contribute the same amounts, but He does expect us to give to the work of the Lord willingly and regularly. In Paul's second epistle to the Corinthians, he explains why they should be generous in giving to the Lord:

> *For you know the grace of our Lord Jesus Christ, that though He was rich, yet for your sakes He became poor, that you through His poverty might become rich* (2 Cor. 8:9).

Contemplating all that the Son of God had to set aside in glory to become God's Lamb for sacrifice (for our sin) should prompt us to want to give back to Him want we can. If we gave Christ everything we have, we still could never repay the debt that He paid on our behalf. Furthermore, Paul reminds them:

> *He who sows sparingly will also reap sparingly, and he who sows bountifully will also reap bountifully. So let each one give as he purposes in his heart, not grudgingly or of necessity; for God loves a cheerful giver* (2 Cor. 9:6-7).

The Greek word rendered "cheerful" is *hilaros*. The English word "hilarious" is derived from *hilaros*. Interestingly, *hilaros* only occurs twice in the New Testament and both incidences relate to giving (Rom. 12:8 is the other). God loves a *hilaros* giver because it is how He gives.

August 3 – Three Tenses of Salvation
(2 Corinthians 1)

No Jew or Gentile in the Church Age is under the Law. Yet, the Law is still holy because it reflects the character of God so we can understand our ungodliness and come to Christ for salvation (Rom. 7:4-6, 12). Although our salvation in Christ is not yet fully received, we must aspire to live out Christ's holiness now. Salvation means "to deliver, to rescue, to pardon, to secure, to make safe." As Paul explains to the Corinthians, believers in the Church Age enjoy the benefits of a three-tense salvation:

> *Yes, we had the sentence of death in ourselves, that we should not trust in ourselves but in God who raises the dead, who **delivered us** from so great a death, and **does deliver us**; in whom we trust that He **will still deliver us*** (2 Cor. 1:9-10).

Christians, through the gospel message, can rejoice that our souls are saved from the **penalty of sin**, and through the Holy Spirit we now have **power over sin**. Furthermore, we are to anticipate a future day when we will be saved from **the presence of sin**. At that moment a believer's body will be transformed into holy humanity. Nothing of the flesh nature inherited from Adam will remain, and we will be removed from the presence of sin (i.e., from the corruption of the world) to ever be with the Lord (1 Thess. 4:17). So a Christian **has been saved** (John 5:24; Eph. 2:8), **is being saved** (Phil. 2:12; Rom. 8:24), and **will be saved** (Rom. 13:11; 1 Thess. 5:9). Through trusting the gospel message, we, in the Church Age, are born again and receive eternal salvation through the Holy Spirit. Those in the dispensation of the Law were not indwelt by the Holy Spirit as believers are today; therefore, they did not have the power to overcome the sinful impulses from within (Rom. 7:9-19). Additionally, we have the hope of being with the Lord forever and that should have a sanctifying effect on the way we live out our salvation for Christ today. John puts the matter this way:

> *Beloved, now we are children of God; and it has not yet been revealed what we shall be, but we know that when He is revealed, we shall be like Him, for we shall see Him as He is. And everyone who has this hope in Him purifies himself, just as He is pure* (1 Jn. 3:2-3).

August 4 – From Glory to Glory
(2 Corinthians 3)

After being alone with God on Mount Sinai for forty days, Moses returned to the camp carrying the two stone tablets of the Law. There was no need to break these tablets as he entered the camp – the people were patiently waiting for him. Moses did not realize it, but he soon learned from the reaction of others that his countenance shone brightly; his face had retained a measure of God's glory. Understandably, the people, and even his own brother Aaron, were afraid to come near him.

After Moses spoke to Aaron and the elders, then the people knew it was safe to approach Moses. Yet, when Moses was among the people, he covered his face with a veil, but whenever he went into the tabernacle he removed it. Did he do this to settle the anxieties of others or was there another reason? Paul answers this quandary:

Unlike Moses, who put a veil over his face so that the children of Israel could not look steadily at the end of what was passing away. But their minds were blinded. For until this day the same veil remains unlifted in the reading of the Old Testament, because the veil is taken away in Christ. But even to this day, when Moses is read, a veil lies on their heart. Nevertheless when one turns to the Lord, the veil is taken away (2 Cor. 3:13-16).

Moses covered his face, not to make the Israelites more comfortable in his presence, but rather so they would not notice that the brilliance of his face diminished over time. Why was this important? Moses brought the Israelites the Law, but though it reflected God's righteous character, it did not convey the full measure of God's goodness in resolving their sin. The Law showed and condemned human sin, but did not provide man power to overcome it. Hence, just as the reflected glory of God faded from Moses' face, the Law also had a diminishing glory.

In time, the Old Covenant (the Law) would be replaced by the New Covenant sealed with Christ's own blood. This truth was conveyed to the Jews when the Lord Jesus presented Himself to them as their Messiah. When Christ sojourned among the Jews, He removed the veil that was over the Law in order to show its fading glory. Yet, instead of trusting Him, the Jews covered their own hearts with the same veil; nationally speaking, they still remain in blindness today (Rom. 11:7).

August 5 – A New Creation
(2 Corinthians 5)

As a new creature in Christ, a believer is to fully consecrate his or her spirit, soul, and body for God's purposes by abhorring evil in thought and deed (1 Thess. 5:23). The matter hinges on the believer's understanding that who and what he or she was positionally in Adam is dead (Eph. 4:22; Rom. 6:6). All that we were before Christ is no more – it died with Him at Calvary. Because we have been legally declared dead, we may receive a new life – His life. We must now endeavor to live His life in practice and not follow our own ambitions.

> *For the love of Christ compels us, because we judge thus: that if one died for all, then all died; and He died for all, that those who live should live no longer for themselves, but for Him who died for them and rose again. Therefore, from now on, we regard no one according to the flesh. Even though we have known Christ according to the flesh, yet now we know Him thus no longer. Therefore, if anyone is in Christ, he is a new creation; old things have passed away; behold, all things have become new* (2 Cor. 5:14-17).

Those who trust the Lord Jesus alone for salvation get a new beginning. They become a new creation (2 Cor. 5:17) and possess eternal life with Christ (John 5:24). Spiritually speaking, they shall never die (John 10:28). This is the principal message of the Bible. Creation itself is God's grand stage to accomplish His plan of redemption for mankind. Through Christ, the redeemed will ultimately enjoy God's self-expression of all that He is and forever bask in His glory. In a coming day all those who are new creatures in Christ will be able to enjoy His new creation for eternity!

Jesus, Thou art all compassion; pure, unbounded love Thou art,
Visit us with Thine affection, enter every longing heart.
Firstfruits of Thy new creation, faithful, holy, may we be,
Joyful in Thy great salvation, daily more conformed to Thee:
Changed from glory into glory, till in heaven we take our place,
Then to worship and adore Thee, lost in wonder, love, and praise.

— Charles Wesley

226

August 6 – Ambassadors for Christ
(2 Corinthians 5)

Paul informs us of an important role that all believers are to perform during their earthly sojourn – we are ambassadors for Christ:

Now then, we are ambassadors for Christ, as though God were pleading through us: we implore you on Christ's behalf, be reconciled to God. For He made Him who knew no sin to be sin for us, that we might become the righteousness of God in Him (2 Cor. 5:20-21).

Christians are heavenly representatives of Christ on earth (Phil. 3:20). As faithfully as Christ declared the name of His Father during His earthly sojourn, the Christian is now to reveal to the world the name of the Lord Jesus Christ. This was Paul's prayer for the young believers at Thessalonica: *"That the name of our Lord Jesus Christ may be glorified in you, and you in Him, according to the grace of our God and the Lord Jesus Christ"* (2 Thess. 1:12). Christ is our Lord and Master; we glorify Him by learning more of Him and willingly submitting to His Word and example. *"The disciple is not above his Master: but every one that is perfect shall be as his Master"* (Luke 6:40; KJV). He is the perfect Master (Teacher) and we should endeavor to be His perfect servants.

Paul instructs Timothy as to what is necessary for Christians to adequately display the name of Christ: *"Let everyone who names the name of Christ depart from iniquity"* (2 Tim. 2:19). Children imitate famous musicians by lip-syncing their songs on the radio, but believers cannot pretend to be holy; their conduct will either honor a sin-hating Savior or endorse a Savior-hating system of sin. To declare the name of Christ is a high honor, but to associate with His name is the highest call to honor Him. There is only one way to become a Christian – to trust in the Lord Jesus Christ for salvation alone and be born again (John 1:12-13, 3:3). Spiritual birth implants the eternal life of Christ within the believer – this is the life God wants us to live out daily. So, to be identified as "a Christian" is one and the same as acknowledging Christ's call to live as He did, that is, to be like the Master in all things! May we live worthy of Christ's example and calling for our lives.

August 7 – As Sorrowful, Yet Always Rejoicing
(2 Corinthians 6)

Paul spoke of incredible difficulties he faced in serving the Lord, but then concluded, *"As sorrowful, yet always rejoicing"* (2 Cor. 6:10). The Lord had delivered him from many life-threatening circumstances (2 Cor. 11:23-28). He also told the Corinthians that though it had cost him much to labor among them, he had maintained a glad state of mind. Paul could have complained, but instead he chose to rejoice in laboring to bring the Corinthians to maturity. The Greek word *chairo* rendered "rejoicing" in the above verse may refer to an act of gladness, or rejoicing, or joy as in the following verses:

*And I will **very gladly** spend and be spent for your souls; though the more abundantly I love you, the less I am loved* (2 Cor. 12:15).

*For **we are glad** when we are weak and you are strong. And this also we pray, that you may be made complete* (2 Cor. 13:9).

Even during ominous circumstances, the Lord told His disciples to rejoice in their afflictions and that their reward was waiting for them:

Blessed are you when men hate you, and when they exclude you, and revile you, and cast out your name as evil, for the Son of Man's sake. Rejoice in that day and leap for joy! For indeed your reward is great in heaven, for in like manner their fathers did to the prophets (Luke 6:22-23).

Against incredible challenges, Nehemiah led his countrymen to rebuild the entire wall around Jerusalem in only fifty-two days. A short time later the Jewish nation was under deep remorse after Ezra confronted their sins. Nehemiah then encouraged the people, *"Do not sorrow, for the joy of the Lord is your strength"* (Neh. 8:10). Similarly, David wrote: *"Delight yourself also in the Lord, and He shall give you the desires of your heart"* (Ps. 37:4). The Lord Jesus, Paul, Nehemiah, and David all have the same message: When insurmountable problems weigh your soul down, choose to rejoice in the Lord. Rejoicing during arduous times demonstrates real faith in God because we are not trying to insert our preconceived solutions into His Sovereign purposes.

August 8 – Do Not Be Unequally Yoked
(2 Corinthians 6)

On one particular occasion during Christ's earthly sojourn He invited anyone in His audience that was burdened in life to come to Him (Matt. 11:28-30). The Lord said that He was gentle and lowly in heart and that anyone choosing to be yoked with Him would find rest for their souls. He closed His invitation by saying, *"For My yoke is easy and My burden is light"* (Matt. 11:30). Being yoked with Christ enables believers for service, for without Him we can do nothing pleasing to God.

Christians are chosen in Christ to receive God's goodness, but it is not because of our personal righteousness that we receive God's favor. It is because of our holy standing in Christ. Practically speaking, being yoked with Christ means that we must not walk ahead or behind Him, as this would create a tiring situation for us. Walking in step with Him (i.e., in His will) is nearly an effortless task, as He then pulls along our burdens. To be yoked with Him also means that we must be a holy people, which means having no fellowship with unrighteousness, including no close associations with children of the devil. It was on this latter point that Paul admonishes the carnal believers at Corinth:

> *Do not be unequally yoked together with unbelievers. For what fellowship has righteousness with lawlessness? And what communion has light with darkness? And what accord has Christ with Belial? Or what part has a believer with an unbeliever? And what agreement has the temple of God with idols? For you are the temple of the living God. As God has said: "I will dwell in them and walk among them. I will be their God, and they shall be My people." Therefore "Come out from among them and be separate, says the Lord"* (2 Cor. 6:14-17).

The only safeguard against evil is to remain near the Lord, for *"evil company corrupts good habits"* (1 Cor. 15:33). The devil often lures God's people into unnatural unions with his own children through religious causes and social gatherings. These things are valued by churchianity, but not by the Lord, if He cannot attend also. Satan uses benevolent objects and religious grounds to influence believers to leave a true work of God for what is not. The busy doings of religion are a poor substitute for Spirit-led ministry that counts for eternity!

229

August 9 – Godly Sorrow
(2 Corinthians 7)

Paul labored in the letter known as 1 Corinthians to put the local assembly into godly order. He confronted their personal and corporate behaviors, carnal mindsets, and bad doctrine. The apostle succeeded in making them *"sorry in a godly manner"* (2 Cor. 7:9). After hearing that they had responded well to his rebuke, Paul wrote them again to encourage them: *"For godly sorrow produces repentance leading to salvation, not to be regretted; but the sorrow of the world produces death. ...you sorrowed in a godly manner"* (2 Cor. 7:10-11).

This pattern of cleansing is needful in the lives of all believers; we must both recognize and then repudiate the uncleanness of the flesh. Often we are grieved in our conscience after doing or saying something without understanding the reason why. Thankfully, through continued exposure to God's Word, seeking the Lord's wisdom in prayer (Jas. 1:5), and the conviction of the Holy Spirit, believers are enabled to better understand what God disapproves of and then to reject it.

The next phase of cleansing is to confess and repent of known failures which have been exposed by God's Word and morally understood (Jas. 1:21-23). As Paul told the Corinthians, true repentance is repentance that should not be repented of. It is more than telling God, "I know this is wrong, I am sorry – please forgive me." True repentance includes an aspiration to, by the grace of God, not repeat the same sin.

As soon as one is conscious of sin, the sin should be confessed – in so doing Christ promises to both forgive and to cleanse the guilty conscience: *"If we confess our sins, He is faithful and just to forgive us our sins, and to cleanse us from all unrighteousness"* (1 Jn. 1:9). Of course, God desires His children not to sin (1 Jn. 2:1) so that He can walk together with them in the light of divine truth (1 Jn. 1:6-7). But when we do sin (venture into darkness), there is an immediate solution – His cleansing permits us to walk with Him again in the light. This permits the Christian life to be one of ongoing separation from the world while still permitting evangelical connections in the world.

Today believers can rejoice that Christ has delivered them not only from consequences of their sins, but also from sin's present claims and influences. Christ's purification permits heaven-bound pilgrims to journey through our sin-defiled world as heavenly-minded strangers.

August 10 – Beware of False Prophets
(2 Corinthians 11)

Paul warned the Corinthians that Satan often transforms himself into an angel of light and his servants into ministers of righteousness because he knows it is easier to deceive God's people in their work than it is to dissuade them from their purpose:

For such are false apostles, deceitful workers, transforming themselves into apostles of Christ. And no wonder! For Satan himself transforms himself into an angel of light. Therefore it is no great thing if his ministers also transform themselves into ministers of righteousness, whose end will be according to their works (2 Cor. 11:13-15).

False prophets plagued Israel throughout the nation's history, and they still infest Christendom today, surmises H. A. Ironside:

In every age when God has been dealing with His professed people because of their sins and apostasy, there have been such false prophets who have sought to lull the offenders to sleep in a false confidence, assuring them that all is well and there need be no fear of judgment falling upon them. How these prophets abound in Christendom today! With the Judge standing at the door, they continue to cry, "Peace, peace, when there is no peace!"[32]

This problem is compounded by the fact that God's prophets always seemed to be greatly outnumbered by their counterparts. The ministries of Elijah (1 Kings 18), Micaiah (1 Kings 22), and Jeremiah (Jer. 20) serve as good examples. Time and again, God's prophets have suffered greatly for their faithfulness to be a voice for God among a throng of dissident and hostile people. Because the Jews have throughout their history looked for signs to substantiate their faith, they have invariably fallen into the trap of ignoring God's immutable Word. False prophets can powerfully represent a virtual reality of the truth. Sadly, false brethren and self-ordained prophets, with their overbearing, self-promoting evil practices, continue to plague God's people today.

Discernment is not a matter of simply telling the difference between right and wrong; rather it is telling the difference between right and almost right.

— C. H. Spurgeon

August 11 – My Grace Is Sufficient for You
(2 Corinthians 12)

The Lord delights to demonstrate His power through the weakness of His people (1 Cor. 1:26-31). When men say "not possible," God often does the impossible that He might be known. Human weakness provides a wonderful opportunity for God to add honor to His own name. Great things occur from God's point of view when small people faithfully do seemingly small things for God. Whether it is a teenager taking down a giant with a stone and sling or a lad's lunch multiplied to feed thousands of hungry people, God specializes in using what is weak and unfitting to do the incredible. The Lord Jesus reminded Paul of this truth after he had prayed three times to have the thorn in his flesh removed: *"My grace is sufficient for you, for My strength is made perfect in weakness"* (2 Cor. 12:9). Paul's response is praiseworthy:

> *Therefore most gladly I will rather boast in my infirmities, that the power of Christ may rest upon me. Therefore I take pleasure in infirmities, in reproaches, in needs, in persecutions, in distresses, for Christ's sake. For when I am weak, then I am strong* (2 Cor. 12:9-10).

Paul would gladly remain weak so that the power of Christ would be more obvious in him. In this sense, the day of small things is but the beginning of greater things where God is concerned. When little men think of themselves as small, an infinite God goes big!

The Lord Jesus conveyed this idea in His *Sermon on the Mount*: *"Blessed are the poor in spirit, for theirs is the kingdom of heaven. Blessed are those who mourn, for they shall be comforted. Blessed are the meek, for they shall inherit the earth"* (Matt. 5:3-5). The Lord does not need our wealth or religious feats; He simply wants our hearts soft, pliable, and beating for Him. Once Paul understood why he must continue suffering with his infirmity, he was pleased to do so. The Lord delights to demonstrate His power through the weakness of His people, and it liberates our minds to realize that this is always best for us because it honors Him. If you do not think you have much to offer the Lord, you are just the kind of person He is looking for to honor Himself.

August 12 – Live by the Law, Die by the Law
(Galatians 3)

The Law was a conditional covenant between God and the Jews. God revealed a special set of commandments for the Jews to follow in order to please Him; if they obeyed it, they would be justified in His sight and be blessed by Him. While in Egypt, the Israelites had been redeemed by the blood of the Passover Lamb because they exercised faith and obeyed God's Word. But afterwards God taught them through His Law that no one could earn a righteous standing before Him, because no one could keep the Law; hence, the Law condemned them:

> *For as many as are of the works of the law are under the curse; for it is written, "Cursed is everyone who does not continue in all things which are written in the book of the law, to do them." But that no one is justified by the law in the sight of God is evident, for "the just shall live by faith." Yet the law is not of faith, but "the man who does them shall live by them." Christ has redeemed us from the curse of the law, having become a curse for us (for it is written, "Cursed is everyone who hangs on a tree")* (Gal. 3:10-13).

Undoubtedly, the Jews at Sinai and at various seasons afterwards sincerely wanted to obey all that God had commanded them in His Law, but time would show their utter failure to do so. In the following centuries, Jewish religious leaders added their *Oral Laws* to God's Law, creating an even more cumbersome system of "doings" in an attempt to cleanse their guilty consciences through doing good works. Consequently, all such efforts to justify oneself eventually lead to one outcome – some form of idolatry (i.e. esteeming something or someone more reliable than God for salvation). Jehovah could not tolerate this grievous sin and therefore punished His covenant people by scattering them among the nations, where they are to this day.

Today, the Jewish nation is still held in the bondage of legalism. The Jewish rabbis do not teach that blood sacrifices are necessary to atone for sin, but that repentance, good deeds, and prayer have atoning value and thus replace the animal sacrifices demanded by Scripture. But these sacrifices were pictures of the future, once-for-all blood sacrifice of Christ, which provided complete propitiation for man's sin. Their choice is to live by the Law and die by the Law or to choose Christ, who died to fulfill the Law that they might live in Him.

233

August 13 – The Ongoing Battle Will End
(Galatians 5)

Every earth-bound believer is presently engaged in an ongoing battle that rages within our members. Each of us naturally inherited through our parents a nature from Adam that opposes the things of God. Although our Old Man, who we were in Adam, positionally died at Calvary, we still have his carnal wherewithal within. Thankfully, the new nature that believers received at regeneration cannot sin (1 Jn. 3:9). Paul tells us that this nature continues to war against our flesh nature within: *"For the flesh lusts against the Spirit, and the Spirit against the flesh; and these are contrary to one another, so that you do not do the things that you wish"* (Gal. 5:17). There is nothing in the old nature that can please God (Rom. 8:8) – only when our vessels are under God's control do we have the capacity to please Him.

This is not to say that the unregenerate cannot do good things, such as obeying God's design for marriage, instead of continuing in fornication. Yet, the motives of the flesh ruin what outwardly appears as a good deed to us. For example, if a young man decided to help a little old lady across the street, we might think that to be a good deed. But what if, while escorting the elderly woman across the street, the young man is thinking, "I hope someone notices me serving this old lady," or, "I hope she will tip me after I do this for her." The carnal essence of our flesh nature taints everything we do, which makes what we do unfit for the Lord's praise. Since only God can love unselfishly, we need His Spirit in us to do those things which perfectly please Him.

The Holy Spirit enables believers to lay hold of our spiritual possessions in Christ while we travel along the unencumbered path of righteousness, but our flesh will always be blocking the way of such a journey. Hence, it must be fought, beaten, and driven out of the way again and again. There are no other paths leading to spiritual blessings in Christ – the enemy must be engaged and defeated in His strength.

This battle will continue on the personal level until each believer experiences death or glorification. In heaven we will never have to suffer another stinking thought, carnal appetite, ungodly word, or selfish deed. The battle will continue on all fronts until God removes all evil from His presence in a future day, but in Christ and through the Holy Spirit we can be more than conquerors today (Rom. 8:37)!

234

August 14 – Bear One Another's Burdens
(Galatians 6)

Moses reminded his countrymen that *"the poor will never cease from the land; therefore I command you, saying, 'You shall open your hand wide to your brother, to your poor and your needy, in your land'"* (Deut. 15:11). Even under the stringent particulars of the Law, God desired for His covenant people to assist one another in economic hardships, rather than take advantage of each other. Moses promised that such generosity would be reimbursed by the Lord (Deut. 15:10).

Centuries later, Solomon would affirm the same promise: *"He who has pity on the poor lends to the Lord, and He will pay back what he has given"* (Prov. 19:17), and, *"He who gives to the poor will not lack, but he who hides his eyes will have many curses"* (Prov. 28:27). The Lord always provides resources for His children to worship Him and to give to others – that is, if we have willing hearts to honor Him with what He has graciously given us.

Although Deuteronomy 15:11 does not legally apply to Christians today, it does highlight what God deems appropriate conduct for His people throughout all ages, that is, to rally around and help each other during times of distress: *"Bear one another's burdens, and so fulfill the law of Christ"* (Gal. 6:2). The Greek word rendered "bear" means "to carry" and the word translated "burdens" implies a crushing load. There are times in life when we may be unexpectedly buried by a crushing load; it is at those times believers are to support each other. Paul speaks of a different load (a soldier's backpack) in Galatians 6:5. This represents the daily tasks each soldier of the cross is to expected to accomplish for the Lord; no one is to take that assigned burden from us.

The early Church cared for their poor widows (Acts 6:1; 1 Tim. 5:3-5). These Christians did not value their possessions (of which they were merely God's stewards) more than each other (Acts 4:32). As a result of this loving unselfishness, all of the Lord's people were wonderfully sustained: *"nor was there anyone among them who lacked"* (Acts 4:34). They experienced exactly what both Moses and Solomon promised and laid up treasures in heaven in the process (Matt. 19:21). God forbid that we, who have received so much goodness in Christ, should *"oppress one another"* by withholding back our temporal possessions from our brethren in need (Lev. 25:14, 17).

August 15 – Circumcision Avails Nothing
(Galatians 6)

During the dispensation of the Law, the Jews were bound to circumcise their male infants eight days after birth. God had given Abraham and his posterity circumcision as a reminder of His covenant (Gen. 17). A dispensation is an economy of truth that God reveals to man, holds him accountable to, and then punishes him for failing to obey it (1 Cor. 9:17; Eph. 3:2; Col. 1:25). A dispensation is not a period of time, for often God's economies of truth overlap, but certainly each dispensation has its working in time.

The new stewardship of truth given to the Jews at Sinai by Moses was for them only; it was not given to the Gentiles (Acts 15:10). In the dispensation of the Church, Paul referred to this fact to exhort the Gentile believers in Galatia not to give ear to the Judaizers: *"For in Christ Jesus neither circumcision nor uncircumcision avails anything, but a new creation, and as many as walk according to this rule, peace and mercy be upon them"* (Gal. 6:15-16). These legalists were teaching that salvation was by grace through Christ, but that a believer had to continue to keep the Law to maintain his or her salvation. As the Galatians had never been under the Law, it was irrational for the Judaizers to place them under its bondage now, especially since the Law only condemned as no one could keep it.

Hebrews contains the Jewish complement of this message: they were no longer under the Law; the entire system had been replaced by what it anticipated in Christ. The Law was not dead, for it still declares the righteousness of God, but the Jews were dead to it, in that they had been liberated by Christ from its condemning outcome (Rom. 7:4-6). Thus, the Church Age marks the end to the dispensation of the Law. The purpose of the Law was, and still is, to show sin (Rom. 3:20) and to point the sinner to the solution – God's grace through Christ: *"For the law was given through Moses, but grace and truth came through Jesus Christ"* (John 1:17).

The Lord's first parable of the new patch on an old wine skin was to inform His audience that no religious system can mingle the Law with grace. Each has its distinct purpose, the former to show sin and the latter to be God's means of extending salvation to those who desire it.

236

August 16 – In Heavenly Places
(Ephesians 1)

The kingdom gospel message the Lord Jesus and His disciples preached throughout Israel offered a literal, political, earthly kingdom to the Jewish nation. It was not received at that time because they rejected the spiritual ramifications necessary to enter it, namely, repentance and spiritual revival in Christ. Instead, Israel crucified their Messiah, God's Lamb, according to God's providential plan (1 Pet. 1:19-20). The kingdom offer is consistent with what the Jews both longed for and fought for throughout much of the Old Testament – their land inheritance promised to Abraham in Genesis 15. God's promises to Israel have an earthly focus, but Christ's promises to the Church are for a heavenly inheritance. Paul writes:

Blessed be the God and Father of our Lord Jesus Christ, who has blessed us with every spiritual blessing in the heavenly places in Christ (Eph. 1:3).

For our citizenship is in heaven, from which we also eagerly wait for the Savior, the Lord Jesus Christ, who will transform our lowly body that it may be conformed to His glorious body. (Phil 3:20-21).

In the Church Age, believers do not labor for a *place* of rest as Israel did and still does; our rest and inheritance are in a *Person* – Christ in heavenly places. This is why Paul could pray for fellow believers, *"The Lord of peace Himself give you peace in every way"* (2 Thess. 3:16) and also share his life's aspiration with them:

Not that I have already attained, or am already perfected; but I press on, that I may lay hold of that for which Christ Jesus has also laid hold of me. Brethren, I do not count myself to have apprehended; but one thing I do, forgetting those things which are behind and reaching forward to those things which are ahead, I press toward the goal for the prize of the upward call of God in Christ Jesus (Phil. 3:12-14).

Christ is the believer's inheritance and resting place. The practical blessing of those present, heavenly possessions granted the believer in Christ will be practically experienced through faith and obedience as one engages in active conquest now through His resurrection power.

237

August 17 – "To the Praise of His Glory"
(Ephesians 1)

After Paul speaks of the wonderful blessings those who have been redeemed by Christ have in Him, Paul highlights why the Lord still has His Church in the world instead of with Him in heaven: *"that we who first trusted in Christ **should be to the praise of His glory** ... having believed, you were sealed with the Holy Spirit of promise, who is the guarantee of our inheritance until the redemption of the purchased possession, **to the praise of His glory"** (Eph. 1:11-14).

The main reason that the Lord still has His Church on earth is to make Him look good – to be *"the praise of His glory."* Through our spiritual sanctification the Lord gets more glory from us as we become more like Him (Rom. 8:29). Believers should sin less with spiritual maturity (Rom. 6:1), though sinless perfection will not be achieved until we experience glorification at His coming (1 Jn. 3:2-3). Believers are marked by righteous living (i.e., they do not practice sin; 1 Jn. 3:8-9); however, the unregenerate habitually practice sin without remorse – the fallen nature within them rules their behavior (1 Jn. 3:10).

The prophet Isaiah informed his countrymen of God's future plans to use Babylon to chasten them for their idolatry so that they would know that He was the true God. Jehovah wanted to show them that no idol could foreknow or accomplish such things and that He would not tolerate them giving His glory to their images: *"For My own sake, for My own sake, I will do it; for how should My name be profaned? And **I will not give My glory to another"** (Isa. 48:1). The prophet then reveals God's solution for how His covenant people could express His glory:

> *"**Come near to Me**, hear this: I have not spoken in secret from the beginning; from the time that it was, I was there. And now the Lord God* [God the Father] *and His Spirit* [the Holy Spirit] *have sent Me* [God the Son]." *Thus says the Lord, your Redeemer, the Holy One of Israel:* "I am the Lord your God, who teaches you to profit, who leads you by the way you should go" (Isa. 48:16-17).

Nearness to Christ enables us to experience Him and permits us to express His glory. Seeing God's dealings with the Jew and His desire to honor His own name through them should prompt all believers today to consider what we do and say, and to stay near to the Lord Jesus.

August 18 – Sealed and Guaranteed
(Ephesians 1)

There are a number of one-time acts that the Holy Spirit does at a believer's conversion. Spiritual baptism, indwelling, anointing, cleansing, regeneration, and the bestowing of spiritual gifts are some, to name a few. Also, the Holy Spirit seals and secures the new believer by taking up permanent residency within him or her. The Holy Spirit, Himself, is God's guarantee that He will finish what He has started. In a coming day, the Lord Jesus will return to claim His purchased possession that was previously redeemed by His blood. Paul writes:

In Him you also trusted, after you heard the word of truth, the gospel of your salvation; in whom also, having believed, **you were sealed with the Holy Spirit** *of promise,* **who is the guarantee** *of our inheritance until the redemption of the purchased possession, to the praise of His glory* (Eph. 1:13-14).

Even as the testimony of Christ was confirmed in you, so that you come short in no gift, eagerly waiting for the revelation of our Lord Jesus Christ, **who will also confirm you to the end,** *that you may be blameless in the day of our Lord Jesus Christ. God is faithful, by whom you were called into the fellowship of His Son, Jesus Christ our Lord* (1 Cor. 1:6-9).

Similarly, Levitical priests were sealed by God; that is, they would be protected by Him from outside harm while fulfilling their office. Numbers 16 records a revolt against Moses, God's chosen leader of the nation, and Aaron, God's chosen high priest for the nation. Korah, Dathan, Abiram, and others sought to intrude into the priesthood – it cost them their lives. In the believer's case, God does not promise immunity from physical harm, but the Christian's eternal security is indeed assured. The Holy Spirit Himself is the seal of God (Eph. 1:13).

This eternal seal is likened to the wax seal placed on a letter or scroll in ancient times. Such a seal protected and secured the letter from being opened, and it also indicated who the originator and owner of the letter was. In some cases, seals were used to indicate approval of a contract or an agreement. Through the sealing ministry of the Holy Spirit the believer is both approved of and secured in Christ forever!

239

August 19 – Christ the Head of the Church
(Ephesians 1)

The Lord Jesus Christ is the head of the Church and the center of her Body-life (Eph. 1:22-23; Col. 1:18; Acts 20:7). This can be biblically expressed by breaking bread each week in remembrance of Christ. In so doing, believers declare to all who observe that Christ is the gathering focus of the Church (Luke 22:19; Acts 2:42, 20:7). God the Father is honored when the Church worships His Son (John 5:22-23). The Church is to worship God, and to adore Christ as its Head.

Sadly, Christ's headship can be also distorted by unbiblical behaviors such as having elected church officials, and maintaining denominations and centralized headquarters. Rather, under Christ's authority as Head, believers are to gather in autonomous groups according to His order for His Body (1 Cor. 14:23, 33).

Local churches are to be interdependent on each other, but no group of believers has the authority to control any other local church. This is demonstrated by the outcome of the Jerusalem Counsel in Acts 15. The apostles and elders convened this meeting to discuss whether or not Gentile believers should be circumcised. Though a doctrinal decision was affirmed at this meeting, counsel, not a mandate, was provided for the various Gentile churches to consider. The apostles and elders described how the Gentiles should behave among Jewish believers, but no attempt was made to enforce the ruling. Letters were sent out to various churches, who then considered the ruling and its implications.

Unfortunately, today much of the Church has compartmentalized into denominational organizations which govern a collective of churches. The ideological principles as to why these organizations were initially formed define what, or who, is important to them. Some identify themselves by a particular doctrine (e.g., the Baptists), or to a form of church government (e.g., the Presbyterians), or to evangelical methods (e.g., the Methodists), or a person (e.g., Lutherans). Others gather under the focus of spiritual gifts, social cliques, schooling preferences and family ties. Scripture does uphold the doctrines of believer's baptism, spiritual gifts, plural church oversight, and differing evangelical methods, but we do not gather to these things; we gather in the name of Christ. To come together for any other reason is to ignore our Head and to supplant His centrality in the meeting.

August 20 – The Head Is Coming for His Church
(Ephesians 1)

Paul tells us that not only do all believers compose the Body of Christ, but that He, as the Head of that Body, must return physically to the Body so that *"fullness of Him who fills all in all"* can be enjoyed:

What is the exceeding greatness of His power toward us who believe, according to the working of His mighty power which He worked in Christ when He raised Him from the dead and seated Him at His right hand in the heavenly places, far above all principality and power and might and dominion, and every name that is named, not only in this age but also in that which is to come. And He put all things under His feet, and gave Him to be head over all things to the church, which is His body, the fullness of Him who fills all in all (Eph. 1:19-23).

Relationally speaking, Christ is not complete without His bride, so believers are to eagerly long for all that Christ accomplished at Calvary to come to fruition in God's timing. The Lord Jesus Himself waits with blissful anticipation to be with His glorious bride and to establish His eternal kingdom (Isa. 53:11). Until summoned home by the call of the archangel and the trump of God, may each believer count on the faithfulness of God to enter into His rest. This serenity of mind is enjoyed only through ongoing dependence and ceaseless vigilance, for the adversary remains active to distract us from fully resting in Christ.

The challenge, then, in any fearful disaster or sorrowful event, is to maintain an unruffled mind by determining to rest in Christ in heavenly places (Eph. 2:6). That is where all our spiritual resources are presently found (Eph. 1:3). All beneficial spiritual exercise then begins with resting in Christ. We are not to resort to carnal weapons to resolve our difficulties, nor to become depressed because our expectations are not met. We understand that whatever situation we face, He also faces and He is in full control. With our final rest still before us, let us take full advantage of the divine rest available for us today in the Lord Jesus.

Through Him, we can lay hold of the settled mind in unsettling times. There is but one hiding place for the threatened, one solace for the brokenhearted, and one salve for the wounded soul – the Lord Jesus Christ. Whatever you go through – He also goes through with you. Believer, stay near to Him and remember that He is coming for you!

August 21 – The Unity of All Believers
(Ephesians 4)

While in prayer, the Lord Jesus alluded to the truth of Body unity in John 17:21-23. Paul further explains this incredible spiritual oneness: *"For by one Spirit we were all baptized into one body – whether Jews or Greeks, whether slaves or free – and have all been made to drink into one Spirit. For in fact the body is not one member but many"* (1 Cor. 12:13-14). *"Endeavoring to keep the unity of the Spirit in the bond of peace. There is one body and one Spirit"* (Eph. 4:3-4).

The Lord affirmed the oneness and equal-standing of all believers when He told His disciples, *"But you, do not be called 'Rabbi'; for one is your Teacher, the Christ, and you are all brethren"* (Matt. 23:8). Christians are identified by biblical names such as Christians, believers, saints, and brethren. No denominations, cliques, or separate followings should be found in the Body of Christ. Paul asked the Corinthians, who were bestowing honor to various preachers instead of following Christ, *"Is Christ divided?"* (1 Cor. 1:13). The act of identifying with anyone or any organization instead of Christ is completely unbiblical. Harry A. Ironside's response to the question to what denomination he belonged stresses this point. He answered, "I belong to the same denomination that David did," and then quoted Psalm 119:63, *"I am a companion of all them that fear Thee and of them that keep Thy precepts."*[33]

In the practical sense, Christian fellowship (i.e. what we share together in the commonwealth of Christ) is dependent on how much we determine we have in common with other believers. While it is true that we will not be able to have the same degree of fellowship with all believers, we should strive to walk as far as we can with all those who have been redeemed by the precious blood of Christ. So often believers cast others aside because of some difference in thinking, though they hold much more in common than what they disagree about – this wrong mindset hinders the fellowship Christ desires for the members of His body to enjoy. The fact of the matter is that those in the Church are not going to agree on everything on this side of glory (Eph. 4:13). Once in God's presence, we will find out that none of us had it all right. Coming into perfect unity with all Christians will be one of the purest blessings of heaven. Until then, let us strive to walk as far as we can with all believers with the limitation being sound morality and doctrine.

August 22 – Mentoring as Christ Did
(Ephesians 4)

The Lord Jesus demonstrated by the care for His own disciples that mentoring others for the kingdom is not accomplished through training programs. One does not become, for example, an evangelist by completing an accredited program resembling that of secular professions. Evangelism is a gift, not a profession. At regeneration, each believer receives a spiritual gift (or gifts) from the Holy Spirit for the purpose of building up the Church (1 Cor. 12:4, 11). Moreover, every believer has been called by God to perform a specific function within the Church. A believer's effectiveness in this service will depend on his or her spiritual maturity and the development and use of his or her spiritual gift(s).

There are two main objectives in preparing the next generation to serve Christ: training in righteousness (2 Tim. 3:16-17) and equipping for ministry (Eph. 4:12-13). The first passage emphasizes *"instruction in righteousness, that the man of God may be complete, thoroughly equipped for every good work* (2 Tim. 3:16-17). The Greek work translated "instruction" in 2 Timothy 3:16 is *paideia*, which means "education or training; disciplinary correction." Christians have the responsibility of training those who are younger in the Lord in the way of righteousness as parents rear their children (Prov. 22:6). The second verse focuses on *"the equipping of the saints for the work of ministry, for the edifying of the body of Christ"* (Eph. 4:11-12). The Greek word translated "equipping" in Ephesians 4:12 is the noun *oikodome*, which means "building" or "edifying." Paul explains that all Christians are called to edify in love other members of the Body (Eph. 4:15-16).

These two passages show us the inseparable link between godly character and God-honoring service. Ministry which does not reflect the character of Christ does more harm than good. This is why the work of mentoring must focus on both character development and preparation for ministry, which is accomplished through an interactive and personal relationship between mentor and mentee. The Lord Jesus made the character of His Father known to everyone He came in contact with through His life and His works. Likewise, the passion of every believer should be that Christ might be manifest to the world by our joyful disposition, steadfast morality, and genuine care for others.

August 23 – The Effective Working of Every Part
(Ephesians 4)

All believers should engage in Spirit-led worship and service (Eph. 5:18-20). All believers are equipped with spiritual gifts to serve and edify the body of Christ (1 Cor. 12:4-7). Only when all believers use their spiritual gifts with the full measure of faith that God gives will the Church reach its full function to serve Christ (Rom. 12:3 and 1 Pet. 4:10). Paul explained this truth to the Church at Ephesus:

> *Speaking the truth in love, may grow up in all things into Him who is the head – Christ – from whom the whole body, joined and knit together by what every joint supplies, according to the effective working by which every part does its share, causes growth of the body for the edifying of itself in love* (Eph. 4:15-16).

The Lord Jesus gave some individuals, such as evangelists and teachers, as gifts to the Church for a particular reason: *"for the equipping of the saints for the work of ministry, for the edifying of the body of Christ"* (Eph. 4:12). Every believer in the body of Christ has a work of ministry, the benefit of which will bless the entire body. As believers rightly use their spiritual gifts, they equip others in the body to do ministry also, which then passes the original blessing along to other believers in order to further edify the body.

Visualize for a moment several children standing perfectly still in a wading pool while another child jumps into the pool. The resultant wave glides across the surface of the water and eventually bounces off every child in the pool. Each time the wave comes in contact with a child, it is also reflected back across the pool; eventually it also makes contact with every other child in the pool, and so on. This wave phenomenon illustrates how the initial edification of one member in the body equips other members to minister to the body; the blessing then continues to spread throughout the Church. This enables individuals to reach their full potential in Christ and to fulfill God's sovereign purpose for their lives. Those older in the Lord can help younger believers to recognize, to exercise, and to develop their spiritual gift(s) to achieve this goal. The church meetings should not be dominated by the most-gifted saints, but rather they should be giving opportunity and help to those who need to develop their work of ministry in the Body.

August 24 – Put On Christ
(Ephesians 4)

The apostle challenges the believers at Ephesus to exhibit the behavior of Christ in all their actions. They had learned about the Lord and also knew what He expected; therefore, through the power of the Holy Spirit they were to imitate Christ in their speech and deeds:

> *But you have not so learned Christ, if indeed you have heard Him and have been taught by Him, as the truth is in Jesus: that you put off, concerning your former conduct, the old man which grows corrupt according to the deceitful lusts, and be renewed in the spirit of your mind, and that you put on the new man which was created according to God, in true righteousness and holiness. Therefore, putting away lying, "Let each one of you speak truth with his neighbor," for we are members of one another* (Eph. 4:20-25).

All that believers do in this world is to project an accurate display of Christ's character. This enables the lost to see what Christ is truly like so that they will want Him too. The Holy Spirit enables believers to declare the true righteousness and holiness of Christ. Amazing!

This wonderful priestly ministry means that there are conducts believers cannot engage in. Paul mentions lying. Lying to and deceiving others is an affront to the truth, and thus to the God of truth (Ps. 31:5). Solomon reminds his son that there are seven things God hates: a proud look, a lying tongue, murder, devising wicked schemes, a swift inclination to do mischief, a false witness, and those who sow discord among God's people (Prov. 6:16-19).

Lying is never permissible for the child of God (Eph. 4:25). Rather, believers are to speak the truth in love, or be silent and entrust the consequences of either of these honorable responses to the Lord (Eph. 4:15). When things go wrong, we should not go wrong with them! The belt of truth is spiritual armor that should be worn by believers at all times (Eph. 6:14). The moment that we start to flavor or spin the truth, to deceive others or make ourselves look better than we are, we cease to accurately represent the Lord. While in the flesh, we can do nothing to please the Lord, which means no good can come from our behavior: *"So then, those who are in the flesh cannot please God"* (Rom. 8:8).

August 25 – Walking With God
(Ephesians 4 -5)

The word "walk" is used in a metaphorical way throughout the Bible to speak of a certain course of life or one's conduct in life – how we live our lives. Ephesians chapters 4 and 5 contain the most densely populated occurrences of the word "walk" in the New Testament. Ponder Paul's medley of exhortations concerning the walk of the believer. We are to walk worthy of our calling in Christ (Eph. 4:1), in love, as Christ did (Eph. 5:2), as children of light (Eph. 5:8), and circumspectly and wise (Eph. 5:15). We are not to walk the way the Gentiles do in the vanity of their minds, or as fools (Eph. 5:15), or the way we formerly did in darkness (Eph. 5:8). Thankfully, we have God's Word to tell us exactly what conduct He expects from us. When we yield to the Word of God and the Spirit of God, we walk as God desires us to: *"Walk in the Spirit, and you shall not fulfill the lust of the flesh"* (Gal. 5:16-17).

In order to walk with the Lord, we must be in agreement with Him on the matter of sin. For, *"can two walk together except they be agreed?"* (Amos 3:3). We read in 1 John 1:5-7 that walking with God requires walking in the light of divine truth. A willingness to walk in the truth brings happy fellowship with God and with other believers doing the same. We must have light to walk safely. When we choose to walk in the dark, we are inviting injury and the chastening hand of God.

As His children, we receive our Father's blessing and care while walking in the light with Him. But He also expresses His love towards His children through parental reproof when we wander from the path of righteousness. The apostles warn us: *"Be you therefore followers of God, as dear children"* (Eph. 5:1); *"as obedient children, not fashioning yourselves according to the former lusts in your ignorance"* (1 Pet. 1:14); *"for whom the Lord loves He chastens"* (Heb. 12:6). Solomon wrote that *"a wise son makes a father glad"* (Prov. 15:20). The Lord Jesus, as God's divine Son, always made His Father glad. The Lord said, *"the Son can do nothing of Himself, but what He sees the Father do; for whatever He does, the Son also does in like manner"* (John 5:19). Christ is our perfect example to follow if we want to walk with God and make Him glad too. Christ promised, *"He who follows Me shall not walk in darkness, but have the light of life"* (John 8:12).

August 26 – The Will of God (Part 1)
(Ephesians 5)

"The will of God" and the related phrases "the Lord's will," "the Lord will," and "Your will" occur thirty-four times in the New Testament. Nineteen times the sovereign plan of God to accomplish a distinct purpose is in view. There are four references to the will of God being done or that it shall be done, and seven references to believers doing God's will. Scripture further declares that the expressed will of God should be understood, and three times it is specifically declared for all believers to know.

The term relates to a sovereign God accomplishing His purposes in time, whether it be through a specific event, or in conforming the behavior and attitudes of believers to be like that of His Son. Several times in Scripture "the will of God" refers to the overall holy behavior that all believers should exhibit. For those aspects of God's will which are not fully revealed, the believer learns to trust God's guiding hand. In this way, God works on our attitudes and motives, and refines the quality of our faith. As an example, God is *"long-suffering towards us, not willing that any should perish"* (2 Pet. 3:9). How can God desire something, but yet not force it to happen? It is a mysterious unfolding of His foreknowledge and predestined blessings in Christ which are guaranteed to benefit those who, in time, repent and receive His Word. Thankfully, we don't have to completely understand the mind of God to obtain His blessing; God simply wants us to trust Him for what cannot be fully understood and obey what He has revealed to us. For those aspects of God's will which are clearly revealed, the believer learns to yield to the Lord – our conduct is brought into alignment with His will. This pleases God and promotes Christ-likeness, which will be the ultimate outcome of our salvation (Rom. 8:29).

Paul instructs believers to *"be not unwise, but understanding what the will of the Lord is"* (Eph. 5:17) in order to *"prove what is that good, and acceptable, and perfect, will of God"* (Rom. 12:2). Consequently, Paul exhorted the believers at Colosse, *"stand perfect and complete in all the will of God"* (Col. 4:12). Knowing, yielding to, and demonstrating the will of God is the goal of the Christian life. In summary, we are *to learn* the revealed will of God (Ps. 143:10) and *to delight* in doing it (Ps. 40:8).

August 27 – The Will of God (Part 2)
(Ephesians 5)

We have a superb example in the Lord Jesus of both knowing and doing the will of God: *"Then I said, 'Behold, I have come – In the volume of the book it is written of Me – to do Your will, O God'"* (Heb. 10:7). But following the Lord's example of doing God's will is not easy; rather, it is impossible without relying on God's grace. Doing the will of God does not come naturally to us; in fact, our nature opposes God's will (Gal. 5:17). Any selfish motive or action to abide in the will of God will fail miserably. The only way to remain in fellowship with the Lord is to yield to His will – to do that which delights Him.

As pertaining to the revealed will of God, what does God expect of all true Christians? The following behaviors are the expressed will of God for all believers. Before reviewing the list ask yourself, "Do I want to do the will of God?" If the answer is "yes," then read on. If the answer is "no," ponder the words of the Lord Jesus: *"Why call Me, Lord, Lord, and do not the things which I say?"* (Luke 6:46). In other words, "Don't call Me Lord if you are not going to do what I say!" Though the whole of Scripture declares the will of God, the following are specific statements pertaining to the Lord's will for all Christians:

1. Serve and please the Lord instead of men (Eph. 6:6).
2. Do not be conformed to the world (Rom. 12:2).
3. By well-doing put to silence the ignorance of foolish men (1 Pet. 2:15).
4. Abstain from fornication (1 Thess. 4:3).
5. In everything give thanks (1 Thess. 5:18).
6. Suffer for well doing, rather than for evil doing (1 Pet. 3:17).
7. Do not be controlled by the lusts of the flesh (1 Pet. 4:2).

A true believer will long to know the will of God and then do the will of God. Love for the Lord Jesus Christ prompts obedience: *"If you love Me, keep My commandments"* (John 14:15). The believer is challenged to live for and invest into eternity. John wrote, *"And the world passes away, and the lust thereof: but he that doeth the will of God abides forever"* (1 Jn. 2:17). All that is of this world is going to vanish someday – only what is done for Christ has lasting value. May each of us know and yield to the revealed will of God; it is the only way to experience Christ and please God during our earthly sojourn.

August 28 – Be Filled with the Holy Spirit
(Ephesians 5)

Paul exhorts believers *"do not grieve the Holy Spirit of God"* (Eph. 4:30) and *"do not quench the Spirit"* (1 Thess. 5:19). Because the Greek verb in the latter verse is in the present tense and imperative mood, the phrase could easily be rendered, "stop quenching the Spirit." Wuest's Expanded Translation reads, "Stop stifling and suppressing the Spirit"! The Holy Spirit is likened to a flame (Isa. 4:4; Matt. 3:11; Rev. 4:5). He warms our hearts, enlightens our minds, and empowers the believer's spirit, but He can be resisted. It is the effectual working of the Holy Spirit that Paul warned against hindering or even snuffing out.

Although the Holy Spirit is always present in the believer, when the believer chooses to sin, it is as if he or she had thrown a wet blanket over His energizing capacity. When an individual trusts Christ as his or her personal Savior, the Holy Spirit responds by regenerating that person (Tit. 3:5). That new believer becomes an available vessel in the hands of Almighty God to fill and pour out of as He chooses.

As the believer submits to the known will of God, the Holy Spirit responds by filling that individual and equipping him or her with divine power for service. This can be clearly seen from the dawning days of the Church Age (Acts 1:4 with 1:12 and 2:1-4; Acts 4:23-32; Acts 6:9-10 with 7:55; Acts 9:6 with 9:17). Submission leads to Spirit filling, which results in fruitfulness. Thus, the believer is commanded to *"be filled with the Holy Spirit"* (Eph. 5:18). Paul informs us in Romans 6 that as we *know* and personally *yield* to truth we *present* our bodies to God as a living sacrifice. We enable the Holy Spirit by losing ourselves through submission and yielding ourselves to God's revealed truth.

Paul declares to Timothy that when we make the choice to flee ungodliness, we become vessels of honor available for God's sovereign use (2 Tim. 2:20). According to God's foreknowledge of both our failures and our obedience, He has preordained us to specific works to accomplish. This is why Peter exhorts Christians to *"make your calling and election sure"* (1 Pet. 1:10) and Paul instructs them to walk in the good works that God has foreordained (Eph. 2:10). We must truly lose our life to gain the vitality God desires for our spiritual life in Him (Luke 9:24). It is only by the empowerment of the Holy Spirit that our testimony can shine forth the wonderful splendor of Christ (Zech. 4:6).

August 29 – A Sweet Aroma to God
(Ephesians 5)

The work and worth of the Lord Jesus was previously typified through the Levitical offerings and sacrifices in order to point the Jews to their Messiah. The incense burnt on the Golden Altar of Incense in the tabernacle ascended upward to God and served as a reminder of God's appreciation for His Son's excellence in word and deed. Another example of this type of appreciation is revealed in unique incense that was to be set before the Lord in the Most Holy Place (Ex. 30:34-35). It was to have equal amounts of sweet spices that were to be ground together and then salt and frankincense were to be added to the powder.

Spices release their maximum fragrance when crushed in this manner. Likewise, the horrific events of Calvary only served to manifest the sweet aroma of Christ's perfections before the Father. The outward battering of His person only further revealed the inward quality of His divine character. For this reason, the Israelites were not to try to create the perfume for themselves. No one was permitted to breathe in its aroma – the incense was for God alone (Ex. 30:37-38).

Its specific ingredients and its restricted use all point to the precious nature of the perfume to God; thus, it was to have its place before Him in the Most Holy Place of the tabernacle. This incense was God's alone, for only God can fully appreciate the deep mystery of godliness pertaining to the Lord Jesus (1 Tim. 3:16). There, in the utter privacy of the tabernacle, a mere two hundred twenty-five square feet of holy ground upon a minute planet within a vast universe, God the Father would breath in that sweet reminder of His Son, the love of His heart, and would be refreshed in a way that no human can fully understand.

With this understanding we can better appreciate Paul's exhortation: *"Therefore be imitators of God as dear children. And walk in love, as Christ also has loved us and given Himself for us, an offering and a sacrifice to God for a sweet-smelling aroma"* (Eph. 5:1-2). When we walk in selfless love as Christ did, we remind God of His Son's self-sacrificing offering. Spiritually speaking, we may now offer discreetly prepared selfless sacrifices on the Altar of Incense (who is Christ Himself in glory). At such times, a pillar of sweet aroma ascends into the very nostrils of God in heaven where He breathes it in and is refreshed at the remembrance of His own Son's self-effacing sacrifice.

August 30 – Preparing a Spotless Bride
(Ephesians 5)

Paul told the believers at Corinth about their spiritual espousal with Christ: *"For I am jealous for you with godly jealousy. For I have betrothed you to one husband, that I may present you as a chaste virgin to Christ"* (2 Cor. 11:2). He also wrote the saints at Ephesus about this *"great mystery ...concerning Christ and the Church"* (Eph. 5:32).

> *Christ also loved the church and gave Himself for her, that He might sanctify and cleanse her with the washing of water by the word, that He might present her to Himself a glorious church, not having spot or wrinkle or any such thing, but that she should be holy and without blemish* (Eph. 5:25-27).

Believers should never forget who they were without Christ: condemned rebels, dead in trespasses and sin, enslaved to sin, and heading to hell (Eph. 2:1-3). Likewise, we should never think lightly of who we are in Christ: a forgiven, alive, cleansed people who the Lord Jesus wants as a spotlessly pure bride for Himself in heaven (Eph. 5:27). This means we must fully consecrate our spirit, soul, and body to Christ by abhorring evil in thought and deed (1 Thess. 5:23). What we were in Adam is dead and gone; it died with Christ at Calvary (Eph. 4:22). Being legally declared dead means we can receive a new life in Christ through rebirth. Hence, we should endeavor to live daily as He would, which means we cannot pursue our own ambitions or lusts.

> *For the love of Christ compels us, because we judge thus: that if one died for all, then all died; and He died for all, that those who live should live no longer for themselves, but for Him who died for them and rose again"* (2 Cor. 5:14-15).

From Christ's perspective, a believer commits spiritual adultery when he or she lives a carnal life in lieu of a crucified life. James affirms this same reality when he labeled worldly-minded believers as *"adulterers and adulteresses"* (Jas. 4:4). He said that such *"a double-minded man* [is] *unstable in all his ways"* (Jas. 1:8). To live with any other aspiration than to please the Lord (to be His spotless bride) will end badly for us. Let us never forget who we were and are now.

August 31 – Admonish Your Children
(Ephesians 6)

Paul instructs children to honor and obey their parents *"in the Lord"* (Eph. 6:1-3). The stipulation phrase, *"in the Lord,"* implies children are to serve their parents as unto the Lord in matters of righteousness, but not in matters of sin. There is a blessing tied with obeying this commandment: *"that it may be well with you and you may live long on the earth."* In general, those who despise authority and are rebellious usually reap the consequences of their carnality and die earlier or at least live lesser lives than if blessed by God.

After admonishing children to obey their parents, the fifth of the Ten Commandments, Paul admonishes fathers, *"Do not provoke your children to wrath, but bring them up in the training and admonition of the Lord"* (Eph. 6:4). Fathers are never to abuse their leadership role in the family, for God will hold them accountable (e.g. 1 Pet. 3:7). Whenever God gives authority, there is always accountability with Him (e.g., Heb. 13:17). Rather, fathers are to train their children for the Lord, for he desires a "godly offspring," not just reproduction (Mal. 2:15). Children do not naturally know the way they should go; they must be shown what God expects through a godly example (Prov. 22:6). Moses promised the Israelites that God would respond favorably to genuine devotion and faithful obedience. For that to happen, the Jews must faithfully teach their children His Law and also obey it (Deut. 6:20-24). If they did this, then they could have great confidence in the Lord to bless them: *"Then it will be righteousness for us, if we are careful to observe all these commandments before the Lord our God, as He has commanded us"* (Deut. 6:25).

Similarly, Christian parents must know the Lord and His Word to properly teach their children to know and love Him too. If we neglect this duty, the Lord will impose harsher measures to ensure that He is known by our children. This means that the Bible should never be neglected in the home, but rather should be the rulebook for all family matters. A Christian family is not a household of Christians, but a Christian household. It is more than Christ dwelling within the hearts of family members; it is a family that is pursuing the heart of God. If the Bible is not at the center of family life and all home affairs, that home cannot be called a true Christian home.

September 1 – Standing Strong in the Lord
(Ephesians 6)

Paul revealed several mysteries of God (previously concealed truths about Christ and His Church) in his epistle to the Ephesians. The apostle wanted them to finish well, so first he taught them to "sit" with Christ in heavenly places (Eph. 1-3), and then about the necessity to "walk" with Him in holiness (Eph. 4-5). He concludes by telling them how to "stand" strong in the Lord against spiritual wickedness (Eph. 6).

The Believer's Position in Christ. To "sit" in the heavenly places (Eph. 2:6) means to rest in our identification with Christ. Sitting means no strain on the legs (no walking or standing): We are to rest in faith without expending fleshly energy. Christ usually waits until we rest in Him before acting to rescue us from our difficulties.

The Believer's Life in the World. To "walk" has two aspects: First, it means to complete (i.e., *walk in*) what God has divinely arranged for us to do (Eph. 2:10). Second, walk, and the more common application, means to "order one's behavior." We are not to walk like we did before (Eph. 4:17), but rather as selfless, cross-bearing children of light (Eph. 5:8). This is a life worthy of our union in Christ.

The Believer's Attitude Towards the Enemy. To "stand" means we are to resist and withstand satanic powers in high places (Eph. 6:11-14). Gospel work is offensive in nature because it must confront sin, but the focus of Ephesians 6 is how to withstand satanic attack:

Finally, my brethren, be strong in the Lord and in the power of His might. Put on the whole armor of God, that you may be able to stand against the wiles of the devil. For we do not wrestle against flesh and blood, but against principalities, against powers, against the rulers of the darkness of this age, against spiritual hosts of wickedness in the heavenly places (Eph. 6:10-12).

To war against spiritual wickedness in heavenly places, we must rely on a higher authority than the enemy's – thus, the paramount importance of Christ's priestly ministry. This means that believers must use all the spiritual armor that God supplies (Eph. 6:13-17) and approach Christ in heavenly places to receive the resources they need to "stand" against darkness and wickedness. Only then can we *"be strong in the Lord and in the power of His might"* (Eph. 6:10).

253

September 2 – Garments of Glory and Beauty
(Philippians 2)

The Day of Atonement was an annual reminder of human sin and that the blood of animals did not satisfy God's anger over sin or purge the sinner's guilty conscience. The entire feast pointed the Jews to God's ultimate provision in Christ, who would accomplish both. The limited access to the Holy Place also reminded the Jews that God was intrinsically holy and man was inherently corrupt. It is what Aaron does faithfully on behalf of the people, not who he is personally, which distinguishes him as a picture of Christ's future priesthood. What Aaron was personally in the Levitical priesthood is contrasted with the personal excellence of Christ as the eternal High Priest in Hebrews 5 and 7. For example, Aaron derived his *"glory and beauty"* from the garments he wore (Ex. 28:2), but the glory of the Lord Jesus emanates from His very person. Aaron's beauty and glory only lasted as long as he lived and wore the priestly garments, but the Lord Jesus is the *"Lord of Glory"* (1 Cor. 2:8) from eternity past and will be forevermore.

Aaron had two sets of priestly garments, but he was to exchange his garments of *"glory and beauty"* for the simple white linen outfit and miter only once a year on the Day of Atonement. Although this raiment is referred to as *"holy"* (Lev. 16:4), there was neither glory nor beauty associated with atoning for the sins of the people. In type, this pictures the Holy One (Luke 1:35, 4:34) who willingly put aside His glorious appearance, left heaven, and came to earth as God's holy sacrifice to suffer death to provide propitiation for human sin:

> *Christ Jesus, who, being in the form of God, did not consider it robbery to be equal with God, but **made Himself of no reputation**, taking the form of a bondservant, and coming in the likeness of men. And being found in appearance as a man, **He humbled Himself** and became obedient to the point of death, **even the death of the cross*** (Phil. 2:5-8).

On the Day of Atonement, Aaron wore his simple white linen coat and miter and was permitted to sprinkle animal blood on the Mercy Seat to atone for Israel's sin that year; the same process had to be repeated every year. But at Calvary, the Lord Jesus (God in the flesh) was stripped of His garments and shed His own blood to seal the New Covenant forever – what wonderful garments of glory and beauty!

September 3 – Christ's Lordship
(Philippians 2)

In a future day, the words of the Lord Jesus Christ will be proven true: *"My judgment is just"* (John 5:30) and *"The Father judges no one, but has committed all judgment to the Son"* (John 5:22). Only a just and impartial Judge can uphold the righteousness and holiness of God in rewarding and condemning others. Paul declared that we will all answer to the just Judge: *"For it is written: 'As I live, says the Lord, every knee shall bow to Me, and every tongue shall confess to God.' So then each of us shall give account of himself to God"* (Rom. 14:11-12). The Lord will reward believers at His Judgment Seat and will also punish the wicked at His Great White Throne (Rev. 20:11-15). On that day, no one will argue with His justice or their sentence:

> *Therefore God also has highly exalted Him and given Him the name which is above every name, that at the name of Jesus every knee should bow, of those in heaven, and of those on earth, and of those under the earth, and that every tongue should confess that Jesus Christ is Lord, to the glory of God the Father* (Phil. 2:9-11).

Paul had just written about Christ leaving heaven to become a man to be God's sacrifice for human sin. But the depths of His humiliation are reversed to the heights of heaven in His exaltation. The Greek verb translated "should confess" is in the middle voice, which means those being judged will confess on their own that Jesus is Lord; they are not forced to do so. The majesty of Christ will be so spectacular at the Great White Throne that even the most evil people in human history will fully agree that He is Lord. In a coming day everyone will proclaim that Jesus Christ is Lord! Those who previously embraced Him as Savior will gladly do so for eternity, but those who rejected Him in the first life, will bring honor to Him in the second death.

We should not think that the Lord derives pleasure by casting the wicked into the Lake of Fire, which was originally prepared to punish Satan and his angels (Matt. 25:41). Yet, God will use this abode of torment to also punish those who continue the devil's rebellion by rejecting God's offer of salvation in Christ. The Lord desires all men to repent and to turn to Him by faith that they might be declared righteous in His sight (2 Pet. 3:9). But Christ will be honored by all regardless.

September 4 – The Peace of God
(Philippians 4)

The Lord Jesus not only made peace with God, but now offers us the peace of God. He not only offers salvation of the soul, but of the mind as well. *"Therefore, having been justified by faith, we have **peace with God** through our Lord Jesus Christ"* (Rom. 5:1). *"And **the peace of God**, which surpasses all understanding, will guard your hearts and minds through Christ Jesus"* (Phil. 4:7).

The Greek word translated "peace" is *eirene*. It is derived from a verb meaning to "bond together." It literally means to "be made at one again," as reflected in Acts 7:26 when Moses sought to make two quarreling Israelites *"at one again."* *Eirene* is almost always translated "peace" in Scripture, but on rare occasions it is rendered "rest," "quietness," and "at one again." In application then, Romans 5:1 means that we are "one again" with God when we believe the gospel message – this is the saving of the soul. However, Philippians 4:7 refers to the saving of the mind – it is achieved when we are "one again" with Christ in His thinking, affections, and attitudes (the relevance of John 16:33).

The Lord shows the significance of being one with Him in salvation and in mind during His first visit with His disciples on resurrection day (being afraid they had gathered behind locked doors): *"Jesus came and stood in the midst, and said to them, 'Peace be with you.' When He had said this, He showed them His hands and His side. Then the disciples were glad when they saw the Lord. So Jesus said to them again, 'Peace to you! As the Father has sent Me, I also send you'"* (John. 20:19-21). Why did the Lord say *"Peace be with you"* twice?

At Christ's initial appearing, His disciples were discouraged and fearful. The Lord knew that they needed to have His peace within before they could convey His message of peace outwardly. Once the disciples had been with the Lord (i.e., one with Him again), their hearts were glad. Now, having peace within, the Lord could send them out to preach a message of peace to others. It is impossible to convey God's peace to others unless the believer has laid hold of the peace of God. Being one again with Christ brings peace to the soul. If we are fretful, we should ask ourselves, "Where is my thinking not one with Christ?" By *"looking to Jesus, the author and finisher of our faith"* (Heb. 12:2) we demonstrate His peace in such a way that the lost will want it too.

September 5 – Contentment
(Philippians 4)

When difficulties come, remembering that God is sovereign over His creation and His past faithfulness will help settle our minds. Recalling to our minds God's sovereignty should defeat feelings of jealousy and discontentment. God is in control and everything is as He allows it. Nothing is permitted to happen, including our trials, which does not first have His stamp of approval and His wise guiding hand. Paul found this mindset helpful in learning contentment during periods of lack:

> *Not that I speak in regard to need, for I have learned in whatever state I am, to be content: I know how to be abased, and I know how to abound. Everywhere and in all things I have learned both to be full and to be hungry, both to abound and to suffer need.* ***I can do all things through Christ who strengthens me*** (Phil. 4:10-13).

At this very moment we have exactly what the Lord wants us to have to live for Him. If He wanted us to have more money or resources, we would. The reason we suffer lack at times is that the Lord is teaching us that we do not need what we are yearning for, or that we would be a poor steward of it, if He gave it to us, or that He is teaching us lessons concerning budgeting and giving. The Lord knows what He is doing, and His doings serve our best *interest*. So let us appreciate what we have and give thanks for it, assess our present condition with a spiritual mindset, adjust where we lack, and accept everything as from the Lord. This is how we learn contentment in Christ.

This mindset will keep bents of coveting and unrighteous jealousy in check. King Saul, even after understanding that the kingdom had been promised to David, was lifted up in pride and jealousy. Saul could not accept God's sovereign rule or the just punishment he deserved for his own blundering mistakes. If we understand that we have exactly what God desires us to possess and our neighbors have exactly what God bestows to them, what room is there for envy and coveting in our thinking, for *"what do you have that you did not receive?"* (1 Cor. 4:7). Let us remember that God is always *"good and does good"* (Ps. 119:68).

257

September 6 – Reviving Knowledge
(Colossians 1)

The paramount reason to study Scripture is to learn what God reveals about Himself. Knowledge that "puffs up" is not the goal, but rather awareness of God's greatness which prompts us to fall on our faces in wonder and awe before Him. The reason Paul prayed that the Colossian believers would be *"increasing in the knowledge of God"* is that he knew such knowledge would lead them into spiritual wisdom, strength, and fruitfulness (Col. 1:9-11). Paul recognized that as the believers experienced Christ in this way, they would experience His reviving power also. Whenever a believer's understanding of Christ slips, or his or her desire to know Him more intimately wanes, something has gone very wrong. Understanding who Christ is, and what He has done and will do, promotes our spiritual vitality. Most of our doubts and anxieties arise from a diminished view of God's true nature and of the power of His gospel message centered in His Son.

Consequently, those with a degraded estimation of God's Son will usually live defeated lives because they also underestimate the strength of the devil and the danger his cunning devices pose. These spiritually despondent souls fall prey to the whims of the enemy, and then fail to learn from their disappointing experiences and rise in grace to victory. Whether we tumble or stumble, it is wise to learn from our mistakes, but past failures should not hinder Christians from pressing onward in their heavenly calling. Falling is a normal part of learning to walk properly; it is not falling that makes us a failure, but rather, it is remaining down after the fall: *"A righteous man may fall seven times and rise again, but the wicked shall fall by calamity"* (Prov. 24:16). There are just consequences for falling, but there are even more for wallowing in self-pity and rejecting Christ's help in time of need.

It is one thing to know Christ is divinely omnipresent; it is quite another to have His abiding presence and to appreciate His handiwork in all that we do; this is a distinguishing characteristic of a true revival.

Revival is the manifestation of the glory, power, and blessing of the Son of God among His people. Revival is ultimately Christ Himself, seen, felt, heard, living, active, moving in and through His body on earth. Revival is not some emotion or worked-up excitement; it is rather an invasion from heaven which brings to man a conscious awareness of God (S. Olford).

258

September 7 – Knowledge to Knowledge
(Colossians 1)

Paul's prayer for the believers at Colosse emphasizes their need for increasing knowledge of Christ and experience in Christ to mature in service for Christ:

> *For this reason we also, since the day we heard it, do not cease to pray for you, and to ask that you may be filled with the knowledge of His will in all wisdom and spiritual understanding; that you may walk worthy of the Lord, fully pleasing Him, being fruitful in every good work and increasing in the knowledge of God; strengthened with all might, according to His glorious power, for all patience and longsuffering with joy; giving thanks to the Father who has qualified us to be partakers of the inheritance of the saints in the light* (Col. 1:9-13).

Note the progression from the knowledge of God, to the wisdom of that knowledge, to the outworking of both in fruitfulness, which then leads to further knowledge of God. Not only were the believers to know the truth of Scripture, but they were also to grow in wisdom (the practical application of understood truth).

The link between practicing and experiencing truth to learn wisdom was evident in the life of the Lord Jesus. Though He was full of truth (John 1:14), yet Scripture says that He increased in wisdom and favor with God (Luke 2:52) and learned obedience by doing the Father's will for His life (Heb. 5:8). How can the One who knows all things learn something new and the All-Wise God increase in wisdom? The full answer is not revealed to humanity, but somehow the Son of God in human form experienced the process of learning in the same way you and I do. This highlights the necessity that each person must personally experience the truthfulness of God's Word in his or her own life.

For example, tribulations practically test our faith and work into our faith a quality of patience that could not be achieved otherwise (Rom. 5:3; Jas. 1:3). The Bible tells us to persevere with patience, but until the trial comes we neither know how we will handle it, nor the benefit of God's grace in that situation. The experience then exposes our spiritual vitality for what it is and hopefully teaches us to rely on the Lord's help in a way we did not before. If the Word of God is properly applied during the trial, the entire experience promotes our spiritual growth.

September 8 – By Him Were All Things Created
(Colossians 1)

We read in Genesis 1:1, *"In the beginning God created the heavens and the earth."* The Hebrew word *bara* is translated *created* in this verse. Interestingly, this word is always used in connection with God's creative handiwork; it does not speak of human productivity. Only God can call into existence that which had no previous existence; only the Creator can create life. We understand from Genesis 2:7 how the first man was created: *"And the Lord God formed man of the dust of the ground, and breathed into his nostrils the breath of life; and man became a living being."* When God breathes on something, that which is breathed on receives life (either physical, Gen. 2:7, or spiritual, John 20:22). David tells that God simply spoke creation into being (Ps. 33:6-9).

Lucifer (Satan) is also a created being (Ezek. 28:12-15), which means there must be a superior Being to explain his existence. This explains Satan's limitation in mimicking the plague of the gnats which God brought on Egypt through Moses (Ex. 8:16-19). God caused gnats to materialize from the dust of the earth and life suddenly came from what was not living. Satan cannot create life, for he is a created being.

In the New Testament we learn that the Son of God was intimately involved with the creation process. Speaking of the Lord Jesus Christ:

> In the beginning was the Word, and the Word was with God, and the Word was God. He was in the beginning with God. **All things were made through Him, and without Him nothing was made that was made.** In Him was life, and the life was the light of men (John 1:1-4).

> **For by Him [Christ]** **all things were created** that are in heaven and that are on earth, visible and invisible, whether thrones or dominions or principalities or powers. **All things were created through Him and for Him. And He is before all things, and in Him all things consist.** And He is the head of the body, the Church, who is the beginning, the firstborn from the dead, that **in all things He may have the preeminence** (Col. 1:16-18).

Scripture confirms that all things were created by the Lord Jesus in accord with the will of His Father and through the power of the Holy Spirit. Hence, the essence of all life is in Christ; apart from Christ there is no life. Clearly, the Son of God existed before anything was made.

September 9 – Rooted and Built Up in Christ
(Colossians 2)

The Colosse believers were being pressured by Gnostics to think less of Christ and to gain wisdom through human reasoning. Given this dangerous influence, Paul reveals his passion for the Colosse believers:

> *The knowledge of the mystery of God, both of the Father and of Christ, in whom are hidden all the treasures of wisdom and knowledge. Now this I say lest anyone should deceive you with persuasive words. ... As you therefore have received Christ Jesus the Lord, so walk in Him, rooted and built up in Him and established in the faith, as you have been taught, abounding in it with thanksgiving* (Col. 2:2-7).

In spiritual matters, there is nowhere else to go for understanding than Christ, for in Him are the vast treasuries of divine wisdom and knowledge. However, as evidenced by his deceitful work in Eden, Satan constantly works to cast doubt in the minds of men as to the validity of God's revealed Word. Not only does the first question in the Bible belong to the devil, but the first effort to deceive does also: *"Then the serpent said to the woman, 'You will not surely die'"* (Gen. 3:4). He added the word "not" to what God said to change the meaning of God's decree. Satan spoke of physical death; God spoke of spiritual separation from Him. Adam and his wife believed the devil and every cemetery today is proof that God told the full truth and that Satan is a liar.

The word "deceive" means "to impute around the truth." This is what Satan does; he puts what he wants us to believe near God's revealed truth in order to entice us to not be "rooted and built up" in God's foundation of truth. In Christ is absolute truth; therefore, let our faith rest on the foundation of Christ alone. If so grounded, we will be less likely to fall prey to threatening accusations and secular reasoning. The value of our service relates directly with having fellowship with God in spirit and in truth. If we become satisfied with the goodness of God's blessings and yet lose sight of what He desires for us, we will become feeble and powerless. God strengthens those who want to be guided into the knowledge of Himself and the purposes of His grace. The devil cannot overcome those who are rooted in God's Truth – the Lord Jesus Christ (1 Pet. 5:8-9)!

September 10 – Shadows of Things to Come (Part 1)
(Colossians 2)

While confronting the dangerous philosophies of the Gnostics, Paul warned the believers at Colosse not to value superficial things that would cause them to devalue Christ, their Head (Col. 2:14-23). He reminded them that feasts and festivals under the Law had been abolished by Christ: *"Regarding a festival or a new moon or Sabbaths, which are a shadow of things to come, but the substance is of Christ"* (Col. 2:16-18). These observances had served their intended purpose already by foreshadowing certain aspects of their coming Messiah. Now that He had come, the shadows of things did not matter anymore.

One of the best examples of these shadows is found in the Feasts of Jehovah. The seven Feasts of Jehovah provide an exceptional prophetical blueprint of God's means of reconciling the nation of Israel to Himself forever. Every aspect of this blueprint centers in the work of Christ. The following are the four Spring Feasts of Jehovah and what each typifies prophetically: Christ's death, burial, resurrection, and the beginning of the Church Age.

Passover (1st month, 14th day): This pictures Christ on the cross on Friday; this was the day the Passover lambs were slain and was also the day when the Lamb of God was slain for the sin of the world (1 Cor. 5:7).

Unleavened Bread (1st month, 15th day): This speaks of Christ in the grave on Saturday; like the bread, Christ's body had neither life while in the grave nor had it been previously influenced by sin (i.e., Christ lived an unleavened life).

Firstfruits (1st month, 16th day): This typifies Christ's resurrection on Sunday; He was the firstfruits from the dead (1 Cor. 15:20).

Pentecost (fifty days after Firstfruits): This pictures the formation of the Church (Christ's body of believers), fifty days after Christ's resurrection. The events at Pentecost conveyed a final ultimatum to Israel: repent or suffer God's judgment (Acts 2). Judgment came to Jerusalem in 70 A.D.

September 11 – Shadows of Things to Come (Part 2)
(Colossians 2)

We continue with the prophetic framework of the Feasts of Jehovah from the previous devotion. Below are the final three feasts in the fall. The Church Age is represented by the gap between the spring and autumn feasts. (This also relates to the interval between Daniel's 69th and 70th weeks; Dan. 9:24-27.) The autumn feasts speak of Israel's future acknowledgement of Christ as Messiah, their restoration to Him, and the blessings of His Millennial Kingdom. It is noted that this framework provides a clear picture of a Pre-Tribulation rapture of the Church. The autumn feasts prophetically pertain to Israel only.

Trumpets (7th month, 1st day): This refers to the time when Christ will gather all the Jews back to Israel and under His rule (Matt. 24:29-31; Ezek. 39:28-29). The Church will be with Christ in heaven prior to this event.

The Day of Atonement (7th month, 10th day): This pictures the future event when the Jews will repent and receive Jesus Christ as their Messiah (Heb. 9:28; Zech. 12:10).

Tabernacles (7th month, 15th day): This announces the future release of the Jews from the Antichrist's rule during the Tribulation Period, and the blessings of Christ's rule during His Millennial Kingdom.

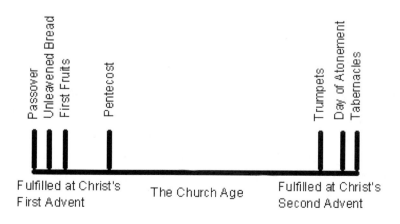

September 12 – The Motive for Forgiveness
(Colossians 3)

There are primarily two Greek words in the New Testament that are translated "forgive." *Aphiemi* primarily means "to send forth" or "to send away" or by implication "to forgive." *Aphiemi* is associated with the act of forgiving 48 times in the New Testament, but oddly it is only employed four times in the Epistles to speak of forgiveness. It views God's willful action of sending away the remembrance of our sin as illustrated in Psalm 103:12: *"As far as the east is from the west, ao far has He removed our transgressions from us."* Or in Hebrews 10:17: *"Their sins and their lawless deeds I will remember no more."* We must realize that it is humanly possible to forgive and not forget, and to forget and not forgive; hence, forgetting is not forgiving. Forgiving declares that the wrong has been put away and will not be remembered.

The second Greek word used to speak of forgiveness is *charizomai* which means, "to bestow a favor unconditionally or to freely release." It is rendered "forgive" 14 of the 24 times found in the New Testament, but 12 of these instances are in the Epistles. Why is one word for *forgiveness* found mainly in the Gospels and the other in the Epistles?

We are taught the mechanics of forgiveness in the Gospels: (1) How to resolve personal conflicts (Matt. 15:15-17). (2) That we should immediate *release* (send away) offenses to the Lord to judge rather than taking vengeance on our offenders (Luke 23:34) or defending our reputations. Offenses remain in the background of our thinking until repentance occurs; this permits us to think objectively – what is best for the offender and God's honor. (3) When to *declare* forgiveness and when we are not to, lest we endorse the sin of the offender (Luke 17:3).

In the Epistles, we are taught the motive to forgive: *"Bearing with one another, and forgiving one another, if anyone has a complaint against another; even as Christ forgave you, so you also must do"* (Col. 3:13). *"Be kind to one another, tenderhearted, forgiving one another, even as God in Christ forgave you"* (Eph. 4:32). Given all that we have done against the Lord and yet have been forgiven, we should be eager show God's forgiveness to those who have repented of the wrongs against us. Afterwards the issue should not be revisited. God is slow to anger, but quick to forgive and so should we (Ps. 145:8).

September 13 – To Wait for His Son
(1 Thessalonians 1-5)

Believers in the Church Age are sealed by the Holy Spirit (Eph. 1:13) and are therefore exempt from divine wrath forever. Having responded to the gospel message, believers in the Church Age will be removed from the earth before God refines and restores His covenant people to Himself during the Tribulation Period (Rom. 11:25). Hence, Christians are commanded to wait for Christ's imminent return to the clouds, at which time they will be suddenly translated from the earth (1 Thess. 4:13-18), will receive glorified bodies (1 Cor. 15:51-51), and then will be escorted back to heaven and to be examined at the Judgment Seat of Christ (Rom. 14:10-12). Works done for Him and in the power of the Holy Spirit will be rewarded by Him (1 Cor. 3:11-15; 2 Cor. 5:10).

The Church will not suffer God's wrath during the Tribulation Period, but rather will be kept out of it:

*Much more then, having now been justified by His blood, **we shall be saved from wrath** through Him* (Rom. 5:9).

*And to wait for His Son from heaven, whom He raised from the dead, even Jesus who **delivers us from the wrath to come*** (1 Thess. 1:10).

*For God did **not appoint us to wrath**, but to obtain salvation through our Lord Jesus Christ* (1 Thess. 5:9).

I also will **keep you from** the hour of trial which shall come upon the whole world, to test those who dwell on the earth (Rev. 3:10).

Because Christ has suffered God's full wrath over human sin, those who have received His pardon through Christ will never come under His judicial wrath – ever! This is the same pattern for other saints also. Therefore the Church must be taken from the earth to Heaven before Christ opens the first seal on the scroll initiating the Tribulation Period (Rev. 6:1). Likewise, surviving tribulation saints and those Jews of spiritual Israel will be spared death when God judges the nations at the end of the Tribulation Period. God's wrath is against wickedness, not against His redeemed (Zech. 12:8-9).

September 14 – The Day of the Lord
(1 Thessalonians 5)

The Day of the Lord is an Old Testament term that speaks of those times when Jehovah intervened in a visible and powerful way to judge the wicked on earth. This meaning continues into the New Testament and speaks of the Tribulation Period and the Millennial Kingdom of Christ. Hence, Paul told the believers at Thessalonica that the lost would not be expecting this worldwide judgment: *"For you yourselves know perfectly that the Day of the Lord so comes as a thief in the night. For when they say, 'Peace and safety!' then sudden destruction comes upon them"* (1 Thess. 5:2-3). The apostle then told them that they would not be a part of this judgment, as the Church would be taken up to be with Christ before the Day of the Lord (1 Thess. 4:13-18, 5:4-5).

After the judgment of nations which concludes the Tribulation Period, Jerusalem will be the religious center of the world (Isa. 2:1-5). Christ will reign from there and all the nations will come there to praise, worship, and learn of Him. There will be no war or violence, only peace. All the earth will see the glory of the Lord Jesus (Isa. 60:18-20) and any nation opposing Him will be laid waste (Isa. 60:12). The Day of the Lord speaks of the era in which all this will come about.

Ultimately, it will be God alone who will be exalted on earth. When the Lord comes to establish His kingdom, the wicked will seek to escape *"the terror of the Lord, and the glory of His majesty"* by hiding under rocks or in caves (Isa. 2:10-11). John alludes to this when he foretells that rebels on the earth will attempt to hide from the Lamb's face to avoid His wrath (Rev. 6:14-17). There is a coming day when all the arrogant and the proud will see the glory and power of the Lord Jesus Christ and realize too late that they cannot escape His judgment, for *"the Lord alone shall be exalted in that day"* (Isa. 2:11, 17).

Peter foretold that *the Day of the Lord* and the Millennial Kingdom conclude with destruction of the earth (2 Pet. 3:10), and will be followed by *the Day of God*, often referred to as *the eternal state* (2 Pet. 3:12). Isaiah states that *"all the host of heaven shall be dissolved, and the heavens shall be rolled up like a scroll"* (Isa. 34:4). Afterwards, God will judge the wicked at the Great White Throne judgment (Rev. 20:7-21:1) and then create a new heaven and new earth (Isa. 65:17). The Day of the Lord, Christ's day of vindication, is near!

September 15 – "Rejoice Always"
(1 Thessalonians 5)

Though the shortest verse in the Greek New Testament, *"Rejoice always"* (1 Thess. 5:16) declares one of the most important decrees in Scripture. Joy removes burdens from the soul. God's family should be a happy family, meaning we all must contribute to the atmosphere of joy. As believers are only on the earth for one purpose, to make God look good, there is no room for "doom and gloom" attitudes: *"Yet if anyone suffers as a Christian, let him not be ashamed, but let him glorify God in this matter"* (1 Pet. 4:16). As a believer chooses to rejoice in the Lord during trials, God often responds with a miraculous solution to honor Himself and to end our trial. Here are two examples:

Pagans at Philippi accused Paul and Silas of wrongdoing. They were not extended the right of a fair trial, but instead were beaten, chained, and put into prison. In the inner prison, the air circulation was poor. The stench of open wounds, feces, body odor, and the smoke from torches made it difficult to breathe. How did these two servants of the Lord respond to this cruel situation? *"But at midnight **Paul and Silas were praying and singing hymns to God**, and the prisoners were listening to them"* (Acts 16:25). They prayed and rejoiced in their God through singing. How did the Lord respond to their prayers and rejoicing? He brought a great earthquake, which released them from their captivity and then provided an opportunity for the jailer and his whole family to hear and believe the gospel message.

How did the apostles respond after they had been arrested, beaten, and threatened by the Pharisees for preaching Christ? *"They departed from the presence of the council, **rejoicing that they were counted worthy to suffer shame for His name.** And daily in the temple, and in every house, they did not cease teaching and preaching Jesus as the Christ"* (Acts 5:40-42). Despite the warning against preaching Christ, the apostles continued to do so, and the Church multiplied. Instead of choosing to be depressed or bitter about their stripes, the disciples determined to rejoice in their Savior. It may be that our rejoicing does not specifically or immediately bring relief or conclusion to our difficulty, but God has promised to work a greater good and glorify Himself through every situation (Rom. 8:28). Rejoicing in the Lord exhibits faith in God's sovereign control over every matter of life.

267

September 16 – "Pray Without Ceasing"
(1 Thessalonians 5)

Nehemiah, the king's cupbearer, was so deeply affected by the dismal report on Jerusalem that he immediately petitioned the Lord for help while fasting *"day and night"* for four months (Neh. 1). This does not mean Nehemiah prayed nonstop during this interval, for he was the king's servant, but rather, that he engaged in the type of prayer Paul exhorts the believers at Thessalonica to engage in: *"Pray without ceasing"* (1 Thess. 5:17). This did not mean that Paul was expecting them to be in prayer every moment of every day, as that would not be humanly feasible.

The Greek word *adialeiptos*, which is rendered "without ceasing," implies that our prayers should be "constantly recurring" rather than "continuously occurring." It would be impossible to pray twenty-four hours a day, seven days a week. But it is possible to have an actively recurring prayer life. To "pray without ceasing" means to stay in contact with God in such a way that our praying is like a long conversation with short pauses: we never sense a break in communion. The believer should pray at regular times and as exercised when needs arise (to confess sin, to make intercession, to seek grace in a time of need). The Lord should never be far from our thoughts, for He is always willing to bend His ear to the pangs of a humble heart: *"Lord, You have heard the desire of the humble; You will prepare their heart; You will cause Your ear to hear"* (Ps. 10:17). The Lord knows the desire of our hearts and grants the humble that desire. For example, Paul prayed for the souls of the nation of Israel – that they might be saved (Rom. 9:1-3, 10:1). Paul also informed the Gentiles that they came to Christ as a result of God answering the prayers of Jewish Christians (2 Cor. 9:14). Warren Wiersbe wrote: "Prayer is not an escape from responsibility; it is our *response* to God's *ability*."[34] True prayer energizes us for service and to battle the enemy. Hudson Taylor, who labored for the Lord as a missionary in China in the mid-nineteenth century, had three important principles concerning prayer:

1. You can work without praying, but it is a bad plan.
2. You cannot pray in earnest without working.
3. Do not be so busy with work for Christ that you have no strength left for praying. True praying requires strength.[35]

September 17 – "In Everything Give Thanks"
(1 Thessalonians 5)

To the Thessalonians, Paul instructs: *"In everything give thanks; for this is the will of God in Christ Jesus for you"* (1 Thess. 5:18). **"In everything** give thanks" is not necessarily "for" everything, but Paul also wrote the Ephesians to be *"giving thanks **always for all things** to God the Father in the name of our Lord Jesus Christ"* (Eph. 5:20).

Why are we to give thanks in and for every situation? Because as children of God *"we know that all things work together for good to those who love God, to those who are the called according to His purpose"* (Rom. 8:28). This means that God has uniquely permitted every situation to express His sovereign purposes to honor Himself, to proclaim the good news of His Son, and to both bless and perfect us in the process. In other words, whether in faithfulness or declension the Lord has us exactly where He wants us. This means that we can have hope in every situation that our sorrows and suffering have a purpose.

Going through life with a mindset of wanting to see a half-full glass instead of a half-empty glass in every situation protects our mind. The reality of our circumstances has not changed, but our perception of what God might do through them guards our hearts from anxiety and depression. A thankful and critical mind frame cannot exist together.

The prophet Daniel is a good example of a man who walked with God having a thankful disposition. Because he was a godly man, no one could accuse him of wrongdoing. So jealous, evil men devised a plan to ensnare the king's ego and ensure Daniel's death (Dan. 6). Daniel's adversaries knew that he would not obey the law forbidding prayer that they had tricked the king into approving. After hearing of the edict, Daniel did not appeal the matter to the king, but went into an upper room of his home and prayed to God through an open window.

Daniel enjoyed an open-window relationship with God, so instead of complaining about the unjust situation, Daniel committed the situation to God with thanksgiving! In the end, God was exalted by the king, and not Daniel but his adversaries were fed to the lions. How often the Lord's people become rattled by circumstances and rush into the throne room of grace in hopeless panic, as if God is unaware of what is happening in our lives or is somehow not in control. God's peace resides within His sovereign control over all things.

September 18 – "Test All things"
(1 Thessalonians 5)

Paul includes this statement in his barrage of imperative exhortations to the church at Thessalonica, *"Test all things; hold fast what is good"* (1 Thess. 5:21).

In responding to His disciples' question about things to come, the Lord Jesus confirmed that in the latter days of the Church Age false doctrine would be widespread. Besides this mass deception, many would come claiming to be the Christ (Matt. 24:5). With the coming of the Lord Jesus being imminent today, His warning two thousand years ago, *"Take heed that no one deceives you"* (Matt. 24:4), could never be more critical to obey. "No one" means well-meaning preachers (and authors) too, as Paul did say *"test all things."* Sometimes even well-known brethren can teach what is wrong and cause believers to do what displeases the Lord. We have only to turn to Galatians 2 in our Bibles to find Paul withstanding Peter for his hypocrisy of not eating with Gentile believers. Such intrusions of darkness on the children of light come from the flesh and the devil, not the Lord. Paul did test and hold to what was good, and thankfully Peter received what was good for him too. But Peter, having been wrong and rebuked for it, later wrote in the Spirit *"our beloved brother Paul."* No doubt Peter was thankful for a brother who tested all things and loved him enough to rebuke him when he had not been diligent and careful.

Given the darkness of the hour, may we test everything according to God's Word, lest we be deceived by our God-hating adversary, who wants only to cause us harm and to degrade the name of Christ. If brethren attempt to lead us away from the truth, they must be resisted, for to leave the truth is to depart from the presence of Christ!

In his hatred of Christ, the devil will seek to rob us of the truth, or, failing to do this, he will seek to bring dishonor upon the Name of Christ and discredit the truth by bringing about moral breakdown among those who hold the truth. The more truth we have, the greater the dishonor to Christ if we break down by the allowance of the flesh. We must therefore be prepared to face conflict, and the more truth we have, the greater will be the conflict.

— Hamilton Smith

September 19 – Consecration Demanded
(1 Thessalonians 5)

The ordinances within Deuteronomy 14 indicate God's desire for His covenant people to remain separated from the Canaanite pagan culture of that day. The Jews were God's chosen people and God had marked them out to be distinct among the nations. Accordingly, their mourning customs, their diet, and their giving to the Lord were all to be consecrated to Him. If Israel obeyed God's Law, the Jewish nation would look, act, and think differently than everyone else. Their attire (which included a blue fringe), their food, their farming methods, their slaughtering of animals, their family structure, and their system of worship all declared that they were unique among all people.

While the Church is not under the same Levitical particulars, the concepts of separation from evil and worldliness are widely upheld in the New Testament. For example, James proclaims that worldliness is enmity with God (Jas. 4:4), and Paul reminds Christians to *"abstain from all appearance of evil"* (1 Thess. 5:22). No matter the age or dispensation God's people find themselves in, holiness and full dedication to the Lord is expected!

The Old Testament laws showed the extent to which Jehovah was jealously guarding His covenant people; He did not want them near what was unclean, lest they be tempted to defile themselves. Thus, contact of any kind with what God deemed as unclean was forbidden. The Jewish dietary laws have been abolished by the New Covenant secured by the Lord Jesus Christ (Mark 7:14-23; Acts 10:9-13). However, God's desire for His people to remain morally clean and set apart for Him is not abolished. Much sin in the Church today would be avoided if God's people were constantly mindful of what was clean and unclean to the Lord. May God give us grace to *"abhor what is evil and cling to what is good"* (Rom. 12:9-10), and wisdom to refrain from engaging in anything that even has even the slightest hint of evil.

Through philosophy and deception, Satan works to confuse our minds as to the order that God has decreed for us. Just as the Israelites were not told all the "whys" for the unusual practices they were to obey, neither is the Church; God just expects us to yield to what He commands – thus marking us as the most peculiar people on earth!

September 20 – Dealing With the Unruly
(2 Thessalonians 3)

Paul instructed how to handle unruly saints who were threatening the order and peace of the Church at Thessalonica:

> *But we command you, brethren, in the name of our Lord Jesus Christ, that you withdraw from every brother who walks disorderly and not according to the tradition which he received from us. ... For we hear that there are some who walk among you in a disorderly manner, not working at all, but are busybodies* (2 Thess. 3:6-11)

A busybody is someone who injects their own interests, not the Lord's concerns, into your affairs. Such unruly behavior within a local church harms body-life and leads to disunity, division, and often corruption of what is important to the Lord. At such times a purifying action is needful to remedy the problem. Paul acknowledges this mysterious truth of Church body-life: *"For none of us lives to himself, and no one dies to himself"* (Rom. 14:7). *"And if one member suffers, all the members suffer with it; or if one member is honored, all the members rejoice with it"* (1 Cor. 12:26). Hence, we should never think that our personal sins do not have ramifications for others. The choices we make today affect our family members, our local churches, and indeed all the brethren. When the Body suffers, Christ suffers, and that is why this subject matter is important to Him – He loves His Church!

When a believer continues in willful sin, he or she should be rebuked (1 Tim. 5:20; 2 Tim. 4:2; Tit. 3:10-11). A rebuke is a stern warning to the offending party to repent; it should carry the threat of punishment for continued wrong behavior (Rev. 3:19). If people, even elders, continue in sin, they must be stopped. Strong measures are warranted. This disgraceful conduct cannot be tolerated in the church. As a sanctified Body gathered to the Lord, the local assembly should completely avoid those who have been warned but continue to be disorderly (2 Thess. 3:11, 14, 15), divisive (Rom. 16:17), or factious (Titus 3:10-11). *"Cast out the scorner, and contention will leave; yes, strife and reproach shall cease"* (Prov. 22:10). The purpose of this shunning is to help another person see that he or she is out of fellowship with God, and therefore out of fellowship with His people. This action is motivated by love and not pity; that is, we want to do what is best for the unrepentant individual, not what will ease his or her sorrow.

272

September 21 – "The Household of God"
(1 Timothy 3)

Because Paul was separated from Timothy, Paul desired to write his spiritual son on an important matter: *"I write so that you may know how you ought to conduct yourself in the house of God, which is the church of the living God, the pillar and ground of the truth"* (1 Tim. 3:15-16). The Household of God did not refer to a building where the Church gathered, but rather to the saints themselves (Eph. 2:19).

We read in Acts 2:42 that the New Testament Christians continued in activities such as teaching, prayer, fellowship, and the Lord's Supper. In the Greek text, there is a definite article before the word "fellowship" in this verse, meaning that there was one particular fellowship that the Church was to enjoy – Christ's fellowship. The Church is a living body composed of many members who enjoy divine fellowship with each other. Local churches were commanded to receive other believers who desired to take part in the privileges and responsibilities of church fellowship (Rom. 15:7) and those received into the local church fellowship were instructed not to neglect it (Heb. 10:25). Each individual church fellowship is a local manifestation of Christ's fellowship within the Church as a whole.

Accordingly, membership in a local church is never taught in Scripture. Rather, those who had a consistent profession of faith (Acts 2:41-42), were morally sound in life (2 Thess. 3:10-11; 1 Cor. 5:11), who were sound in doctrine (2 Thess. 3:6, 14; Titus 3:9-10), and who agreed to submit to the church elders as unto the Lord (1 Thess. 5:12; Heb. 13:17) were received into local church fellowships. Church membership stresses an individual's rights and affirms a person's salvation, though he or she may not be saved. The New Testament pattern of reception puts the emphasis on personal acceptance of the privileges and responsibilities which accompany family life in an assembly of believers. Those who take themselves out of fellowship with Christ through unrepentant sin are to be removed (1 Cor. 5:5). They are to be dealt with in love through various stages of church discipline. The Church is God's instrument to teach all those who witness its behavior that God is Holy. The Lord Jesus desires to extend joyful and empowering fellowship to all those who seek to be holy through remaining in fellowship with Him (1 Pet. 1:16).

September 22 – "The Mystery of Godliness"
(1 Timothy 3)

The first three humans to walk on this planet entered the world in different ways: Adam became a living soul after God breathed a spirit into a heap of dust He had gathered from the earth. Eve was created from materials taken from Adam's side. Cain was a product of human procreation. The Lord Jesus entered the world by a fourth means, a virgin birth. The means by which one enters the world does not determine if one is human or not, for Adam, Eve, Cain and Jesus Christ were all human.

Satan was defeated at Calvary (John 12:31) and further humiliated at the resurrection of Christ (Eph. 1:19-21). His only recourse since those triumphant events has been to cast doubt on the work and Person of Christ. Any teaching which undermines the divine Person and the moral perfection of Christ is an attack at the very foundation of the Christian faith; if no flawless Christ, if no divine nature – then no salvation. The Lord said, *"if you do not believe that I am [He], you will die in your sins"* (John 8:24). *He* in this verse is not in the Greek text.

There are various erroneous teachings concerning the Person of Christ. Some say Christ is not fully God, nor fully man. Others teach that Christ became some hybrid creature, a created being, between God and man, but neither God nor man. Christ is not diminished deity added to a human personality; God literally and personally became a human, without emptying Himself of any divine attributes (John 1:14).

"Great is the mystery of Godliness. God was manifest in the flesh" (1 Tim. 3:16). Christ was fully man, but He had a unique human nature, different from our nature. Because there is no definite article in the Greek before "flesh," this verse is better rendered, *"God has been manifested in flesh."* God was manifest "in flesh," not "in the flesh." The Lord Jesus was veiled in flesh (Heb. 10:20); He was made flesh (John 1:14) but was not in the flesh – the nature of His flesh did not rule Him; it served Him. The Lord was holy humanity (Luke 1:35).

When Adam sinned, he made a transition from *innocent humanity* to *condemned humanity* and was judged by God. Everyone coming from Adam is condemned as well (Rom. 5:12-14). Through the obedience of Christ came the offer of grace, forgiveness and restoration (Rom. 5:15-21). Those believing on Christ become *redeemed humanity* and wait to become *glorified humanity* (as Christ is now) at His return.

September 23 – "Godliness With Contentment"
(1 Timothy 6)

Paul instructed Timothy on the important virtue of contentment:

*Now **godliness with contentment is great gain**. For we brought nothing into this world, and it is certain we can carry nothing out. And having food and clothing, with these we shall be content. But those who desire to be rich fall into temptation and a snare, and into many foolish and harmful lusts which drown men in destruction and perdition. For the love of money is a root of all kinds of evil, for which some have strayed from the faith in their greediness, and pierced themselves through with many sorrows* (1 Tim. 6:6-10).

Paul suggests that any ungodly deed we can imagine has been pursued for the love of money. Sadly, many people are neither content nor thankful for what God has provided them. They often covet money and err from the faith. If God wanted us to have more than what we have, He would gladly give it to us. God wants us to have what would be good for us to have: *"Every good gift and every perfect gift is from above, and comes down from the Father of lights"* (Jas. 1:17). Being thankful for what God does provide defeats the temptation to be dissatisfied. This is why Paul told the Philippians that he had learned to be content no matter if he lacked or had plenty: *"Not that I speak in regard to need, for I have learned in whatever state I am, to be content: I know how to be abased, and I know how to abound"* (Phil. 4:11-12).

Murmuring and complaining must be replaced by thanksgiving and contentment, which are closely related. The most common cause of sin seems to be dissatisfaction, with selfishness and pride trailing close behind. When we are not content with what we have, we murmur against God. Murmuring is half-uttered complaints that God fully hears anyway. It results from looking earthward and backwards instead of Godward and forward. Looking for earthly solutions and comparing today with where we were yesterday will result in complaining. But looking to the Lord and His promises in hopeful expectation of what He will do tomorrow results in joyful contentment today.

Paul exhorts us to *"do all things without complaining"* (Phil. 2:14). If we are complaining, we are upholding ourselves before others and that cannot be called service to the Lord.

September 24 – If Rich, Serve Others

(1 Timothy 6)

Having just taught that *"godliness with contentment is great gain"* and having warned that seeking wealth often enables unchecked lusting that results in a shipwrecked testimony, Paul provides an additional exhortation for those who were already rich:

> *Command those who are rich in this present age not to be haughty, nor to trust in uncertain riches but in the living God, who gives us richly all things to enjoy. Let them do good, that they be rich in good works, ready to give, willing to share, storing up for themselves a good foundation for the time to come, that they may lay hold on eternal life* (1 Tim. 6:17-19).

It is not a sin to be rich, for such things are bestowed by God alone, but to trust in one's wealth to fix personal problems or to indulge in worldliness is sin. What we have is exactly what God wants us to have and is for the purpose of serving Him, helping others, and providing for our basic necessities. If our needs are satisfied, we are to labor in order to provide help for those in need (Eph. 4:28). As the Israelites learned in Moses' day, wealth not consecrated to God soon leads to idolatry. As an idol is anything that draws our affection from God, the warning could never be more relevant than it is today. The Western culture is immersed in much stuff and it is strangling the life out of the Church.

The Lord Jesus used the parable of the *Unjust Steward* in Luke 16 to instruct His audience as to what their attitude towards riches should be. A steward was caught embezzling his master's wealth. Knowing that he would soon have to give an account of his actions and would then lose his job, he settled many of his master's accounts for less than what his debtors owed. He thus gained the favor of these individuals who he hoped would show him kindness in the future. The Lord did not commend the steward for his crookedness, but for his forward thinking. The Lord then noted that the unregenerate are often better at using what they have to invest in the future, than God's people are. Hence, He exhorts us to *"make friends for yourselves by unrighteous [money]"* while secular riches still have value. In other words, be future thinking – invest into eternity what God has given you now because in a coming day it will have no ability to earn you anything of real value.

276

September 25 – "If We Endure"
(2 Timothy 2)

Because Paul was sold out to Christ, he spoke out for Christ. "Proclaiming His name" and "suffering for His name" go hand in hand; these realities cannot be separated. *"If we endure, we shall also reign with Him. If we deny Him, He also will deny us"* (2 Tim. 2:12). The Lord explained the connection to His disciples on the eve of Calvary. He told them that the world hated Him and would hate them also, and informed them that they would be persecuted by the world, for *"all these things they will do to you for My name's sake"* (John 15:21).

Many in the early church were so enthralled with Christ that they considered it a great privilege to suffer for His sake. In doing so, they were enabled to more closely identify with the Lord. This was Paul's desire – to know Christ more deeply through suffering for Him: *"That I may know Him and the power of His resurrection, and the fellowship of His sufferings, being conformed to His death"* (Phil. 3:10).

The apostles had been warned once already by the Pharisees not to preach Christ, but despite the threat they continued to be obedient to the Lord's commands. After being arrested a second time, we read that the Sanhedrin had them beaten and then commanded them not speak in the name of Jesus Christ before letting them go. What did they do? *"So they departed from the presence of the council, rejoicing that they were counted worthy to suffer shame for His name. And daily in the temple, and in every house, they did not cease teaching and preaching Jesus as the Christ"* (Acts 5:41-42). They had settled the death question and determined that preaching Christ was more honorable than living without proclaiming the value of His name (1 Pet. 4:14).

The assurance of God's Word gave the apostles hope for the future and joy while suffering for their Savior. Hence, the Lord's disciples faced death with the same hope and joy that their Savior did, and so can we. Aegeas crucified Andrew, Peter's brother, for his faith in Christ. Seeing his cross before him, Andrew bravely spoke, "O cross, most welcome and longed for! With a willing mind, joyfully and desirously, I come to thee, being the scholar of Him which did hang on thee: because I have always been thy lover, and have coveted to embrace thee."[36] Andrew could approach his cross with expectancy and joy, because he had watched the Lord Jesus do the same at Calvary.

September 26 – "We Shall Reign With Him"
(2 Timothy 2)

Having first addressed the important matter of believers enduring for Christ now, he speaks of one of the blessings of doing so later: *"If we endure, we shall also reign with Him"* (2 Tim. 2:12). Only Spirit-controlled believers could exhibit the code of behavior appropriate to reign with Him in His kingdom. The Lord originally spoke of this fact during His Sermon on the Mount message, which promised Kingdom blessings for those that were with Him (Matt. 5-7). For Israel, this will be the fulfillment of the Messianic prophecy of Isaiah: *"Behold, a king will reign in righteousness, and princes will rule with justice"* (Isa. 32:1). Christ will reign in righteousness and those entering His kingdom will be those who pursue justice and purity. This will include Gentiles who did not side with the Antichrist and who lived through the Tribulation Period, the restored nation of Israel, and glorified saints (Old Testament believers, the Church, and previously martyred Tribulation saints). Some within the Jewish nation – *"princes will rule with justice"* (Isa. 32:1), glorified Tribulation saints (Rev. 20:4), and the Church will rule and reign with Christ during the Kingdom Age.

Think of a world which has no political agendas, no warring factions, no unethical dealings, and is void of rebels and wickedness. Such a utopia will exist in Christ's kingdom; furthermore, citizens of His kingdom will be protective of each other. Isaiah says that subjects of the King will be like a shelter in a windstorm to each other, and they will seek to refresh each other, like a rock casting its shadow or a cool drink of water for those suffering in desert heat (Isa. 32:1-2). This attitude is just one of the evidences that the Spirit of God has free recourse to bless humanity during the Millennial Kingdom.

Isaiah says that in the Kingdom Age the inhabitants of the earth will see, hear, and discern spiritual things properly (Isa. 32:1-8). They will know and choose to obey God's laws; ungodliness of any sort will not be tolerated. Rather, subjects of Christ will seek to care for those in need, and will pursue righteousness; God promises that such a person has His favor and will continue to stand with His blessing.

John also provides a promise to overcomers: *"He who overcomes shall inherit all things, and I will be his God and he shall be My son"* (Rev. 21:7-8). We shall reign with Christ and inherit all that He has!

September 27– Destined to Suffer (Part 1)
(2 Timothy 3)

Paul knew a good deal about being persecuted for the name of Christ and therefore had something he desired his spiritual son Timothy to understand: *"Yes, and all who desire to live godly in Christ Jesus will suffer persecution"* (2 Tim. 3:12). It is a promise of God that if we live to serve Christ, we will suffer for it. Dear believer, do not expect anything less and you will not be disappointed. Prepare your mind for the struggles ahead, and do not get bogged down in self-pity or grapple with despair when those forecasted storms of life arrive.

Many of our failures can be attributed to having the wrong view of what we experience in our wilderness journeys. If new converts would realize that they are destined for disappointments, hardships, and persecution because of their identity in Christ, then every provision of God's grace in the wilderness would be answered with joyful praise. But if new believers begin their pilgrimage heavenward expecting ease in the world, the coming relentless hardships will be overwhelming.

From this perspective the *Prosperity Gospel* message often preached today will always have an appeal to the flesh. However, those desiring the benefits of the cross, but denying its demands will eventually be disappointed (Luke 9:23-26). Those who try to live with one foot in the world and one in the church will also experience failure, for there can be no mixing of the two; one is earthly and the other heavenly. C. H. Mackintosh also highlights the crippling influence of the *mixed* mindset on those who would seek to follow the Lord:

> There is nothing more damaging to the cause of Christ or to the souls of His people than association with men of *mixed* principles. It is very much more dangerous than having to do with open and avowed enemies. Satan knows this well, and hence his constant effort to lead the Lord's people to link themselves with those who are only half and half; or, on the other hand, to introduce spurious materials – false professors – into the midst of those who are seeking, in any measure, to pursue a path of separation from the world.[37]

Every Christian who righteously suffers for the cause of Christ will be rewarded: *"If we suffer, we shall also reign with Him"* (2 Tim. 2:12; KJV). So though we are destined for trouble, we should not despair.

September 28 – Destined to Suffer (Part 2)
(2 Timothy 3)

We continue contemplating Paul's charge to Timothy: *"Yes, and all who desire to live godly in Christ Jesus will suffer persecution"* (2 Tim. 3:12). This is a facet of the Christian experience for which all believers need to be mentally prepared (1 Pet. 1:13), and one which they ought to rejoice in (Acts 5:40-42, 16:23-25). Paul told the saints at both Philippi and Thessalonica (who were being persecuted for their faith) that suffering patiently was evidence (a proof) of their salvation.

If you are an evangelist faithfully sharing the gospel message, a preacher that shares the full counsels of God, or a shepherd who faithfully uses God's rod to lead, comfort, and correct, then you already know that you will suffer for doing what God wants you to do. If we do anything for the Lord, we should expect to be misunderstood, criticized, and even slandered. Evaluate criticism for potential constructive benefits, especially when it comes from those who love you unquestionably, and then cast the rest aside and forget about it. And if you are prompted to critique another, do not do so unless it pains you to do so; that would be the right attitude. However, if you have even a hint of pleasure in doing it, then it would be best to keep still. Why? This is because our flesh naturally opposes the things of God (Gal. 5:17), and *"the wrath of man does not produce the righteousness of God"* (Jas. 1:20). Paul did not even judge the value of his own ministry because he knew his flesh was biased (1 Cor. 4:2-4). A spiritual person wants to edify others, not hurt them for the sake of personal vindication or self-justification.

> Abraham Lincoln once said, "If I tried to read, much less answer, all the criticisms made of me, and all the attacks leveled against me, this office would have to be closed for all other business. I do the best I know how, the very best I can. And I mean to keep on doing this, down to the very end. If the end brings me out all wrong, ten angels swearing I had been right would make no difference. If the end brings me out all right, then what is said against me now will not amount to anything."[38]

When living for Christ becomes arduous, let us remember that it is God and not our accusers who control the worth of our service!

September 29 – A Poured-Out Drink Offering
(2 Timothy 4)

Our wonderful God knows that one of the best ways to reveal Himself and His truth to us is through personal experience. This means that His messengers will often suffer hardship, pain, and rejection. God Himself sent His own Son from the heights of heaven to be born of a virgin, to suffer the contradiction of sinners for decades in order to personally convey His message of love and life. How did mankind recompense Him? Man mocked His Son, spit on Him, beat Him, whipped Him, and then nailed Him to a tree to suffer an agonizing death. Yet, it was God's plan for Christ to be accursed and to taste death for every man (Heb. 2:9). By doing so He became the sole Mediator between a holy God and sinners destined for hell (1 Tim. 2:5). God personally knows the pain and suffering which sin causes in ways we never will, and yet the Lord Jesus was faithful to stay His course, and He promises to assist us to do the same:

No temptation has overtaken you except such as is common to man; but God is faithful, who will not allow you to be tempted beyond what you are able, but with the temptation will also make the way of escape, that you may be able to bear it (1 Cor. 10:13).

I can do all things through Christ who strengthens me (Phil. 4:13).

Looking unto Jesus, the author and finisher of our faith, who for the joy that was set before Him endured the cross, despising the shame, and has sat down at the right hand of the throne of God (Heb. 12:2).

Seeing Christ's supreme example and knowing of His boundless provision of grace, Paul was determined to finish well. Hence, at the end of his life he could declare: *"I am already being poured out as a drink offering, and the time of my departure is at hand. I have fought the good fight, I have finished the race, I have kept the faith"* (2 Tim. 4:6-7). God had answered Paul's prayer years earlier: *"That I may know Him and the power of His resurrection, and the fellowship of His sufferings, being conformed to His death"* (Phil. 3:10). This is the highest aspiration that any believer can have. May it be ours also!

281

September 30 – Nothing Man Does Is Pure
(Titus 1)

The fallen nature of man enslaves him to sin (Rom. 6:19), and thus he will naturally endeavor to pull others under its influence and to enslave them too. As a result, natural man yearns to control and to use others for his advantage, rather than to serve and assist them. Even when natural man does assist others, it is still unacceptable to God because his motivation is impure; he either desires to gain something from his effort, to earn spiritual promotion, or to merit some reward. This is all humanized religion, but the fact remains that outside of Christ man can do nothing to please God. Paul affirmed this truth to his spiritual son Titus: *"But to those who are defiled and unbelieving nothing is pure; but even their mind and conscience are defiled. They profess to know God, but in works they deny Him, being abominable, disobedient, and disqualified for every good work"* (Tit. 1:15-16).

Consequently, the sum of all the good works a sinner does in his lifetime is still counted as filthy rags to God. Understanding this truth, the remnant exclaims: *"But we are all like an unclean thing, and all our righteousnesses are like filthy rags; we all fade as a leaf, and our iniquities, like the wind, have taken us away"* (Isa. 64:6). Barnes comments, "No language could convey deeper abhorrence of their deeds of righteousness than this reference – it is undoubtedly to the *vestis menstruis polluta* [used menstruation rags]."[39] Just as a powerful storm blows away the leaves of trees, the remnant of Israel realized that they had been swept away by their own sins. This verse graphically conveys how offensive our sin is to God and also how putrid to Him are all our "good works" apart from His enablement and control.

Today, people often minimize or excuse their sin with expressions such as: "I did my best, but that was not good enough," "I didn't mean to do anything wrong," "I just made a mistake," or "God made me this way." Sometimes, errors and failures are not sinful in nature, but it is morally wrong to label what is sin merely as "an error in judgment." Solomon tells us the danger of not being real with God about the matter of sin: *"He who covers his sins will not prosper, but whoever confesses and forsakes them will have mercy"* (Prov. 28:13). God's Word shows us what sin is and also how deceitful and offensive it is to God, that we might know that only He could ever have the means of forgiving us.

October 1 – "The Blessed Hope"
(Titus 2)

The word "hope" in the New Testament is almost exclusively used to speak of Christ's coming for His Church – the rapture. There is *"one hope"* (Eph. 4:4), and it is *"looking for that blessed hope, and the glorious appearing of the great God and our Savior Jesus Christ"* (Tit. 2:13). This event is the believer's greatest hope. The expectation of imminently and suddenly being "caught up" into the blissful presence of the Lord Jesus should thrill the soul of every believer.

John reminds us not to lose sight of this event, for not only will thinking about it provide joy during dark times, but it will also promote holy living. *"Beloved, now we are children of God; and it has not yet been revealed what we shall be, but we know that when He is revealed, we shall be like Him, for we shall see Him as He is. And everyone who has this hope in Him purifies himself, just as He is pure"* (1 Jn. 3:2-3). What was the expectation of the early Church apostles?

John writes: *"It is the last times"* (1 Jn. 2:18). *"He shall appear that we may have confidence and not be ashamed before Him at His coming"* (1 Jn. 2:28).

Paul writes: *"Then we which are alive and remain shall be caught up together with them in the clouds, to meet the Lord in the air: and so shall we ever be with the Lord"* (1 Thess. 4:17). *"We also eagerly wait for the Savior, the Lord Jesus Christ, who will transform our lowly body that it may be conformed to His glorious body, according to the working by which He is able even to subdue all things to Himself"* (Phil. 3:20-21).

James writes: *"The coming of the Lord is at hand"* (Jas. 5:8).

Peter writes: *"But the end of all things is at hand"* (1 Pet. 4:7). *"But the day of the Lord will come as a thief in the night ... looking for and hastening the coming of the day of God"* (2 Pet. 3:10, 12). Note: *the Day of Christ* (the rapture of the Church) precedes *the Day of the Lord* (i.e., Tribulation Period and Kingdom Age), which precedes *the Day of God* (the eternal state).

Because the Lord did not reveal the "when" of His coming for the Church, the apostles lived each day in earnest expectation of soon being with the Lord Jesus in glory – and so should we!

October 2 – "Spoken to Us by His Son"
(Hebrews 1)

The writer of Hebrews speaks of the Lord Jesus as being "the Apostle" of God: *"Wherefore, holy brethren, partakers of the heavenly calling, consider the Apostle and High Priest of our profession, Christ Jesus"* (Heb. 3:1). As prophet (or "apostle"), He is literally the "sent One" from the Father to perfectly represent God to mankind and to reveal God's plan of salvation.

For this reason, John refers to the Son of God as "the Word" (John 1:1; 1 Jn. 1:1); the Son became a man to bring God's message of peace to humanity. Jesus Christ is a living message; He embodies the word and goodness of God. All that Christ did and said on earth was the message God wanted conveyed to man. Hence, the writer of Hebrews begins His epistle by declaring the glory of Christ in three ways:

> *God, who at various times and in various ways spoke in time past to the fathers by the prophets, has in these last days spoken to us by His Son, whom He has appointed heir of all things, through whom also He made the worlds; who being* **the brightness of His glory** *and* **the express image of His person**, *and* **upholding all things by the word of His power**, *when He had by Himself purged our sins, sat down at the right hand of the Majesty on high* (Heb. 1:1-3).

When the word "glory" is associated with God in Scripture, it usually refers to one of three things: His outshining radiance, His holy character, or His all-mighty power. The writer begins his letter by affirming Christ's deity. Jesus Christ is the brightness (the radiance) of God's glory and the express image of God's person (i.e., Christ reflects God's character and authority), and that Christ upholds all things by the word of God's power. (He, in Himself, possesses the power of God.)

The Lord Jesus, in His life, conveyed the incomprehensible glory of God to humanity in a unique fashion. In all things that Christ did and said, He declared the goodness, holiness, and righteousness of God. His sinless life reproved the self-righteous and His wise words refuted human reasoning. His miracles and authority over the demons declared God's omnipotence. God's Son, the heir of all things, is now rightfully seated at God's right hand in heaven. There is a Man in the glory who in every way continues to declare God's glory.

October 3 – Eternal Sonship
(Hebrews 1)

The term "begotten" commonly used in Scripture refers to the relationship of a father to his son in the ancestral sense. "Begotten" can also speak of uniqueness as determined by the context of the passage. The writer of Hebrews applies the expression to the Lord Jesus:

> *For to which of the angels did He ever say: "You are My Son, today I have begotten You"? And again: "I will be to Him a Father, and He shall be to Me a Son"? But when He again brings the firstborn into the world, He says: "Let all the angels of God worship Him"* (Heb. 1:5-6).

In verse 5, the Lord was begotten again, referring to His *unique resurrection.* Obviously the Lord Jesus was not born again, so "begotten" must have a wider sense than mere physical birth. In verse 6, the term begotten is used to speak of the Lord's *unique incarnation.* Hebrews 11:17 refers to Isaac as Abraham's only begotten son, yet Abraham had several other sons, including Ishmael (who was born before Isaac); here the term clearly expresses uniqueness (i.e. Isaac was the unique son of promise and Ishmael was not). God's Son is also unique; Jesus Christ is His Son of promise (John 3:16).

There are many other Scriptures which address the eternal sonship of the Lord Jesus Christ. For example, John 16:28 teaches that Christ came forth from the Father, while John 17:5 and 24 indicate that there was a Father/Son relationship in the Godhead even before the creation of the world. Hebrews 1:2 also states that the Son created all things. God gave His Son (John 3:16), implying that Christ was God's Son before He was given – He did not give one that would become His Son, but was already His Son. Isaiah 48:16-17, Psalm 40:6-8, and Hebrews 10:6-9 also confirm this same understanding. There are many passages which speak of the Father "sending" the Son; these all imply that Christ existed as God's Son prior to His earthly mission (John 20:21; Gal. 4:4; 1 Jn. 4:10, 14). Clearly, the Son eternally existed in the bosom of the Father (1 John 1:18) and He alone enjoyed the fellowship of that relationship prior to His incarnation. Obviously, there cannot be eternal Fatherhood without an Everlasting Son.

October 4 – The Son's Acquired Glory
(Hebrews 1)

Besides referring to His unique resurrection, "begotten" is also linked with the Son's incarnation. J. N. Darby comments about the divine glories associated with Christ, God's Son and Messiah in Hebrews 1:5-6:

> This glory is twofold, and in connection with the twofold office of Christ. It is the divine glory of the Person of the Messiah, the Son of God. The solemn authority of His Word is connected with this glory. And then there is the glory with which His humanity is invested according to the counsels of God – the glory of the Son of man; a glory connected with His sufferings and in all the temptations to which the saints, whose nature He had assumed, are subjected.[2]

> *"Thou art My Son, this day have I begotten Thee."* It is this character of Sonship, proper to the Messiah, which, as a real relationship, distinguishes Him. He was from eternity the Son of the Father, but it is not precisely in this point of view that He is here considered. The name expresses the same relationship, but it is to the Messiah born on earth that this title is here applied.[3]

The glory related to the divine essence of Christ is unchanging, but the glory associated with His Messiahship was earned through faithful devotion and great sacrifice. Therefore, we have God's subsequent declaration after Christ's ascension to heaven: *"Your throne, O God, is forever and ever; a scepter of righteousness is the scepter of Your kingdom"* (Heb. 1:8). He is "the King of Glory" – "The Lord of Hosts" (Ps. 24:7-10).

The writer of Hebrews declares, *"He [Christ] has by inheritance obtained a more excellent name than they [the angels]"* (Heb. 1:4). Christ's holy morality was demonstrated during His earthly sojourn; His intrinsic glory is that which is essential to Him as the Son of God. Having fully completed the work of redemption, God the Father rewarded His Son with a position of glory. This acquired glory demands the respect of every knee and every tongue. God is insulted when we do not keep the King of kings and Lord of lords in the highest estimation. Diminished appreciation for the Savior always leads to our spiritual stagnation and, in time, a sorrowful outcome (Heb. 5:12-6:1)!

October 5 – Let All Worship Him
(Hebrews 1)

In Hebrews 1, the Father commands the angels, His ministering spirits, to worship His Son: *"Let all the angels of God worship Him"* (Heb. 1:6). Then addressing His Son as God, God the Father proclaims:

Your throne, O God, is forever and ever; a scepter of righteousness is the scepter of Your kingdom. You have loved righteousness and hated lawlessness; therefore God, Your God, has anointed You with the oil of gladness more than Your companions (Heb. 1:8-9).

The Old Testament states that there is only one God and that He will not share His glory with another (Isa. 42:8, 48:11) and that He alone is to be worshipped (Ex. 20:1; Deut. 5:7). The Lord Jesus also affirmed to Satan that only the Lord God should be worshipped (Matt. 4:10). Yet, God the Father commands the heavenly angels to worship the Lord Jesus Christ who is seated with the Father on His throne. Having been highly exalted after finishing the work of Calvary, the Father tells His Son to *"sit at My right hand, till I make Your enemies Your footstool"* (Heb. 1:13). Christ is to be adored, revered, and worshipped by all. When He comes into His earthly kingdom, this will become a permanent reality; no rebellious attitudes will be tolerated.

Even during Christ's earthly sojourn the Gospels record that some recognized His divinity and worshipped Him. This was appropriate, as only God is to be worshipped, and those who honor Christ, honor the Father. The Magi from the East worshipped the Lord Jesus as a young child (Matt. 2:11). A healed blind man worshipped the Lord Jesus after learning that He was the Son of God (John 9:38). Mary anointed Him with expensive ointment as an act of worship (John 12:3).

In a coming day, all the hosts of heaven will worship the Lamb, the Lord Jesus Christ (Rev. 5:12-14, 19:10). Since only God is to be worshipped, and God the Father is pleased when His Son is worshipped and appreciated by all, the Lord Jesus is indeed God Himself. Paul puts the matter this way: *"Christ came, who is over all, the eternally blessed God"* (Rom. 9:5).

October 6 – The Captain of the Host
(Hebrews 2)

The Greek word *archegos* is found four times in the New Testament and each occurrence speaks of the Lord Jesus. Luke refers to Christ as the *Prince* of Life (Acts 3:15) and a *Prince* (Acts 5:31). The writer of Hebrews ascribes the titles of *Captain* and *Author* to Him:

> *For it was fitting for Him, for whom are all things and by whom are all things, in bringing many sons to glory, to make the **captain** of their salvation perfect through sufferings* (Heb. 2:10).

> *Looking unto Jesus, the **author** and finisher of our faith, who for the joy that was set before Him endured the cross, despising the shame, and has sat down at the right hand of the throne of God* (Heb. 12:2).

Both verses speak of the Lord's victorious campaign against the ruler of this world (the devil) at Calvary. Therefore, Christ is the King of the saints (Rev. 15:3) and commands the armies of heaven. We find this imagery at both ends of Scripture. Joshua met the Commander in Chief of Israel's army privately on the eve of the battle against Jericho:

> *When Joshua ... lifted his eyes and looked, and behold, a Man stood opposite him with His sword drawn in His hand. And Joshua went to Him and said to Him, "Are You for us or for our adversaries?" So He said, "No, but as **Commander of the army of the Lord** I have now come"* (Josh. 5:13-14).

The Hebrew word *sar* rendered "commander" here is translated as "prince" in Isaiah 9:6. Isaiah also refers to the Lord as *"the Prince of Peace"* and *"a leader and commander for the people"* (Isa. 55:4). Indeed, the Warrior before Joshua was God's Commander of His army. Realizing this, Joshua fell to the ground and worshipped the One who held the drawn sword before him. Being on holy ground, Joshua was told to loosen the shoes from his feet and he did so. By this command, the One speaking to Joshua identified Himself as Jehovah God.

The Bible closes with the majestic scene of the *Lord of lords and King of kings* leading His heavenly armies to earth to vindicate His name (Rev. 19). There is nothing wimpy or feminine about the Lord Jesus, as often depicted in art. He is a courageous, victorious Warrior.

288

October 7 – "My Brethren"
(Hebrews 2)

As with the *friend* terminology discussed previously, no reference may be found in Scripture which implies that Christ is our brother; believers are always referred to as His brethren (Matt. 12:50, 23:8). For example, the writer of Hebrew writes: *"For both He who sanctifies and those who are being sanctified are all of one, **for which reason He is not ashamed to call them brethren**: 'I will declare Your name to My brethren; in the midst of the assembly I will sing praise to You'"* (Heb. 2:11). Clearly, we are set apart in Him to enjoy an intimate relationship with Him; He is not set apart by us!

In speaking to the Pharisees, the Lord clarified the matter of who His brethren were – those who would willingly submit to God's will and honor Him:

> But He answered them, saying, "Who is **My** mother, or **My** brothers?" And He looked around in a circle at those who sat about Him, and said, "Here are **My** mother and **My** brothers! For whoever does the will of God is **My** brother and **My** sister and mother" (Mark 3:33-35).

The biblical focus of the Lord's *brethren* terminology was for us to better grasp who we are in Him and then show our appreciation of being associated with Him by doing His will. When Christians call on the Lord of Glory with unbiblical and often casual expressions such as "my Big Brother," it demonstrates a level of ignorance that borders on violating the second of the Ten Commandments. In other words, such language creates an imaginary image of God which fits human liking, but is unfitting for the Lord's exalted station.

Let us be careful not to lower the Lord to our human level of reckoning through casual speech and flippant terminology. The Lord Jesus has worked diligently to bless us with all spiritual blessings in heavenly places in Himself and we are to rest in the heavenlies with Him. In Him, we are children of God. In Him, we are His friends. In Him, we are His brethren. In Him, we have everything that is good!

October 8 – Three Rests
(Hebrews 4)

The writer of Hebrews affirms that when men cease working to earn heaven and simply rest by faith in the finished work of Christ, they enter God's rest of salvation (Heb. 4:1-7, 10). This follows God's example of laboring six days in the work of creation to enter into His rest the seventh day – one must cease working to rest. The rest of the gospel secures peace with God, but not necessarily the peace of God. The latter is gained through the practical experience of going on with the Lord in faith. This was the primary lesson the Israelites were to learn in Canaan. Sadly, they did not keep going with the Lord after the initial conquest and over time many of them lost their rest because they failed to secure their God-given possession in faithful obedience.

Thus, the writer explains that Canaan, in present-day application, does not picture God's heavenly and peaceful abode, for the Israelites had to engage in hard fighting for years to conquer their enemies and lay hold of their God-given possession (Josh. 11:23, 13:1; Heb. 4:8, 11). Joshua understood that Canaan was not to be the final resting place for God's people: *"For if Joshua had given them rest, then he would not afterward have spoken of another day. There remains therefore a rest for the people of God"* (Heb. 4:8-9). The Greek word translated "rest" in verse 9 is *sabbatismos*, and is only found here in the New Testament. *Sabbatismos* literally means "a keeping of the Sabbath" and speaks of the future "battle-free" rest believers will enjoy with God in heaven forever. But as in the days of Joshua, the earthly sojourn of faithful believers today will undoubtedly be fraught with conflict (2 Tim. 3:12), but hopefully not against each other (Gal. 5:15).

For earth-bound believers, heaven is still future, which means the battle against spiritual wickedness in high places is still ongoing (Eph. 6:12). Engaging in spiritual warfare is the believer's great opportunity to learn of and lay hold of all his or her spiritual blessings in heavenly places in Christ (Eph. 1:3). When at last the Bright and Morning Star standing alone in the dreary predawn hue becomes the rising sun in its full glory, then all of our earthly school days will be done. On that day, while basking in the inconceivable bliss of God's glory, then Joshua's promise will be fulfilled: *"Not a word failed of any good thing which the Lord had spoken ... all came to pass"* (Josh. 21:45). Rest indeed!

October 9 – We Cannot Hide From God (Part 1)
(Hebrews 4)

The writer of Hebrews tells us that it is just not possible to hide anything from the Lord: *"There is no creature hidden from His sight, but all things are naked and open to the eyes of Him to whom we must give account"* (Heb. 4:13). The Lord is omniscient and it is the self-righteous man who thinks he can avoid being seen, being caught, being judged for sin (Rom. 2:1-4). No one can hide from the Lord or escape His jurisdiction, *"for the eyes of the Lord run to and fro throughout the whole earth, to show Himself strong on behalf of those whose heart is loyal to Him"* (2 Chron. 16:9).

Omniscience means "all-knowing." God in Himself possesses perfect knowledge. God cannot learn; He has never learned anything and cannot be instructed by another. The prophet Isaiah contemplated the vastness and magnificence of creation and then asked his audience who could have instructed God in such things: *"Who has directed the Spirit of the Lord, or as His counselor has taught Him? With whom did He take counsel, and who instructed Him, and taught Him in the path of justice? Who taught Him knowledge, and showed Him the way of understanding?"* (Isa. 40:13-14). The answer is no one. Paul echoes the same sentiment in Romans 11:33-36. God is the definer of absolute truth and therefore has no need to learn – He already knows. God knows everything, and His knowledge is infinite. It is impossible for God to not know. Even when we have concealed our sin from everyone else, God knows all about it; we cannot hide from Him.

The omniscience of the Lord Jesus was demonstrated throughout His earthly ministry many times. Here are a few examples: *"But Jesus knew their thoughts, and said to them..."* (Matt. 12:25). *"When Jesus perceived in His spirit that they reasoned thus within themselves..."* (Mark 2:8). *"But Jesus did not commit Himself to them, because He knew all men, and had no need that anyone should testify of man, for He knew what was in man"* (John 2:24-25).

How silly for people to think that the omniscient Son of God would not know their most secret thoughts. Neither should we try to conceal from the Lord Jesus what He already knows all about. May we be transparent and honest with Him now; otherwise, He will be obliged to confront us later at His Judgment Seat. Nothing evades His sight!

October 10 – We Cannot Hide From God (Part 2)
(Hebrews 4)

We continue to ponder the silliness of thinking that we could ever hide our secret sins from an all-knowing, all-seeing God, for *"all things are naked and open to the eyes of Him to whom we must give account"* (Heb. 4:13). Even those deep secrets that no one else knows about, God looks down from heaven and says, "I see exactly what is lurking in the dark recesses of your heart – you cannot hide it from Me, so why try?"

David fully understood this attribute of God and welcomed His examination: *"O Lord, You have searched me and known me. You know my sitting down and my rising up; You understand my thought afar off"* (Ps. 139:1-2). Because David realized every aspect of his life was searched out, planned, and meticulously controlled by the Lord, he could praise the Lord for His wondrous works and invite further inspection and refinement of his inner man (Ps. 139:23-24). Hamilton Smith reminds us that godly saints desire this type of spiritual scrutiny and enhancement:

> The godly man welcomes the searchings of God into the inmost recesses of his heart, desiring that he may be delivered from every evil way and led "in the way everlasting." In the experience of the psalmist, the consciousness of the omniscience of God at first plunges his soul into the deepest distress as he thinks of his own broken responsibilities towards God. When, at length, he realizes that God's "works" and God's "thoughts" are toward him in grace, the omniscience of God becomes the source of his deepest comfort.[40]

Divine inspection of David's heart would both prove his loyal devotion to the Lord and permit God to further test and enrich David's character. He knew he could not hide his thoughts and doings from the Lord, so he desired to transform all his contemplations and deeds to those that would please Him. This is the proper response to the omnipresent, omniscient, omnipotent God. Concerning one's devotion to the Lord, David shows us that there is no middle ground; we should loathe what the Lord disapproves of and yearn for what pleases Him.

The greatness of a man's power is the measure of his surrender.

— William Booth

October 11 – "Come Boldly to the Throne"
(Hebrews 4)

Consecrated believers are invited to *"come boldly to the throne of grace, that we may obtain mercy and find grace to help in time of need"* (Heb. 4:16). James reminds us that *"the effective, fervent prayer of a **righteous** man avails much"* (Jas. 5:16). A powerful, effectual prayer life is one of the rewards of living a consecrated life of faith. The veil separating man's access to God has been rent, and each believer now has the great privilege of humbly walking beyond the thick cloud of darkness into the spectacular brilliance of God's presence to enjoy fellowship with Him. The writer of Hebrews refers to this as *"the new and living way"* of approaching God – this new way is available to all who have trusted Christ as Savior:

> *Therefore, brethren, having boldness to enter the Holiest by the blood of Jesus, by a new and living way which He consecrated for us, through the veil, that is, His flesh, and having a High Priest over the house of God, let us draw near with a true heart in full assurance of faith, having our hearts sprinkled from an evil conscience and our bodies washed with pure water* (Heb. 10:19-22).

Paul knew that real spiritual power was supplied through answered prayers and since we battle spiritual wickedness in high places, believers must get up into heavenly places by this new and living way and beseech the Lord's help. He, therefore, instructed the saints at Thessalonica to *"pray without ceasing"* (1 Thess. 5:17) and the believers at Ephesus to pray always *"with all prayer and supplication in the Spirit, being watchful to this end with all perseverance and supplication for all the saints"* (Eph. 6:18). God's people have the opportunity to lift their hands to God in prayer anytime and anywhere to ask for wisdom and grace in any situation. But our lifted hands must be holy (i.e. reflecting a pure heart), and we must pray without doubting and without wrath (no works of the flesh can be present). It is evident from the weak condition of the Church that much of our praying does not comply with these criteria. From a practical standpoint, unconfessed sin, wrong motives, and carnal intentions stagnate the flow of God's blessings into our lives (Jas. 4:1-3).

October 12 – Apostle and High Priest
(Hebrews 5)

In His role as Son of Man, the Lord holds two offices: priest and prophet. *"Therefore, holy brethren, partakers of the heavenly calling, consider the Apostle and High Priest of our confession, Christ Jesus"* (Heb. 3:1). As prophet, or apostle, He is the sent One from the Father to perfectly represent God to mankind. As priest, Christ perfectly represents man to God. The writer of Hebrews informs us why Christ must be the Son of Man to be our High Priest:

> For every high priest **taken from among men** is appointed for men in things pertaining to God, that he may offer both gifts and sacrifices for sins. He can have **compassion on those who are ignorant** and going astray, since **he himself is also subject to weakness** (Heb. 5:1-2).

Christ being *holy humanity* demonstrated compassion for others and felt the infirmities of mankind, yet not in sin. Hebrews 4:15 reads, *"For we have not a high priest not able to sympathize with our infirmities, but tempted in all things in like manner, sin apart"* (JND). *"We are, yet"* commonly inserted in this verse is not in the Greek text. The latter part of this verse is often used to teach that Christ was sinless despite testing. Though this is true, it is not the fullness of what the writer is declaring. The passage is not highlighting the sinless perfections of Christ but His inherent impeccability. Christ was tested in every way you and I are, except in sin because there is none in Him. Our hearts are rotten to the core; we are *"deceitful above all things, and desperately wicked"* (Jer. 17:9), but Christ's heart was perfectly pure.

The Lord experientially knows what it is like to live on a sin-cursed earth, to endure the contradiction of sinners, to be hungry, weary, and thirsty, to be betrayed by a friend, and to be wrongfully treated for doing good. As our High Priest, we can solicit Him for grace to endure such things (Heb. 2:17, 4:14). Yet, though He understands the suffering that our sin causes, He cannot relate to our sinful impulses, lusting, and selfishness. Since God cannot condone sin, we cannot approach our heavenly High Priest for help or sympathy in matters of sin. Instead, we must permit the Holy Spirit to thrust us through with God's Word to mortify such behavior. Let us be careful not to have a distorted view of Christ's humanity or we will degrade His priesthood also.

October 13 – The Priesthood of Christ
(Hebrews 5)

As priest, Christ perfectly represents man to God: *"For every high priest taken from among men is appointed for men in things pertaining to God, that he may offer both gifts and sacrifices for sins"* (Heb. 5:1). A High Priest, then, stands between God and man, and must have a perfect connection with both in order to perform his duties properly. For this reason, the Aaronic priesthood and its offerings were inferior. Every priest after the order of Aaron was a sinner, and the blood of the bulls and goats that was presented by them in the temple on behalf of sinners could only atone for (cover) sin. Animal blood cannot cleanse a sinner's guilty conscience or provide propitiation for sin (Heb. 9:14).

Consequently, a new High Priest and new Sacrifice were necessary: Christ was both (Heb. 7:27, 9:11-15, 24-26). He was *"a merciful and faithful High Priest in things pertaining to God, to make propitiation for the sins of the people"* (Heb. 2:17). So while Christ's priestly work of providing propitiation for sinners is complete (Rom. 3:25; 1 Tim. 2:5), His continuing work as Priest is not. There are two main facets of Christ's ongoing priestly ministry, namely, He is our *High Priest* and our *Advocate*. (Christ's advocacy will be discussed later in 1 John 2.)

The Priesthood of the Lord Jesus Christ fulfills a number of Scriptural types. In keeping with the priestly type of Christ presented in Melchizedek, the Lord is *"without genealogy, having neither beginning of days nor end of life"* (Heb. 7:3). This pictures the uniqueness and eternality of the High Priest needed in heaven – One who could intercede on the behalf of all the redeemed still alive on earth. Scripture does not record Melchizedek offering a sacrifice, but rather bringing a memorial of a sacrifice to Abraham, as pictured in the bread and wine (Gen. 14:18). After the Lord's resurrection, He entered into the eternal priestly office typified by Melchizedek, but in the power of an endless life; thus, there is a continuing memorial of His sacrifice in heaven.

We have the wonderful privilege of soliciting our High Priest in heaven for grace that we do not sin, for forgiveness when we do sin, and for consolation when we suffer because of others' sin. Let us not approach the throne of grace with thoughts which degrade the character of our Great High Priest, but rather let us fully recognize His holy nature and profit from His gracious ministry.

October 14 – Christ "Learned Obedience"
(Hebrews 5)

If the Lord Jesus, being the Son of God, is omniscient, how do we understand the writer's statement in Hebrews 5 about the Lord *learning* obedience?

Though He was a Son, yet He learned obedience by the things which He suffered. And having been perfected, He became the author of eternal salvation to all who obey Him (Heb. 5:8-5).

If the Son of God knows all things, how can He learn anything? Furthermore, how did He as God *"[increase] in wisdom"* (Luke 2:52)?

The answer to both questions rests in our understanding that to be our perfect High Priest, He had to *experience* to understand what it means to live and suffer as a human in a sin-cursed world (Heb. 4:15). Because the Lord did not use His deity to satisfy His human needs, we know that He can legitimately invite us to solicit Him for grace whenever we are in legitimate need. If He had cheated, then He would not *experientially* have been shown to be a High Priest that understands our needs and suffering. Accordingly, He learned to suckle, eat, crawl, walk, talk, etc. in the same way you and I did. As divinity He knew of these already, but experientially these were learned in His humanity. For example, in His youth the Lord had to learn the books of the Hebrew Bible, how to look up passages in the Bible, and then He had to memorize and meditate on what He read. We have to do the same thing to learn what God desires for us to know, the only difference being that the Lord was not hindered by sin within His members as we are. Sin within us hinders our retention and recall of what is of God.

In a mysterious way, God the Son withheld from utilizing what He knew in order to demonstrate human learning. This should not surprise us, for in like manner an all-knowing God chooses not to remember our past sins once properly handled (Ps. 103:11; Jer. 31:34). In some instances, God's sovereign purposes can only be accomplished when an all-knowing God chooses not to act on what He knows. Thankfully, He knew us before He laid the foundations of the world and then He acted to bring us to Himself. Be thankful that we have an all-knowing Savior who *learned obedience by the things which He suffered.*

October 15 – Backsliders Are Warned (Part 1)
(Hebrews 6)

Throughout Scripture, God never referred to His covenant people as "being backslidden," but He did call them "backsliding" when appropriate to speak of their evil doings, not their state. Jeremiah told the Southern Kingdom that they were a "backsliding" people thirteen times, which is the number signifying rebellion in Scripture. Backsliding is not a matter of ignorance; rather, it results when God's people willfully and actively turn from understood truth. Backsliding, then, is a conscious choice of a child of God to discontinue fellowship with God, to become fruitless, and to invite God's chastening hand.

The writer of Hebrews conveys the same truth in the Church Age:

*For it is impossible for those who were once **enlightened**, and have **tasted** the heavenly gift, and have become **partakers** of the Holy Spirit, and have **tasted** the good word of God and the powers of the age to come, if they fall away, to renew them again to repentance, since they crucify again for themselves the Son of God, and put Him to an open shame* (Heb. 6:4-6).

This passage is difficult to understand, but the verb tenses in the original language indicate that the writer is stating that as long as someone willfully chooses to fall away (backslide), it is impossible to renew that person through repentance to a state of spiritual fruitfulness. In fact, trying to please God while in such a rebellious state mocks the power of the Lord's redemptive blood and puts Him to open shame. All of the Greek verbs in Hebrews 6:4, "enlightened," "tasted," and "become partakers," are aorist passive participles, which indicates that these actions have already occurred. The word "tasted" is exactly the same Greek verb used in Hebrews 2:9 to acknowledge the fact that Christ suffered death for every man; the word does not denote a partial experience, but a complete one. The Greek verb for "enlightened" is the same one translated as "illuminated" in Hebrews 10:32, where it is employed to speak of the spiritual sight God gives to believers. The third Greek verb in this description, "partakers," is rendered "companion" in Hebrews 1:9. The meaning is much more absolute than just a taste of truth limited to some pre-conversion work of the Spirit. Hebrews 6:4 states that those who had tasted and were enlightened were also companions with the Holy Spirit; this refers to true believers in active rebellion against God, not apostates that were never saved.

October 16 – Backsliders Are Warned (Part 2)
(Hebrews 6)

If the Hebrews 6:4-6 is warning believers against backsliding and not addressing unsaved apostates, how are we to understand the statement *"if they fall away, to renew them again to repentance"*? Again, reviewing the original language is helpful in ascertaining the passage's context. In Hebrews 6:6, the verb rendered "falling away" is an aorist, active participle meaning that these backsliding believers caused themselves to fall away previously and still remained in that condition. Additionally, the Greek verb *parapito*, not *apostasia*, is used here to indicate the action of falling. Its root *pipto* is employed to describe the Lord Jesus falling to the ground in the garden to pray (Mark 14:35). The remaining verbs translated in these phrases "to renew," "they crucify again," and "put Him to an open shame" are present, active participles which indicate an active, ongoing process is in view. If perfect tense verbs had been used, then the subject would be engaged in an "unchangeable activity," but the use of present tense conveys the idea that as long as the subject chooses to be falling away, they would also suffer ongoing consequences.

To summarize, the writer of Hebrews is saying that as long as backsliding believers choose to fall away, they actively put Christ to shame and cannot be brought to repentance or fruitfulness. One cannot turn back to the Lord (i.e. repent) if he or she is actively backsliding away from Him. Those living in a falling away spiritual condition are "near to cursing," but are not cursed (Heb. 6:8). Backsliding believers are not fruitful, nor can they be; yet, fruit *should* accompany salvation (Heb. 6:9). A believer in this condition has a burned up testimony which ruins their ministries and disgraces Christ (Heb. 6:8; John 15:4-6). Those who are actively falling away from the truth are said to be "rejected" according to Hebrews 6:8. The same word is translated "castaway" in 1 Corinthians 9:27 (KJV), where Paul was surely not speaking of losing his own salvation; rather, the term refers to the loss of one's testimony and one's opportunity for profitable ministry that occurs as a result of giving in to carnal lusting. The bottom line: Any child of God who willfully forsakes going on with the Lord will be miserable, fruitless, and cause the name of Christ to be disdained.

October 17 – Backsliders Are Warned (Part 3)

(Hebrews 6)

James Vernon McGee provides this summary of Hebrews 6:4-6:

> In Hebrews 6, we find genuine believers, because they are identified as such in many ways. ... You will notice that it is said of these people that they are dull of hearing (Heb. 5:11) – it does not say that they are dead in trespasses and sins (Eph. 2:1). And in Hebrews 5:12 it says that *"when for the time ye ought to be teachers, ye have need that one teach you...and are become such as have need of milk...."* They need to have milk because they are babes. An unsaved person doesn't need milk; he needs *life*. He needs to be born again.
>
> The whole tenor of the text reveals that he is speaking of rewards which are the result of salvation. In verse 6 he says, *"If they shall fall away, to renew them again unto repentance"* – not to salvation, but to *repentance*. Repentance is something that God has asked believers to do [e.g. the Lord told five of the seven churches of Asia Minor to repent (Rev. 2-3)]. So the writer of Hebrews is talking about the *fruit* of salvation, not about the *root* of salvation. Notice verse 9 again: *"But, beloved, we are persuaded better things of you. And things that accompany salvation"* [he hasn't been discussing salvation but the things that accompany salvation]... the whole tenor of the passage is that he is warning them of the possibility of losing their reward.[41]

Unfortunately, the Jewish nation had been actively backsliding and, thus, consequently fruitless much of their history. With this historical example in mind, Paul warned the Church against making the same mistake, using the figure of an olive tree whose branches were pruned away and a wild olive branch (Gentile believers) was grafted into it. If God did not spare the natural olive branches (speaking of rebellious Jews), how much more likely would He be to punish, if needed, the wild branch (i.e. Gentile believers) that were grafted into the blessings of the Abrahamic covenant (Rom. 11:17-21). God's severe dealings with His covenant people serves as a solemn warning for the Church to take heed and not to duplicate the backsliding ways of the Jewish nation. Our God is a consuming fire (Heb. 12:29), and He is very jealous of where we place our affections (1 Cor. 10:22). Thankfully, He loves us too much to permit us to leave Him without consequences!

299

October 18 – "Two Immutable Things"
(Hebrews 6)

For when God made a promise to Abraham, because He could swear by no one greater, He swore by Himself, saying, "Surely blessing I will bless you, and multiplying I will multiply you." And so, after he had patiently endured, he obtained the promise. For men indeed swear by the greater, and an oath for confirmation is for them an end of all dispute. Thus God, determining to show more abundantly to the heirs of promise the immutability of His counsel, confirmed it by an oath, that by two immutable things, in which it is impossible for God to lie, we might have strong consolation" (Heb. 6:13-18).

The writer says that the New Covenant was confirmed by two immutable things – God's word and His oath, neither of which can fail. God had previously promised to institute a New Covenant with the houses of Judah and Israel (Jer. 31:31-32; Heb. 8:8) in order to fulfill His promise to Abraham made millennia ago. That is why the prophet Jeremiah could foretell of an everlasting covenant resulting in eternal blessing to the Jews (Jer. 32:40). This promise is literal and has yet to be fulfilled. For example, the prophet Isaiah connects this covenant with God's promise to erect an eternal city where the Jewish remnant will dwell (Isa. 48:2; 52:1). The prophet Ezekiel refers to the New Covenant as a *"Covenant of Peace"* with the Jewish nation (Ezek. 34:25). Isaiah proclaimed that through this covenant, *"Israel shall be saved in the Lord with an everlasting salvation"* (Isa. 45:17).

The Old Covenant was conditional in nature; the Jews had to keep God's Law to receive God's blessing (Heb. 8:9). The New Covenant sealed by Christ's blood accomplished what the previous covenant could not, propitiation for sins. The New Covenant is unconditional in nature and would be the means by which God would honor His covenant with Abraham.

God had given His word and oath on enacting this covenant. In other words, God the Father was staking His name, His word, His oath, and His honor on the faithfulness of His Son to complete His mission at Calvary and establish the New Covenant. God literally gave His precious Word (His Son) to keep His promise to Abraham. Indeed, we agree with Paul: *"For all the promises of God in Him are Yes, and in Him Amen, to the glory of God through us"* (2 Cor. 1:20).

October 19 – Our Refuge
(Hebrews 6)

The writer of Hebrews mentions the only reference to a "refuge" in the New Testament to speak of the believer's place of security, justice, and rest found in Christ: those *"who have fled for refuge to lay hold of the hope set before us"* (Heb. 6:18). This *refuge* ties back to the six Cities of Refuge in Canaan after the Israelites obtained their possession from God, through conquest (Num. 35).

All six cities were evenly spread from north to south on both sides of the Jordan River. All six cities were to uphold the righteousness of God in the land and the path to justice was to be readily found. The gates to the Cities of Refuge were always to be open, so that every manslayer might find protection until justice could be determined (Deut. 19:3). When someone sought refuge in a City of Refuge, no retaliation by the relatives of the deceased was permitted. Appointed judges would then hear the case in the public place of decision – the gate of the city. Everyone was to uphold the ruling of the judges.

The writer invokes the imagery of this Refuge to speak of the eternal security believers have because of their union with Christ (Heb. 6:18). For those who cease to work for heaven and choose to rest in Christ alone for salvation – He becomes their rest (Heb. 4:1-5, 10). Christ is the City of Refuge for all believers. Through spiritual baptism we become one with Him and become safe and secure in Him forever.

At Christ's coming our earthly sojourn will conclude and our bodies will experience glorification. In this spiritual sense, believers, who are also spiritual priests, are safe in their City of Refuge until they can come into their final rest, for their High Priest will never die (2 Cor. 5:8). Today, the Cities of Refuge represent the gracious, ongoing work of God to bring condemned sinners into a safe and secure resting place to escape judgment. Those who openly admit their guilt before a Holy God can flee to a refuge far safer than any City of Refuge – Christ Himself. The Lord Jesus has already suffered for the condemned and in Him alone do we find divine peace with God.

The hope of the manslayer, incarcerated in a city of refuge, was for the death of the high priest, but the believer's hope in Christ today is much better. Our High Priest will never die, and when He comes again in glory, we will be liberated from a world ruled by the god of this age!

October 20 – Our Anchor and Forerunner
(Hebrews 6)

This hope we have as an anchor of the soul, both sure and steadfast, and which enters the Presence behind the veil, where the forerunner has entered for us, even Jesus" (Heb. 6:19-20).

The passage informs us that Christ is the Forerunner of the journey before us and the anchor in God's presence to ensure we arrive safely – this is our hope. The forerunner in a footrace ran ahead of the actual competitors to ensure that they knew the course and would not get disqualified by veering off of it. Every aspect of Christ's life on earth demonstrated the value of remaining on the narrow path of holiness and pointed the way to the finish line. The Lord safely journeyed through potential worldly hazards and sinful pitfalls in order that we might have a life-pattern to follow. He was not disqualified through any missteps, but in fact was proven to be wise and sinless in all that He did.

Besides being the forerunner, the Lord Jesus is also our Anchor in the presence of God. Before highways were built and tractor-trailers began carrying goods along the Caribbean coastline, small sailing ships loaded with large cargoes brought goods into coastline harbors for distribution. Occasionally, as these approached a harbor, there would be insufficient breeze for the ship to enter it. A small boat with a line attached was then rowed to the dock's mooring. Once there, a heavy cable was attached to the line and pulled back to the ship while the other end was securely anchored to the dock. The ship's crew then assembled on deck and literally pulled the cargo ship into port. They showed their faith in the anchor by working together towards the goal of being where the anchor was. In this illustration the small boat was the forerunner; it not only indicated the route to take, but its arrival ensured that the anchor would permit the larger ship to arrive at the dock safely. Likewise, the Lord Jesus is our Forerunner and Anchor. He has shown us the way to go and has entered within the veil (i.e., into God's presence in heaven) to ensure we all get home safely. Likewise, He calls us to exercise faith and work with Him until we are with Him.

Tempters seek to lure astray, storms obscure the light of day:
But in Christ I can be bold; I've an anchor that shall hold.

— W. C. Martin

October 21– The New Covenant
(Hebrews 8)

God promised to institute a New Covenant with Israel that would give them eternal salvation, a new and clean heart, and cause the Holy Spirit to indwell them forever (Jer. 31:31-40; Ezek. 34:25). The first covenant revealed man's sin and brought condemnation as no one could keep it (Rom. 3:20). Christ sealed the New Covenant with the house of Judah and the house of Israel with His own blood (Luke 22:20; Heb. 8:8). Paul explains that Gentiles have been brought into the good of this New Covenant as a second benefactor (Eph. 2:14-3:12). Since Christ is the Mediator of this covenant, the Church's claim to the Lord Jesus as High Priest is as strong as any redeemed Jew (Heb. 4:14):

> *For if that first covenant had been faultless, then no place would have been sought for a second. Because finding fault with them, He says: "Behold, the days are coming, says the Lord, when* **I will make a new covenant with the house of Israel and with the house of Judah** *– not according to the covenant that I made with their fathers ... because they did not continue in My covenant, and I disregarded them, says the Lord. For this is the covenant that I will make with the house of Israel after those days, says the Lord: I will put My laws in their mind and write them on their hearts; and I will be their God, and they shall be My people. ... He says, "A new covenant," He has made the first obsolete.* **Now what is becoming obsolete and growing old is ready to vanish away** *(Heb. 8:7-13).*

About four years after these words were penned, God completely removed the religious practices of the Old Covenant from Israel, which in reality had been replaced by Christ's New Covenant forty years earlier. The Jews had rejected the terms of this covenant which required them to receive Christ as their Messiah. By the destruction of Jerusalem and the temple, God put to an end the religious system that the Jews had developed from the Levitical order (Gal. 1:13-14). No more ceremonial lip service devoid of any spiritual value would be tolerated. By the New Covenant, God will forgive the sins of Israel and Judah, pour out His Spirit on them, and restore them to Himself. Although during the Church Age some Jews have come to faith in Christ, the nation as a whole will not turn to Him until His second advent to the earth at the end of the Tribulation Period (Zech. 12:10; Rom. 11:7-25).

October 22 – A Better Sacrifice in a Better Sanctuary
(Hebrews 9)

On the Day of Atonement, Aaron sprinkled the blood of a bullock and a goat on and before the Mercy Seat in the Most Holy Place of the tabernacle to atone for the nation of Israel's sin that year; this means of making atonement had to be repeated every year. But at Calvary, the Lord Jesus shed His own blood to seal the New Covenant forever. His loud cry, *"It is finished!"* uttered just before He relinquished His life, was an eternal declaration of what He had accomplished on our behalf. God's judicial wrath for human sin was appeased through His Son's sacrifice which was presented before God in His heavenly sanctuary:

> *But Christ came as High Priest of the good things to come,* **with the greater and more perfect tabernacle** *not made with hands, that is, not of this creation. Not with the blood of goats and calves, but with His own blood He entered the Most Holy Place once for all, having obtained eternal redemption. For if the blood of bulls and goats and the ashes of a heifer, sprinkling the unclean, sanctifies for the purifying of the flesh,* **how much more shall the blood of Christ, who through the eternal Spirit offered Himself without spot to God, cleanse your conscience from dead works to serve the living God?** *And for this reason He is the Mediator of the new covenant, by means of death, for the redemption of the transgressions under the first covenant, that those who are called may receive the promise of the eternal inheritance* (Heb. 9:11-15).

Aaron had to repeat the blood sacrifices day by day and year by year because the blood of bulls and goats could only cover sin temporarily until the revelation of what these sacrifices pictured: the ultimate solution for human sin. Through Christ's sacrifice, righteous justice for sin was answered, and by His blood those who trust Him for salvation are purged from filth and guilt and become clean vessels fit for God's use. Christ has opened a way (the only way) for man to pass within the heavenly veil and enter the very place from where Christ originally came and where His blood was presented (Heb. 6:18-20).

In comparison to the Old Covenant, Christ's priesthood is better than Aaron's, His blood offered better than that of animals, and His sanctuary better than any veiled-off earthly tent/building ever could be. Why would any Jewish Christian want to go back to what was inferior?

October 23 – Three Deaths
(Hebrews 9)

Several types of death are spoken of in Scripture, but there are three deaths, or literally, "separations," that are most significant to all mankind. We are all born *spiritually dead*; that is, we are spiritually separated from God. Then, when *physical death* occurs, our soul and spirit separate from our body. If physical death occurs while a person is still spiritually dead, *eternal death* (judgment in Hell) is assured. Hebrews 9:27 proclaims, *"It is appointed unto men once to die, but after this the judgment."* The only exception to this is that God may demonstrate His grace by applying the blood of Christ to the souls of those who died in the womb or early in life, before they understood the moral law within them and God's solution to their sin problem (2 Sam. 12:23). Though condemned in Adam, God calls these young ones "innocent" (Jer. 19:4). But as adults and older children, the unsaved are just one heartbeat, one breath away from an eternal destiny of woe.

When did death begin? God had informed Adam shortly after his creation, *"Of every tree of the garden you may freely eat, but of the tree of the knowledge of good and evil you shall not eat, for in the day that you eat of it you shall surely die"* (Gen. 2:16-17). Life was wonderful in Eden until that horrible day that changed the course of humanity forever. Satan solicited Eve to eat the forbidden fruit so that she might be like God. Eve, then Adam, chose to believe the "father of lies" instead of God. The same satanic deception and desire for knowledge presently blinds many from heeding the offer of Christ that would liberate their souls from the bondage of sin and eternal death.

After Adam and his wife disobeyed God and ate of the forbidden tree, their fellowship with God was instantly severed. They now felt uneasy with God and even tried to hide from Him. Feelings of guilt, shame, and impending judgment relentlessly pounded their awakened conscience. God judged them and thrust them out of the garden to struggle for survival on a cursed planet. Instead of significance, they felt rejection. Gone too was their security; they were now on their own, having to rely on their own strength and self-control to live. In a brief moment their secure and unhindered communion with God was severed. They felt rejection, shame, and feebleness. Sin and death walk hand in hand, and only trusting Christ can alleviate the pangs of both.

October 24 – Five Offerings in One (Part 1)
(Hebrews 10)

Long ago, David prophesied of the One who would willingly come in faithful obedience to God to fulfill what is typified in each of the five priestly offerings described in Leviticus chapters 1 through 7:

Sacrifice [zebach] and offering [minchad] You did not desire; My ears You have opened. Burnt offering [olah] and sin offering [chataah] You did not require. Then I said, "Behold, I come; in the scroll of the book it is written of me. I delight to do Your will, O my God, and Your law is within my heart" (Ps. 40:6-7).

The writer of Hebrews quotes from Psalm 40 to confirm that Christ's sacrifice at Calvary on behalf of humanity was a direct fulfillment of David's prophecy. God the Father did not want us to miss the link between the willing Servant and the suffering Son of God:

For the law, having a shadow of the good things to come, and not the very image of the things, can never with these same sacrifices, which they offer continually year by year, make those who approach perfect. For then would they not have ceased to be offered? For the worshipers, once purified, would have had no more consciousness of sins. But in those sacrifices there is a reminder of sins every year. For it is not possible that the blood of bulls and goats could take away sins. Therefore, when He came into the world, He said: "Sacrifice and offering You did not desire, but a body You have prepared for Me. In burnt offerings and sacrifices for sin You had no pleasure. Then I said, 'Behold, I have come – in the volume of the book it is written of Me – to do Your will, O God'" (Heb. 10:1-7).

A comparison of Psalm 40 and Hebrews 10 clearly reveals that the One who had His ear opened to be marked as a servant in Psalm 40:6 is the same One who offered His entire body, indeed His life (John 10:11), to God and fulfilled the complete meaning of all five Levitical sacrifices. The first three offerings, the burnt, the meal, and the peace offerings were voluntary and a sweet savor to God. However, the sin and the trespass offerings were demanded and hence were non-sweet-savor offerings. These distinctions show Christ's willingness to be the sin sacrifice God demanded to be offered on behalf of humanity.

October 25 – Five Offerings in One (Part 2)
(Hebrews 10)

The Hebrew words employed in Psalm 40 directly relate to all the Levitical offerings: *zebach* pertains to the *peace* offering, *minchad* the *meal* offering, *olah* the *burnt* offering, and *chataah* the *sin* offering. Although distinct, the sin and trespass (*'asham*) offerings were often connected together: *"The trespass offering is like the sin offering; there is one law for them both"* (Lev. 7:7). Portions of the New Testament also refer to the Lord Jesus in the language of the Levitical offerings.

And walk in love, as Christ also has loved us and given Himself for us, an offering and a sacrifice to God for a sweet-smelling aroma (Eph. 5:2).

But this Man, after He had offered one sacrifice for sins forever, sat down at the right hand of God, from that time waiting till His enemies are made His footstool. For by one offering He has perfected forever those who are being sanctified (Heb. 10:12-14).

The five Levitical offerings present different facets of Christ's life on earth and His sacrifice at Calvary: the burnt offering speaks of Christ's devotion to the Father as an offering totally consumed for God, the meal offering reflects the fine moral character of Christ and His sufferings prior to the cross, the peace offering acknowledges the communion of God with man through Christ, the sin offering pictures God's own payment for the offense of man's sin, and the trespass offering relates to restitution for the damage that sin causes. In all of these, the Person and work of Christ are presented and appreciated.

Before the foundations of the earth were laid, God had already predetermined the incarnation, death, resurrection, and exaltation of His Son, in order to rescue a fallen race, which as of yet He had not even created (1 Pet. 1:20). God foreordained that an innocent and perfect God-man would, as a substitute, suffer the death that you and I deserved in order that we might have an opportunity to escape death, be forgiven, and be restored to our Creator. Who but God could have devised such a plan? *"Oh, the depth of the riches both of the wisdom and knowledge of God! How unsearchable are His judgments and His ways past finding out!"* (Rom. 11:33).

October 26 – Five Offerings in One (Part 3)
(Hebrews 10)

As just mentioned, Leviticus chapters 1 through 7 specifically describe five offerings crucial for maintaining Jehovah's presence among His covenant people. Three offerings (the burnt offering, the meal offering, and the peace offering) were designated as sweet aroma offerings because they were associated with one's choice to freely praise and thank God for His goodness. These present Christ's devotion and excellences, and indicate our approach to God is through Him on the basis that the price of sin has already been paid. When God looked down on the Levitical sacrifices, He could see His Son's finished work on man's behalf because He is not bound by time.

The final two offerings, the sin and trespass offerings, were demanded by God because of the offerer's sin, and thus were deemed non-sweet aroma offerings. In these offerings the perfections of Christ, though apparent and needful, are not the emphasis; rather, He is extolled as the suffering Sin-bearer who satisfies God's demand for justice and also offers restitution for sin's damage (Isa. 53:10).

This entire sacrificial system was replaced some two thousand years ago by what it symbolized, that is, Christ's achievements in redemption (2 Cor. 3:11-14). This being the case, a believer in the Church Age has much more scriptural revelation with which to behold the Savior in the sacrifices than the Jews did. We are utterly amazed God would stoop so low as to represent such spectacular wonders of His Son in the slaughtered animals, the splattering of blood, the wringing off of heads, the smoke of burning fat, and the stench of smoldering flesh. However distasteful all this may seem to our dignified humanity, this is exactly the point we are to appreciate. How much more repugnant would it be for the Creator of all things to personally experience all that is pictured in the Levitical sacrifices!

The writer of Hebrews confirms the purpose of these Old Testament pictures and lessons is to further our appreciation of the Lord Jesus Christ and His finished propitiatory work (Heb. 10:1-4).

All the shame men heaped upon Thee, Thou didst patiently endure;
Not the pains of death too bitter our redemption to procure.
Wondrous Thy humiliation to accomplish our salvation:
Thousand, thousand praises be, precious Savior, unto Thee (E. Homburg).

October 27 – "The Reproach of Christ"
(Hebrews 11)

The book of Hebrews provides insight as to why Moses chose to identify with God's covenant people instead of with the Egyptians:

> *By faith Moses, when he became of age, refused to be called the son of Pharaoh's daughter, choosing rather to suffer affliction with the people of God than to enjoy the passing pleasures of sin, esteeming **the reproach of Christ** greater riches than the treasures in Egypt; for he looked to the reward. By faith he forsook Egypt, not fearing the wrath of the king; for he endured as seeing Him who is invisible* (Heb. 11:24-27).

First of all, Moses understood who he was and he chose to identify with God's suffering people. Moses was willing to forsake riches and status to suffer *the reproach of Christ* in the world. Notice that the text does not say Moses suffered *reproach for Christ*. That activity refers to those who share Christ's message with others and suffer for doing so (1 Pet. 4:4). This is not what Moses suffered, as he did not know who Christ was at this time or what His future message to Israel would be.

Christ departed heaven to take up a lowly existence on the earth in order to identify with those He came to save. Though Moses did not suffer because of his testimony for God, he did honor God by foreshadowing Christ's suffering by identifying with God's people. Somehow he understood that there was a day of reckoning with God, and was determined that it would be better for him to identify with God's people and forsake the splendor of Egypt, rather than to be associated with a dismal system of rule which brutalized God's people.

Today, believers have the privilege of suffering both *the reproach of Christ* and *reproach for Christ*. Believers should lose interest in this passing world that they reside in as they discover their true citizenship is in Christ in heavenly places. God's people are referred to as pilgrims and strangers (Heb. 11:13). Pilgrims belong where they are going and strangers do not belong where they are at. To suffer the reproach of Christ then is to follow His example of humbling Himself to identify with those that were His. Rather, than communing with condemned worldlings, we must closely identify with God's people and be willing to go on with them through thick and thin, no matter what the cost!

October 28 – The Rod of a Loving Father
(Hebrews 12)

The writer of Hebrews in quoting Proverbs 3:11-12 reminds his audience that God loves His children very much, and is even willing to prove His love by chastening them when necessary:

"My son, do not despise the chastening of the Lord, nor be discouraged when you are rebuked by Him; for whom the Lord loves He chastens, and scourges every son whom He receives." If you endure chastening, God deals with you as with sons; for what son is there whom a father does not chasten? But if you are without chastening, of which all have become partakers, then you are illegitimate and not sons. Furthermore, we have had human fathers who corrected us, and we paid them respect. Shall we not much more readily be in subjection to the Father of spirits and live? For they indeed for a few days chastened us as seemed best to them, but He for our profit, **that we may be partakers of His holiness**. Now no chastening seems to be joyful for the present, but painful; nevertheless, afterward **it yields the peaceable fruit of righteousness** to those who have been trained by it (Heb. 12:5-11).

God's chastening of His children is a proof of His love for them. God loves us too much to leave us the way we are. While no chastening is pleasant at the time, those who yield to God's correction are made to be partakers of His holiness and to yield the peaceable fruit of righteousness. In other words, the result of achieving oneness with the Lord and restored fruitfulness makes God's chastening desirable.

Thankfully, though we fail the Lord at times, He does not forsake us. Paul reminded Timothy of this wonderful truth: *"If we are faithless, He remains faithful; He cannot deny Himself"* (2 Tim. 2:13). We have the Lord's promise to bring us safely through to the conclusion of our salvation – glorification with Christ: *"Being confident of this very thing, that He who has begun a good work in you will complete it until the day of Jesus Christ"* (Phil. 1:6). The Lord is faithful to His Word and to us also, even when we do not go on with Him in faith. God is going to demonstrate His love to us no matter what we do, but it would be less grieving to Him to freely bless us rather than to lift up His rod of correction and deliver blows. The Lord Jesus is the ultimate example of the wise Son and the only divine blow He ever received was ours.

October 29 – No "Root of Bitterness"
(Hebrews 12)

Pursue peace with all people, and holiness, without which no one will see the Lord: looking carefully lest anyone fall short of the grace of God; **lest any root of bitterness springing up cause trouble,** *and by this many become defiled* (Heb. 12:14-16).

Bitterness is a chronic and pervasive state caused by smoldering resentment. The Greek work *pikria* rendered "bitterness" in this text refers to poison. Bitterness is a lingering hostile and agitated mental disposition caused by a poisonous frame of mind. Bitterness causes people to agonize over hurtful events or perceived ills to the point they become repulsive and cold in demeanor. Bitterness causes depression, anxiety, pessimism, and poor mental and physical health; it wrecks relationships and hinders communion with God. Bitterness is a choice to be sidelined from experiencing God and His goodness. Interestingly, the writer borrows the expression "root of bitterness" from Deuteronomy 29:18; there, it refers to the negative influence of idolatry among God's people. By one person (the root) evil spreads its influence. Bitterness is the opposite of God's grace working within us; rather, it robs us of the peace and virtue God wants to display to others.

Bitterness can occurs when expectations are not met, especially when being mocked (1 Sam. 1:10). Bitterness can occur when immense loss happens, especially if others infer that you are being punished by God (Job 7:11). Bitterness can occur when we suffer unjustly because of what others have done (Ezekiel suffered hardship because others had sinned; Ezek. 3:14). Bitterness can occur if we do not release offenses to the Lord as they occur (i.e., we internalize our anger; Eph. 4:31-32).

Sadly, bitterness is not a private matter; it affects all relationships: *"The heart knows its own bitterness, and a stranger does not share its joy"* (Prov. 14:10). We can avoid bitterness by (1) thanking the Lord for a closer identification with Him, for He was also wrongly ill-treated (1 Pet. 2:19-21); (2) recognizing that we live in a cursed world in which all sin, meaning that no one is completely blameless; (3) not permitting another's bitterness to infect us (like a virus); (4) practicing the release of offenses immediately to the Lord; (5) thanking God for what we do have; (6) remembering that the Lord Jesus has waited over 2000 years for vindication: Can we not wait with Him for all to be set right?

October 30 – "Let Us Hold Fast"
(Hebrews 12)

Although the dispensation of the Law has been replaced with the stewardship of grace, the Law still declares God's moral standard for right and wrong today; the Ten Commandments show us our sin (Rom. 3:20) and affirm our need of a Savior (Gal. 3:24-25). Accordingly, God's message of salvation (under the New Covenant) is different today than at Sinai, but God Himself does not change (Mal. 3:6). He is still holy and demands holiness in His people today:

> *As obedient children, not conforming yourselves to the former lusts, as in your ignorance; but as He who called you is holy, you also be holy in all your conduct, because it is written, **"Be holy, for I am holy"*** (1 Pet. 1:14-16).

Christians would do well to remember the awe-inspiring scene that transpired on Mount Sinai in Numbers 19 and 20. Moses' entrance before God at Sinai was so threatening that he said, *"I am exceedingly afraid and trembling"* (Heb. 12:21). Yet, believers in the Church Age can boldly, with confidence and assurance, approach the same awesome God that Moses stood before in terror. How is this possible? Because Christ is the Mediator of the New Covenant and through the sprinkling of His own blood He has opened the way for us to approach Almighty God and call upon Him as *Abba* Father (Rom. 8:15; Heb. 12:24). In light of this, what exhortation does the writer of Hebrews offer to believers? *"Let us hold fast the confession of our hope without wavering, for He who promised is faithful"* (Heb. 10:23). Dear believer, be holy, for God is a consuming fire (Heb. 12:29), and hold fast to Christ – He is the means and the assurance of all good things to come!

God has not changed; He hates sin as much today as when the children of Israel were before Him at Sinai. He is still a sin-hating God and we dare not test His merciful patience by endorsing sin with compromising conduct; rather, let us live out our confession of faith.

There is a danger of forgetting that the Bible reveals, not first the love of God, but the intense, blazing holiness of God, with His love as the center of that holiness.

— Oswald Chambers

November 1 – The Immutable Son
(Hebrews 13)

In recent years there have been some who would agree that the trinity is a biblical doctrine, but yet would reject the eternal Sonship of Christ (i.e. they say that although the second Person of the Godhead existed, He did not become the Son of God until His incarnation). Some teach that He did not even become aware of His calling until after His birth. A fundamental ontological principle of existence is that if the essence of something can change, that particular entity is dependent upon a higher being. Only a fully independent being can be God – for only God is fully self-sufficient and not subject to the cause and effect influences of others or of natural law.

However, the writer of Hebrews not only affirms the eternal sonship of Christ, but he also affirms the immutability of Christ (i.e., that He does not change): *"Jesus Christ is the same yesterday, today, and forever"* (Heb. 13:8). The Lord Jesus Christ said, *"I am the first and the last"* (Rev. 1:8, 11, 22:13). Hence, only an eternal and immutable Savior could promise those He loves, *"I will never leave you nor forsake you"* (Heb. 13:5).

Christ, as God, must be unchanging in nature and essence or He is not God, for God cannot change what He is (Mal. 3:6). God is not subject to any superior being or cause-and-effect relationship. In the Lord's incarnation He took on a different form, but His essence was unchanged. Other Persons of the Godhead also can change their appearance without changing their essence. For example, we see the Holy Spirit in the form of a dove (John 1:32), and as seven flames of fire before the throne of God (Rev. 4:5); also, John witnessed the hand of God the Father materializing while seated on His heavenly throne (Rev. 5:1). In these examples, God the Father and the Holy Spirit took on forms which were not natural for a spirit-being to have, nevertheless Their character and attributes remained unchanged. When members of the Godhead chose to appear in different forms (usually to convey information to humanity), it does not impact who They are intrinsically – God cannot cease being God.

November 2 – "The Great Shepherd"
(Hebrews 13)

The shepherding trilogy of Psalm 22, 23, and 24 foretells the future work of the Lord Jesus in relationship to those He would save. In Psalm 22, the Lord is presented as the "Good Shepherd" who willingly gave His life for the sheep at Mount Calvary. John speaks to us about the life-sacrificing work of the Good Shepherd and how the Lord's sheep know His voice and enter His fold of safety (John 10).

In Psalm 23, the present sanctifying work of the Lord Jesus leading is pictured – He is faithfully leading His sheep through the valley of shadows and providing for all their needs. The writer of Hebrews highlights this ongoing ministry of the Lord Jesus who is proclaimed to be the "Great Shepherd":

Now may the God of peace who brought up our Lord Jesus from the dead, that great Shepherd of the sheep, through the blood of the everlasting covenant, make you complete in every good work to do His will, working in you what is well pleasing in His sight, through Jesus Christ, to whom be glory forever and ever. Amen (Heb. 13:20-21).

The Great Shepherd has experienced resurrection and in the power of that life equips and enables His sheep to do the work that He has for them. Furthermore, all the works that believers accomplish through His resurrection power are well pleasing to Him. Presently, the Lord is faithfully leading us through the valley of shadows to His glorious, heavenly home. During our pilgrimage with the Lord, we must remember that though shadows can scare us, they cannot hurt us. Accordingly, we must ignore the shifting shadows of humanism, deception, and intimidation and just go on with our faithful Shepherd.

Finally, Psalm 24 speaks of the Lord gathering up His people to Mount Zion, heaven. This shepherding ministry of Christ is acknowledged by Peter; He is the "Chief Shepherd" who will return and gather His sheep to Himself (1 Pet. 5:4). This is speaking of the return of Christ to the air to "snatch away" from the earth those who have truly believed on Him. As the prophetic trilogy of Psalms 22-24 predicted the death, burial, resurrection, and exaltation of Christ, the Holy Spirit caused the New Testament apostles to pick up each aspect of the Lord's shepherding ministry to show its direct fulfillment.

November 3 – "Be Doers of the Word"
(James 1)

Initially, Israel, God's covenant people, were to represent Him to the nations. The Jewish nation had been raised up by God, planted in a specific land for the purpose of testifying to the world of the one true God. However, as Paul notes in the book of Romans, they failed miserably to accurately reflect Jehovah's goodness to the nations:

You who make your boast in the law, do you dishonor God through breaking the law? For "the name of God is blasphemed among the Gentiles because of you," as it is written (Rom. 2:23-24).

The Jews thought that they were a special people because God had given them His Law and its badge – circumcision. Paul, however, clarifies that it was not merely having the Law and being physically circumcised that would mark them as a peculiar people in the world, but keeping God's Law would. Regrettably, because they merely taught the tenets of the Law and then broke the Law in practice, their testimony of God was blasphemed among the Gentiles.

This realization serves as a strong reminder to believers in the Church Age, for we too can cause others to blaspheme the name of Jesus Christ when we poorly represent Him. All that we do for Christ in this world is to accurately represent His character and His Word. James concisely summarizes the appropriate conduct of children of God: *"But be doers of the word, and not hearers only, deceiving yourselves"* (Jas. 1:22). To name Christ as Savior and then to reject His call to holy living effectively blasphemes the name of Christ in the world.

This must have been a problem in the early Church, for Paul exhorts believers more than once to put away all evil speech and blasphemies: *"Let all bitterness, wrath, anger, clamor, and evil speaking* [literally blasphemies] *be put away from you, with all malice"* (Eph. 4:31). *"Put to death your members which are on the earth: fornication, uncleanness, passion, evil desire, and covetousness, which is idolatry"* (Col. 3:5-6). Our willful refusal to do what God commands and expects of us causes His name to be slandered. The Church should consider the example of God's chastening of Israel for not representing Him properly among the nations and be determined to be "doers of [His] word"!

315

November 4 – Beware of Man's Wrath
(James 1)

The epistle of James is packed with tidbits of wisdom concerning how believers can better reflect God's character in their behavior. For example, the apostle instructs believers about their speech and anger:

> *So then, my beloved brethren, let every man be swift to hear, slow to speak, slow to wrath;* ***for the wrath of man does not produce the righteousness of God*** (Jas. 1:19-20).

Our anger in action will not have a profitable outcome unless it is being controlled by the Spirit of God; only then will our behavior honor the Lord. This means that we need to understand God's anger and attempt to reproduce its benefits in what we do and say. God is longsuffering, and His judgments are tempered with mercy, in that God's anger had to be "aroused" or "kindled" (KJV) before it results in righteous indignation. Not only is God slow to be angry, but once provoked to anger, His anger fully develops before action is rendered. God's anger requires sufficient kindling before flaming vengeance is released. God shows us that righteous provocation and a period of anger development are necessary before proper action is discharged.

We should understand that God is not angry by nature; He must be provoked to anger (Deut. 4:25, 9:18). His anger has a building up time before causing Him to act (Ex. 4:14). Thankfully, our God is slow to anger (Ps. 103:8-9, 145:8) and He is quick to forgive (Ps. 86:5). We would do well to imitate God's example; our anger-motivated behavior must have a present, righteous purpose!

Living a Christ-centered and disciplined life will reduce the number of occasions on which we feel unnecessarily angry. While in close fellowship with the Lord, the power of the Holy Spirit will effectively control and mold our anger to accomplish the righteousness of God. God's wrath always upholds His righteousness: *"For the wrath of God is revealed from heaven against all ungodliness and unrighteousness of men, who suppress the truth in unrighteousness"* (Rom. 1:18). And as Paul confirms, *"the wrath of God is coming upon the sons of disobedience"* (Col. 3:6). If God is not controlling our behavior when we get angry, we will needlessly hurt others, damage relationships, and impede the work of Christ.

November 5 – Believe, Counted, Righteousness
(James 2)

Paul and James are like two bookends about the same truth. Paul emphasizes saved by grace through faith. In full agreement, James adds, but faith never stands alone; it has good works. James quotes Genesis 15:6 to make his point: *"Abraham believed God, and it was accounted to him for righteousness"* (Jas. 2:23). Faith is the ability of the soul to reach beyond what can be verified by the human senses and to trust what cannot be confirmed through reason. Hebrews 11:3 reminds us that it is only by faith that we know that the visible things we see did not originate by chance from what is visible, but from the hand of the invisible Creator. This is why one must have faith to please God, *"for without faith it is impossible to please Him"* (Heb. 11:6).

God performed no signs and wonders for Abraham to prove His promise of a vast posterity. God simply reconfirmed His word to Abraham. That was good enough for him – he simply trusted God and believed. God responded by accrediting a standing of righteousness to Abraham's account. This accrediting of divine righteousness to a sinner who exercises faith is seen throughout the Bible (e.g., Rom. 4 and 5). Obviously, God wanted no confusion on this matter, for the words "believe," "counted," and "righteousness" all occur for the first time in Scripture in one verse (Gen. 15:6) and in one Divine decree just after the first mention of "the word of the Lord" in the Bible (Gen. 15:1).

Genesis 15:6 then appears three times in the New Testament: Romans 4:3, Galatians 3:6, and James 2:23. In Abraham's case, what preceded imputed righteousness? His faith. In Noah's case, what preceded imputed righteousness? God's grace (Gen. 6:8). Combining these two important truths we have: *"For by grace you have been saved through faith, and that not of yourselves; it is the gift of God, not of works, lest anyone should boast"* (Eph. 2:8-9). Both God's means of salvation through grace and man's responsibility to lay hold of this gift by personal faith are presented in the first book of the Bible, Genesis.

May we read these Scriptures, and their truths believe,
Own our need as sinners, and God's Son receive;
In assurance resting, His commands obey,
And in His grace growing, live for Him each day.

— A. P. Gibbs

317

November 6 – God Hates Worldliness
(James 4)

The apostle pulls no punches in explaining how much God hates worldliness in the believer's life. James vividly likeness worldliness to committing spiritual adultery against Christ, thus invoking the Lord's jealously and anger:

> *Adulterers and adulteresses! Do you not know that friendship with the world is enmity with God? Whoever therefore wants to be a friend of the world makes himself an enemy of God* (Jas. 4:4-5).

Worldliness is any sphere from which the Lord Jesus is excluded. Ponder for a moment how the world's standard of success is in direct opposition to what the Lord Jesus taught:

The world wants to be served, but Christ says humble yourself and serve others.

The world says save your life, but the Lord says lose your life to gain one worth living.

The world exclaims "live for the moment," but Christians are to live for eternity.

The world says live for self, but the Lord says lose your life for Him.

The world is into power, but the Lord uses weak things to confound the mighty.

The world permits greed to rule distribution, but Christians are to give according to need.

The world says acquire wealth, but God teaches us not to seek to be rich.

The world uses money and power to rule, but Christians are to pray and to use Scripture in love to serve others.

The world says retaliate and get even, but the Lord teaches us to repay evil with good and be forgiving.

The world uses violence, but Christians are to turn the other cheek.

So why is it that the world stands in opposition to Jesus Christ and His message? Why is it permissible to speak of world religions, but not to mention Christ's name? It is because Satan is behind the scene, controlling the various systems of the world, and he despises Christ and those who identify with Him. Those living for Christ and not temporal things are a constant reminder to the devil of his defeat at Calvary.

November 7 – Grace to the Humble

(James 4)

Both James and Peter proclaim the same truth concerning pride and humility: *"God resists the proud, but gives grace to the humble"* (Jas. 4:6; 1 Pet. 5:5). Solomon wrote, *"When pride comes, then comes shame; but with the humble is wisdom"* (Prov. 11:2). David declared, *"The sacrifices of God are a broken spirit, a broken and a contrite heart"* (Ps. 51:17). The opposite of pride is a broken spirit and a contrite heart. Matthew Henry explains this important realization:

> We must be clothed with humility, *for the proud in spirit* are those that cannot bear to be trampled upon, but grow outrageous, and fret themselves, when they are hardly bested. That will break a proud man's heart, which will not break a humble man's sleep. Mortify pride, therefore, and a lowly spirit will easily be reconciled to a low condition.[42]

> He that has a low opinion of his own knowledge and powers will submit to better information; such a person may be informed and improved by revelation: but the proud man, conceited of his own wisdom and understanding, will undertake to correct even divine wisdom itself, and prefer his own shallow reasonings to the revelations of infallible truth and wisdom. Note, we must abase ourselves before God if we would be either truly wise or good: *"For the wisdom of this world is foolishness with God"* (1 Cor. 3:19).[43]

True humility is selfless behavior that honors the Lord and yearns to serve others. From Genesis to Revelation, the Bible declares God's contempt for pride and His commitment to judge it. As the proverb says, *"Pride goes before destruction and a haughty spirit before a fall. Better to be of a humble spirit with the lowly, than to divide the spoil with the proud"* (Prov. 16:18-19). To be broken before the Lord is to be a qualified recipient of His grace. Our failures should lead to personal brokenness, which should then cause us to cast ourselves upon the Lord in a way that we were hesitant to do beforehand. Our victories, won by His grace, only prompt us to praise His name! The outcome of testing, then, is that the believer knows and trusts the Lord with a greater patience and confidence than he or she did before. This is why the Lord longs for us to come to Him in brokenness with all of life's burdens.

November 8 – "If the Lord Wills"
(James 4)

James provides a practical warning against saying what we will do or what will happen ahead of time as if we are in control of all the particulars of what will happens to us:

> *Come now, you who say, "Today or tomorrow we will go to such and such a city, spend a year there, buy and sell, and make a profit"; whereas you do not know what will happen tomorrow. For what is your life? It is even a vapor that appears for a little time and then vanishes away. Instead you ought to say, "If the Lord wills, we shall live and do this or that"* (Jas. 4:13-15).

As God is the One who controls all the events of our existence, only He can say with surety what will happen in the future. Because we have limited control of our circumstances, we should refer to our intensions, but then uphold God's sovereignty over us by saying "in the will of the Lord." This is why the Lord Jesus forbids us from making vows today as the Jews were accustomed to doing under the Law (Matt. 5:33-37).

Vows in the Old Testament might be to abstain from something (Ps. 132:2-5), or to promise things or services to the Lord (Lev. 27). The fulfillment of such vows then became the substance of things prompting common joy among God's people; thus David wrote, *"I will pay my vows before them that fear Him"* (Ps. 22:25). And Psalm 116:14 reads, *"I will pay my vows to the Lord now in the presence of all His people."* However, in the Church Age, the pattern of those things associated with the vows under the Law are fulfilled in Christ. In the Church Age, it is not the completion of personal vows that cause us to fear the Lord or to have joy in the Lord – we have Christ, and He accomplishes those things and He is our joy.

So let us heed James' warning; we cannot promise or declare what we may do ahead of time because we do not control the future. While a vow may be viewed as a legitimate expression of one's devotion to God, it would be better to express one's aspiration to serve God in prayer and through pursuing a consecrated life, rather than committing to some particular course of action which is not fully within one's control. In this way we agree with the Lord Jesus, *"Your* [God's] *will be done"* (Matt. 26:42).

November 9 – Effectual Praying
(James 5)

What type of man or woman bends the ear of God? Isaiah informs us: *"But on this one will I look: On him who is poor and of a contrite spirit, and who trembles at My word"* (Isa. 66:2). James puts the matter this way: *"The effective, fervent prayer of a righteous man avails much"* (Jas. 5:16). When believers walk in integrity with God and are burdened over what concerns Him, God is inclined to honor their prayers for the honor of His own name: *"Now this is the confidence that we have in Him, that if we ask anything according to His will, He hears us* (1 Jn. 5:14). Believers today can have this same assurance in the Lord. Not only does James tell us about effectual praying, but he also informs us of what type of wrong attitudes concerning prayer hinder God's blessings:

If any of you lacks wisdom, let him ask of God, who gives to all liberally and without reproach, and it will be given to him. But let him ask in faith, with no doubting (Jas. 1:5-6).

You do not have because you do not ask. You ask and do not receive, because you ask amiss, that you may spend it on your pleasures (Jas. 4:2-3).

The reason many of God's people today do not see the hand of God moving in their lives is that they are not dependent on Him. Either they do not pray, or they cannot do so in genuine faith, or they do so with impure motives (i.e., they lust for what is outside of God's will).

Speaking to His disciples shortly before His death, the Lord Jesus promised them: *"And whatever things you ask in prayer, believing, you will receive"* (Matt. 21:22). This is not a "blab it and grab it" reality, but rather affords assurance that our prayers offered in faith and in the will of God will be answered for the glory of God (John 14:13; 1 Jn. 5:14). The Father desires to honor His Son through answering our prayers. Thankfully, there are still a few today with clean hands and pure hearts that regularly beseech the Lord to revive His Church and to show Himself strong in a world that desperately needs to see Christ. He is the ultimate solution to all of our problems, and thus, in Him, we find the answers to all our effective, fervent prayers.

November 10 – "Hope to the End"
(1 Peter 1)

Scripture reveals that God's future plan for glorifying the Church is quite different than His agenda for restoring the nation of Israel to a position of honor and blessing. Hosea refers to this latter event as *"a door of hope"* for Israel (Hos. 2:15). Prophecy not only bestows hope to the Jewish nation, but should also excite every Christian to love *"the blessed hope,"* the appearing of the Lord Jesus Christ (2 Tim. 4:8)! Consequently, both the nation of Israel and the Church have all their hopes in Christ!

Writing to encourage persecuted believers scattered throughout the Roman Empire, Peter conveys a message of hope:

> *Blessed be the God and Father of our Lord Jesus Christ, who according to His abundant mercy has begotten us again to **a living hope through the resurrection of Jesus Christ from the dead**, to an inheritance incorruptible and undefiled and that does not fade away, reserved in heaven for you, who are kept by the power of God through faith for salvation ready to be revealed in the last time* (1 Pet. 1:3-5).

> *Therefore gird up the loins of your mind, be sober, and **rest your hope fully upon the grace that is to be brought to you at the revelation of Jesus Christ**; as obedient children, not conforming yourselves to the former lusts, as in your ignorance* (1 Pet. 1:13).

Believers were to literally *"hope to the end"* (KJV) because of their forthcoming resurrection through Christ at the revelation of Christ. Paul also declares that the believer's hope is solely based on Christ: *"To them God willed to make known what are the riches of the glory of this mystery among the Gentiles: which is Christ in you, the hope of glory"* (Col. 1:27). In Christ, the believer is ensured an extraordinary future!

Solomon declares, *"Hope deferred makes the heart sick"* (Prov. 13:12). Hope is rejoicing now in the future promises of God. Jeremiah, while suffering for the Lord, rightly summarizes the matter of hope for all of God's people: *"Blessed is the man who trusts in the Lord, and whose hope is the Lord"* (Jer. 17:7). Trusting and hoping are different; yet, exercising faith now is inseparably tied with hoping for the future.

November 11 – The Precious Blood
(1 Peter 1)

The Lord Jesus Christ was the ransom God paid for human sin – He *"tasted* [experienced] *"death for everyone"* (Heb. 2:9). While Old Testament sacrifices merely atoned for sin (i.e., provided a temporary covering), John tells us that Christ's sacrifice was the propitiation which satisfied God's wrath concerning all of humanity's sin for all of time (1 Jn. 2:2). Likewise, Paul writes:

Being justified freely by His grace through the redemption that is in Christ Jesus, whom God set forth as a propitiation by His blood, through faith, to demonstrate His righteousness, because in His forbearance God had passed over the sins that were previously committed, to demonstrate at the present time His righteousness, that He might be just and the justifier of the one who has faith in Jesus (Rom. 3:24-26).

Through Adam's sin, the special creature formed in His own image and likeness was lost to God (Gen. 1:26), but by the blood of Christ, God is able to restore all that was lost in Eden. The shed blood of the Lord Jesus is the only basis on which God the Father can redeem sinful man; hence, Christ's blood is more valuable than all the precious metals and gems in all the earth combined:

You were not redeemed with corruptible things, like silver or gold, from your aimless conduct received by tradition from your fathers, but with the precious blood of Christ, as of a lamb without blemish and without spot. He indeed was foreordained before the foundation of the world, but was manifest in these last times for you who through Him believe in God, who raised Him from the dead and gave Him glory, so that your faith and hope are in God (1 Pet. 1:18-21).

His sacrifice was *foreordained*; none of the events associated with Calvary were an accident, including the disdain, brutality, and betrayal of God's own Son. The devil did not outsmart God or catch Him by surprise. Rather, that horrific day had been intricately prearranged before the foundation of the world; however, God's redemptive purposes were kept secret until accomplished in Christ (1 Cor. 2:8-9). The innocent took the place of the condemned (Col. 2:12), so that the guilty could have the opportunity to be redeemed and be made clean.

November 12 – The Rock of Offense
(1 Peter 2)

Peter quotes several Old Testament prophecies which foretold of Israel's estimation of their Messiah at His first advent; they would find Him offensive and stumble over (reject) His message. However, in God's providential purposes, this treatment of His Son would result in Him being the cornerstone of a new, living tabernacle for God – the Church:

Coming to Him as to a living stone, rejected indeed by men, but chosen by God and precious, you also, as living stones, are being built up a spiritual house, a holy priesthood, to offer up spiritual sacrifices acceptable to God through Jesus Christ. Therefore it is also contained in the Scripture, "Behold, I lay in Zion a chief cornerstone, elect, precious, and he who believes on Him will by no means be put to shame." Therefore, to you who believe, He is precious; but to those who are disobedient, "The stone which the builders rejected has become the chief cornerstone," and "A stone of stumbling and a rock of offense" (1 Pet. 2:4-8).

Isaiah foretold that it would be God alone who sets the cornerstone and foundation of salvation and all who trust in it (Him) will not be ashamed for doing so: *"Behold, I lay in Zion a stone for a foundation, a tried stone, a precious cornerstone, a sure foundation; whoever believes will not act hastily"* (Isa. 28:16). Notice that the cornerstone is tried, precious, and sure, and therefore typifies Christ's faithfulness, proven impeccability, and fruitful ministry.

The Lord Jesus Christ is often likened to a stone in Scripture to portray either His character, His work, or how others respond to Him. For example, He was the Rock struck by God's rod in the wilderness to provide life-sustaining water (Ex. 17:1-6). He was the Rock of Offense, the rejected Cornerstone, over which the Jewish nation stumbled at His first advent to earth (1 Pet. 2:6-8). He is the Rock of Strength (Deut. 32:4) and the Foundation Stone of the Church (1 Cor. 3:11). For those who will not trust in Him, He will be the Smiting Stone (Dan. 2:44-45) and a Grinding Stone (Matt. 21:44-45). Those who trust in God's cornerstone alone for salvation will experience God's eternal peace and joy – these will be gladly broken upon their divine Stone (Luke 20:28)!

November 13 – Believer-Priests
(1 Peter 2)

During the Church Age, all believer-priests (i.e., Christians) are the temple of God and are able to lift up worship and living sacrifices heavenward to Him wherever and whenever they desire (1 Pet. 2:5, 10; Heb. 10:22; Rev. 1:6). One of the ways that believers worship the Lord is to reject the world's values and attractions by renewing our minds on what is true and spiritual (Rom. 12:1-2). The apostles highlight the wonderful nature of our priesthood made possible through the finished work of Christ:

> *Coming to Him as to a living stone, rejected indeed by men, but chosen by God and precious, you also, as living stones, are being built up a spiritual house, a holy priesthood, to offer up spiritual sacrifices acceptable to God through Jesus Christ* (1 Pet. 2:4-5).

> *Therefore, brethren, having boldness to enter the Holiest by the blood of Jesus, by a new and living way which He consecrated for us, through the veil, that is, His flesh, and having a High Priest over the house of God, let us draw near with a true heart in full assurance of faith, having our hearts sprinkled from an evil conscience and our bodies washed with pure water* (Heb. 10:19-22).

> *To Him who loved us and washed us from our sins in His own blood, and has made us kings and priests to His God and Father, to Him be glory and dominion forever and ever. Amen* (Rev. 1:5-6).

As believer-priests we are equipped to offer worship and praise to God. Additionally, the high moral character of Christ is exhibited and ascends to God as a living sacrifice when believer-priests are controlled by the Holy Spirit in thought, word, and deed. In this sense, every moment of every day can be a worship experience with the Lord (John 4:23-24). To want what God wants and to say "no" to what He disapproves of are a pleasing sacrifice to Him. It is a sacrifice because it costs us something: our desires that are contrary to His holy will. May we be God-fearing, Christ-loving, Bible-believing, Spirit-controlled Christians who remind everyone of the Lord Jesus!

November 14 – Suffering Precedes Glory (Part 1)
(1 Peter 2)

The Lord Jesus gave us a pattern of ministry to follow: patient laboring and suffering in the work of God now results in honor and glory later.

> *For this is commendable, if because of conscience toward God one endures grief, suffering wrongfully. For what credit is it if, when you are beaten for your faults, you take it patiently? But when you do good and suffer, if you take it patiently, this is commendable before God. For to this you were called, because Christ also suffered for us, leaving us an example, that you should follow His steps* (1 Pet. 2:19-21).

How did Christ suffer? Christ did nothing wrong, but released wrongs done against Him to His Father to judge. Christ did not seek justice at that time, but suffered willingly in the Father's will. Christ did not seek to vindicate Himself, but kept to His ministry. The devil often gains a victory over believers by sidetracking them from the Lord's work into wasting time defending themselves. In the work of God, it is our character that is important, not our reputation. Let us remember that Jesus Christ has waited over two thousand years to vindicate His good name; can we not wait a little while with Him for all things to be set right? How we respond when wronged is much more important than asserting the facts to right the wrong (1 Cor. 11:19).

The Lord is watching and He knows the quality of our work and will reward it appropriately and abundantly in a coming day:

> *For our light affliction, which is but for a moment, is working for us a far more exceeding and eternal weight of glory* (2 Cor. 4:17).

> *For I consider that the sufferings of this present time are not worthy to be compared with the glory which shall be revealed in us* (Rom. 8:18).

> *For God is not unjust to forget your work and labor of love which you have shown toward His name, in that you have ministered to the saints, and do minister. And we desire that each one of you show the same diligence to the full assurance of hope until the end, that you do not become sluggish, but imitate those who through faith and patience inherit the promises* (Heb. 6:10-12).

November 15 – Suffering Precedes Glory (Part 2)
(1 Peter 2)

A wonderful pattern of calling-serving-suffering is witnessed in the call of Isaiah as a prophet in the Old Testament (Isa. 6). After seeing the glory and holiness of God sitting on His throne, Isaiah keenly felt his sin and pronounced a woe on himself, instead of Israel. God responded to Isaiah's humility by demonstrating His ability to purge his sin by the pressing of a coal from the altar to Isaiah's lips. Then the Lord inquired openly: *"Whom shall I send, and who will go for Us?"* (Isa. 6:8). This inquiry prompted Isaiah to instantly reply, *"Here am I, send me."* It is important to observe that God did not give the call for service, nor did Isaiah respond to it, until his sin had been dealt with.

Having realized his doomed position before a holy God and then experiencing God's mercy and cleansing, Isaiah became a clean vessel, fit for service. Notice that Isaiah did not suggest to the Lord what kinds of ministries he would enjoy doing. Nor did he even ask the Lord what He would have him do. Isaiah was completely available and willing to do whatever God told him to do. This is evidence of true salvation – a willingness to serve no matter the cost to the servant personally.

Peter understood that if a believer lives for Christ, he or she will suffer for it. But as mentioned in the previous devotion, such suffering would be a sweet savor in the nostrils of God because it would remind Him of the way His Son suffered for doing His will (1 Pet. 2:20-22).

> *For it is better, if it is the will of God, to suffer for doing good than for doing evil. For Christ also suffered once for sins, the just for the unjust, that He might bring us to God, being put to death in the flesh but made alive by the Spirit* (1 Pet. 3:17-18).

Yet, there is another benefit of suffering with endurance in the will of God. Paul told the saints at both Philippi and Thessalonica that suffering patiently for the cause of Christ was a token of (a proof of) their salvation (Phil. 1:28; 2 Thess. 1:5). Naturally speaking, it is not possible to suffer patiently for doing what is right; however, it is possible for a Christian who draws on supernatural power from on high. Thus, suffering patiently in the will of God becomes an influential testimony of the power of God to the lost; in fact, this was the testimony that brought one thief, crucified with the Lord, to repentance.

327

November 16 – "The Chief Shepherd"
(1 Peter 5)

As previously mentioned, a shepherding trilogy is contained in the New Testament to speak of God's Servant-Shepherd, the Lord Jesus: He is the "Good Shepherd" who lays His life down for the sheep (John 10:9-11). He is the Great Shepherd who protects, cares for, and sanctifies His Sheep (Heb. 13:20-21). He is the Chief Shepherd who will return and gather His sheep unto Him (1 Pet. 5:4). In the latter reference, Peter challenges other church elders to follow Christ's example of shepherding God's flock in their charge:

Shepherd the flock of God which is among you, serving as overseers, not by compulsion but willingly, not for dishonest gain but eagerly; nor as being lords over those entrusted to you, but being examples to the flock; and when the Chief Shepherd appears, you will receive the crown of glory that does not fade away (1 Pet. 5:2-4).

The Lord Jesus is the Arch Shepherd and when He returns for His Church all of His under-shepherds (church elders) who cared for His sheep well will be rewarded with the Crown of Glory.

After Ezekiel blasted Israel's selfish and lazy shepherds in his day (and their inevitable accountability with God), he foretold what God's coming Servant-Shepherd would be like. The coming, true Shepherd would rescue God's sheep, speaking of a refined remnant of Israel. He will be a just and righteous Ruler over the restored Jewish nation regathered to the land of Israel in a future day (Ezek. 34:11-31). L. E. Cooper identifies eight character traits of this promised future King-Shepherd from this text: He has a special relationship with Yahweh. He will feed His sheep. He will gather His sheep together. He will reestablish His people peacefully in their land. He will rule with justice and compassion. He will personally judge His people. He will be the only true shepherd. He will mediate a covenant of peace.[44]

While these virtues and actions were all evident to some extent during the Lord's first advent, each will be completely fulfilled in His second advent. The Shepherd-King will gather His covenant people out of all nations and then feed and protect them as only the true Shepherd can. In His kingdom, the Lord Jesus Christ will watch over and care for not just Israel, but all who have been added to His flock (John 10:16).

November 17 – Beware of False Prophets
(2 Peter 1)

Peter fervently warned believers about being deceived by false prophets and then foretold the doom of these deceivers:

But there were also false prophets among the people, even as there will be false teachers among you, who will secretly bring in destructive heresies, even denying the Lord who bought them, and bring on themselves swift destruction. And many will follow their destructive ways, because of whom the way of truth will be blasphemed. By covetousness they will exploit you with deceptive words; for a long time their judgment has not been idle, and their destruction does not slumber (2 Pet. 2:1-3).

Paul warned the elders at Ephesus that false teachers would secretly come among them as wolves to devour the flock (Acts 28:15-17). Similarly, Moses sternly warned the Israelites centuries earlier to avoid the corrupting influences of false prophets (Deut. 13:1-5). False prophets and dreamers of dreams would come among them with signs and fanciful messages to deceive them. God would permit this to happen in order to test the Israelites' love for Him and their allegiance to His Law (Deut. 13:4).

Moses then provided instruction for identifying false prophets, which is still valid today: First, a miracle did not prove truth, as Satan is capable of accomplishing supernatural feats, if permitted by God. Second, a false prophet would be identified if his message was contrary to a revelation already given by someone verified to be a true prophet of God (Isa. 8:21). Third, whatever a true prophet of God says would happen, will always happen; if not, the speaker was a false prophet as God only speaks the truth. Fourth, a true prophet of God will always lead His people into repentance and humility before God, never away from the Lord. False prophets may for a time feign humility and morality (Matt. 7:15), but they are inherently self-exalting (i.e., they compete for God's honor) and self-gratifying (often immoral; 2 Pet. 2:10, 14) and will eventually lead the Lord's people away from Him.

Dear believer, be aware of anyone who tries to lead you away from Christ by displacing Him, or by corrupting His Word or His person! Cling to Him above all else.

November 18 – Growing in Knowledge and Grace
(2 Peter 1)

As we increase in our knowledge of Christ and rely more upon His grace, we are transformed to become more like Him. Adam forfeited God-likeness in Eden through sin, but through Christ's obedience, the believer has the present opportunity to regain it. In Peter's second epistle, he clearly links the knowledge of Christ with spiritual fruit-bearing: *"For if these things* [i.e., faith, virtue, knowledge, self-control, patience, godliness, brotherly love, and love from 2 Peter 1:5-7] *be in you, and abound, they make you that ye shall neither be barren nor unfruitful in the knowledge of our Lord Jesus Christ"* (2 Pet. 1:8). *"But grow in grace, and in the knowledge of our Lord and Savior Jesus Christ"* (2 Pet. 3:18). Concerning the latter verse, William MacDonald offers the following comments:

> There must be a twofold growth – in grace and in knowledge. Grace is the practical demonstration of the fruit of the Spirit. Growth in grace is not increased head knowledge or tireless activity; it is increasing likeness to the Lord Jesus. Knowledge means acquaintance with the Lord through the Word. Growth in knowledge means increasing study of and subjection to His words, works and ways.[1]

In fact, five times in his second epistle, Peter refers to directly knowing Christ as the means of spiritual fruitfulness or to not knowing Christ as the cause of spiritual deadness. In these exhortations, the Greek word for knowledge is *epignosis*, which means "to have full discernment of." But how is it possible to have full discernment of Christ – to intimately know Him thoroughly?

Learning the Person of Christ will radically diminish our angry feelings, bring security to our natural impulses of expression, and guide righteous behavior. The answer to the question the Savior asked of others, *"What do you think about the Christ?"* (Matt. 22:42), is really the key to growing in knowledge and grace, and becoming more like Him.

The Christian who has stopped repenting has stopped growing.

— A. W. Pink

November 19 – Walking With God in the Light
(1 John 1)

In the system of the Law, the Lord Jesus was represented in the sweet savor sacrifice of the *peace* offering (Lev. 3). The peace offering did not relate to Christ's suffering for human sin – it represented the future cleansing power of Christ's blood that is provided for us to maintain fellowship with God. Having already borne our sins, Christ has secured our *peace with God*; this opens the way for us to enjoy the *peace of God* while in happy fellowship with Him. And we are encouraged to do so, but God cannot come into the darkness to have fellowship with us; we must walk with Him in the light of divine truth (1 Jn. 1:7). Thankfully, when we do sin, there is a provision for cleansing through the effectual power of Christ's blood. As we confess sin to the Lord, His blood has the power to repeatedly wash and cleanse us from all the stain of sin:

> *If we say that we have fellowship with Him, and walk in darkness, we lie and do not practice the truth. But if we walk in the light as He is in the light, we have fellowship with one another, and **the blood of Jesus Christ His Son cleanses us from all sin**. If we say that we have no sin, we deceive ourselves, and the truth is not in us. **If we confess our sins, He is faithful and just to forgive us our sins and to cleanse us from all unrighteousness*** (1 Jn. 1:6-9).

John does *not* say that God cleanses our unrighteousness when we pray to ask forgiveness of our sins. Rather, it is when we "confess" our sins to Him that we are purified and are returned to fellowship with God again. The act of confessing means that we stand with God against ourselves, that is, we agree with Him that our wrong behavior was sinful and that we are genuinely sorry for offending Him.

Confession is the responsibility of the believer, and cleansing is what only God can do. Both acts must be performed on an ongoing basis as we have a constant need for *"the blood of Jesus Christ His Son [which] cleanses us from all sin"* (1 Jn. 1:7). This passage does not pertain to eternal salvation (the believer's relationship with God) – that is secured in Christ (John 5:24, 10:28-29); the focus here is how the believer can maintain fellowship with God. We are to walk in the light with God and confess to Him when we have strayed into the darkness.

331

November 20 – Our Advocate – Part 1
(1 John 2)

Besides being our heavenly High Priest (Heb. 4:14), Christ is also our legal representative or "advocate" before the Father: *"These things I write to you, so that you may not sin. And if anyone sins, we have an Advocate with the Father, Jesus Christ the righteous"* (1 Jn. 2:1). This is a special comfort to every believer, especially knowing that Satan slanders us before God's throne day and night (Rev. 12:10). The English term "advocate" is only translated once from the Greek word *parakletos*, which is translated as "comforter" four times in John's gospel account in reference to the Holy Spirit. The role of advocate (or comforter) is to legally plead a case or to speak on the behalf of another in a court of law – a legal intercessor. Thayer's Greek definition describes the meaning as "Christ's pleading for pardon of our sins before the Father."[45] When does Christ plead our case? Is it when we acknowledge and confess our sins? First John 2:1 states that Christ is our advocate when we sin, not when we confess our sins, though we certainly should repent and confess our sins. Concerning the Lord Jesus' continuing ministry of advocacy, S. Emery writes:

> His valid ministry, therefore, on our behalf, is not on the basis of an effective, verbal and persuasive pleading before the Father, but on the basis of a perfect satisfaction for all our sins ever before the Father's face. He is our propitiation of undiminishing value. ... His very presence before the Father is the plea. Continuance in the family of God is never in question, but forgiveness of our sins and cleansing from all unrighteousness are experienced only when we make confession (1 Jn. 1:9).[46]

When a believer sins, Satan may abruptly call God's attention to the despicable deed, but Christ, being on the throne with His Father, immediately addresses the offense. He concedes the ungodly behavior of the believer but then asserts that the penalty for that lawless deed has already been paid by Himself at Calvary. In this way, all the heavenly hosts see that God is righteous and that He has accounted justly for every sin that His children have done. God hates sin, but because He judged Christ for sin, He can extend the repentant sinner a full pardon and family status as His adopted child with full privileges (Rom. 8:15).

November 21 – Our Advocate – Part 2
(1 John 2)

Christ pleads for us on the grounds of justice, of righteousness, of His obedience, and of His endurance of sin's full penalty; thus a just acquittal is assured. Through the continual advocacy of Christ (1 Jn. 2:1), we never need to fear the judicial penalty of our sins being laid on us. Accordingly, we should be prompted to live in holiness before our Father so as to stay in fellowship with Him and to not provoke His chastening hand. Our souls have been liberated through the work of Christ to serve God out of love and not out of fear of judgment, for judgment is past and true love does not fear (1 Jn. 4:18).

I hear the accuser roar, of ills that I have done;
I know them well, and thousands more, Jehovah findeth none.
Though the restless foe accuses – sins recounting like a flood,
Every charge our God refuses; Christ has answered with His blood.

— Unknown

Understanding the continuing drama in heaven should cause the child of God to keep "short accounts" with the Lord. As soon as one is conscious of sin, the sin should be promptly confessed. God desires His children not to sin (1 Jn. 2:1). But when we do sin, *"if we confess our sins, He is faithful and just to forgive us our sins, and to cleanse us from all unrighteousness"* (1 Jn. 1:9). Let the child of God stay in active fellowship with his Father by holy living and confessing the moment he or she stumbles in thought or deed.

The judgment of sin at Calvary and the empty tomb of Christ sufficiently answer any judicial claim the enemy may levy against a redeemed soul. Neither Satan nor the world has any claim on the Christian, for positionally speaking, he or she has died and has been buried with Christ (Rom. 6:3-6). All our adversary's accusations against us are completely answered by our Advocate, Jesus Christ: His suffering and death were just payment for all of our offenses, and His resurrection proves that God was satisfied with His redemptive work.

November 22 – You Have an Anointing
(1 John 2)

Priests, prophets, and kings were often anointed with oil when consecrated to serve the Lord. The Lord Jesus Himself was anointed by the Holy Spirit at the commencement of His ministry (Matt. 3:16; Acts 10:38). Likewise, each believer is anointed and called to serve the body of Christ according to God's will (Eph. 2:10). *"Now He who establishes us with you in Christ and has anointed us is God, who also has sealed us and given us the Spirit in our hearts as a guarantee"* (2 Cor. 1:21-22).

Not only does this anointing separate out the believer for God's purpose, but the anointing actually provides divine discernment of the truth, which enables the believer to follow after God's will in his or her ministry. John instructed the believers, *"Beloved, do not believe every spirit [teacher], but test the spirits, whether they are of God; because many false prophets have gone out into the world"* (1 Jn. 4:1). He also informed them of an anointing that they had received at spiritual rebirth from the Holy Spirit. There is no need to pray for this anointing as some do; every believer already has it. It is always spoken of in the past tense and has the purpose of giving spiritual discernment as to what is truth and what is false.

> *But **you have an anointing from the Holy One, and you know all things.** I have not written to you because you do not know the truth, but because you know it, and that no lie is of the truth"* (1 Jn. 2:20-21).

> *These things I have written to you concerning those who try to deceive you. **But the anointing which you have received from Him abides in you, and you do not need that anyone teach you; but as the same anointing teaches you concerning all things, and is true,** and is not a lie, and just as it has taught you, you will abide in Him* (1 Jn. 2:26-27).

With this spiritual resource each believer can validate what is truth and what is deception by the illumination of God's Word: *"Your word is a lamp to my feet and a light to my path"* (Ps. 119:105). As believers, we have what we need to learn the truth about Christ and His will for our lives. But we must remember that slothfulness will either lead us into spiritual despondency or deception.

November 23 – A Son Given and a Child Born
(1 John 4)

About seven centuries before the birth of Christ, the prophet Isaiah uttered a delightful prophetic message to foretell the coming of God's Messiah to Israel:

> *For unto us a Child is born, unto us a Son is given; and the government will be upon His shoulder. And His name will be called Wonderful, Counselor, Mighty God, Everlasting Father, Prince of Peace. Of the increase of His government and peace there will be no end, upon the throne of David and over His kingdom, to order it and establish it with judgment and justice from that time forward, even forever. The zeal of the Lord of hosts will perform this* (Isa. 9:6-7).

The *"For unto us"* supplies the basic premise on which the prophecy rests: the Child born and the Son given would be for Israel. The two initial expressions confirm both the humanity and the deity of the coming Savior, says H. A. Ironside:

> The "child...born" refers to His humanity. As we have already seen, He was to come into the world as the virgin's Son. As such He was true Man – spirit, soul, and body. The "son...given" refers to the Savior's deity. He was born of Mary, but without a human father. The eternal Son of the Father, Christ came from the glory that He had with the Father throughout all the past eternity. The Son was given in grace for our redemption.[47]

The double reference to the first advent of the Lord Jesus is of great importance. The Holy Spirit carefully chose the specific phrases and their order. The Lord was not "a child given," nor "a son born" – He was the unique child born, because He was the unique Son given. John tells us that the spirit of Antichrist is evident when one denies that God's Son *came* from heaven to the earth to be born of a virgin:

> *By this you know the Spirit of God: Every spirit that confesses that Jesus Christ has come in the flesh is of God, and every spirit that does not confess that Jesus Christ has come in the flesh is not of God. And **this is the spirit of the Antichrist, which you have heard was coming, and is now already in the world*** (1 Jn. 4:2-3).

335

November 24 – Fellow Workers for the Truth
(3 John)

By commending beloved Gaius in a personal letter (preserved in Scripture for us), we understand the type of generous and hospitable behavior the Lord expects of His saints towards His servants:

> *I rejoiced greatly when brethren came and testified of the truth that is in you, just as you walk in the truth. I have no greater joy than to hear that my children walk in truth. Beloved, you do faithfully whatever you do for the brethren and for strangers, who have borne witness of your love before the church. If you send them forward on their journey in a manner worthy of God, you will do well, because they went forth for His name's sake, taking nothing from the Gentiles. We therefore ought to receive such, that we may become fellow workers for the truth* (3 Jn. 2-8).

Christians are the Lord's representatives on earth (2 Cor. 5:20) and God provides for His own. God always supplies for the work He orders. This support usually comes through the Lord's people; for example, we read the saints at Philippi had fellowship with Paul in the gospel several times (Phil. 4:15-19). John's letter also shows us that in the early days of the Church, itinerant workers were supported by their hosting families as they traveled to spread the gospel message; they took nothing from those they desired to see won to Christ (2 Cor. 11:8).

Gaius provides a good pattern to follow in the care of the Lord's servants. He extended hospitality to itinerant church workers and then did not send them away empty-handed (also see Tit. 3:14). At times workers may need to engage in secular employment for financial reasons (Acts 18:3), but nowhere in Scripture do we see them making public appeals for their own financial support. Commended workers serve the Lord (Acts 14:26), and thus the Lord wants His people to freely and amply provide for them in His name (Phil. 4:10-19; Col. 4:17). Those who have been blessed by the Lord's servant's ministry have a "duty" to bless them in return (Rom. 15:27). This arrangement permits His workers to do His bidding and for the Lord to endorse their efforts by attending to their daily needs. Serving the Lord Jesus is not a career to be chosen, but a heavenly calling to be fulfilled! A work done for Christ, His way, will never lack His resources to accomplish it.

November 25 – "The Way of Cain"
(Jude)

The Lord's half-brother Jude warned believers of false teachers that were trying to lead them away from Christ. He wrote: *"Woe to them! For they have gone in the way of Cain"* (Jude 11). A brief review of what we learn about Cain in Genesis 4 will enable us to better understand Jude's warning. In that chapter, we are introduced to Adam and Eve's first two sons: Cain a "tiller of the ground" and Abel the "keeper of sheep." Yet, it becomes obvious that the choice of their professions depended not on accidental circumstances, but according to their character and views of life. Alfred Edersheim writes:

> Abel chose the pilgrim-life, Cain that of settled possession and enjoyment of the earth. The nearer their history lay to the terrible event which had led to the loss of Paradise, and to the first giving of the promise, the more significant would this their choice of life appear. Quite in accordance with this, we afterwards find Cain, not only building a city, but calling it after the name of his own son, to indicate settled proprietorship and enjoyment of the world as it was.[48]

Abel was a "keeper of sheep." He took the best sheep of his flock and approached God by offering a burnt sacrifice. God had respect for Abel's offering because it pictured the future death of His beloved Son, the Lord Jesus. Abel did not know about His future Savior or how He would be judged for his sins, but in faith he simply did what pleased God. His brother Cain, however, was a "tiller of the ground" and brought to God what he had labored for – the fruit from a cursed ground. What Cain offered to God represented his accomplishments (good works) and not an innocent substitute to bear judgment in his place – there was no life in the fruit. Cain chose to worship God his way or, as Jude puts it, "the way of Cain." In Cain, we have the first system of theology apart from atonement of sin through blood sacrifice. Cain's way denied the guilt of man and his need for a Savior; Cain's way is the wide way leading to hell!

Believers today should want to follow the pilgrim lifestyle of Abel. Our days on the earth are few; we are just passing through. Let us not get settled down and invest or delight in a world that is cursed, under judgment, and shall be destroyed in a coming day.

November 26 – "The Error of Balaam"
(Jude)

The pagan prophet Balaam who successfully corrupted the Israelites nearing Canaan (Num. 25) is mentioned three times in the New Testament. Peter and Jude wrote of Balaam in the context of false teachers leading God's people astray, and our Lord rebuked the church at Pergamos for embracing *"the doctrines of Balaam"* (Rev. 2:12).

> *They have forsaken the right way and gone astray, following the way of Balaam ... who loved the wages of unrighteousness* (2 Pet. 2:15).

> *Woe to them! For they ... have run greedily in the error of Balaam for profit* (Jude 11).

The *"way of Balaam"* was an indictment against the false teachers in Peter's day who pursued the *"wages of unrighteousness"* (2 Pet. 2:15). Like covetous Balaam, these false teachers were attempting to represent God for financial profit. While God did speak through Balaam to Balak, he was nonetheless an impure vessel in God's hands. Peter likens the character of Balaam to false teachers in the Church Age who use religion as a cover for their self-seeking ways. The outcome of their teaching is all the same – to lead God's people into sin and away from Him, instead of drawing them nearer to Him (2 Pet. 2:14).

Jude speaks of *"the error of Balaam,"* which wrongly assumed that God had to judicially curse His people on the basis of their spiritual and moral failure. Balaam understood neither God's merciful character, nor His means of righteously judging sin through a substitute. Blood atonement under the Law pictured God's ultimate means of propitiation for human sin that would be achieved by the sacrifice of His Son.

Balaam instructed Balak to seduce the Israelites to commit idolatry and immorality with the daughters of Moab, so that God would be forced to punish them. While *"the way of Balaam"* speaks of his corrupt motives and *"the error of Balaam"* his wrong assessment of God's character and ways, *"the doctrine of Balaam"* refers to the willful teachings to purposely cause the corruption of God's people.

The Lord hates all of it! As a corrupt prophet who did not know God, Balaam eventually reaped what he had sowed and perished among the very people whom he sought to assist. And it always must be so!

November 27 – "The Rebellion of Korah"
(Jude)

Jude completes his trilogy of woes against false teachers by noting their end...they will perish in God's judgment just as rebellious Korah and his followers did in Numbers 16 (Jude 11). Korah led a rebellion against God's appointed leadership (Moses) and priesthood (Aaron and his sons) by suggesting that Moses and Aaron were limiting others from serving as priests before God. Moses responded to the indictment by reminding Korah of the privileged role in the tabernacle that God had assigned him as a Kohathite and then warns him not to rebel against it by seeking the priesthood (Num. 16:8-11). Korah used the truth of *sonship* (i.e., all God's people are sanctified and thus equal) to argue against God's order of *headship*. God made us, redeemed us, called us, and equipped us to serve Him the way He determines best. It is a terrible blunder to suppose that all believers are called to positions of prominence or that we can select our role within His Body.

Rather, Christ alone is to have preeminence in the Church – He is the head! Furthermore, every believer's role in the Body is appointed by Him (Eph. 2:10, 4:11) and all must adhere to His order for the Church (1 Cor. 14:33-34). Every Christian is therefore responsible to act in accordance with this divine principle, and to testify against everything that denies it. On this point, C. H. Mackintosh writes:

> The fact of the ruin of the professing Church is no reason whatever for abandoning the truth of God, or sanctioning any denial of it. The Christian is always solemnly bound to submit himself to the revealed mind of God. To plead circumstances as an excuse for doing wrong, or for neglecting any truth of God, is simply flying in the face of divine authority, and making God the Author of our disobedience.[49]

Korah was called into Levitical ministry, but not to the Levitical priesthood. Korah did not want to minister in his calling, but sought what he could not be, a priest. While today all believers are ministers to Christ (1 Pet. 4:10) and believer-priests to God (Rev. 1:6), there is but one Great High Priest – the Lord Jesus Christ (1 Tim. 2:5; Heb. 4:14). Woe to those who intrude on His priestly office and assume a position before men that is not theirs. Such pomposity will surely result in God's condemnation, for God hates the rebellion of Korah.

November 28 – Visions of Heaven
(Revelation Introduction)

God used prophetic visions and dreams, angelic visits, and pre-incarnate appearances of the Son of God, most of which are recorded in the Old Testament, to open our understanding of heavenly things. For example, Isaiah saw a vision of God and His heavenly throne room (Isa. 6:1-8); also in a vision, Ezekiel saw the Lord, His throne, and heavenly creatures about it (Ezek. 1). Then, there are the personal testimonies of people such as Elisha, who watched his mentor Elijah ascend into heaven in a fiery chariot (2 Kgs. 2:1-11), and Moses, who, on the mount, witnessed incredible sights beyond this world, and Paul who was caught up into the third heaven (God's spiritual domain) and saw things that he could not speak of (2 Cor. 12:2-4).

John was also taken up into heaven and told to write down what he saw, but yet, in some matters he was instructed not to record what he had witnessed (Rev. 4:1-2, 10:4). All this is to say that there is a good deal of biblical information which allows us to understand what God wants us to comprehend about heaven. What He has not revealed to us, we are not responsible to understand, nor is it likely that we could anyway (Deut. 29:29; Amos 4:13).

When John wrote the book of Revelation, he was an elderly man who had been banished to the Isle of Patmos by the Roman Empire. He was spiritually caught up into heaven to preview the prophetic messages that he was to write down (Rev. 1:1, 10, 4:1-2).

Paul, on the other hand, when transported into God's presence, did not know whether he was in or out of his body. Yet, he was fully conscious of the Lord's presence, and allowed to see and hear most sacred things, though he was not permitted to speak of them to others. What is clear from Paul's experience, and should be an encouragement to all believers, is that though he did not know what form he was in while in heaven, he was fully aware of the Lord's presence there. This tells us that whether the believer's soul is in heaven before or after his or her resurrection occurs, the Lord's presence will be enjoyed in either case (2 Cor. 5:8; Phil. 1:23). Being with the Lord is the thrill of heaven and what all true believers long for.

November 29 – Symbols From Heaven
(Revelation 1)

Moses was to construct the tabernacle and its furnishings according to the pattern that God showed him, which was a mere shadow (an abstract copy, if you will) of the heavenly things which already existed (Heb. 8:5). John was also shown heavenly things through the use of symbolic depiction: *"The Revelation of Jesus Christ ... things which must shortly take place. And He sent and **signified it** by His angel to His servant John"* (Rev. 1:1). What John heard and saw is retained for us to appreciate in writing, but in the form of symbolic depiction.

Besides the divine message contained in the Bible's narrative, God also uses numbers, symbols, metals, colors, names, etc. to convey information. These more abstract forms of revelation do not substitute for or supplement the clear teaching of Scripture, but rather reiterate the clear message of Scripture through metaphor. When God initially introduces an object, a number, a color, etc. in a metaphoric presentation, that symbolic meaning is held consistently throughout all sixty-six books of the Bible. Understanding the meanings of these consistent symbols permits us to decipher the book of Revelation.

For example, let us briefly consider the subject of numerology. In Scripture, numbers one through forty are used in a consistent way when a metaphoric meaning is intended. Though most numbers in Scripture have a literal meaning, some numbers also serve a figurative purpose. The Lord Jesus, the Lamb, is described as having *seven* horns before the throne of God in Revelation 5:6. It is not likely that the Lord Jesus Christ will physically look like this in heaven. Rather, the seven horns symbolically represent His omnipotence, as *seven* is used throughout Scripture as the number of *perfection*, while a *horn* represents *power*. He is also described in the same verse as having seven eyes; as an *eye* represents *sight*, we understand this description to speak of the Lord's divine omniscience – He knows and sees all things.

The consistent use of symbols, numbers, analogies, names, first-mention occurrences, the fulfilled prophetic types and shadows, plus the plain and consistent teachings of the Bible prove it to be the orchestrated genius of one Mind. It stands to reason, then, that we must know what several biblical symbols signify to better understand the meaning of heaven as shown to us in the book of Revelation.

November 30 – Vindication Imminent
(Revelation 1)

Before speaking of Christ's Second Advent to war against the Antichrist, Daniel is first transported into God's heavenly throne room, in the same way John is before receiving the vision of the Apocalypse (Rev. 4:1). Interestingly, both John and Daniel first describe the glory of God the Father, "the Ancient of Days" (Dan. 7:9-10; Rev. 4:2-3), before honoring God's Son, the Lamb (Dan. 7:13-14; Rev. 5:5-6). Like Daniel, John also recognizes an innumerable host of attendants about God's throne, except John includes redeemed saints among the throng of angelic beings, who are praising God and His Lamb (Rev. 5:11-12).

Before John is shown the visions of the coming Apocalypse, he is first afforded a spectacular vision of the glorified Christ poised to return to earth and vindicate His name. It was a sight so awesome and terrifying that John fell to the ground like a dead man:

> Then I turned to see the voice that spoke with me. And having turned I saw seven golden lampstands, and in the midst of the seven lampstands one like the Son of Man, clothed with a garment down to the feet and girded about the chest with a golden band. His head and hair were white like wool, as white as snow, and His eyes like a flame of fire; His feet were like fine brass, as if refined in a furnace, and His voice as the sound of many waters; He had in His right hand seven stars, out of His mouth went a sharp two-edged sword, and His countenance was like the sun shining in its strength. And when I saw Him, I fell at His feet as dead (Rev. 1:13-16).

Christ's brilliant countenance, white hair, and golden band about His waist all symbolically portray His purity and holiness. Fire and bronze speak of judgment throughout Scripture, and that is what is in the Lord's eyes and this is the purpose for which His feet will soon take Him. He is wearing a long judicial robe and speaks with majestic authority, like the roar of many waters; He is clearly the Supreme Judge over the earth. The entire scene expresses that Christ is ready to vindicate His name by returning to the earth to defeat evil, to deliver those who are loyal to Him, and to fulfill all God's covenants with the Jewish patriarchs by establishing His kingdom.

December 1 – "The Alpha and the Omega"
(Revelation 1)

During John's encounter with the radiant Lord Jesus in Revelation 1, the Lord affirms His deity twice by asserting He is the *"Alpha and the Omega"*:

> *"I am the Alpha and the Omega, the Beginning and the End," says the Lord, "who is and who was and who is to come, the Almighty"* (Rev 1:8). *I am the Alpha and the Omega, the First and the Last* (Rev. 1:11).

The Lord Jesus is again identified as *the Alpha and the Omega* in the final chapter of Scripture (Rev. 22:6, 13). Alpha is the first letter in the Greek alphabet, and omega is the last. Thus, the reference to these two letters figuratively represents God as the Beginning and the End. God is eternal, the source of life, the originator of all that has ever been created, thus, the only true God. In the New Testament, only the book of Revelation applies the title "the Beginning and the End" as a name for God (Rev. 1:8; 21:6). John declares the same truth by referring to the Lord Jesus as the Alpha and Omega (Rev. 1:8; Rev. 22:13).

The expression "the Alpha and the Omega" is similar to our English expression "from A to Z" which means "the entire thing – the whole alphabet." As God's Alphabet, Christ is God's entire communication. He is "the Word of God." *"Beginning at Moses and all the prophets, He expounded unto them, in all the Scriptures, the things concerning Himself"* (Luke 24:27).

Those who deny Christ's deity would say that it is Jehovah speaking in verses 8 and 11 and not Christ, but that denies the clear context of the passage, as John is describing the glorious posture of the Lord Jesus poised to vindicate Himself. It also creates a difficulty when the one speaking touches a frightful John and says: *"Do not be afraid; I am the First and the Last. I am He who lives, and was dead, and behold, I am alive forevermore. Amen. And I have the keys of Hades and of Death"* (Rev. 1:17-18). This begs the question: "When did the First and Last (God) die and come back to life?" The only answer to this question is at Calvary and three days later, respectively. Hence, Jesus Christ is God!

December 2 – Overcomers Will Be Rewarded
(Revelation 2)

The prophet Isaiah foretold that God's suffering Servant would be raised from the dead, exalted, and recompensed for His faithfulness; additionally, He would share the benefits of His victory with those who trust in Him: *"Therefore I will divide Him a portion with the great, and He shall divide the spoil with the strong, because He poured out His soul unto death"* (Isa. 53:12). This prophecy expresses the ancient idea that a victor would share with his fellows the spoils of those he conquered. The New Testament conveys this same meaning. The Lord Jesus taught that *"no one can enter a strong man's house and plunder his goods, unless he first binds the strong man. And then he will plunder his house"* (Mark 3:27). On the night before His crucifixion the Lord also foretold that He would conquer Satan to accomplish the release of those in his death grip: *"Now is the judgment of this world; now the ruler of this world will be cast out"* (John 12:31). By securing a means of salvation for humanity, the triumphant Savior despoiled Satan of many souls that were following him into the Lake of Fire. Christ is now leading "captivity captive" (those who were once in Satan's clutches) heavenward and bestowing to them the wealth of heaven, which was not available to them previously (Eph. 1:3, 4:8).

Christ is the Victor, and God has given Him the plunder of the defeated, but who are "the great" and "the strong" in Isaiah 53:12? The Septuagint's rendering of the verse: "I will give him the mighty for a portion" and "He shall divide the spoils of the mighty." The idea is that those Christ died to make righteous will be His inheritance and He will share the spoils of the defeated with them. God will certainly ensure that the rewards His Son receives will be worthy of the death He died.

However, there is a practical application also, if we understand "the great" to refer to those made righteous by Christ and then remain "strong" in Him. Then the verse would speak of Christ rewarding proportionally those who have borne reproach for His Name in the world which hated and crucified the Lord. This is the idea that John conveys: Overcomers are promised paradise with God, not to be hurt by the second death, and special intimacy with the Lord in heaven (Rev. 2:7, 11, 17). The Lord values those who follow His example of faithfulness and persistence; they will be rewarded appropriately.

344

December 3 – Beware of the Nicolaitans
(Revelation 2)

In writing to the churches of Asia Minor, the Lord minces no words in conveying His disdain for the Nicolaitans: *"But this you have, that you hate the deeds of the Nicolaitans, which I also hate"* (Rev. 2:6). *"Thus you also have those who hold the doctrine of the Nicolaitans, which thing I hate"* (Rev. 2:15). But who were these Nicolaitans?

The term "Nicolaitans," derived from *Nikolaos*, means "victorious over the people," and referred to those individuals who ruled the laity. At the time Revelation was written, a ruling body of clergy had evidently conquered the people in some areas and assumed rule over them. The Lord Himself used strong language against those who seized the rule over His people, saying He *hated* both their deeds and their doctrine. Their self-promoted status and professionalism worked to displace Christ's headship and to limit other believer-priests from using their spiritual gifts to honor Christ and edify His Church. Christ is Head of His Body – all believers are merely members of that Body.

Nowhere in Scripture do we read of a clerical position over the people, except when it rebukes those who had wrongly assumed one, such as Diotrephes (3 Jn. 9), and the Nicolaitans. The New Testament reveals ministries and offices that individuals were associated with, but no believer was given a personal title as part of his or her fulfillment of these. For example, there were apostles, elders, deacons, evangelists, pastor-teachers, etc. in the early Church, but no disciple of Christ was referred to by a title before his or her name. All believers have a common designation in Christ and have been equipped by the Holy Spirit to serve Christ. Thus, no one should seek titles or use terminologies that elevate themselves to unbiblical roles in the Church.

Although the Lord raises up elders to oversee local churches (Acts 20:28), these men are not the Pastors of the church (that is Christ's title alone in Scripture). Christ does give His Church men and women that are gifted as shepherds (Eph. 4:11). Some men with this gift will be used in church leadership, but not all elders have this pastoral gifting. Those in church leadership have a ministry for the Chief Shepherd, not an elevated position above fellow-believers. Whatever authority the church elders have springs forth from lives of godliness and subjection to the Lord, and not from human ambitions, certificates, or titles.

December 4 – God's Book of Names
(Revelation 3)

Expecting couples often rely on a book of names to spawn ideas for naming their babies. Yet, can you imagine browsing through a book which contained every name from every culture, throughout all of time? Scripture informs us that God maintains such a record.

One of God's books of names is first referred to by Moses, after the Israelites had created a golden calf and worshipped it at Mt. Sinai (Ex. 32). Moses had been with the Lord for forty days on Sinai, but ventured down its slopes to confront the people. The calf was destroyed and 3,000 people perished that day in judgment. The next day, Moses reminded the people that they had committed a great trespass against God, and said he would return to Mount Sinai to intercede on their behalf and to learn from the Lord how atonement could be offered for their sin (Ex. 32:30-35). Moses then ascended Mount Sinai again.

Moses asked the Lord to blot his own name out of His book if the nation as a whole could be spared judgment. Like Paul centuries later (Rom. 9:3), he pled for God to condemn him so that mercy could be granted to the Israelites. These were hypothetical prayers, for both men knew their divine callings and that God could not condemn those He had declared righteous, but their pleas did demonstrate their supernatural compassion for their countrymen. Evidently, Moses knew that God kept a roster of the names of everyone He would create, (including those who perish in the womb), in a book entitled *The Book of the Living* (Ex. 32:32-33). David refers to this same book in Psalm 69:28, and then again in Psalm 139:15-16. Psalm 139 confirms that this book contains the specific details of everyone prior to their conception.

This Book of the Living is likely what John is referring to in Revelation 3:5: *"He who overcomes ... I will not blot out his name from the Book of Life; but I will confess his name before My Father."* John assures us that the names of the faithful (true believers) are not blotted out of this book. On the other hand, unbelievers' names are blotted out of *The Book of the Living* as they die because they did not receive God's forgiveness for their sins while they were living (Heb. 9:27). This means that when it is reviewed at the Great White Throne Judgment (after the earth's destruction), it will contain only the names of those who have been declared righteous in Christ.

December 5 – He Who Opens and Shuts Doors
(Revelation 3)

The Lord Jesus told His disciples: *"Your Father knows the things you have need of before you ask Him"* (Matt. 6:8). John reminded the church at Philadelphia that it is the Lord Jesus alone who opens and closes doors of opportunity for believers: *"These things says He who is holy, He who is true, 'He who has the key of David, He who opens and no one shuts, and shuts and no one opens'"* (Rev. 3:7). This means that the Lord Jesus knows fully what we need and is fully able to provide it.

In the Church Age, all who are born again become temples of the living God and are indwelt with the Spirit of God (1 Cor. 6:19-20). This allows the human spirit to directly commune with God the Father; this is accomplished through the intercession of His indwelling Spirit (Rom. 8:26) and through the mediation of His Son (1 Tim. 2:5). This means that if we walk in the purity of our priesthood, the moment our hearts become burdened over what burdens God's heart, He is prompted to act for the honor of His name. It is comforting to know that when we do not know what to pray, or are so downhearted we are incapable of forming words in prayer, the Spirit of God intercedes perfectly on our behalf.

This means that we should not rush ahead of the Lord to try to fix our problems by perceived solutions; rather, we should ask and wait on the One who opens and closes doors to direct our way. Often what we first think is undesirable becomes the Lord's means of guiding us into what He has for us. God's blessing is often forfeited because Christians impetuously run ahead of the Lord to engage in some religious cause or some seemingly good deed which the Lord does not endorse. Nehemiah prayed and fasted for four months before God's door of opportunity was opened for him. He knew he could not resolve Jerusalem's problems, so he waited patiently for the Lord to answer his prayers. His example shows us how utterly defenseless the enemy is when Christ opens the doors of opportunity in response to our earnest praying.

The habit of regular, lingering prayer, more than anything else, makes any Christian a dangerous, holy weapon in the hand of God.

— J. Sidlow Baxter

347

December 6 – You Are Poor, Blind, and Naked
(Revelation 3)

The believers at Laodicea were materialistic, self-centered, and spiritually superficial. Their miserable condition prompted the Lord's rebuke: *"You are wretched, miserable, poor, blind, and naked – I counsel you to buy from Me gold refined in the fire, that you may be rich; and white garments, that you may be clothed, that the shame of your nakedness may not be revealed; and anoint your eyes with eye salve, that you may see"* (Rev. 3:17-18). Because those in the Church at Laodicea were not living for Christ, God's righteousness was not displayed in their lives. Spiritually speaking, they were poor, blind, and naked! While all the redeemed in heaven will be wearing white robes and have human form (Rev. 4:4, 19:14), some saints will outshine others with the splendor and glory of Christ.

In heaven, the bride of Christ must have righteous attire; she is *"arrayed in fine linen, clean and bright, for the fine linen is the righteous acts of the saints"* (Rev. 19:8). While all believers in the Church have been positionally declared righteous in Christ, each believer has the opportunity to labor in righteousness for Christ. Those things which are done in accordance with revealed truth and in the power of the Holy Spirit have eternal value; the outshining of these righteous acts are what the believer is adorned with throughout eternity.

After glorification, some saints will shine brighter than others, just as some stars in the nighttime sky are more brilliant than others (1 Cor. 15:40-42). This acquired glory directly reflects the righteous acts (good works) that are done for Christ presently (Rev. 19:8). Eternal glory has a weight to it; in other words, its quality is measurable (2 Cor. 4:17) and can be earned by believers through selfless service for Christ now.

Thus, to be appropriately dressed for eternity, believers should secure for themselves a covering of eternal glory, which consists of genuine righteous deeds. Such beneficial personal behavior on earth will provide believers with differing reflections of God's glory in heaven forever (Rev. 3:18). Without being justified in Christ, no one can enter into heaven, and only by doing righteous acts by His power do believers contribute to their eternal attire of glory. This means that all believers will reflect God's glory throughout eternity to some degree. May we endeavor to dress for heaven now!

December 7 – Knocking on Your Heart's Door
(Revelation 3)

The Lord concludes His letters to the seven churches with an invite:

Behold, I stand at the door and knock. If anyone hears My voice and opens the door, I will come in to him and dine with him, and he with Me (Rev 3:20).

The Lord was knocking on the door of believers' hearts who were a part of the lukewarm, materialistic church at Laodicea. He is a perfect gentleman and will not force Himself upon those who would rather live without Him, that is, who would rather live for themselves. Yet, His love is patient and He continues knocking and asking for access so that He might enjoy full communion with those He loves. Those who open the door of their hearts to Him eagerly receive His rule, and will enjoy His peace and blessing also. Unfortunately, there is much lethargy in the Church today, and few permit the Savior in to dine with them. Thankfully, the Lord will always be found in the midst of His people attending to their needs (Matt. 18:20) – this is what the Great Shepherd does (Heb. 13:20-21). Those who willingly gather to Him instead of venturing into the world to find answers and gratification will never suffer the frantic anxiety of not knowing where their Beloved is.

Much of the modern Church is stranded in the spiritual doldrums of complacency or being comfortably pampered. Those who have been redeemed and cleansed by the blood of Christ must venture out into the world and tell others of their wonderful Savior. To be witnesses for Christ, we must demonstrate His goodness and holy character through selfless deeds; this is how others will become familiar with our Beloved. Everything about the Lord Jesus is wonderful, which means others, if given the opportunity, will find Him lovely too. Being self-focused and spiritually despondent has a tremendous cost – communion with the Beloved is lost. May every believer reckon himself or herself dead to self and alive in Christ (Gal. 2:20). Then we too will have the right realization of our relationship: *"I am my beloved's, and my beloved is mine"* (Song 6:3). We are Christ's before all else. Moreover, He is ours; there is no possibility of disappointment on our part. So when He comes knocking to possess more of us, we must let Him in.

December 8 – The Voice of a Trumpet
(Revelation 4)

Twice John refers to the voice of Christ as sounding like a trumpet:

I was in the Spirit on the Lord's Day, and I heard behind me a loud voice, as of a trumpet, saying, "I am the Alpha and the Omega, the First and the Last" (Rev. 1:10-11).

After these things I looked, and behold, a door standing open in heaven. And the first voice which I heard was like a trumpet speaking with me, saying, "Come up here, and I will show you things which must take place after this" (Rev. 4:1).

During the wilderness years of the Israelites, two silver trumpets were blown by the priests for various reasons, but chiefly to declare the mind of God to His people (Num. 10:3-8). Later, the trumpets would be blown over sacrifices, on feast days, and when kings were anointed, but God's initial purpose for the trumpets was to call the people together, to move them out, or to sound an alarm. Given their intended purpose, the two silver trumpets represent God's ability to gather His people to Himself and then cause them to move forward in faith, that is, to go on with Him. If both trumpets sounded a summons, then the entire congregation of Israel was to come promptly before the Lord, but if only one trumpet was blown, only the leaders needed to respond.

In a spiritual sense, the Lord Jesus continues to direct the affairs of His redeemed today as He once did by two silver trumpets. John even likens the sound of the Lord's voice to that of a trumpet. In this sense, the Lord summons the local assembly together on the first day of the week (Acts 20:7; 1 Cor. 14:23). This is a call that must not be ignored (Heb. 10:25). The Lord beckons all the redeemed to remember Him often through the breaking of the bread (Luke 22:19-20; 1 Cor. 11:23-25). Also, believers today are waiting for the blast of the trumpet that will signal the Lord's coming for them. Then we will move out, in an upward direction, and ever be with Him: *"For the Lord Himself will descend from heaven with a shout, with the voice of an archangel, and with the trumpet of God. And the dead in Christ will rise first. Then we who are alive and remain shall be caught up together with them in the clouds to meet the Lord in the air"* (1 Thess. 4:13-18).

350

December 9 – God's Throne Room – Part 1
(Revelation 4)

John was permitted to see God's throne in heaven and records what he saw in Revelation 4. In that chapter, John mentions the throne of God twelve times and is careful not to describe anything else he saw except in its relationship to the throne. To emphasize this connection, Jim Flanigan observes John's use of five prepositional clauses:

Upon the Throne — Deity sitting in inscrutable splendor.
Round about the Throne – a rainbow, and twenty-four crowned elders, and four strange living creatures.
Out of the Throne – lightning, and thundering, and voices.
Before the Throne – seven lamps of fire, a sea of glass, and the proffered crowns of the elders.
In the midst of the Throne – the four living ones, who also surround the Throne; and ... the Lamb (Rev. 5).[50]

In summary, nothing is described in this heavenly scene apart from its connection with God's throne. Why? Because God is sovereign over all things; He is accountable to no one. Everything which exists is dependent upon Him. Without God on His throne, nothing else would matter. This is why the first sight that John describes after being caught up into heaven by the Holy Spirit was God on His throne:

And He who sat there was like a jasper and a sardius stone in appearance; and there was a rainbow around the throne, in appearance like an emerald. Around the throne were twenty-four thrones, and on the thrones I saw twenty-four elders sitting, clothed in white robes; and they had crowns of gold on their heads. And from the throne proceeded lightnings, thunderings, and voices, seven lamps of fire were burning before the throne, which are the seven Spirits of God (Rev. 4:3-5).

The priority of what John describes is important. Some think that it will be streets of gold, foundations of precious stones, and pearly gates that will make heaven special; however, heaven would not be a spectacular domain at all if God were not there. John, therefore, begins his revelation with the most spectacular sight in heaven – God the Father on His throne and His Son, the Lamb, is with Him (Rev. 5:6).

December 10 – God's Throne Room – Part 2
(Revelation 4)

John describes the outshining of God's holy essence – His spectacular glory. The prophet relates this visible manifestation of God's radiance to the colors reflected from a jasper and a sardius stone. Jasper is used twice in Revelation 21 as a symbol of God's glory in connection with the New Jerusalem, God's eternal, heavenly city (Rev. 21:10-11). In fact, the walls of this city are made entirely of jasper (Rev. 21:18). Jasper is a crystalline form of silica containing fine minerals of quartz and moganite. It is neither transparent nor translucent, meaning that all visible light reaching its surface is either absorbed or reflected back to us in the colors red, yellow, brown, green, and sometimes blue. Sardius is a red stone. There is no form on the throne to describe, only a dazzling spectacle of various hues of light emanating from it. Sardius and jasper were the first and the last precious stones in the High Priest's breastplate (Ex. 28:17-20). These mentioned in tandem picture of God's immutable and eternal glory.

John also saw a rainbow encircling the throne. God promised Noah that He would never destroy the earth again by water; the rainbow was given to mankind as a symbol of that covenant. The circle never stops and thus represents eternity. The compound symbol indicates that God's promises are eternal – He is a covenant-keeping God.

Around God's throne were twenty-four other, smaller thrones on which twenty-four elders were seated. These represent the redeemed just resurrected from the earth, which would include, but may not be limited to, the Church (Rev. 5:9). These were clothed in white raiment and were wearing gold crowns upon their heads (Rev. 4:4). Though there are likely many rewards for faithfulness, five are mentioned in Scripture: **The Crown of Glory** will be given to church elders who shepherd well (1 Pet. 5:4). **The Crown of Life** will be given to those who endure trials because they love the Lord (Jas. 1:12). **The Crown of Rejoicing** will be given to those who were soul-winners for Christ (1 Thess. 2:19; Phil 4:1); this crown may be more encompassing, such as a reward for spiritual growth in general. **The Crown of Righteousness** will be given to those who long for His appearing (2 Tim. 4:8). **The Incorruptible Crown** will be given to those who control fleshly desires through the Holy Spirit (1 Cor. 9:25). The Lord rewards faithfulness!

December 11 – The Twenty-Four Elders
(Revelation 4)

The crowns, or rewards, were given by the Lord Jesus Christ to the elders, His saints, for their honorable service to Him. The rewards that are earned during this lifetime provide the believer with a greater appreciation for the Lord, a greater capacity to worship Him throughout eternity, and, indeed, a greater capability to enjoy heaven (Rev. 4:11).

As both the twelve apostles and the twelve tribes of Israel are clearly tied to the New Jerusalem in Revelation 21, it is my opinion that the same numerical representation of *twenty-four* is used here to express that all those who have been redeemed up until this point in time have experienced glorification (Rev. 5:8-10). This would include the Old Testament saints, who were mainly connected with the nation of Israel, and the Church in the New Testament. *"And all these, having obtained a good testimony through faith, did not receive the promise* [speaking of Old Testament saints], *God having provided something better for us, that they should not be made perfect apart from us"* (Heb. 11:39-40). The Lord Jesus told His disciples that they would be seated about Him on twelve thrones in a future day. *"Assuredly I say to you, that in the regeneration, when the Son of Man sits on the throne of His glory, you who have followed Me will also sit on twelve thrones, judging the twelve tribes of Israel"* (Matt. 19:28). In the scene before us (Rev. 4 and 5), the Lord Jesus is still on His Father's throne (Rev. 3:21); that is, He is still waiting to establish His kingdom on earth. After that occurs, He will sit on His own throne in Jerusalem. The twenty-four elders on their thrones in heaven are also anticipating their opportunity to rule and reign with Christ in His kingdom.

The elders in this scene have already been rewarded for faithful service and seated in a place of honor about the throne of God and the Lamb. This event refers to the Judgment Seat of Christ, which occurs immediately after the rapture of the Church from the earth (1 Cor. 3:11-15; 2 Cor. 5:10; Rom. 14:12-14). This is a remarkable scene as humans were created to govern the world, not heaven, and humans have a lower position in creation than the angels (Gen. 1:26; Heb. 2:6-8). Yet, we never read of angels seated on thrones in Scripture, nor do they rule and reign with Christ as redeemed humanity will; they were created as eternal beings to serve God and will remain unchanged forever.

December 12 – Lightnings and Thunderings
(Revelation 4)

John continued his description of God's throne room:

And from the throne proceeded lightnings, thunderings, and voices. Seven lamps of fire were burning before the throne, which are the seven Spirits of God (Rev. 4:5).

The apostle observed that there was continual lightning, thunder, and voices proceeding out from God's throne. This description creates an unsettling disposition about the scene. We are left wondering if this ominous panorama depicts God's throne presently or relates to the future period in which John was observing it, which was just after the end of the Church Age (Rev. 4:2), and just prior to the Tribulation Period (Rev. 6:1). William Kelly answers this quandary:

Do thunderings and lightnings and voices proceed from the throne of God at this present time? ...Certainly not. The throne of God now is a throne of grace, to which we come boldly (Heb. 4:14-16). ... Clearly the thunderings and lightnings and voices are the expression of God's displeasure and judicial feeling, so to speak, towards things and people upon the earth.[51]

That this scene represents the future reality of looming worldwide judgment seems to be a logical conclusion, given the testimony of Scripture as a whole. Once in fellowship with God, Moses and the elders of Israel ate a meal before the Lord's throne on Mt. Sinai and all was quiet (Ex. 24:9-12). Neither Stephen nor Paul mentioned anything about thunder, lightning, and voices during their glimpses of God's throne during the Church Age. Yet, with the redeemed surrounding the Lamb in heaven and on the eve of His pouring out judgment on the wicked, God's throne rumbles.

Crown Him with many crowns, the Lamb upon His throne;
Hark! How the heavenly anthem drowns all music but its own!
Awake, my soul, and sing of Him who died for thee;
And hail Him as thy matchless King through all eternity.

— Matthew Bridges

December 13 – The Seven Lamps of Fire (Part 1)
(Revelation 4)

Next John mentions *"seven lamps of fire were burning before the throne, which are the seven Spirits of God"* (Rev. 4:5). These seven torches or flames before the throne represent the Holy Spirit and the fullness of His perfecting work. The number seven is God's number and represents perfection, completeness, and holiness. The Golden Lampstand in the tabernacle and, later, the temple was patterned after this scene. Through the number seven, the light of the lampstand (representing Christ's testimony of truth) is shown to be divine in origin. Likewise, the resource enabling the seven flames to illuminate the tabernacle (the oil) is also shown to be divine in nature. As in Zechariah's vision of the two olive trees that supplied oil to a lampstand, the Holy Spirit is depicted in the pure oil. Speaking of the oil, the Lord told Zechariah: *"Not by might nor by power, but by My Spirit"* (Zech. 4:6). The lampstand, then, speaks of God's perfect revelation of truth in Christ through the power of the Holy Spirit.

We often speak of *types* of Christ in Scripture, which are usually seen in either *people* or *objects*: He is typified in an ark, a rock, a rod, a door, an arm, a shepherd, a veil, etc. The reason types from these two categories are used to speak of Christ is that objects and people are used to accomplish a work, and these picture the Son performing the Father's will. The Holy Spirit, however, as shown in the scene before us, is generally depicted in *active fluids.* He is described as flowing olive oil (Zech. 4), blowing wind (John 3), and rushing water (John 7). John describes Him as seven flames of fire before God's throne.

The Holy Spirit, in these types, is not visibly seen doing the Father's will, but rather enabling and accomplishing the task at hand in a powerful and invisible fashion. Accordingly, the forever-burning fire on the Golden Altar and Lampstand in the temple portray the continual work of the Spirit of God to illuminate Christ to others and to offer up the believer's labors of love as a sweet aroma to God. Thus we see that the selection of types and shadows to portray the members of the Godhead reflect their particular role in the Trinity: the Father wills, the Son performs the Father's will, and the Spirit enables the Son to accomplish the Father's will.

December 14 – The Seven Lamps of Fire (Part 2)
(Revelation 4)

Throughout Scripture, the roles within the Godhead are consistently represented: God the Father declares the will of God (He directs), God the Son executes the will of God, and the Holy Spirit enables and ratifies the will of God to be done, usually through the Son. Each Person of the Godhead acts to the praise of God's glory (Eph. 1:6, 12, 14). The fact that the Father chooses does not imply that the Son and the Holy Spirit do not have individual wills – for They do – but they always align with the Father's (John 6:38; 1 Cor. 12:11). The fact that the Holy Spirit issues power to ratify God's will does not mean that the Son does not have power to invoke miracles – He does, for *"in Him all things consist"* (Col. 1:17). Luke 5:17 serves as an example of the Son doing a miracle in His own power.

Isaiah foretold that the Messiah would not only be a descendant of David but would be endowed with the Spirit of the Lord (Isa. 11:2). Accordingly, the One ruling over the Apocalypse that John is now describing would have the full plenitude of the Holy Spirit's divine power, which Isaiah describes in seven distinct ways to express His perfection: The Spirit of Jehovah, the Spirit of wisdom, the Spirit of understanding, the Spirit of counsel, the Spirit of might, the Spirit of knowledge, and the Spirit of the fear of Jehovah (Isa. 11:2). John, describing God's throne room in heaven, refers to the Holy Spirit in a similar way: *"Seven lamps of fire were burning before the throne, which are the seven Spirits of God"* (Rev. 4:5). At His second advent, the Son will accomplish the will of the Father in the full wisdom, counsel, power, etc. of the Holy Spirit.

The cults teach that the Holy Spirit is neither divine nor a person. The Jehovah's Witnesses believe that the Holy Spirit is an invisible force that produces visible results, while Mormons teach that the Holy Spirit is an influence of God completely distinct from God the Father and His son Jesus (whom they identify as one of the Father's many spiritual children). However, Scripture teaches that the Holy Spirit is much more than a mere influence or force which God uses to accomplish His will, for the Spirit has a will of His own (1 Cor. 12:11). These groups also deny the deity of Christ and, accordingly, the triune nature of God. God is thrice Holy – the Father, the Son, and the Spirit.

December 15 – The Sea of Glass
(Revelation 4)

John also describes a sea of glass before God's throne (Rev. 4:6). The laver in the tabernacle (Ex. 38) and later in the temple were patterned after this crystal sea, yet these earthly lavers held water, not glass, so a clear distinction is being made between the type and the antitype, as seen by John. The Bronze Laver in the tabernacle courtyard was constructed of polished bronze and filled with water. The Bronze Laver was located between the entrance of the tabernacle and the Bronze Altar where burnt sacrifices were offered to God. The worth of blood and water are set forth in the pattern of the Altar and the Laver; in the former, blood cleanses sin, and in the latter, water washes away defilement. The blood on the Altar flowed from smitten animals and the water in the Laver came from the smitten rock. Both the animals slain and the rock struck are types of Christ (1 Cor. 10:4; John 7:38).

To worship the Lord in the tabernacle, Levitical priests had to first put a lamb on the Bronze Altar and then wash their hands and feet at the laver before entering into the tabernacle (Ex. 30:17-21). The priests had earlier undergone a one-time complete bath at the door of the tabernacle. This pictures the one-time regeneration of a believer by the Holy Spirit (Tit. 3:5). However, no priest could serve the Lord without washing his hands and feet every time he entered the tabernacle. This action typifies the believer's desire to confess sins on an on-going basis in order to be forgiven, to have his or her conscience cleared of guilt, and to be restored into fellowship with God (1 Jn. 1:9). No priest dared come before the Lord without first washing his hands and feet and no believer-priest today can be a daily, living sacrifice or offer acceptable praise, service, or worship to the Lord until he or she has first stopped at the Laver, that is, to first confess his or her sins to Christ.

What is the significance between the Bronze Laver of water and the sea of glass in heaven? As long as there is a Christian on earth, the practical aspects of cleansing defilement from the believer's life would be a necessary ministry of Christ's intercession and Word, as pictured in the Laver. But now that the Church had passed from the scene of her earthly defilement into heaven, she had no more need of the Laver. The clear, ripple-free sea of glass in heaven declares that those in heaven are perfectly cleansed and that all is at peace in God's presence.

December 16 – The Four Living Creatures (Part 1)
(Revelation 4)

John turns his attention from the sea of glass before God's throne to four spectacular creatures flying about it:

> *And in the midst of the throne, and around the throne, were four living creatures full of eyes in front and in back. The first living creature was like a lion, the second living creature like a calf, the third living creature had a face like a man, and the fourth living creature was like a flying eagle. The four living creatures, each having six wings, were full of eyes around and within. And they do not rest day or night, saying: "Holy, holy, holy, Lord God Almighty, who was and is and is to come!"* (Rev. 4:6-8).

Besides this reference to the four living creatures, the Bible informs us that there are classes of spiritual beings that exist in heaven. Besides Michael the archangel, there are cherubim (Gen. 3:24; Ezek. 1:5-14, 10:7), seraphim (Isa. 6:1-7), the four living creatures just described, and a host of innumerable angels with various functions and roles (Ps. 103:19-22). Furthermore, God describes to us what many of these spiritual beings do and how they appear before God's throne in heaven. For example, the angel Gabriel announced the births of both the Lord Jesus and John the baptizer. The four living creatures and seraphim have the occupation of flying about God's throne and praising His name, while cherubim are protectors of God's glory (i.e., they keep what is defiled from entering too close to and being consumed by God's holiness). Why did God afford us all these details?

Clearly, the Father is calling our attention to His Son through the appearance of these extraordinary heavenly creatures. That is, their intrinsic glories are concealed by their wings to ensure our attention remains focused on the Lamb of God, the Lord Jesus Christ. For example, the Seraphim have six wings, but only use two for flying (Isa. 6). The Cherubim were given four wings, but they also use only two for flying (Ezek. 1). God intended them to use their remaining wings to cover their own intrinsic glories while in His presence, thus assuring that only He would be adored and worshipped in heaven. Normally, these spiritual beings gladly cover themselves in God's presence, but there was a time when Lucifer, a special covering cherub, refused to cover himself and was lifted up in pride against God (Ezek. 28:13-16).

December 17 – The Four Living Creatures (Part 2)
(Revelation 4)

Returning to the spiritual creatures in heaven, we notice that not every part of these heavenly creatures is to be concealed with their wings; their feet, eyes, and faces are not to be covered and, in fact, should not be, for an emulated glory of Christ is being proclaimed through their visibility. What reflects Christ's glory in these creatures is seen, but what would compete with His glory is not described and we are not to be concerned with it. This exercise of revealing God's glory and concealing competing glories in God's presence is something that the Church is to remember and practice on earth; in so doing, we pattern the holy scene now occurring in heaven (1 Cor. 11:3-16). The angels learn about submission through this practice (1 Cor. 11:10).

The scriptural accounts of the cherubim in Ezekiel 1 and 10, of the seraphim in Isaiah 6, and of the four living creatures in Revelation 4 all disclose that these beings have four kinds of faces. Apparently, the cherubim each have all four, that is, the face of a lion, the face of an ox, the face of a man, and the face of an eagle. The faces of these beings reflect the same glories of the Lord Jesus that are presented in the main themes of each Gospel:

The *lion* is the king of the beasts, which reflects Matthew's perspective of Christ as king.

The *ox*, a beast of burden harnessed for the rigors of serving, pictures Mark's presentation of Jesus Christ, the servant.

The face of the *man* clearly agrees with Luke's prevalent theme of the Lord's humanity.

Lastly, the *eagle* flies high above all the other creatures – the divine essence of the Savior is in view here, as in the epistle of John.

The many eyes of the cherubim describe Christ's omniscience and their bronze feet convey His divine authority to judge the wicked in flaming vengeance (Rev. 1:15). All that the Bible describes to us about heaven, whether in structures, furnishings, or angelic beings, is for the purpose of calling our attention to God's Son!

December 18 – The Lamb
(Revelation 5)

As John declared years earlier, the Lord Jesus *was "the Lamb of God, which takes away the sin of the world"* (John 1:29). As God's only sacrificial Lamb, Christ was blameless and perfect, and the only acceptable substitutional sacrifice for man's sin. The Lord Jesus commonly referred to Himself by titles which referred to His mission to earth, such as "the Son of Man." However, other than His forerunner, John the Baptist, who spoke of Him as *"the Lamb of God,"* others did not speak of Christ in this way. We should remember what the Lord has accomplished for us at Calvary, but also be careful not to address Him now with expressions of His humiliation (e.g., "the Son of Man").

The only exception to this scriptural pattern is when the Bible affirms that a title of humiliation has become a title of exaltation; "Lamb" is an example of this. God's Lamb is prominent in Scripture, with one-fourth of all references to the word "lamb" being found in the book of Revelation. Revelation chapters 4 and 5 describe the throne room scene in heaven just before the Tribulation Period begins. The twenty-four elders (i.e., the redeemed) sing praises to the Lamb: *"You are worthy, O Lord, to receive glory and honor and power..."* (Rev. 4:11). Then, the elders are joined by the four living creatures in another declaration of praise: *"You are worthy..."* (Rev. 5:9). Then, all the angelic hosts of heaven join the elders and the four living creatures in uttering a sevenfold song of praise: *"Worthy is the Lamb who was slain to receive power and riches and wisdom, and strength and honor and glory and blessing!"* (Rev. 5:12). Finally, this innumerable-member choir is joined by every earthly creature to bring the praise of God's Lamb to a climax: *"Blessing and honor and glory and power be to Him who sits on the throne, and to the Lamb, forever and ever"* (Rev. 5:13).

Furthermore, the power and authority of the Lamb is evident to those on earth during the Tribulation Period. The wicked were terrified after seeing the face of the Lamb peering down at them from heaven (Rev. 6:16). Later, John sees a vision of the Battle of Armageddon: *"These will make war with the Lamb, and the Lamb will overcome them, for He is Lord of lords and King of kings; and those who are with Him are called, chosen, and faithful"* (Rev. 17:14). May every child of God honor God's Lamb – our Lamb, our Savior, and our Lord forever.

December 19 – The Tribulation Period
(Revelation 6-19)

God will judge the nations for their wickedness and refine and restore the Jewish nation to Himself during the seven-year Tribulation Period. There will be twenty-one specific judgments by God upon the earth mentioned in Revelation chapters 6 through 16. During this time, the Antichrist and the powers of darkness will be rampant on the earth; there will be much destruction and a horrific holocaust: In Revelation 6, we are told that one fourth of the world's population will die from pestilence, war, and famine. Revelation 9 states that one third of mankind will be destroyed by fire. Two hundred million soldiers will be annihilated at the battle of Armageddon (Rev. 9:16). Moreover, in Revelation 7 and 13, we learn that an innumerable host of people from all nations will be martyred by the Beast for not receiving his mark.

Furthermore, Iraq, Iran, Egypt, Turkey and Russia (*Rosh*) invade Israel during the middle portion of the Tribulation Period (Ezek. 38 and 39). These armies will be annihilated by Christ's intervention through nature; only a remnant will be allowed to escape back to the north (Joel 2:19-20). Zechariah 13:8-9 confirms that two thirds of the Jews will die during the Tribulation Period; the remaining Jewish remnant will be refined and restored to God as His chosen people (Rom. 11). There will be numerous other judgments upon the earth that will also cause death and misery. The earth will not be the place to be during the Tribulation Period, as perhaps eighty percent of the world's population will perish.

Through various judgments during the Tribulation, Christ will take away from man what man has ignorantly claimed as his own. He has labored, stolen, cheated, murdered, etc. in order to gain wealth, power, prestige, and sensual gratification. But conditions in this epic period will be such that death will be welcomed, as even life's basic necessities will be scarcely found (Rev. 6:6, 8:10-11). The prophet Isaiah (Isa. 2:19) and John describe the response of the wicked at this time: "*And the kings of the earth, the great men, the rich men, the commanders, the mighty men, every slave and every free man, hid themselves in the caves and in the rocks of the mountains, and said to the mountains and rocks, 'Fall on us and hide us from the face of Him who sits on the throne and from **the wrath of the Lamb!** For the great day of His wrath has come, and who is able to stand?'*" (Rev. 6:14-17).

December 20 – Internalizing God's Word
(Revelation 10)

While caught up in the spirit into heaven, John saw a mighty angel, who represented Christ's majestic sovereignty (Rev. 10:1-7). A voice from heaven instructed John to take the little book in the angel's hand and eat it: *"Take and eat it; and it will make your stomach bitter, but it will be as sweet as honey in your mouth"* (Rev. 10:9). John did so and his stomach became bitter. The angel told him why he was asked to eat the little book: *"You must prophesy again about many peoples, nations, tongues, and kings"* (Rev. 10:11). John was now better equipped to reveal the deeper things of God to the Church.

Over six centuries earlier a similar situation happened to the prophet Ezekiel. God desired His prophet to willingly open his mouth and eat (i.e., receive) whatever He put there (Ezek. 2:8). Shortly after this, the Lord commanded Ezekiel to literally eat the scroll that was in His hand. By doing so, Ezekiel was internalizing the divine message he was to passionately communicate to God's rebellious people (Ezek. 3:1-2). The scroll tasted sweet as honey in his mouth, though the content of its message was bitter judgments. It was nonetheless God's Word, and Ezekiel was reminded that its source (God) was sweet.

Then, a few years before Ezekiel's commissioning, the prophet Jeremiah also joyfully ate God's Word, which sustained and delighted his soul (Jer. 15:16). This divine provision empowered him to shun the company of evildoers and fools in order to sit alone with the Lord and be guided by Him. Because Jeremiah was in such close communion with God, he too felt God's indignation against Judah (i.e. he could better identify with God's righteous anger over their sin).

Those sharing God's Word today cannot expect to have any divine power unless they have first fed upon God's Word and permitted the Spirit of God to have His way. What God reveals must be lived out before it can be spoken out in power: *"The judgments of the Lord are true and righteous altogether. More to be desired are they than gold, yea, than much fine gold: sweeter also than honey and the honeycomb"* (Ps. 19:9-10). God's Word and His work are a direct reflection of His character; that is, they are what He is: perfect, sure, right, pure, clean, true, and righteous. God's statutes are more precious than gold, sweeter than honey, and ensure a prodigious reward if obeyed.

December 21 – The Lamb's Book of Life
(Revelation 13)

The Lord Jesus told His disciples in Matthew 10:20 to rejoice because their names were written in heaven. The Greek verb translated *"written"* in this passage is in the perfect tense, which means it can be rendered as Kenneth Wuest does in his expanded translation: *"your names have been written in heaven and are on permanent record up there."*[52] This statement may refer either to *The Book of the Living* (discussed earlier) or to *The Lamb's Book of Life*, which is a timeless roster of all the redeemed – all that will be saved throughout time (Rev. 21:27). Revelation 13:8 and 17:8 also refer to *The Lamb's Book of Life*.

The Book of the Living, though written before time began, has its fulfillment in time. *The Lamb's Book of Life*, also written before creation, has its verification at the Great White Throne judgment. The former book has names blotted out of it as the lost die, while the latter remains unaltered – only the names of the redeemed are written in it. *The Book of Life* (or *The Book of the Living*) initially contained the names of all those who would ever live, but those not coming to salvation never had their names written in *The Lamb's Book of Life*. Because the names of the lost, when they die, are blotted out of the former book, both books will match at the Great White Throne Judgment; their records will be in perfect agreement. The one shows God's foreknowledge; the other, His record of human responsibility.

Because of Moses' great love for God's people, he was willing to be blotted out of *The Book of the Living* (Ex. 32:32-33) in order to secure forgiveness for the Israelites. Moses was willing to suffer in the place of sinners. God's later working in human affairs would be characterized by a similar message: the Lord Jesus willingly took the place of condemned sinners at Calvary in order to secure the opportunity for them to be forgiven and restored to God.

Although Moses pictures the Lord Jesus' willingness to take the place of the condemned, Moses himself was a sinner and, therefore, could not be a substitute in judgment for anyone else. Only through a righteous substitute could an unrighteous person be justified before God. Hence, it is only Christ's intercession and substitutional judgment at Calvary on our behalf which keeps anyone's name eternally readable in *The Book of the Living* and affirmed in *The Lamb's Book of Life*.

363

December 22 – The Song of the Redeemed
(Revelation 15)

There are many similarities between the events surrounding the plagues of Egypt at Israel's exodus with the apocalyptic judgments John identifies in Revelation. Interestingly, the last song recorded in the Bible is associated with the first song mentioned in Scripture: the song of the redeemed, after their oppressors were vanquished in the Red Sea (Ex. 15), as compared to John's description of this heavenly scene:

> *And I saw something like a sea of glass mingled with fire, and those who have the victory over the beast, over his image and over his mark and over the number of his name, standing on the sea of glass, having harps of God. They sing the song of Moses, the servant of God, and the song of the Lamb, saying: Great and marvelous are Your works, Lord God Almighty! Just and true are Your ways, O King of the saints! Who shall not fear You, O Lord, and glorify Your name? For You alone are holy. For all nations shall come and worship before You, for Your judgments have been manifested"* (Rev. 15:2-4).

This song will be sung again, not by those just escaping death to journey with Jehovah through the wilderness, but rather by those who will journey to Him in heaven through death to escape the Antichrist. These saints will choose death rather than to bow to the Antichrist. The heavenly inheritance sung of by the Israelites long ago will then be theirs to enjoy forever. God's own joy in His redeemed people is enthusiastically expressed in song directly after the Tribulation when He will sing over them and quiet them with His love (Zeph. 3:17).

The twelve Tribes of Israel were numbered when they departed Egypt under Moses' leadership. Similarly, during the first part of the Tribulation Period, there will be 144,000 Jews (12,000 Jews from each tribe) who are counted and sealed to be witnesses for the Lord: *"And I heard the number of those who were sealed. One hundred and forty-four thousand of all the tribes of the children of Israel were sealed"* (Rev. 7:4). We later find these faithful Jews, after having completed their mission on earth and being martyred, in heaven singing a new song in the presence of the Lamb (Rev. 14:1-5). What the Jews first sang after their deliverance from Pharaoh in Egypt will be expressed again to the Lord after being saved from the Antichrist on the earth.

December 23 – The Kingdom Age
(Revelation 20)

By the end of the Tribulation Period, rebellious man will have nothing. Christ will demonstrate His control over all things and then purify the earth in order to usher in the Kingdom Age (Dan. 2:35, 44-45; Rom. 8:21). Then, the earth and all its inhabitants will enjoy 1,000 years of blessing under Christ's rule without evil or satanic opposition:

> *Then I saw an angel coming down from heaven, having the key to the bottomless pit and a great chain in his hand. He laid hold of the dragon, that serpent of old, who is the Devil and Satan, and bound him for a thousand years; and he cast him into the bottomless pit, and shut him up, and set a seal on him, so that he should deceive the nations no more till the thousand years were finished. But after these things he must be released for a little while (Rev. 20:1-3).*

What will the Kingdom Age be like? From Isaiah 2:1-5 and 66:20, we learn that Jerusalem will be the religious center of the world. Christ will reign from there and everyone will come there to praise, worship, and learn of Him. There will be no war or violence, only peace. All the earth will see the glory of the Lord Jesus. Isaiah 4:2-4 informs us that the Jews who live through the Tribulation will gaze upon Christ (the Branch of the Lord) and appreciate His splendor, glory, fruitfulness, and beauty. So great will be the glory of the Lord on the earth that there will be no need for the sun or moon to illuminate it (Isa. 60:18-20).

In the Kingdom Age, strange phenomena in nature will be observed as the curses that were put on the earth as a result of man's sin are lifted (Rom. 8:21-22). A handful of seed casually scattered on a mountaintop will produce a great harvest (Ps. 72:16), longevity of life will be restored to humanity (Isa. 65:20), weapons will be used as agricultural implements (Mic. 4:3), and a spirit of peace and tranquility will rest upon the whole earth (Isa. 11:9). The wolf and the lamb shall dwell together, as will the kid of the goat with the leopard, and the calf with the lion (Isa. 11:6-7). Small children shall play by the home of the asp and at the adder's den without being afraid (Isa. 11:8). The glory of the Lord will be displayed upon the world as abundantly as *"the waters cover the sea"* (Isa. 11:9). During the Kingdom Age, any nation opposing the Lord Jesus will be laid waste (Isa. 60:12).

December 24 – The First Resurrection (Part 1)
(Revelation 20)

Though the resurrection of the condemned occurs all at once at the Great White Throne judgment (Rev. 20:11-15), the *resurrection of life*, also called the *first resurrection* (Rev. 20:5-6), occurs for the righteous at several distinct points in time prior to the Great White Throne judgment. The Eternal State, the everlasting reality of a new heaven and new earth without sin follows this final judgment. Time ceases to have meaning after this. Christ was raised from the dead three days after He gave His life as a ransom for humanity at Calvary. Though there had been six bodily resurrections recorded in the Bible previously, Christ was the first individual to experience glorification (to receive a glorified body which would be suitable for the dynamics of heaven). The number seven is used in the Bible to symbolize completeness and perfection and Christ, the seventh human raised from the dead, was the first to experience perfect resurrection; as Paul puts it, the Lord Jesus was *"the firstfruits of the dead"* to appear before God in heaven (1 Cor. 15:20-23).

Shortly after Christ's resurrection, some deceased believers were also raised from the dead, probably as further validation of Christ's own resurrection. They either underwent a bodily resurrection (like Lazarus' resurrection recorded in John 12) or glorification (the same type of resurrection that Christ experienced) – Scripture does not specify which type. If this were only a bodily resurrection, those saints would have had to die a second time. It seems unlikely that God would have allowed these saints to enjoy fellowship with Christ in paradise and then put them back on the earth again to live a normal human existence in a sin-cursed world.

The next stage of the first resurrection will be when Christ returns for His Church. He will descend into the clouds and all true believers (both those who have died and also those still alive) will be quickly caught up from the earth to experience glorification (1 Thess. 4:13-18; 1 Cor. 15:51-52). At that moment, all Christians (and perhaps Old Testament saints as well, per Heb. 11:39-40) will receive the same kind of perfect body that the Lord did after His resurrection (Phil. 3:21; 1 Jn. 3:2). This spectacular event ends the Church Age and will be followed by a devastating period on earth called the Tribulation Period.

December 25 – The First Resurrection (Part 2)
(Revelation 20)

After all true Christians (i.e. those who had been born again and are indwelt by God) have been removed from the earth, the Antichrist will be allowed to rule the world for seven years (2 Thess. 2:4-7; Daniel 9:27). God will pour out great wrath upon the earth at this time and Satan will attempt to gain as many followers as possible and slaughter those who will not take his mark and pledge allegiance to the Antichrist (Rev. 12:12, 13:11-18). As previously mentioned, the holocaust of life during this time will be horrendous; the Lord Jesus said that if He should tarry longer than the appointed time for His return to the earth, humanity would be wiped out (Matt. 24:21-22). Although two thirds of all Jews will be murdered during the Tribulation Period (Zech. 13:8-9), God will protect a remnant of His covenant people from the Antichrist (Rev. 12:13-17) in order to fulfill remaining promises to Abraham and David (Gen. 15:18-2; Ps. 89:3-4; Luke 1:32-33, 67-79).

The good news is that many of the earth's inhabitants will choose to be beheaded by the Antichrist (Rev. 20:4) rather than take his mark of identification and worship him (Rev. 7:9-14). Those who heard the gospel message of Jesus Christ during the Church Age will not be given the opportunity to receive salvation during the Tribulation Period – sadly they will take *"the mark of the beast"* and follow him into destruction (2 Thess. 2:10-12). Because they rejected God's Son's offer of salvation and opted instead to pursue pleasure in unrighteousness, God will not permit them to understand the truth in order to be saved.

Instead, those martyred for choosing to worship God rather than the Antichrist will experience the first resurrection at the end of the Tribulation Period when Christ returns to the earth (Rev. 7:9-14, 20:4). The Antichrist and his followers will be judged, wickedness removed, and Christ will establish His millennial kingdom on earth:

Then I saw the souls of those who had been beheaded for their witness to Jesus and for the word of God, who had not worshiped the beast or his image, and had not received his mark on their foreheads or on their hands. And they lived and reigned with Christ for a thousand years. ... Blessed and holy is he who has part in the first resurrection. Over such the second death has no power, but they shall be priests of God and of Christ, and shall reign with Him a thousand years (Rev. 20:4, 6).

December 26 – The Final Rebellion
(Revelation 20)

Revelation 20:1-8 informs us that Satan will be bound in the bottomless pit during Christ's reign on earth. However, at the end of that time he will be released to again test man's resolve to follow God. Even after one thousand years of peace and prosperity, the devil will successfully deceive the nations of the earth to rebel against Christ. One might ask, "Why would God allow Satan to lead such a rebellion against His own Son? Why not just destroy Satan and be done with wickedness?" Unfortunately, wickedness would not expire with the end of Satan, for his rebel spirit entered into the world in Eden and intruded into humanity (1 Jn. 2:16). Death and rebellion have been passed down to every generation since that time (Rom. 5:12). Summarizing the state of the human heart, the prophet Jeremiah wrote, *"The heart is deceitful above all things, and desperately wicked; who can know it? I, the Lord, search the heart, I test the mind, even to give every man according to his ways, according to the fruit of his doings"* (Jer. 17:9-10). Before destroying Satan, God will allow him to test the human heart's fortitude for godliness. The Lord will find humanity lacking. While enjoying God's fellowship in a perfect environment, both the first man (Adam) and the last humans on earth before it is destroyed (Rev. 20:11, 21:1; 1 Pet. 3:10) are shown to be incapable of pleasing God when tempted to sin against Him.

Man, left to himself, will always go his own way; he will turn away from God (Isa. 53:6). God provided a righteous solution for human rebellion by judging His Son Jesus Christ in our place and giving those who would trust in Him eternal life. Those who will not trust in God's means of salvation in Christ will experience eternal death in hell. So, no matter when individuals live, no matter what dispensation of accountability is present when they lived, all the redeemed (those justified by faith) will experience the first resurrection and enter into the Eternal State. All others will receive resurrected bodies before being judged by Christ and subsequently being cast into the Lake of Fire. These are the only two types of eternal resurrections that the Bible identifies – one to everlasting life and one to everlasting torment and separation from God.

December 27 – The Second Resurrection
(Revelation 20)

Satan's final rebellion will end when the earth is destroyed at the conclusion of Christ's Millennial Kingdom. At that time, God will judge the wicked and cast them into the Lake of Fire. This spiritual abode is often referred to as "hell," and was originally created for the purpose of punishing Satan and his fallen angels (Matt. 25:41). Before God creates a new heaven and earth, He will resurrect those who would not receive the truth of salvation by faith. God is a good record-keeper and is faithful to uphold His Word. A number of books will be opened at this divine trial to demonstrate that God is fully cognizant of sin and just in punishing the wicked for their sins. In fact, the wicked, knowing their own guilt, will not attempt to plead their case before Him (Ps. 64:1; Rom. 3:19). Consequently, all who are tried at the Great White Throne Judgment are found guilty of violating God's perfect, righteous standard – their own works condemn them before a holy God.

God's minimum requirement to enter into heaven is sinless perfection. Committing just one sin during an entire life will prevent entrance into God's presence, that is, unless one has been declared righteous in Christ. Though the Christian is not sinless, he or she has a position of sinless perfection in Christ, and indeed, because of that union should sin less (Rom. 6:1-4). As no one can undo one morally wrong act through the performance of many good ones, it is impossible to enter heaven by doing good works (Rom. 4:3-4; Eph. 2:8-9).

To believe that one is deserving of heaven through doing good deeds is an offensive notion to God, for that would mean that His judgment of His own Son on our behalf did not sufficiently satisfy His righteous demand for justice. This mindset means that individuals are really trusting in themselves and not in Christ alone for salvation. It is the erroneous message of world religion that you can improve your own spiritual essence or position through personal effort – essentially, you do not need a Savior. World religion says, "do, do, do," while biblical Christianity proclaims, "done, done, done." The former promotes personal effort for salvation, while the latter acknowledges that only personal faith in a Savior can save. Accordingly, everyone resurrected to stand before God at the Great White Throne Judgment will be found guilty and cast into the Lake of Fire (Rev. 20:11-15).

December 28 – The Lake of Fire
(Revelation 20)

The Bible provides a vivid description of the Lake of Fire (i.e., Hell), the ultimate fate of those who reject God's truth:

- *"Shame and everlasting contempt"* (Dan. 12:2)
- *"Everlasting punishment"* (Matt. 25:46)
- *"Weeping and gnashing of teeth"* (Matt. 24:51)
- *"Unquenchable fire"* (Luke 3:17)
- *"Indignation and wrath, tribulation and anguish"* (Rom. 2:8-9)
- *"Their worm does not die* [putrid endless agony]*"* (Mark 9:44)
- *"Everlasting destruction"* (2 Thess. 1:9)
- *"Eternal fire ... the blackness of darkness forever"* (Jude 7, 13)
- *"Fire is not quenched"* (Mark 9:46)

Revelation 14:10-11 tells us the final, eternal destiny of the sinner: *"He shall be tormented with fire and brimstone ... the smoke of their torment ascended up forever and ever: and they have no rest day or night."* The Bible's teaching of an eternal place of punishment for unforgiven sinners offends people; consequently, many are watering down the truth by teaching that hell is a state of non-existence or quick annihilation. Misrepresenting the truth in an attempt to avoid its consequences is not a good idea. Truth enables man to face reality and realize that hiding from an omniscient, omnipresent God is impossible.

The Lord Jesus spoke often of hell, addressing the subject of afterlife torment over seventy times. In accordance with God's foreordained plan of salvation, the Lord Jesus bore our hell at Calvary and appeased God's righteous anger for our sin so that we would not have to suffer judgment throughout eternity. He did not frighten people without reason. He lovingly warned them about their deadly disease (sin) and the fatal consequence of the disease (hell), and pleaded with them to internalize the cure (to exercise faith in Him for salvation).

God does not force anyone to receive His solution for sin against his or her will. Heaven would be hell if you didn't want to be there, but hell will not be heaven for those who reject Christ. The Lord Jesus said Himself, *"I am the Way, the Truth, and the Life. No one comes to the Father except through Me"* (John 1:14). Jesus Christ is God's Truth!

December 29 – The New Jerusalem
(Revelation 21)

The Bible begins and ends with a wedding. Both weddings occur in a beautiful garden and in the presence of God. In Genesis 2, the first wedding is of Adam and Eve in the Garden of Eden. The last wedding in the Bible is the marriage of the Lamb and His bride (the redeemed; Rev. 19:7-10). They enjoy communion together before the tree of life and at the very throne of God (Rev. 22:1-5). Because the New Jerusalem is full of redeemed people, an angel referred to the city as the Lamb's bride while speaking to John: *"'Come, I will show you the bride, the Lamb's wife.' And he carried me away in the Spirit to a great and high mountain, and showed me the great city, the holy Jerusalem, descending out of heaven from God"* (Rev. 21:9-10). Abraham knew about God's eternal city and was looking forward to seeing it (Heb. 11:10, 16). John describes the city descending down from heaven:

> *Her light was like a most precious stone, like a jasper stone, clear as crystal. Also she had a great and high wall with twelve gates, and twelve angels at the gates, and names written on them, which are the names of the twelve tribes of the children of Israel. ... Now the wall of the city had twelve foundations, and on them were the names of the twelve apostles of the Lamb. ... The city is laid out as a square; its length is as great as its breadth ... twelve thousand furlongs. Its length, breadth, and height are equal. Then he measured its wall: one hundred and forty-four cubits, according to the measure of a man, that is, of an angel. The construction of its wall was of jasper; and the city was pure gold, like clear glass. The foundations of the wall of the city were adorned with all kinds of precious stones. ... The twelve gates were twelve pearls: each individual gate was of one pearl. And the street of the city was pure gold, like transparent glass* (Rev. 21:10-21).

All three dimensions of the city are 1500 miles, but the height of its wall is nearly insignificant in comparison, only measuring 210 feet. This would seem to indicate that protection of the city is not a concern, but rather the glory of it should be easily viewed by all, including those in hell. The city has twelve foundations of precious stones and twelve pearl gates, but only one street, and it is paved with gold. In this city, no matter how one enters it, all ways lead to the city's illuminating focal point – the throne of God, for *the Lamb is its light* (Rev. 21:23).

December 30 – The Eternal State
(Revelation 21-22)

Because of Christ's reign, conditions on the earth will be wonderful during the Kingdom Age. However, this era should not be confused with the Eternal State, in which there is a new heaven and earth with no evil present (Isa. 65:17). Peter identifies the former as the Day of the Lord (2 Pet. 3:10), and the latter as the Day of God (2 Pet. 3:12). Peter also states that at the end of the Day of the Lord (i.e., at the end of Christ's millennial kingdom), the heavens and the earth shall pass away with a great noise and their elements shall melt with fervent heat and be burned up (2 Pet. 3:10). Isaiah states that *"all the host of heaven shall be dissolved, and the heavens shall be rolled up like a scroll"* (Isa. 34:4). He later foretells that after the millennial kingdom, God will create a new heaven and new earth (Isa. 65:17).

Following this creative feat, Paul states that there will be a divine audit to confirm that Christ has completely dealt with all sin and has restored creation to perfection and to its proper association with God. All the damage caused by sin will be corrected and then God will be all in all (1 Cor. 15:26-28). It is likely that in the eternal state previous distinctions such as Old Testament saints, the Church, Tribulation saints, the nation of Israel, etc. will be remembered, but not emphasized. These distinctions served God's purposes in time while He was unfolding His great plan of salvation in various stages, but will not be significant in eternity (1 Cor. 15:26-28; Rev. 21:24-27, 22:1-5).

There are several clear distinctions in Scripture between the Kingdom Age and the Eternal State. For example, the seas and oceans we know today will still be present during the Kingdom Age (Isa. 11:9; Ezek. 47:18; Zech. 14:8) but there will not be any seas in the new earth (Rev. 21:1). Likewise, geography on earth today will exist in the Kingdom Age (Joel 3:18; Zech. 14:16-21) but obviously will not in the new earth. The new heaven and earth will be created after Satan's last rebellion is quelled (Rev. 20:7-10), and the planet we live on is obliterated (Rev. 20:11; 2 Pet. 3:10). All this and more Christ will do!

To conclude Scripture, the Lord refers to Himself as *"the Bright and Morning Star"* (Rev. 22:16) and then promises: *"Surely I am coming quickly"* (Rev. 22:20). And we happily agree with John's response, *"Amen. Even so, come, Lord Jesus!"*

December 31 – New Testament Authentication

The whole of the Bible speaks of Christ. The Old Testament provides hundreds of prophecies, allegories, types, and shadows of the coming Messiah so that He would be properly recognized by Israel and indeed the whole world. The Lord Jesus is God's personal message and invitation to mankind to have fellowship with Him!

The New Testament reveals God's Message and Messenger with distinct clarity and as the fulfillment of all the Old Testament predictions and expectations. Hence, we see the Lord Jesus Christ as the spirit of prophecy (Rev. 19:10); all the promises of God are yea in Him (2 Cor. 1:20). The believer's complete identity and existence abides with and in Christ. He is our peace (Eph. 2:14), our joy (John 15:11), and our hope (Tit. 2:13). He is the foundational Stone of our faith (1 Cor. 3:11), the Shepherd and Overseer of our souls (1 Pet. 2:25), the Head of the Church (Col. 1:18), our Great High Priest (Heb. 4:15), our Advocate with the Father (1 Jn. 2:1), and our Savior (Eph. 5:23). He is Lord of lords and King of kings (1 Tim. 6:15), the Judge of all (Matt. 25:31-33), the Alpha and the Omega (Rev. 1:11), the Creator (Col. 1:16-17) and the only begotten Son of God (John 3:16). Without Christ, there is no salvation, no life, and no hope!

For by Him all things were created that are in heaven and that are on earth, visible and invisible, whether thrones or dominions or principalities or powers. All things were created through Him and for Him. And He is before all things, and in Him all things consist. And He is the head of the body, the church, who is the beginning, the firstborn from the dead, ***that in all things He may have the preeminence*** *(Col. 1:16-18).*

Understanding who Christ is and what the believer has in Him should compel every true Christian to follow Paul's own aspiration: *"One thing I do, forgetting those things which are behind and reaching forward to those things which are ahead, I press toward the goal for the prize of the upward call of God in Christ Jesus* (Phil. 3:13-14).

Rejoice ye saints, rejoice in Christ, your glorious Head;
With heart, and soul, and voice, His matchless honors spread;
Exalt His love, proclaim His name, and sweetly sing the Lamb once slain.

— Gadsby's Selection

"Man of Sorrows," What A Name

Man of sorrows what a name
for the Son of God, who came
ruined sinners to reclaim:
Hallelujah, what a Savior!

Bearing shame and scoffing rude,
in my place condemned He stood,
sealed my pardon with His blood:
Hallelujah, what a Savior!

Guilty, vile, and helpless we;
spotless Lamb of God was He,
sacrificed to set us free:
Hallelujah, what a Savior!

Lifted up was He to die;
"It is finished" was his cry;
now in heaven exalted high:
Hallelujah, what a Savior!

When He comes, our glorious King,
all His ransomed home to bring,
then anew this song we'll sing:
Hallelujah, what a Savior!

— P. P. Bliss

Endnotes

1   C. I. Scofield, *The New Scofield Study Bible* (Oxford University Press, New York; 1967), p. 987

2   Samuel Ridout, *The Serious Christian* (Books for Christians, Charlotte, NC; no date), p. 24

3   J. G. Bellett, *The Evangelists, Meditations on the Four Gospels* (Bible Truth Publishers, Addison, IL; no date), Introduction

4   William MacDonald, *Believer's Bible Commentary* (Thomas Nelson Publishers, Nashville, TN; 1989), p. 1198

5   Arthur Pink, *Why Four Gospels?* (Scripture Truth Book Co., Fincastle, VA; no date), pp. 45-46

6   C. I. Scofield, op. cit., p. 994, note 3

7   Arthur Pink, op. cit., pp. 109-110

8   Oswald Chambers, message entitled *Gateway to Heaven*

9   Dr. Howard Taylor, *Spiritual Secret of Hudson Taylor* (Whitaker House, New Kensington, PA; 1996), p. 368

10 Warren Wiersbe, *The Bible Exposition Commentary, Vol. 1* (Victor Books, Wheaton, IL; 1989), p. 416

11 Hamilton Smith, *Classic Christian Commentary – Matthew* (Books for Christians, Charlotte, NC; no date), pp. 1-3

12 Andrew Jukes, *Four Views of Christ* (Kregel Publications, Grand Rapids, MI; 1966), p. 21

13 C. H. Spurgeon, C. H.: *Morning and Evening: Daily Readings* (Logos Research Systems, Inc., Oak Harbor, WA; 1995), December 26 AM

14 Warren Wiersbe, op. cit., p. 259

15 Arthur Pink, *Why Four Gospels?* (Scripture Truth Book Co., Fincastle, VA; no date), p. 75

16 Dr. Howard Taylor, *Spiritual Secret of Hudson Taylor* (Whitaker House, New Kensington, PA; 1996), p. 368

17 Samuel Ridout, op. cit., p. 171

18 Albert Barnes, *Barnes' Notes – The Gospels* (Baker Book House, Grand Rapids, MI; 1884 reprint), p. 293

19 Thomas A. Kempis from Edythe Draper, op. cit.

20 Albert Barnes, op. cit., pp. 273-274

21 Andrew Jukes, op. cit., p. 107

22 Charles Finney, *The Use and Prevalence of Christ's Name* (from *Lectures on the Conditions of Prevailing Prayer* (Oberlin College; 1850 – copyright by Gospel Truth Ministries)

23 A. W. Tozer, from Edythe Draper, *Draper's Quotations from the Christian World* (Tyndale House Publishers Inc., Wheaton, IL)

24   William G. Moorehead, *The Fundamentals of Christianity: The Moral Glory of Jesus Christ* (Biblesoft, Electronic Database, 1997)

25   C. H. Mackintosh, *Genesis to Deuteronomy* (Loizeaux Brothers, Inc., Neptune, NJ; 1972), p. 389

26   C. H. Spurgeon, op. cit., May 29 AM

27   C. H. Mackintosh, op. cit., Num. 21

28   Charles Ryrie, *So Great Salvation* (Victor Books, Wheaton, IL; 1989), pp. 59-60

29   J. A. Motyer, *The Prophecy of Isaiah* (InterVarsity Press, Downers Grove, IL; 1993), p. 121

30   C. H. Mackintosh, *The Mackintosh Treasury* (Loizeaux Brothers, Inc., Neptune, NJ 1976; reprint by Believers Bookshelf Inc.; 1999), p. 794

31   *The American Heritage Dictionary* (Houghton Mifflin Company, Boston, MA; 1978)

32   H. A. Ironside, *Ezekiel* (Loizeaux, Neptune, NJ; 1949), p. 82

33   E. Schuyler English, *H. A. Ironside, Ordained of the Lord* (Loizeaux Brothers Inc., Neptune, NJ; 1976). p. 132

34   Warren Wiersbe, *The Bible Exposition Commentary, Vol. 2* (Victor Books, Wheaton, IL: 1989), p. 416

35   Dr. Howard Taylor, op. cit., p. 368

36   W. Grinton Berry, editor, *Foxe's Book of Martyrs* (Power Books, Old Tappan, NJ; no date), p. 9

37   C. H. Mackintosh, *Genesis to Deuteronomy,* op. cit., Num. 11

38   Gary W. Smith, *Life Changing Thoughts* (Authorhouse, Bloomington, IN; 2009), p. 148

39   Albert Barnes, op. cit., 64:6

40   Hamilton Smith, *The Psalms*, STEM Publishing: http://stempublishing.com/authors/smith/PSALMS.html

41   James Vernon McGee, *Thru The Bible Commentary, Vol. 5*, (Thomas Nelson Publishers, Nashville, TN; 1983), p. 545-546

42   Matthew Henry, *Commentary on the Whole Bible, Vol. 3* (MacDonald Pub. Co., Mclean, VA; 1985), Eccl. 7:7

43   Ibid., 1 Cor. 3:18

44   L. E. Cooper, *The New American Commentary – Ezekiel* (Broadman & Holman Publishers; 1994), pp. 304-305

45   J. H. Thayer, *Thayer's Greek Lexicon* (Biblesoft; 2000)

46   S. Emery, *Treasury of Bible Doctrine – Mediator and Advocate* (Precious Seed Magazine, UK: 1977), p. 210

47   H. A. Ironside, *Isaiah – Rev.* ed. (Loizeaux, Neptune, NJ; 2000), p. 57

48   Albert Edersheim, *Bible History Old Testament* (Hendrickson Publishing, Peabody: 1995), p. 18

49   C. H. Mackintosh, op. cit., Num. 16

50   Jim Flanigan, *Notes on Revelation* (Gospel Tract Pub.; 1987), pp. 40-41

51   William Kelly, *The Elders in Heaven*, STEM Publishing:
     http://www.stempublishing. com/authors/kelly/7subjcts/eldershv.html

52   Kenneth S. Wuest, *The New Testament: An Expanded Translation*
     (Eerdmans Pub. Co., Grand Rapids, MI; 1989), Matt. 10:20

An Old Testament Journey

May We See Christ?

WARREN HENDERSON

May We See Christ – An Old Testament Journey is a sequential study of Scripture containing 366 two-page devotions (758 pages). Besides the plain language of the Old Testament, God has employed a variety of types, symbols, and allegories in a complementary fashion to teach us about His Son. With the light of New Testament truth and the illuminating assistance of the Holy Spirit, we are able to understand and appreciate these fascinating Old Testament pictures. All of God's written Word speaks of Christ to some degree as He is the main emphasis of Scripture. Accordingly, the best reason to embark on this one-year journey is to more clearly see, know, and love Christ. May the Lord richly bless your daily contemplations of the Savior as you expectantly peer into God's oracles and witness the glory of His Son. — Warren Henderson